Contents

Note on Contributors

ARNOLD J. TOYNBEE, whose best-known work is *A Study of History*, was Stevenson Professor of International Relations in the University of London and Director of Studies at the Royal Institute of International Affairs from 1925 to 1955.

Neil McInnes, an Australian journalist now working in Paris, is the author of 'Les débuts du marxisme théorique en France et en Italie', 'Georges Sorel: Aperçu sur les Utopies, les Soviets, et le Droit Nouveau' (published in *Cahiers de l'Institut de Science Economique Appliquée*, Paris), 'Antonio Gramsci', 'Havemann and the Dialectic' (*Survey*, London), etc.

Hugh Seton-Watson is Professor of Russian History in the University of London and author of *The East European Revolution, The Pattern of Communist Revolution, Neither War nor Peace*, etc.

Peter Wiles is Professor of Russian Social and Economic Studies in the University of London and author of *The Political Economy of Communism* and *Communist International Economics*.

Richard Lowenthal is Professor of International Relations in the Free University of Berlin and author of *Ernst Reuter* (with Willy Brandt) and *World Communism: the Disintegration of a Secular Faith*.

Looking Back Fifty Years

ARNOLD J. TOYNBEE

REVOLUTIONS, like wars, are abnormal disturbances of the course of life; and, being abnormal, they are bound to be temporary. Officially, a country may be in a permanent state of revolution. This is the official doctrine in present-day Mexico; yet the Mexico of 1967 is not, in truth, the revolutionary country that Mexico was during the fifteen or twenty years immediately following the outbreak of revolution there in 1910. Every revolution has its trajectory. The shape and the length of the curve will be different in different cases. Yet it does seem to be a general rule that, sooner or later, every revolution eventually comes to rest. The seventeenth-century revolution in England took eighteen years to move from the outbreak of the Civil War in 1642 to the restoration of the monarchy in 1660. The eighteenth-century revolution in France took twenty-five years, 1789–1814, to run its corresponding course. The communist revolution in Yugoslavia took twenty-one years, 1945–1966, to reach the point at which the Communist Party and its executive organs relinquished their revolutionary monopoly of power.

The revolution that broke out in China in 1911 has had a more complicated history. The overthrow of the Manchu dynasty was a normal event in Chinese history. For two thousand years past, dynasties had repeatedly been overthrown when they had been deemed by the Chinese public to have 'exhausted their mandate from Heaven'. The new element in the Chinese revolution of 1911 was that the deposed dynasty was replaced, not by a new dynasty, but by an exotic regime inspired by the western ideology of liberal democracy. This new fact put this twentieth-century Chinese revolution into the same category as the English and French revolutions, or the abortive liberal democratic revolution in Russia in 1917. This first Russian Revolution was, of course, rapidly followed by the Bolshevik Revolution of the same year; and in China, as in Russia, what seemed at one time to have been the beginnings of a liberal democratic westernizing revolution, misfired, to be followed after decades of ruinous turmoil by the triumph of a rival western ideology, communism, which has now been in power for eighteen years. The upheavals and civil wars which began in 1911 with the downfall of the Manchu dynasty, and to which were added intermittent hostilities with Japan, lasted nearly forty years; in Russia only a few months elapsed between the fall of the Tsar and the establishment of the Soviet regime.

By comparison with the course of the Chinese revolution, the course of the Russian Revolution is fairly clear. Here the experiment in liberal democracy was so short-lived that it can be almost ignored. Its successor, the Bolshevik Revolution, that trod closely on the liberal revolution's heels, is the event that counts, and, by this year 1967, half a century has elapsed since its outbreak. How are we to size up the situation in the Soviet Union today, fifty years after? In Russia, as in Mexico, the revolution has obviously shed much of its initial demonic violence. The storm has abated, but can we be sure that it is over? Is there no possibility that it might break out again? These questions need close and earnest consideration. The answers, whatever these may prove to be, are going to affect the course of history, not just in the Soviet Union, but all over the world.

When we are trying to answer these questions in the Russian case, in which the revolution is still current history, it may be helpful to look back on the histories of previous revolutions which, by now, have completed their course. In the light of these previous cases we can perhaps venture on two generalizations. On the one hand, every revolution does change things irreversibly, as every revolution claims to have done. On the other hand, no revolution ever succeeds in making the complete break with the past that every revolution also claims to have made. The irreversibility of a revolution asserts itself if an attempt is made at an integral restoration of the pre-revolutionary state of affairs. When Humpty-Dumpty has had a great fall, all the king's horses and all the king's men cannot put him back again securely in his previous position. They can merely condemn him to suffer a second fall. The Restoration lasted only twenty-eight years in England, and no more than fifteen years in France. In each case it provoked a fresh outbreak of revolution—indeed, a series of fresh outbreaks in the French case. A revolution is a way of bringing about changes that have become imperative, and it will continue to erupt until its work has been completed. At the same time, it is an illusion to imagine that a revolution can create an entirely new Heaven and new Earth. It is notorious, for example, that the ultimate

THE IMPACT OF
THE RUSSIAN REVOLUTION
1917–1967

The Impact of
the Russian Revolution
1917–1967

The Influence of Bolshevism
on the World outside Russia

With an introductory essay by
Arnold J. Toynbee

Issued under the auspices of the
Royal Institute of International Affairs
OXFORD UNIVERSITY PRESS
LONDON   NEW YORK   TORONTO
1967

Oxford University Press, Ely House, London W.1

GLASGOW NEW YORK TORONTO MELBOURNE WELLINGTON
CAPE TOWN SALISBURY IBADAN NAIROBI LUSAKA ADDIS ABABA
BOMBAY CALCUTTA MADRAS KARACHI LAHORE DACCA
KUALA LUMPUR HONG KONG TOKYO

Printed in Great Britain at the Pitman Press, Bath

effect of the French Revolution in the field of administration was to give practical effect, in a more systematic form, to the ideas that were latent in the *Ancien Régime* which the Revolution claimed to have swept away.

These generalizations from past experience may throw some light on the Russian Revolution's probable future course. The founding fathers of the Soviet Union claimed to have abolished Tsarism and capitalism within the Soviet Union's frontiers. Beyond that, they claimed that communism was an ideology that had a unique capacity for unifying mankind. On a world-wide scale, so the Bolsheviks claimed, communism was destined to overcome the vicious traditional divisions between classes, nations, and races (it would overcome the divisions between religions by extinguishing the religions themselves). In making these claims—and they made them with the confidence of sincere conviction—Lenin and his companions were launching a myth that was potent, exhilarating, and infectious. Today, fifty years after, it is already clear that these overweening claims are not going to be made good. Yet, just because the passage of half a century has now given us this hindsight, it has become difficult for us to recapture mentally the atmosphere of the immediate reactions, abroad, to the Bolshevik Revolution of 1917 in Russia.

The immediate repercussions were dynamic, and this, above all, in Europe. Already, before the end of the First World War, Europe had become receptive soil for the sowing of Lenin's dragons'-tooth seed; and, in central and eastern Europe, the defeat of the two Central Powers, and the simultaneous dissolution of one of the two, Austria–Hungary, carried the wartime agony to a climax. Here, next door to Russia, people's minds were now deeply unsettled and confused. The despair into which they had been plunged by terrible experiences was being compensated psychologically by wild hopes for the advent of a secularized version of the millennium. At the turn of the year 1918–19 the Spartacists—the core of the newly-founded German Communist Party—made a desperate attempt at revolution. In 1919 two Central European countries, Hungary and Bavaria, became 'Soviet Republics' on the Russian model; and, though these two regimes were shortlived, the destiny of all Europe still seemed to remain in the balance till the defeat of the Red Army before Warsaw in summer 1920 and the failure of the 'March action' in 1921, when the German communists made another attempt, doomed from the outset, to capture power. Till then, it seemed on the cards that

Europe, at any rate east of the Rhine, might go communist *en bloc*, and if this possibility had become a reality, the consequences would have been momentous, not only for Europe, but for the whole world. The statesmen assembled at Versailles debating the expediency of intervention, were not immune from these anxieties. Far from it. Their fears matched in reverse the hopes of the Bolsheviks. Colonel House wrote in his diary that 'Bolshevism is gaining ground everywhere'; Lloyd George saw Europe 'filled with the spirit of revolution'.

Nor was the Bolshevik myth discredited in Europe by the failure of communism to establish its domination there. In Britain, for instance, the tradition of conducting politics in a constitutional way was piquantly different from the dictatorial methods that, in Russia, the Bolsheviks had inherited from a long line of predecessors. The 'Hands off Russia' campaign, organized in protest against British intervention in the Russian Civil War, received strong trade union support, and there were mutinous incidents among the war-weary French troops and in the French fleet sent to support the opponents of the Bolsheviks. However strong their opposition to the communists at home, most working-class leaders in Britain between the wars were obsessed by the notion that the Soviet Government was in some sense the true representative of the working class. The most bitter opponents of the new Russian regime were for the most part the same people who were most hostile to the labour movement at home; to have joined them in attacking Moscow would have seemed in a sense an act of disloyalty to their own cause. Throughout the 1920s and 1930s, it was embarrassing for a British labour leader to make serious public criticisms of the Bolshevik system. If and when he found himself unable to avoid doing this, he would usually make some kind of preliminary apology for the awkward stand that he was taking. Vestiges, at least, of this attitude outlived the Second World War. This did not prevent the Labour Party from adopting a strongly hostile attitude to those of its members who went over to the communists or appealed and worked for co-operation between the two. From the outset it rejected the British Communist Party's application for affiliation (which Lenin had urged on the reluctant British delegates to the second Comintern congress), and in the thirties it was equally implacable in rejecting the proposal for a popular front. Indeed, it expelled many of the prominent advocates of this. In fact, the Bolshevik myth was finally discredited outside the Soviet Union not by any spontaneous revulsion on the part of the western working class, but by a dramatic volteface in Russian communist domestic politics. After Stalin's death, when Stalin had been exposed and denounced in the Soviet Union by Khrushchev, it at last became virtually impossible, outside the Soviet Union, to cherish the Bolshevik myth any longer. What is remarkable, however, is not that the myth gradually evaporated in Europe, but that it survived there as long as it did.

This is the more remarkable, considering two points that are made in a later chapter of the present book, by Mr McInnes. He points out that already before the Bolshevik Revolution of 1917 in Russia, the western industrial working class had abandoned, in practice, its original ideological objective of overthrowing bourgeois society for the practical objective of winning for itself successive slices of the alluring bourgeois cake. Mr McInnes's second point that is extremely pertinent in this connection is that the authoritarianism and opportunism of the Russian form of communist organization were horrid stumbling-blocks for the communist parties which, after 1917, had been founded in western countries on Russian initiative. Westerners did not cease to be westerners when they became communists, and the western political ideals of acting on principle and of respecting a minority's right to dissent were irreconcilable with Russian authoritarianism.

The factor that has played the greatest part in defeating communist hopes and expectations—and this both in the Soviet Union and everywhere else—has, however, been the triumph of nationalism. Communism has now been worsted by nationalism as decisively as liberal democracy has been. Within the communist part of the world, national rivalries are today as bitter and as divisive as they are within the non-communist part.

There has, indeed, so far, been only one eminent communist who has genuinely been prepared to expend his own country in the cause of propagating communism throughout the rest of the world. This whole-hearted communist was, of course, Trotsky; and it is surely no accident that Trotsky was defeated in his contest with Stalin— the rival statesman whose policy was the inverse one. Stalin sought to make communism serve the national interests of the Soviet Union; and, unlike Trotsky, Stalin was not peculiar. Communists, as well as liberal democrats, usually prove to be nationalists first whenever a conflict of interests arises between their ideology and their country. After this had been demonstrated in the Soviet

Union by Stalin's victory over Trotsky, it was demonstrated again successively by Tito's revolt against Stalin and by communist China's pretension to be the orthodox guardian and exponent of the communist faith—which communist Russia has betrayed, so the Chinese communists maintain. More recently still, we have seen the Soviet Union's east European former satellites taking courage from the examples set by Yugoslavia and by China, and in their turn they are now beginning to reassert their national independence. The communist regimes imposed on them by the Soviet Union survive, but they, too, have proved to be nationalist communist regimes, in which nationalism takes precedence over the professedly ecumenical communist ideology. We may guess that Vietnamese nationalism will also assert itself against any threat of Chinese ascendancy in communist North Vietnam, if and when the United States ceases to press North Vietnam into China's arms.

The passage of time has also confuted Lenin's doctrine that the industrial proletariat of Russia and of the western countries is the natural ally of the Asian and African peoples that are being exploited by imperialism, and that communism is the creed that can link together these two wings of the great army of the victimized. Today the Chinese communists are denouncing the Russian communists as representatives of the affluent white minority of mankind who have entered into a tacit conspiracy with the Americans for preserving this minority's illegitimate privileges. The Chinese have taken over Lenin's doctrine that communism is the non-white peoples' hope, but maintain that only a non-white communist Power can be trusted to champion the non-white peoples' interests honestly. China has, in fact, virtually declared a race-war in Chinese communism's name.

Thus Russian communism has failed to overcome nationalism and racialism, and it has also failed to extinguish the historic religions. In the Soviet Union, Eastern Orthodox Christianity, Baptist Protestantism, Judaism, Islam, and Buddhism have all managed to survive under adversity; and, after all, this is not surprising; for all these traditional religions offer to individual human beings something that the parvenu ideologies do not attempt to provide. The traditional religions offer to the individual some personal consolation and guidance for coping with the tribulations that every one of us encounters in the course of his life.

Fifty years after the Bolshevik Revolution of 1917, it is obvious that Russian communism has failed to attain the positive objectives which it was so confident of attaining at the start. It is also obvious that it has failed to achieve its intended break with the past. If we were to interpret this first half-century of Russian communism's history in Marxian terms, we should diagnose the Russian communist regime's *raison d'être* as being a technological and economic one. The First World War, we should say, revealed the gigantic Russian Empire's shocking technological inferiority to its western neighbour Germany. This relatively small but highly industrialized western country defeated Russia with ease. The subsequent establishment of the communist regime in Russia can be interpreted as Russia's device for catching up, technologically, with Germany and with Russia's other western neighbours. Under the communist regime, Russia has been making a forced march, under effective leadership, towards technological efficiency up to contemporary western standards.

This interpretation of the last half-century of Russian history, with which not all Marxists would agree, and to which many non-Marxists subscribe, does go some way towards explaining why Russia went communist in 1917 and why its original communism has evolved since then in a direction that is a partial reversion to something like a 'bourgeois' regime. At the same time, it shows that Lenin's revolution in Russia was not so radical a break with the past as Lenin himself believed it to be. The war of 1914–18 was not the first Russian experience that had brought to light, through the shock of military defeat, Russia's current technological backwardness by comparison with the western world. Germany's victory over Russia in the First World War had been anticipated by Poland's and Sweden's victories over her in the seventeenth century. Russia's reaction on that earlier occasion had been the grafting of a western regime— 'enlightened autocracy'—on the traditional Russian autocracy in the Byzantine style; this western regime had been adopted in Russia as a political instrument for producing technological results; the purpose had been to bring Russia into line with its western contemporaries in the technological field; and this new regime had been introduced, for this purpose, by a revolutionary man of genius, Peter the Great. On this interpretation of Russian history, Lenin's mission has been a continuation of Peter's mission, and the Bolshevik Revolution of 1917 was a resumption of the revolution that had been started by Peter at the turn of the seventeenth and eighteenth centuries.

In fact, in Russian history, interpreted in these terms, there is a governing factor that was operating before, as well as after, 1917. This governing factor is not one that has originated in Russia in the course of Russia's own native development. It is something that would never have disturbed Russia if it had not had the western world for its next-door neighbour. The constant disturbing factor in Russian history has been the accelerating progress of technology in the western world since the seventeenth century. This dynamic development of western technology has been a challenge to the non-western majority of mankind. It has confronted all non-western peoples with a choice between mastering western technology and falling into subjection to technologically more efficient western Powers. Russia was the first non-western country to face this problem and to try to save its independence by putting itself through a 'crash' programme of technological westernization. The pioneer in this endeavour to cope with western technology was not Lenin, however; it was his seventeenth-century predecessor Peter. It was a stroke of luck for Russia that Peter was a natural-born technocrat who happened to be armed with a Muscovite Tsar's dictatorial powers.

Peter's Russian revolution anticipated Lenin's in another point as well. It was infectious, and this was because it was an attempt to solve a problem that was not Russia's alone, but was common to all Byzantine and other non-western countries as and when they came into collision with the technologically dynamic modern West. Russia's eighteenth-century achievements under its Petrine regime inspired the Turks to follow suit in self-defence, and the Greeks to follow suit in order to liberate themselves from the Turks. Even the Meiji revolution of 1868 in Japan was an indirect result of Peter's pioneer work. The present is not the first time that a revolutionary Russia has suffered from its pupils' ingratitude. Turkey's reaction to the shock of Russia's victory over her in the war of 1768–74 was fundamentally the same as China's reaction now. Turkey's, like China's, aim in imitating Russia's adoption of western technology was to save itself from falling under Russia's dominion.

The two earliest modern revolutions were the sixteenth-century Dutch and seventeenth-century English revolutions. These, being the earliest, had no contemporary external source of inspiration to draw upon. They challenged modern western autocracy in the name of traditional native rights that were legacies from the Middle

Ages. The Dutch and English revolutions were, in theory, expressions of conservatism, though, in seeking to vindicate old rights, they fell into claiming new rights that had no historical precedents. By contrast, the French Revolution did not cast back to France's own medieval past. At least part of its inspiration came from abroad; for it was inspired by the French *philosophes*, and, by 1789, these had been theorizing, for a century, about English post-revolutionary practice. On this point—and it is a point of capital importance—the Russian and Chinese communist revolutions have been of the French, not of the Dutch and English, type. Their theoretical inspiration was derived from foreign precedents, and, by comparison with the English inspiration of the French Revolution, their inspiration has been highly exotic. In borrowing from England, France was borrowing from a fellow member of its own family circle of western peoples. At bottom, French and English traditions and institutions and ideas all had common western roots. On the other hand, the non-western countries that have adopted communism have taken over an ideology that has no roots at all in their own native traditions.

When we survey Russian and Chinese history during the ages before Russia's and China's encounters with the West, we find nothing here that suggests that the Russians or the Chinese would ever have dreamed of communism, in the sense in which it is now understood, if this ideology had not already been manufactured in the West and had not been waiting, ready-made, for non-western peoples to import. Communism, like liberal democracy and enlightened autocracy, is a western invention which can be accounted for only in terms of the western civilization's previous history. The founding fathers of communism, Marx and Engels, were born and brought up in the Rhineland and did their work in England—Marx as a reader in the British Museum library and Engels as the manager of a small factory in Manchester. They were thoroughbred westerners like Cromwell and the Emperor Joseph and Robespierre, and they were not singular in being prophets who were without honour in their own world, but who made their ideological fortunes abroad, quite contrary to their own expectations. Marx did not have his eye on Russia; he felt a nineteenth-century German's contempt for that backward eastern country. Marx expected that England would be the first country to go communist, because England had been the first country to enter on the capitalist phase of an economic and social course of evolution that he believed to be predetermined. If Marx could have lived to see

Russia seize the role of being the first country to make the communist revolution, he would have certainly been astonished and would probably have been displeased; for this first great practical success for Marxism was at the same time a confutation of Marxist theory.

Marxism is not, however, the only creed that has been ousted from its birthplace but has made its fortune on alien ground. Christianity, for instance, was rejected by the Jews but was adopted by the non-Jewish majority of the population of the Roman Empire. Buddhism was eventually rejected in India but was adopted in Eastern Asia. This is no paradox. A religion or ideology attracts adherents where it is able to meet a spiritual or psychological need, and it does not necessarily meet a need in its own homeland. The Jews, being monotheists already, felt no need for the trinitarian dilution of monotheism which Christianity offered. On the other hand, this monotheism with a tincture of polytheism in it did meet the needs of a polytheistic Greco-Roman society that was already groping its way towards a vision of divine unity. The Hindus, being ascetic and metaphysical-minded already, felt no need for the temperate asceticism and minimal metaphysical-mindedness of Buddhism. On the other hand, these characteristically Indian spiritual gifts of Buddhism—offered as they were, by Buddhism, in a moderate dosage —were attractive to the peoples of Eastern Asia because for these peoples, whose native religions and philosophies were for the most part this-worldly and matter-of-fact, Buddhism's Indian other-worldliness filled a spiritual vacuum. In China, this spiritual vacuum had already been partly filled by the transcendental philosophy of Taoism. Buddhism gave to China, in a more imposing form, what Taoism had been seeking to give before Buddhism's arrival there.

Marxism's fortunes have been similar to Buddhism's and Christianity's. In its western birthplace, Marxism has been a drug in the market. It has been just one representative of the modern western world's innumerable brood of social and political ideologies, and, for a majority of westerners, it has been an unattractive ideology. It is cruder, more violent, and more dogmatic than many others of the contemporary western-made ideologies among which a westerner can take his choice; and, since Marx's day, violence has come to make less and less appeal to the western industrial working class, since this class's material conditions were already being improved by non-violent means by the time when Marxist propaganda got under way. Therefore the western-made ideology of Marxism has been rejected by the western world, with the exception of a small western communist minority whose prospects are as bleak as those of the Jewish Christians in Palestine were when Christianity was making its fortune among the non-Jewish majority of the people of the Roman Empire. On the other hand, Marxism attracts non-western peoples by the qualities that repel westerners. Its violence and radicalism offer to non-westerners the prospect that, if they swallow this potent western medicine, it may implant in them the western stamina that all non-westerners need if they are to hold their own in a westernizing world. In other words, Marxism fitted the mood of the non-western peoples when these were ripe for revolting against western dominance. It is a creed of western origin that indicts the western 'establishment'. It is thus able to express a will to revolt against the West in terms that, being western, have prestige—for the West does have prestige, in virtue of its dominance, even among peoples that are striving to bring its domination over them to an end. Psychology counts for more than economics in deciding whether the propagation of a religion or an ideology shall succeed or shall fail. If Marx had thought in psychological terms and not in economic terms, he would not have been surprised to learn that the two leading communist countries today are both non-western.

This may perhaps at least partly explain why communism has captivated Russia and China. We have still to see how long the effects of this powerful western drug are going to take in working themselves off in these two great non-western countries. We have also still to see whether Russia and China are going to succeed or to fail in their efforts to propagate their borrowed western ideology in other non-western countries.

The fact that communism is not a native Russian or Chinese product does not necessarily mean that Russian and Chinese attempts to propagate communism will fail. The ideas of the French Revolution were derived partly from what the French thought were the principles underlying political and constitutional arrangements in England; yet, in the French version of them, these ideas proved to be more catching than their exemplification across the Channel. Today, Russia and China are playing the role of serving as the disseminators of an ideology that they did not originate, and this is not the first time that they have played this part. Russia adopted Eastern Orthodox Christianity from Byzantium and propagated it among the peoples in her Siberian hinterland. China adopted Buddhism from India and propagated it in Korea, Japan, and Vietnam. To propagate an alien ideology is not impracticable; all the same, it is a *tour de force*. The outcome will depend partly on how the missionary people regards itself, and partly on how it is regarded by the foreign peoples whom it is seeking to convert.

In the past, China and Russia have each had confidence in its capacity to sustain the missionary role. The Chinese have thought of China as being 'the Middle Kingdom', that is, the uniquely civilized centre of the human world. They have thought of the Chinese Empire as being 'All that is under Heaven', that is, as being sovereign, or at least suzerain, even over barbarians beyond the pale of civilization (that is, Chinese civilization). What is more, this Chinese claim was accepted by most of the non-Chinese peoples, near or remote, with whom the Chinese came into contact before the British assault on China in 1839—an assault that brought with it a sudden catastrophic change in China's standing in the world. This was not, of course, the first time that China had been assaulted with success. Japanese pirates had raided the country from the sea before the first western ships reached its coasts. Central Asian nomads had conquered it partially, and, in the Mongols' case, completely, from the landward side. But these barbarian naval and military conquerors had continued to feel awe and admiration for China's culture; and China made the same imposing impression on western observers in the thirteenth and fourteenth centuries, when it was under Mongol rule, and again in the modern age, from the sixteenth century down to 1839. Voltaire put China on a pedestal as a model for the West to imitate. Eighteenth-century French *philosophes* abandoned the traditional Christian belief in original sin for the more optimistic, but perhaps less realistic, Confucian faith in the natural goodness of human nature. Even after 1839, the westerners and the Japanese who were now treating the Chinese as 'natives' still continued to appreciate Chinese art.

Thus China enjoyed cultural prestige in the eyes of foreign peoples that were geographically remote and were militarily stronger than China was; and this cultural prestige also imposed itself upon neighbours that offered a stubborn resistance to Chinese political domination. The Koreans, the Japanese, and the Vietnamese readily received from China not only its own cultural products, such as the characters and the Confucian philosophy, but also an Indian religion,

Buddhism, of which China was not the creator but was merely the transmitter.

The Russians, for their part, before they became converts to, and propagators of, communism, had already regarded themselves on two occasions as being the sole residuary legatees of an orthodox faith that had been betrayed by its originators, from whom the Russians had received it. When, at the Council of Florence in 1439, the East Roman Government accepted ecclesiastical union with Rome under the supremacy of the Papacy, the Russians refused to endorse an agreement that they held to be a betrayal of Eastern Orthodoxy; and, after the Ottoman Turkish conquest of Constantinople in 1453, the Russian church considered itself to be the only one of the Eastern Orthodox churches that was still preserving the true faith, immune from both Frankish and Turkish domination. Again, after Peter the Great had, in effect, replaced Eastern Orthodox Christianity by modern western secular autocracy as Russia's state religion, the Russian Tsardom prided itself, in the Napoleonic and post-Napoleonic age, on having been the only absolute monarchy in Europe that had not succumbed to the ideas of the French Revolution.

Russia, however, was much less successful in the pre-communist age than China was in inducing its neighbours to take it at its own high valuation. Its western neighbours held that, though Christian, it was schismatic from the Western Christian standpoint, and that, anyway, it was backward and indeed barbarous. It was more significant still that its fellow Eastern Orthodox Christians, too, looked down on Russia. It was politically independent and powerful, while the Greeks, Bulgars, Serbs, and Georgians were politically subject to Venice, the Ottoman Empire, and the Persian Empire. Yet Russia's political power was outweighed, in these other Eastern Orthodox peoples' eyes, by its cultural inferiority to them. In matters of Eastern Orthodox Christian doctrine and practice, it was still they who set the standard for Russia, not vice versa. Nor did Russia improve its standing in its neighbours' eyes as a result of its reception of secular western civilization in and after the time of Peter the Great. The Petrine revolution did induce the western countries to admit Russia into their society, but they continued to treat it as a backward neophyte who did no credit to the civilization that it was attempting clumsily to adopt.

What are Russia's and China's respective prospects of success in

their present common role of being propagators of communism—
an ideology that was originally alien to both of them alike? Our
guesses at the answer to this question about the future will be
influenced by our knowledge of the two countries' respective pre-
communist pasts. We may perhaps gain some further light if we
recall the reasons for France's success in propagating the partly
alien (that is, English) 'ideas of the French Revolution'.

Like Chinese cultural exports, these French cultural exports
found ready takers, and these among peoples that were up in arms
against being dominated militarily and politically by a foreign
Power. To compare small things with great, France, in the western
world, had been a miniature 'Middle Kingdom' in the Chinese sense
of the term. France's centrality, unlike China's, had not been
uncontested, yet neither Italy in the Middle Ages nor Britain in the
modern age had succeeded in wresting from France its primacy. The
shock that the French Revolution gave to the rest of the western
world could not and did not wipe out the cultural prestige that
France had been accumulating in the course of ages. France continued to have many gifts to give, and these continued to be attractive
to other western peoples, even now that they were being presented in
a revolutionary form.

Revolutionary and Napoleonic France's greatest asset was its
wealth in capable cultivated men of the professional class. The
Revolution gave such men their opportunity; the subsequent French
conquests extended this opportunity's geographical scope. A host
of Frenchmen of this kind rationalized the law and the system of
public administration, first in France itself, and afterwards in Italy,
the Low Countries, western Germany, and Switzerland. Heine, the
Jew for whom the French regime spelled emancipation, has expressed
a feeling that was shared with him by millions of non-Jews in these
countries. It felt as if a stuffy house had suddenly been ventilated by
a great breath of vivifying fresh air. The Napoleonic regime, outside France's pre-revolution frontiers, was short-lived, but its effects
there were enduring. The ending of the French military and political
occupation could not undo the social, cultural, and psychological
consequences of this historic episode.

Here we have an important point in which both Russia and China
in 1967 are at a serious disadvantage by comparison with France at
the turn of the eighteenth and nineteenth centuries. To their credit,
the communist regimes in both countries have been making efforts,

at home, to raise the level of modern education, which, under the pre-communist dispensation, had been low in terms of the average level in the contemporary western world. Russia has now had half a century for increasing its fund of modern-educated citizens; China has had eighteen years. Yet today Russia, as well as China, probably still has a deficit of such citizens for meeting its own domestic requirements. Certainly, neither country has a surplus that it can afford to employ abroad on world-wide propaganda operations. Both the Soviet Union and continental China are, of course, doing propaganda work abroad on a considerable scale, but probably they are doing this to the detriment of their own development at home.

This dearth of competent citizens is one of the factors that, first in Russia and then in China, defeated the attempt to establish a liberal democratic regime and led to the establishment of a communist regime instead. A communist regime can be operated by a small number of competent citizens; a liberal democratic regime requires a much larger number of them to enable it to work successfully. The presence of a communist regime is presumptive evidence of a shortage of citizens of this kind. Conversely, if there is a large number of them, they are unlikely to put up with an authoritarian regime of any kind—communist, military, or dynastic.

This suggests that the present communist regimes in Russia and China are not nearly so well equipped as the revolutionary and Napoleonic regime in France was for propagating their ideology abroad.

If Russia and China are both labouring under this common handicap, which of the two has the better prospects? Probably China, but this only within the limits of the area in which pre-1839 China enjoyed cultural prestige, that is, within the limits of Eastern Asia, which, besides China, includes Korea, Japan, and Vietnam. Today, Eastern Asia harbours nearly half the human race—nearly half, but not more than that.

On a visit to Japan at the end of 1956, I had the impression that, as a result of Japan's failure to conquer China in the war of 1931–45, China's traditional prestige in Japanese eyes had revived. I found that many Japanese of the rising generation were now learning Chinese, in the hope that a knowledge of Chinese might be a passport to a job if trade between Japan and China were to be resumed on a considerable scale. After the defeat of China by Britain in 1839, and again by Britain and France jointly in 1858–60, and after the success of the westernizing Meiji Revolution in Japan in 1868, the Japanese had for a time taken to seeing China through contemporary western eyes and not in the traditional Japanese light. They had come to look upon the Chinese as being backward, helpless, and contemptible 'natives'. Japan's subsequent failure to conquer China, working together with its utter defeat in the Second World War, has, I believe, had the effect of restoring in Japanese eyes the image of China as the great central civilized Power which, before the century of China's temporary humiliation (1839–1945), was traditional in Japan, as well as in China itself. If this is a correct diagnosis, then Japan in the latter part of the twentieth century may prove to be as open to Chinese communist propaganda as it was to Chinese Buddhist propaganda in the earlier part of the sixth century. Of course this does not mean that Japan would submit to Chinese military and political domination. Even if Japan were, one day, to adopt communism from China, it would be a nationalist Japanese communism, and the nationalism in this mixture would prevail over the communism in it if there were to be a clash between the interests of the two ideologies. As a matter of fact, it now seems improbable that Japan will go communist, however high the level to which communist China's prestige in Japan may rise. Post-Second-World-War Japan is making such immense technological and industrial progress under a non-communist regime that communism of any brand seems likely to have little attraction there.

As for Korea and Vietnam, their traditional policy towards China has been the same as Japan's. They have embraced Chinese culture but have resisted Chinese domination, and this traditional attitude of theirs seems likely to persist. In both countries, nationalism seems likely to take precedence over any other ideology. This means that, in both countries, reunification will be the paramount objective, and will be welcomed whether the regime under which it is achieved happens to be a communist or a non-communist one. In Vietnam, whatever the military outcome of the present war, eventual political reunification can be predicted with some confidence; and there, at any rate, it seems probable that reunification, when it comes, will be under a communist regime. But it also seems probable that a communist reunited Vietnam will be just as determined to maintain its independence against a communist China as a communist Yugoslavia is to maintain hers against a communist Russia. This can be predicted because, at present, nationalism is the strongest ideology in the world and no other ideology can hold its own against nationalism if and when there is a conflict of interests.

It looks, then, as if China is likely to recover its historic position of being 'the Middle Kingdom' of Eastern Asia, but it also looks as if it is unlikely to be more successful in the future than it has been in the past in dominating politically its East Asian neighbours, even if these prove to find Chinese culture as attractive today as they found it in the past. Beyond the bounds of Eastern Asia, there seems to be no ground for expecting that Chinese prestige is going to stand high. China's traditional claim to be 'the Middle Kingdom' of Eastern Asia was in consonance with the historical realities. On the other hand, its traditional claim that the Chinese Empire amounted to 'All that is under Heaven' was chimerical. It was founded on Chinese ignorance of half the world—a half of the world in which there was, of course, a reciprocal ignorance of China. Today, China does have a foothold in one little country in this other half of the world. But Albania is the smallest and most backward of all the countries of eastern Europe. Some of the more important east European countries that became the Soviet Union's unwilling political satellites after the end of the Second World War may now be playing China off against the Soviet Union as part of their strategy for recovering their freedom from Russian domination. But obviously none of them is intending to submit to Chinese domination in place of Russian. The mere fact that they are communist countries does not make them willing to be subject to either of the two communist super-powers. Though they are communist, Russia's European allies are nationalist first and foremost. We may therefore expect that China's influence in eastern Europe will be ephemeral, and its prospects in Africa seem to be no brighter on a long view. This or that African country may be willing to accept Chinese aid against some African neighbour with which it has a local quarrel, but, in the long run, China's presence in Africa is surely going to be as unwelcome to Africans as Russia's presence or as the presence of the United States and the ex-imperial west European Powers. The only country outside Eastern Asia in which China's prospects of exercising an enduring influence look promising is a non-communist South Asian country, Pakistan. The common interest that draws China and Pakistan together is a nationalistic one. Both countries have a common enemy in India.

To sum up, China's prospects of being able to extend the range of its political domination seem unpromising everywhere. It has better prospects of re-establishing its cultural influence—but this only in Eastern Asia, not in the other half of the world. If this is the truth, China's prospects, outside its own frontiers, are mediocre. Yet by comparison with Russia's prospects, China's are relatively good. China can look forward at least to recovering its traditional cultural prestige in Eastern Asia, whereas Russia—notwithstanding its recent achievements in atomic weaponry, rocketry, and spaceman-ship—seems likely to continue to be looked down upon, as being culturally inferior, in the other Eastern Orthodox Christian countries, as well as in the West. Even within the bounds of the Soviet Union itself the western provinces are restive under Russian ascendancy, because they feel that Great Russia is relatively backward in civiliza-tion. There is the same feeling in the Soviet Union's two Eastern Orthodox Christian allies, Romania and Bulgaria, and the reaction is still stronger in the three Western Christian countries, Hungary, Czechoslovakia, and Poland. All the east European former satellites of the Soviet Union aspire to regain their complete independence, as Yugoslavia has already gained hers. Russia has never been a 'Middle Kingdom' for any of its neighbours—except, perhaps, for some of the more backward peoples in Siberia, the Caucasus, and Central Asia. This lack of cultural prestige is a formidable handicap for Russia in its present effort to spread its influence round the world.

This view might seem to be belied by the depth and persistence of the devotion to Russia exhibited by some leading western writers, artists, and intellectuals. For the hopes raised by 1917 were not confined to the more radical sections of the organized labour move-ment. On the European continent particularly, and to some extent in the United States, large numbers of writers and artists and intellec-tuals felt deeply drawn to the new regime, and responded to the promise of a new beginning in human history that would substantiate the belief expressed by Marx and Engels when they wrote that with the triumph of socialism mankind would move from the realm of necessity into the realm of freedom. Shaken and outraged by the war, as these western intellectuals were, to them the first act of the new government—the decree on peace passed on the day following the seizure of power—demonstrated both the guilt of their own society and the possibility that its evils could be eradicated. To these convictions were added the infection spread by the excitement and optimism which informed the work of Russian writers and artists in the early years of the revolution, ephemeral though they turned out to be. Together, they generated a sense of commitment to a lofty cause that long outlived its origins. The intellectual life of Europe after the First World War cannot be understood unless the strength of the attraction exercised by the events of November 1917 is given its full due.

In the thirties the myth of 1917 gained a new lease of life. When millions were unemployed and hungry people demonstrated in the streets of London and New York, Paris and Berlin, when the problems of the capitalist system seemed more intractable than ever before and its apparent requirements more nonsensical, when Hitler's party was making its way to power, the need to believe in the existence of a more rational, more humane society, brought new recruits into or near the communist fold. For some, a closer acquaintance with the realities of Soviet life was enough to put an end to their attachment—André Gide is perhaps the outstanding example. In Germany the stupidity of the policy imposed by Moscow on the German Communist Party drove many of its leading intellectuals into opposition. For others—and this seems to have been particularly the case in the United States—the series of public trials and the execution in 1936–39 of so many of the outstanding figures of the revolution, the suicide of others, and the assassination of Trotsky, cut the cord. On those who witnessed them, the realities of communist policy in Spain made a similar impact, and the Soviet-German agreement of 1939 generated another wave of resignations. The same pattern of disillusion and rejection was repeated after the war when Stalin excommunicated Tito, and when Soviet troops crushed the risings in Berlin in 1953 and in Hungary three years later.

Nevertheless, the attraction endures—the names of Picasso and Sartre come to mind (not that either of them has ever formally been a communist). Their case illustrates two curious features of the situation of the *communisant* intelligentsia of the West. First, their support for Russia has very little that is positive about it—this is not the reflection of Russian prestige; it is almost entirely the automatic corollary of their dislike of their own society—Sartre's 'I shall hate the bourgeois to my last breath'. (Among the younger generation this dislike—'alienation', to use the current jargon—takes non-political forms; in politics, as in other respects, they reject the paths chosen by the generation of the thirties.) It is less easy to explain the paradoxical contrast between the style—using the word in its widest sense—of Russian arts and letters, and the style of Moscow's supporters outside the USSR. Long after radical experiments in these fields were suppressed in the Soviet Union, and the dead hand of the bureaucracy imposed its disciplined conformism, many of the least conformist, least disciplined writers and artists outside remained unmoved. Picasso's 'formalism' is anathema to the Union of Soviet Artists; Sartre's existentialism is sometimes condemned, usually ignored, by Soviet philosophers. Brecht is far less often staged in Moscow and Leningrad (for many years not at all) than in New York, Paris, and London. Socialist realism, still the official creed of Soviet literati, finds no room for the innovations and experiments of 'progressive' writers in the West. Composers were at one time asked—indeed instructed—to turn out 'tunes' that would appeal to the widest audience of the toilers. The Russian translation of a Günter Grass novel omits all the 'erotic' passages. And though Louis Aragon may publicly deplore the imprisonment of some Soviet writers and the boycott of others, the need is still strong to preserve the myth, to keep bright the picture of a world that, if not ideal, is better than their own.

Understandably, there is for them something attractive in the importance attached by the Soviet authorities to the artist's function, to his purpose in society, to the services he can perform in education and propaganda, in helping to shape the 'new Soviet man'. The strength of the concern they show, their serious (if misguided) appreciation of what the artist and intellectual can contribute to a country, though it carries with it the acceptance of the tastes and judgments of a philistine bureaucracy, may seem preferable to the position of perpetual suspect outsider whose job is to entertain, divert, and please.

But for the enhancement of its prestige, Russia's greatest asset is the technological and economic progress that it has succeeded in making during the first half century of its communist dispensation. This is no doubt one of the reasons why it is spending on spacemanship resources that, from any other point of view than that of publicity and propaganda, would be better employed on productive public works. Communist Russia's spacemanship is a crude but easily understandable advertisement of its technological success, and this advertisement is calculated to make Russian communism look like a talisman for countries that possess great undeveloped natural resources but that, under non-communist regimes, have failed so far to develop these resources for the benefit of the indigent majority of the population. Venezuela and Libya are examples of such countries in which natural wealth abounds while the mass of the people still remains poor. This is a politically explosive situation, and it is one from which communist Russia might profit politically in virtue of its impressive technological and economic record. Here Russia has a potential political leverage which China does not possess—at any rate, not yet.

An estimate of communist Russia's and communist China's influence on other parts of the world up to the year 1967 would be incomplete and therefore unrealistic if it took account of positive effects only. Negative effects are just as real, and they may eventually turn out, in retrospect, to have been more important. The most potent negative effect of communism outside the communist countries has been in the United States. At the present moment, China, not Russia, is the American people's and government's principal communist bugbear, but it is Russia—which went communist nearly one-third of a century earlier than China did—that has had the portentous effect on the American outlook and on American policy —and this in the domestic American field, as well as in the world-wide ideological, political, and military arena. This effect of the communist revolution in Russia on the United States is of major importance in its influence on the course of the world's history, considering that, as the cumulative result of the two world wars, the United States has become the leading western Power.

The capture of the Russian Empire by communism in and after 1917 was the first event in the Old World, since the creation of the United States, that awoke American minds to an awareness of the possibility that the American way of life, and perhaps even the political independence of the United States, was, after all, not secure. The awakening was sudden, and the subsequent effect of it has been traumatic. This has been a psychologically revolutionary new departure from what had been the prevalent American attitude towards international affairs since the achievement of independence. The United States severed its political ties with Britain after Britain had evicted France from North America. The two events, taken together and followed up by the Louisiana Purchase and the enuncia-tion of the Monroe Doctrine, made the American people feel that they had achieved not only independence but also security within the broad bounds of their own hemisphere. This belief, in its turn, made them feel that they could afford to be indifferent spectators of any events, however earth-shaking, in the Old World.

The most recent and most surprising illustration of this traditional American sense of security was the American people's failure to appreciate the gravity of the German threat to the security of the United States in both the First and the Second World War. In both wars their impulse was to remain neutral, on the assumption that, as far as America's national interests went, it was a matter of indifference for America which of the European contending alliances won. The United States did, of course, eventually intervene in both wars, and in each case its immense industrial potential made Germany's defeat inevitable. Yet probably the United States would not have become a belligerent if it had not been driven into belligerency —by Germany in the first war and by Germany's ally Japan in the second. Even after its experience of the German temper in the two wars, the United States still appears to feel no mistrust of German militarism. Since the Second World War it has deliberately re-armed Germany to serve as its ally against the Soviet Union.

In the two wars, the United States suffered serious injury at German hands. The Germans killed or wounded hundreds of thousands of American soldiers and sank many dozens of American merchant ships. By contrast, no American soldiers have been killed, and no American ships sunk, by Russian hands so far. Again, any atrocities that the Russians may have committed under the Tsarist and the communist regimes in Russia are eclipsed by the atrocities committed by the Germans, especially under the nazi regime. Yet the American people have never been either seriously alarmed, or even passionately indignant, at any German acts. In spite of these acts, the Americans have had a strong desire to think of the Germans as being innocuous and respectable. On the other hand, since Russia went communist in and after 1917, the majority of Americans—though they have suffered no injury at Russian hands—have thought of the Russians as being ogres, and since the end of the Second World War they have eagerly accepted any anti-Russian regime in any country as their ally. However black the record of an anti-Russian regime may be, its anti-Russian attitude is a warrant of respectability in a great many American eyes. This contrast, within the last half-century, between the respective American attitudes towards Russia and towards Germany is startling. It requires explanation; and the explanation is to be found in the violence of the American reaction to the Russian Revolution of 1917.

Since 1917, the traditional policy of the United States has veered round to its extreme opposite. In the days of the Holy Alliance, American sympathy was always on the side of peoples that were struggling to liberate themselves from despotic governments—and this not only in the western hemisphere but all over the world. Read what Metternich wrote to the Emperor Alexander I apropos of the promulgation of the Monroe Doctrine:

These United States of America have astonished Europe by a new act of revolt, more unprovoked, fully as audacious, and no less dangerous than the former. . . . In fostering revolutions wherever they show themselves, in regretting those which have failed, in extending a helping hand to those which seem to prosper, they lend new strength to the apostles of sedition, and reanimate the courage of every conspirator. If this flood of pernicious example should extend over the whole of America, what would become of our religious and political institutions, of the moral force of our governments, and of the conservative system which has saved Europe from complete dissolution?[1]

These words might have been written by John Foster Dulles apropos of the Soviet Union. On the map of the United States you will find a number of places named after nineteenth-century European fighters for freedom. As late as the close of the nineteenth century the United States intervened to liberate Cuba from Spain. As late as that, the American people still thought of themselves as being the champions of freedom—a free people that was eager to see other people win, in their turn, the freedom that the American people had won for themselves. Today, 'so-called wars of liberation' excite far less American sympathy. If they evoke any American action, this takes the shape of an American expeditionary force to extinguish the 'brush-fire'. The American argument is that an insurrection that is liberal at the start may turn communist later, so the United States cannot afford to let even a liberal revolution run its course without American intervention against it. When Fidel Castro took up arms against the Batista regime in Cuba, he did not win the wholehearted American sympathy that had been won by the Cuban insurgents against Spanish rule in the eighteen-nineties. For a brief interval there was indeed a

[1] Quoted by Dexter Perkins in *The United States and Latin America* (Louisiana State University Press, 1961), pp. 46-7.

good measure of support and approval, since the regime against which Castro was revolting had been an abominable one. But these were soon forfeited, and the American attitude settled down to one of deep suspicion and hostility.

This reversal of American policy has been dramatic. What, then, is the explanation? The ultimate explanation is, no doubt, 'the deceitfulness of riches'. Wealth does produce, in its possessors, the unhappy moral effects that are denounced in the Gospels; and, between the date of the United States' achievement of independence and the capture of Russia by communism in 1917, the United States had become an incomparably rich country.

To the minds of well-to-do Americans, communism looked, from the date of its triumph in Russia, like an infectious disease that might prove catching even in the United States itself. When, later, the American people woke up to the truth that the annihilation of distance by the progress of technology had deprived them also of their fancied security against military attack from abroad, there was bound to be a cumulative American reaction. If it was true that the width of the Atlantic and Pacific Oceans no longer gave the United States physical protection against potential attempts from abroad to rob the American people of their wealth, then the United States' traditional policy of isolationism could no longer give her the security she was still determined to have. This novel precariousness of the situation suggested to some American minds—for example, Mr John Foster Dulles—that henceforth, in order to make itself secure at home, the United States must sally out beyond its own frontiers to nip in the bud any subversive movement anywhere in the world, even on the opposite side of the globe. If this policy had been carried out to its extreme logical conclusion, and if the United States had not been a democracy in which issues are freely and vigorously debated, and in which the Administration's will is not law, the United States might have found itself committed to Metternich's policy of worldwide repression—a policy that the American people detested when it was practised by Metternich himself. This would have been calamitous because that policy is bound, by its very nature, to fail sooner or later, as Metternich's own experience has demonstrated. The Metternichian policy is to stop change; and change cannot be stopped, because change is another name for life.

The American people's enrichment would presumably have induced them to adopt a defensive-minded conservative stance sooner or later. But the event that moved the country to become the conscious and deliberate champion of conservatism and to drop its traditional championship of revolution was the Russian Revolution of 1917; and in restrospect the effect of this revolution on the United States may prove to have been more important—and possibly more lasting too—than its effect on Russia itself. Since 1917, the United States has fancied itself in the role of the world's defender against monolithic world communism.

Monolithic world communism was originally a dream of Lenin's, and the passage of half a century has demonstrated that this dream is an illusion. Today, each of the communist countries is just as narrowly nationalistic-minded as each of the non-communist countries, and this is recognized in the communist countries themselves. In the Soviet Union, in the east European countries allied to it, in Yugoslavia, in China, no-one any longer pretends that communism is presenting a united front to the rest of the world. The only country in which Lenin's dream is still haunting people's minds today is—paradoxically—the United States.

This is dreamland, not reality; for communism has proved not to be the world-unifying ideological force that Lenin predicted it would be. It has proved not to be the strongest ideology in the present-day world. It has been defeated by nationalism, and this is unfortunate for mankind; for in the atomic age nationalism is a far more serious threat than communism is to the survival of the human race. There is, however, an impersonal force at work in the present-day world that is still more powerful than nationalism, and that is technology boosted by the systematic application of science. In the modern world, technology is the key to material power, and therefore, on a planet whose habitable surface is partitioned among about 125 local sovereign States, every State must have up-to-date technology. If a country were to fall behind in the race for technological development, it would go under. In order to have up-to-date technology, a country must have efficient technicians, scientists, and administrators. The representatives of these walks of life are birds of a feather, in whatever country they may happen to be working and whatever the ideology that happens to be professed by that country's government. The technicians, scientists, and administrators of the world's 125 States can understand each other; they are, in fact, the nucleus of a new citizen-body—a body of people who are citizens of the world rather than citizens of some fraction of it.

Through the uniform professional action of this nucleus of world-citizens in every country, life is now being standardized in all countries. In consequence, our distinctive ideological labels, which are focuses of such strong emotion, are becoming less and less relevant to the facts of life. No doubt the labels will be retained long after the local ways of life which the labels purport to distinguish have in truth become indistinguishable from each other. These cherished emblems of perilous discord will die hard, but it can be prophesied that they will all die sooner or later—unless, of course, they first inveigle the human race into committing mass suicide by fighting an atomic world war in the near future. We may guess that the United States' anti-communist label will prove rather more durable than the Soviet Union's communist label, but we may also guess that both labels will gradually fade out. By the end of the Union of Soviet Socialist Republics' second half-century of existence, the terms 'Soviet' and 'Socialist' will have become meaningless, because the *de facto* constitutions of the Soviet Union and the United States will have become virtually identical.

We may even guess that, by that date, neither the Soviet Union nor the United States will any longer be sovereign (except, perhaps, in the nominal sense in which each of the component states of the United States is sovereign today). One of the characteristics of the evolution of technology is that, in order to continue to operate effectively, it has to operate on a constantly expanding scale. The day is now not far distant at which the minimum unit of effective technological operation, for all purposes of any importance, will be the entire surface of this planet, together with a thin but progressively thickening envelope of outer space. Technology, like truth (and technology is a prosaic form of truth) is mighty and will prevail. Nationalism seems to have no prospect of being able to stand up to technology, powerful though the hold of nationalism over human hearts still is. Nationalism's only chance of stopping the march of technology would be to make a holocaust of the human race, and in that case nationalism itself, as well as technology, would be consumed in the burning fiery furnace.

The present essay is a general introduction to the theme of this book. Some of the more important aspects of the impact of the Bolshevik Revolution on the world during the first half century after 1917 are discussed in the following essays in detail.

Professor Seton-Watson deals with the political effects of communism on nationalism and imperialism, both inside the Soviet Union and in the rest of the world.

Communism, Professor Seton-Watson points out, has proclaimed itself to be the champion of national self-determination, and, in the Soviet Union, the component nationalities have, in theory, the right to secede. Actually, on the other hand, the Soviet Union has firmly held together the former Tsarist colonial empire. This is, indeed, the one great colonial empire that is still substantially intact. Is the maintenance of the former Russian Empire in the form of the Soviet Union going to be permanent? Or is this empire, too, going to dissolve, as so many former colonial empires have dissolved— partly through the action of communism—within the last half century?

Mr McInnes deals with the effects, on the socialist and labour movement outside the Soviet Union, of the Bolsheviks' capture of the Russian State. He is chiefly concerned with the effects in western countries. He points out that Russia has produced a special Russian type of revolutionary leader and a special Russian conception of the meaning of revolutionary orthodoxy. It is indeed true that the historical figure of Lenin was foreshadowed in Turgenev's imaginary picture of Bazarov in *Fathers and Sons*, while both the self-appointed leader and his despotic method of organization are prefigured by Dostoevsky in *The Possessed*. The leader is not a democratically commissioned representative of the oppressed masses whose wrongs he has set out to redress. He has commissioned himself, and the first and last duty of the rank and file is obedience to him. Orthodoxy means faithfully following the party line along whatever twists and turns it may be given. Nominally the line is determined, from moment to moment, by a majority of the party itself. Actually, it is determined by a small directing inner ring. The essence of orthodoxy is that, however the line may have been determined, it must be followed blindly. In the figure of the leader we may see a descendant of serf-owning Russian nobles who has changed his creed without having changed his behaviour. He expects from his political henchmen the subservience that his forefathers exacted from their serfs. As for the Russian communist conception of orthodoxy, it is reminiscent of the classical Christian conception of it. In the successive church councils that shaped Christian orthodoxy in the course of the fourth and fifth centuries, the shape underwent repeated changes that were nominally approved, on each occasion, by a majority of the fathers, but were usually imposed, in truth, by some domineering minority. Here, too, unquestioning obedience was demanded for each successive decision, however this might have been reached. The vein of authoritarianism in the Christian tradition had not been eroded in the Eastern Orthodox Christian countries by any counterpart of the revolt against the passive acceptance of authority that had begun to assert itself in the West before the close of the seventeenth century. A nineteenth-century Russian revolutionary who had rejected the tenets of Eastern Orthodox Christianity might not have shaken off the Christian tradition of authoritarianism.

One element that communism inherited from its repudiated Christian background was the church's belief in its mission to convert the whole human race. Russian communism is, or at any rate began by being, a missionary religion. This is the aspect of it with which Mr McInnes is particularly concerned in his essay. He brings out the point that the features of Russian communism that were propitious for its victory in Russia have been handicaps for it abroad, and this especially in western countries. Moreover, the western industrial workers had been so successful in gaining an ever increasing share in the amenities of the bourgeois way of life that it had become inconceivable that they would turn back from the revisionist policy that had paid these dividends to a revolutionary policy that would now have jeopardized the workers' own economic and social gains in attacking the bourgeois regime. In fact, the western workers had become bourgeois-minded, whereas in Russia the bourgeois way of life had never gained a firm foothold.

Mr McInnes shows that the main effect of communism on western socialist and labour parties has been to sabotage their left wings and to drive their right wings farther and quicker towards the goal of absorption into bourgeois society—a goal towards which they were already moving and would no doubt have continued to move in any case, even if the advent of communism had not given them an additional push in this direction.

Would it be an exaggeration to say that, in the West, the ultimate effect of the impact of communism has been to make it doubly sure that the future of the West will be a bourgeois one?

Professor Richard Lowenthal analyses the nature and structure of the communist regime in the Soviet Union, and goes on to consider how far this has been taken as a model elsewhere.

He points out that the word 'Soviet', which is part of the official title of the country and of each of its constituent republics, does not correspond to the actual political facts. 'Soviet' means an elected committee, whereas in reality the Soviet government is not amenable to any elected body; it is a totalitarian single-party regime. The party's fiat is, indeed, not merely above the law; it is the law.

The totalitarian system of government was improvised by Lenin in the course of his seizure of power and was a necessary means to this end. He did not create the system out of nothing; he found it ready to hand (to a Russian hand, that is) in the nineteenth-century Russian revolutionary tradition. The nineteenth-century Russian revolutionaries had professed to be carrying out the will of the people, but in truth they had been, not the people's representatives, but self-appointed leaders who imposed their own will on their rank and file. Lenin was familiar with this tradition, and he followed it.

What is remarkable, and unusual, about Lenin's totalitarian regime is its success in surviving. It survived the defeat of the counter-revolutionaries in the Civil War; it survived the New Economic Policy. It succeeded in harnessing the Russian people's economic energies to purposes that were not the people's own, and it was thus able—at a high cost to Russia—to give the Russian economy and society an abiding twist in the direction of the Bolshevik ideology. Lenin and his companions were not visionaries, however. One of the reasons for their success was that they invariably sacrificed their ideology whenever this was proving an obstacle to their retaining their power and making headway with the process of modernization. They did succeed in creating a distinctively Russian new form of government. It was new in the sense that it demonstrated the capacity of ruthless government to drive a coach and horses through social 'laws' that had been thought, by Marx and by the liberals alike, to be immutable by man. The one thing that the Russian communist totalitarian regime has failed to do has been to achieve its professed, and never repudiated, objective of giving power to the proletariat and establishing an egalitarian society.

The Russian-ness of Lenin's communist totalitarianism made the fortune of this form of government in its, and Lenin's, own country. But its strong point at home in Russia has proved to be its weak point in western countries. The arbitrariness of this system of government has made it hard to swallow for western communists, who have been brought up, like other westerners, in the western, not the

Russian, tradition. The Russian model has, in fact, been virtually abandoned by the French and Italian Communist Parties, which are the only two in the West that have come to play an important part in the national life of their respective countries.

On the other hand, totalitarianism of the Russian type has been seized upon, as the very tool that they needed for their purpose, by leaders of revolutionary movements in non-western countries whose objective was to modernize their peoples' lives on capitalist, not on communist, lines. Professor Lowenthal takes Mustafa Kemal Atatürk's political career as a classical example of this. Atatürk suppressed the Turkish communists, but at the same time he followed in Lenin's footsteps in his progressive imposition on Turkey of a totalitarian one-party regime. Mr Lowenthal points out, however, that this non-communist one-party regime in Turkey did not have the staying-power that its communist prototype in Russia has had. Opposition parties were allowed to revive in 1946, and in 1950 the party that had previously held the monopoly of power allowed itself to be put out of office by the verdict of a general election—a concession to liberalism that, in the Soviet Union, was still out of the question on the fiftieth anniversary of the revolution of 1917.

Professor Peter Wiles discusses the Soviet impact on economic policy in non-communist countries. His field is large, and, in each national compartment of it, he goes into illuminating detail. It would be superfluous to try to give a résumé of this in the present introductory essay. Mr Wiles's general conclusion is that the non-communist governments and classes and peoples that have reacted, on the economic plane, to the Soviet impact have, in most cases, had no more than a vague idea of what the Soviet communist doctrines, objectives, and achievements really are. What they have been reacting to is an enigmatic new menacing presence in the world which might bear down upon them, with possibly dire consequences for them, if they did not forestall this danger by moving of their own accord in the direction in which their pursuer would drive them if they were ever to allow him to overtake them.

I have just called Soviet communism a 'new' menacing presence, but it might be more accurate to say that, for Jews, Christians, and Moslems, this is a familiar presence that has merely assumed a new dress. In the world of the Judaic religions, has not Soviet communism been playing the traditional role of the Devil, alias Satan or Iblis? The Devil's traditional service to human beings has been to scare them into doing things that they ought to do rather more quickly than they might have been willing to move if they had not observed that the Devil is on their tracks. If communism is performing this service for the non-communist world, we may presume that capitalism is performing it for communists. This reciprocal service as substitutes for the traditional devil is one of the rare useful functions of the two antithetical ideologies. In an age in which the historic religions are losing their former hold on human consciences, a convincing replacement of a no longer convincing devil may be one of the necessities of social life.

I cannot close this introductory chapter without expressing, on my fellow contributors' part, as well as on my own, our gratitude to Mrs Jane Degras, who has been most generous in bringing her expert knowledge to bear on the subjects with which this book, as a whole, is concerned, and who edited and prepared it for the press.

The Labour Movement
Socialists, Communists, Trade Unions

NEIL McINNES

FIFTY years after the Bolshevik Revolution, the influence of that event on western socialism seems largely spent. After splitting the labour movement in most countries where there was one, and contributing to the further transformation of that movement in ways that will be studied below in greater detail, Soviet Russia and the national communist parties today have virtually ceased to be important external influences on it. As some say, the communist parties are evolving towards the position of left wing of the labour movement. That formulation is unfortunate since the main fact of the situation, the fact that the communists will have most difficulty in admitting, is that there is no longer a proletarian socialist movement in western countries for them to become the left wing of. What is true is that the communist parties, all that remains of the impact of the Bolshevik Revolution inside western societies, are seeking—after almost half a century of bitter rivalry and often bloody conflict—to find grounds for co-operation with the political parties and trade unions that have inherited the names, the vocabulary, and some of the ideas of the Socialist International. This reconciliation, for which the will exists as well on the socialist side, will no doubt be much more difficult, painful, and slow than is imagined by apostles of the 'reunification of the Left', who seem to borrow their oecumenical optimism from similarly inspired theologians dreaming of reunification of the churches. As in that case, literal reunification is, and long will be, delayed by the tendency of party machines and bureaucratic apparatuses to persist in their being. This inertia is never more dogged than when ideologically unjustified; a party, socialist or communist, that has abandoned every point of principle that once made it distinctive, clings hard to its organization because that is all it has left. However, these rearguard operations, though they may last years, do not change the fact that the tendency now is towards a healing of the split that 1917 brought to the socialist movement and that, therefore, the Bolshevik Revolution is henceforth a spent force in this direction.

Yet the notion that what 1917 put asunder can now be brought together again is quite mistaken, for the two wings that parted company just after the First World War have suffered the most extraordinary changes since—and in fact one has ceased to exist all but in name. Bolshevism, for all its mutations, has changed the less. Of course there is an immense gap between the aspirations of the October Revolution and the realities of Soviet power, between the revolutionary movement that western communists imagined they were adhering to in 1919–23 and the actual Leninist regime. But that is not a change over time; that is merely the contrast of illusion with fact. As a political reality, the Russian communist movement shows a striking continuity from 1917 to today, with important changes crowded into the last few years only. By about 1924, the Russian regime and hence the communist parties through which it made its effects felt in the West had assumed a form that remained pretty much unchanged for the next thirty years (granted that one includes among its constant features the ability to perform volte-faces or tactical zigzags of a sort unknown in other movements). Above all, the regime and its foreign agents have remained faithful to a revolutionary mythology which froze, almost fifty years ago, into a conservative force and a blindness to historical change.

As against that constancy and conservatism, the other half (one simplifies: the Left has always been a congeries of sects and party machines) of the socialist movement has been, ever since the split of 1919–23, fully exposed to the vast transformations of western economies and polities. It has had to live—where it has been allowed to live at all, for one must recall that over much of Europe and Latin America and in part of Asia it has been suppressed for part of the fifty years we are speaking of—in an atmosphere of competition, criticism, and more or less free enquiry and political struggle. So inevitably it has suffered considerably more change than a party ensconced in absolute power and devoted to the celebration of a revolutionary liturgy. Indeed, it now bears scant resemblance to the socialist movement of before the Bolshevik Revolution and even less to what was specifically proletarian in that pre-war movement.

These transformations not only make impossible, at their term, the simple reunification of the socialist movement, but they made difficult, during their occurrence, the identification of the influence of the two wings of socialism on each other, amid the confusion of other influences on both. Specifically, and to take up the position from which the question will be studied in what follows, it is hard to separate out the impact of the Bolshevik regime and its communist parties on the western labour movement in a period during which that movement was being hammered by depression, fascism, world war, the development of capitalism, and the transformation of the status of the working classes.

For all that, there are quite clear cases where the communists influenced the adjustment of the western labour movement to these things, and a study of them will be the substance of this essay. In sum, it will be shown that the consistent impact of the Russians and the communists on western socialism was in the direction of hampering a realistic or 'reformist' acceptance of those new facts, while at the same time blocking any revolutionary effort to change them. That is, socialism suffered, as far as it was influenced by the communists after 1917, a dual amputation, on its left and on its right. All the 'infantile maladies' of socialism, the extremist plans for a radical, revolutionary overturn of modern society in favour of proletarian self-government, were purged by communist teaching, example, and interference. At one and the same time, 'integration' of the socialist parties, the trade unions, and the workers generally into the new society was opposed just as vigorously by the communists. Their plainest influence has often been to give a bad conscience (and hence a diminished efficacy) to western socialists seeking to come to terms with a system they could no longer hope and no longer desire to overthrow. As this doubly crippling influence is removed, as the impact of the Bolshevik Revolution on western leftist movements is spent, the first result is of course a quicker and more rational integration into society of those who no longer feel 'outflanked on the left'. Yet a second result that might not be long in manifesting itself could be the release of new radical forces seeking, with more pertinence than Marxist parties obsessed with the problems of another day, to mobilize present discontents in a movement concerned with thorough-going social change. Meanwhile, the outworn revolutionary vocabulary whose irrelevance to western conditions is henceforth admitted even by communists, is taken up by the Chinese for uses that are not yet clear. But it is improbable that this latest raising of the revolutionary banner will have any effect on western socialism remotely comparable to the epoch of 1917.

The influence of 1917 on western socialism was so extensive that there is no need to exaggerate it, as is sometimes done. For example, there is systematic overstatement in an essay—written, admittedly, at the height of the honeymoon of the Soviets and the western Allies[1]—that gives the Bolsheviks credit for the progress of social welfare doctrines in the West and which mistakes temporary wartime expedients like labour direction and governmental economic controls for a permanent Soviet contribution to western political practice. Such policies, and others thought to have the same origin like anti-individualism, non-economic incentives, or impatience with the free interplay of ideas, are part of the common heritage of all varieties of socialism; western socialists did not have to go looking in Moscow for them.

More generally, it is remarkable how many western socialists could show no more concern with 1917 than westerners of other political persuasions, regarding the whole Bolshevik experiment down to the present day as something entirely foreign to socialism as they understood it. This was most evident in countries like Britain, where communism never gained a significant native following, and where Russian events were held of no more interest than several other chapters of international affairs. Thus, an account of the British Labour Party in the 1920s can be written with virtually no reference to the impact of the Bolshevik Revolution[2], for the good reason that the party was evolving in a contrary sense to anything that Russian influence might have decided, that is, away from a narrowly based workers' party towards a national, non-class party. G. D. H. Cole[3] has even suggested that Russian influence was often negative in this respect, making adherents of the Second International 'more dogmatic' in their attachment to parliamentary democracy 'in their reaction against the proletarian dictatorship' preached by the Bolsheviks. At all events, one finds numerous instances of socialist parties, and not only in Britain, simply shrugging off the Bolshevik Revolution as a development that one might regard with more or less sympathy or distaste but in any case as something peculiar to a backward empire with no prior experience of democracy. Such socialists were content to remain extraordinarily ignorant of Soviet

---

[1] E. H. Carr, *The Soviet Impact on the Western World* (London, 1946).
[2] Catherine Anne Cline, *Recruits to Labour: the British Labour Party 1914–1931* (Syracuse, 1963).
[3] G. D. H. Cole, *World Socialism Restated* (London, 1956), p. 7.

Russia until the wartime alliance produced a polite interest, which lapsed with the return of peace. Examples would be the labour parties of Australia and New Zealand, but the same attitude was adopted by those individual socialist leaders in other countries for whom civil liberty had always been an essential component of socialism. Perhaps a certain sense of superiority entered into this attitude, inclining these socialists to put Russian communism in a class with fascism and Hitlerism as foreign commotions that could contain no instruction for western democrats. Yet it was a sure instinct that prompted the judgment that the overthrow of Tsarism and the subsequent industrialization of a backward country by a dictatorship could have no relevance to the progress of western socialism. Wherever attachment to democratic liberties, shared by socialists with liberals of all sorts, took precedence over specifically socialist aims, the Bolshevik experiment was regarded as embarrassing but irrelevant. So one looks in vain for any impact of 1917 on many socialist and labour parties, except for brief periods, such as the post-1948 Cold War, when they found themselves incommoded in their relations with trade unions by a small but active communist infiltration.

Next, there are instances where an apparently intense interest in the progress of the Russian Revolution over the decades has been combined with resistance to communist influence at home and disinclination to change socialist policies in imitation of Russian. What one is encountering here is the function of the myth of Soviet Russia as a workers' paradise. This myth served sections of the western working class as a consoling fantasy in dark days of economic depression and unemployment (which were also the darkest days of Stalin's tyranny over that workers' paradise). Political opponents of socialism naturally enough made capital of western socialists' toleration of these fantasies, denouncing in them the progress of Bolshevik doctrines, but one is bound to notice that they in fact constituted a striking case of unbridled but ineffectual mythopoeia, and thus cannot be counted as a material influence at all. Borkenau noted before the war how

broad strata which were absolutely non-revolutionary in their own countries started sympathising with the Soviet Union. The same feeling was still stronger among those groups of the labour movement, principally among the left-wing socialists, which, while sympathising with revolution, felt that for a long time to come there was little chance for it . . . the appeal of present-day non-revolutionary communism is a strange psychological phenomenon. It is not due to a revolutionary programme, because the communists are no longer revolutionary; it is not due to a moderate programme, because there is no lack of moderate parties of old standing. It is due, however, to the strange merging of an utterly non-revolutionary and anti-revolutionary policy with the belief in the myth that paradise on earth has already been achieved over 'one-sixth of the earth's inhabited surface'. At home, the masses which vote communist would never fight against democracy, for revolution. It is all the more gratifying, therefore, to adore the dictatorship in Russia and to indulge, in its service, in all those impulses of violence, of vilification and extermination of one's adversaries, which cannot be satisfied at home.[4]

In short, one of the most obvious effects of the Bolshevik Revolution on western socialism was to permit utopian daydreaming that was seldom allowed to have any influence over practical political activity.

These reservations made, one may note that in every country where left or labour movements existed before the First World War (and in most where they arose later), the Bolshevik Revolution brought a division into 'socialists' and 'communists'. In some countries one or other of these groups was a small minority of no political importance; the socialists were soon rendered so in Russia itself, and the communists remained so in Britain. But in many other countries, and notably through most of continental Europe, both were substantial enough forces to make their subsequent rivalry, and occasional collaboration in 'united fronts', facts of the first political importance. The labels by which they are designated became household words and were taken to indicate a decisive distinction, though the one communist country between the world wars was the Union of Soviet *Socialist* Republics. The two words 'socialist' and 'communist' have a chequered history, and the latter term, strictly understood, should have had no application to any Marxist doctrine.[5] Marx and Engels chose it for their Communist Manifesto because of the discredit that utopian fantasy had brought upon the other term, yet by the end of the nineteenth century and down to 1914, the word 'communist' had largely lapsed from use because there was no longer the same need to distinguish the socialist movement from speculation by philosophical socialists. Lenin revived 'communist' again when, after the collapse and discredit of the Second International, he sought a label to distinguish his party from the old socialist parties. At the

[4] F. Borkenau, *World Communism* (new edition, Ann Arbor, 1962), pp. 267, 426.
[5] See the present writer's article 'Communism' in the *Encyclopedia of Philosophy* (New York, 1966).

same time, and inconsistently perhaps from the point of view of keeping one clear meaning for the term, Lenin made much of an *obiter dictum* of Marx in the *Critique of the Gotha Programme*. Marx there was seeking to discourage idle communist speculation within the socialist movement, and he said that the slogan of fair and equal shares for all (the age-old programme of philosophical communists) could be inscribed on the socialist banner only in a future that he made sound sadly remote, namely, when socialism had solved the human race's economic problem and when men had undergone a moral regeneration.[6] Lenin picked up this brief aside and blew it up into the dogma of the two stages of post-revolutionary society, with full communism as the second, higher phase. Stalin gave the name 'socialism' to the first phase. The upshot is that both terms are now misnomers for the main branches of the leftist movement: the socialists dissociate themselves from many of the things that the movement for the autonomy of the working class in the last century called socialism, while the communists will readily admit to condemning communism as dangerous fantasy, 'for the time being' at least.

By whatever name its products be known, the split occasioned by the Bolshevik Revolution was momentous. Not, however, because the socialist movement down to that day had been united. It had never known unity though it had always hankered after it and had sometimes pretended to have attained it on the strength of misunderstandings (as, for example, concerning opposition to war). Nor, for that matter, were the grounds of the division forced by Lenin new; the distinction he made between the 'opportunist' socialists and the disciplined communists was familiar, in slightly different terms, to all European leftists. What was new, and what divided the socialist movement as never before, was a specifically Russian combination of revolutionary purity and tactical suppleness that Lenin introduced under cover of a dogmatic theory of political strategy. Lenin, and after him the communist parties, claimed to be able to settle with a scientific certitude questions of practice and of principle that had

---

[6] 'In a higher phase of communist society, after the enslaving subordination of individuals under the division of labour, and therewith also the antithesis between mental and physical labour, has vanished; after labour has ceased to be a means of life and has become itself the primary necessity of life; after the productive forces have also increased with the all-round development of the individual, and all the springs of co-operative wealth flow more abundantly—only then can the narrow horizon of bourgeois law be fully left behind and society inscribe on its banners: From each according to his ability, to each according to his needs'. Karl Marx, *Critique of the Gotha Programme*.

always beset the socialist movement. They claimed to possess a science that showed what, in each concrete historical situation, was the Left and what the Right, what the progressive solution and what the conservative one. This science served as rational justification for what seemed, to western socialists, a fanticism *à éclipse*, a revolutionary extremism and a political purity that could be turned on and off like a tap. The socialist movement had always been familiar with the distinctions made and the lines of division drawn by the Bolsheviks, but it had discussed them in a rational language shared with other western political movements. From 1917 on, or rather from 1919, when the Russians began directly to intervene in the affairs of western socialism, all these issues became justiciable to a 'science of revolution' which was actually an opportunist religion. On this, the western labour movement was riven. So one must look to see what were the sorts of disagreement that marked the pre-war socialist movement, and then contrast them with the great schism that followed the Bolshevik Revolution.

Breaking out in the midst of world war, that revolution found the international socialist movement already divided against itself, but the breaches were of the sort that the return to peace would have healed. The socialist majorities which had rallied to the national cause and voted the war credits (or at least abstained) were divided on straight nationalist lines, and their leaders refused as commerce with the enemy invitations to several abortive international conferences staged after 1915. Only a few socialists maintained this attitude after the war, declining for a time to sit at the same table as the ex-enemy. More profound, and yet no more important because involving fewer people, was the split inside each socialist party between the majority that had put patriotism before international proletarian solidarity and the minority that had preached pacifism—which in the conditions of modern total warfare would soon have led beyond voting against war credits and opposing conscription to 'revolutionary defeatism'. Every belligerent country saw its socialists rent on this issue, but only in Russia and later in Germany did the minority of revolutionary defeatists gain any significant audience. Everywhere else, the mass of the workers followed leaders who, in 1914, may well have 'betrayed' their anti-war declarations of earlier years but had not betrayed the generally patriotic mood of their party members. There developed, with growing war-weariness, widespread impatience with these leaders for failing to echo adequately the yearnings for peace among those who bore the main brunt of the atrocious sufferings of 1915–17. But from there to revolutionary defeatism there was a distance that only Russians could cover, for the evident reason that only Russians did not thereby run the risk of exposing themselves to subjection to a more oppressive regime. French and British socialists preferred bourgeois democracy to the institutions of Imperial Germany, and the Germans in turn preferred these to those of Tsarism. The China of 1914–18 not being that of 1967, Russians had no such preference.

So, although there was much bitter discussion immediately after the war among socialists about responsibilities for the disaster, and although the Russians sought to make this the pretext for a split in the movement and for the founding of a new International, this was not an issue that would have caused a great schism. The truth is that with Jaurès in August 1914 died the illusion of European socialists that they could, or that they would even want to in an acid test, stop war between their various nations; and that illusion has not since reappeared.

The divisions within socialism that were to be more important, as faults in the rock that will split, date back much earlier than 1914. They date back to a central ambiguity of Marx's own political thought, which in this simply reflects the ambiguous situation of the socialist movement in a democracy. On the whole Marx had favoured recourse to political action by socialists, as against the anarchist, mutualist, co-operativist, and utopian strains in socialism. Even so, one must note recurrent anarchist themes in his policy, which are evident in his first work in 1844 and come back in 1871 after the Commune[7]; they are pronounced enough for Sorel to think to find in them 'the Marxism of Marx'.[8] But that aspect of Marxism, and the socialist lineage it expresses, were not to be of importance in the socialist schism of this century, for the Bolsheviks and their social-democratic adversaries agreed in combating anarcho-syndicalism in all its forms and in seeking to reduce trade unions to dependence on political parties formed by socialists. The ambiguity that was to matter was about what sort of politics the movement was to practise, whether it should be frankly revolutionary or whether it should be parliamentary, electoralist, gradualist (to use some of the terms

[7] Maximilien Rubel, *Karl Marx devant le bonapartisme* (Paris, 1960), pp. 153, 156.
[8] G. Sorel, *La Décomposition du marxisme* (Paris, 1908).

that came up in the long debate), in short democratic. Both seemed plausible policies and warrant for each may be found in Marx's writings, a consideration that mattered inside a movement that by 1895 had become self-conscious about its Marxist orthodoxy. Perhaps it is just this fact, that from Marxism may be deduced contradictory, incompatible policies, that one may find in it almost as one chooses a minimum programme and a maximum programme, that explains the great success of Marxism as the common denominator of socialist ideologies from Marx's death in 1883 onwards, so that Jacobins and Blanquists could rub shoulders inside Marxist parties with parliamentary democrats. When Bernstein showed the two contrasting elements in Marxism, 'The one utopian, sectarian, peacefully evolutionist, the other conspiratorial, demagogic, terrorist', Kautsky replied that Marx had reconciled these contraries 'in a higher unity'. That dialectical solution was entirely satisfactory as long as one remained (as of course Kautsky firmly intended to remain) on the plane of mere talk, but it was less so in the conditions of political action. As a guide to action, Marxism, which was claimed by most socialists as their ideology from the start of this century, remained imprecise and contradictory.[9]

Disagreement about socialist policies—revolution or parliamentarism—raged for a quarter of a century before 1914, with the general drift in Europe being towards parliamentarism spiced or flavoured with revolutionary oratory. In practice, the socialist parties were being integrated into the democratic system but they did not always care to admit it. It is well known how, when Bernstein asked the German social-democrats to admit it, they repudiated him and preferred to listen to the revolutionary demagogy of their leaders. Less well known but just as typical is the case of Guesde and Lafargue, whose 1883 *Commentary* on the Minimum Programme of French socialism rang with a spectacular revolutionism, threatened the day when arms would speak more loudly than theories, and poured sarcasm on hopes of change by parliamentary methods. Now, the *Commentary* went on being reprinted (it was up to its fourth reprinting by 1897) with the same date, 22 October 1883, but with gradual changes that ultimately altered its sense: the revolution

[9] Cf. B. Voyenne, 'De Marx à Staline, le destin historique du marxisme', in Robert Aron et al., *De Marx au marxisme: 1848–1948* (Paris, 1948), pp. 27–53; A. Wauters, *L'Evolution du marxisme depuis la mort de Marx* (Brussels, 1924) pp. 72–3; A. G. Meyer, *Marxism: The Unity of Theory and Practice* (Harvard, 1954), pp. 109–27.

receded, parliament acquired some virtue, and every passage liable to scare off electoral support was toned down or removed.[10] Guesde became a Cabinet Minister in 1914, and was one of the leading opponents of French socialist affiliation with Lenin's International in 1920—having entered political life as an apocalyptic revolutionary collectivist forty years earlier. His evolution, and his shyness about confessing to it, typify the stand of European socialism on the central ambiguity of socialist politics, an issue to which Lenin was to present a characteristic solution and one that would split the socialist movement.

Briefly, Lenin's answer was that the socialist cause was to be advanced neither by a party wedded to democratic parliamentary procedures nor by an uncompromising revolutionary force, but by a new agency controlled by professional revolutionaries who could chop and change from one of those policies to the other without ever losing their purity in opportunism, because their tactics were decided by a scientific technology of political action. This new sort of socialist party could, when occasion demanded, appear as electoralist, as parliamentary, and as democratic as the old parties of the Second International, and it could even co-operate with them in defensive phases of the proletariat's action. At the next moment, it could appear as revolutionary, as violent, and as ruthless as the groups that kept alive the characteristically French contribution to socialism, the tradition of violence that runs from the Jacobins via the Blanquists to the anarcho-syndicalists. To be capable of these extreme, and sometimes sudden, mutations, the new party, the communist party, had to be comparatively small and it had to be weeded and purified by recurrent purges, so that it remained always in the condition of a perfect instrument. It was to practise discipline of a sort the socialist parties had never known, nor for that matter military forces, since the iron chain of command was to extend beyond national borders to a central international command.

Many of these notions were familiar, taken separately, to western socialists because they were found in the long and heterogeneous socialist tradition. Not all however: there were some that came from Russia, where autocracy and the national character had given rise to peculiar forms of revolutionism. Less familiar still was the total effect, the fusion of elements drawn from several quarters and com-

---

[10] G. Sorel, 'L'Evoluzione del socialismo in Francia', in *La Riforma sociale*, 1899, pp. 509–25.

bined according to a dogmatic theory about what was going to happen in history in the near future. That is why all western socialists reacted to Leninism as to something utterly new, both those who rejected it as a foreign imposition and those who felt that the failure of socialism in the war and in the post-war labour struggles justified turning to a powerful novelty that seemed to have proven itself in Russia. Before looking at the impact of that original combination on western socialism, one should analyse its principal innovations in socialist theory. These are the notions of professional revolutionary, of political purity, and of that science or technology of revolution that indicated when the instrument was to be used in this way or that.

The professional revolutionary seems to be a peculiarly Russian product, unfamiliar to even the most extremist western socialists. Still, the Jacobin and Blanquist traditions assisted the acclimatization of this model in the West when it arrived at a crucial moment. That moment was when socialists realized that Marx had been wrong in believing that the proletariat would become spontaneously revolutionary in the conditions that capitalism created for it. In fact, it did not even become spontaneously socialist or class-conscious. Since that moment—and these facts were stated by Bernstein and Sorel from the start of the century—orthodox Marxist revolutionism has been known to be without foundation, so the choice for those who did not wish to practise revolutionary demagogy has been between abandoning class-struggle doctrines, on the one hand, and, on the other, embracing one or other of the revolutionary Marxist heresies, anarcho-syndicalism or Leninism. These consist in the assertion that if the working class does not become revolutionary by itself, the only way to get a revolution is for a small number, designated by their superior morality, to lead the workers to revolutionary action even though it does not accord with their apparent or short-term interests. In Leninism, this small number are professional revolutionaries. In anarcho-syndicalism, they are a syndicalist elite. The former has proven by far the more general. Syndicalist elites existed for a time in France and Spain, more briefly in Italy, but they were impossible to transplant and withered in their native soil. The professional revolutionary, in contrast, though of Russian origin, has appeared and thrived in every climate. Indeed, this universality has given twentieth-century history much of its unity, has made it more 'one story' than some earlier ages.

The original Russian professional revolutionary was not necessarily a socialist, for many movements of opposition had this same hard core. It is precisely that neutrality, from a political and ethical point of view, that made the professional revolutionary infinitely more adaptable and more easily exportable than such types as the entrepreneur or the syndicalist; but that neutrality also explains why the communist professional revolutionary so easily degenerated into the Stalinist party bureaucrat, the tempered instrument that can serve conflicting purposes in turn.

The definition of the type is by now familiar. A young man of whatever social class or origin cuts himself off from his folk and his environment to dedicate himself, if need be to the point of martyrdom, to the violent overthrow of the existing order by a small, strictly disciplined group that hopes to be able to lead masses to revolt. 'The organization of professional revolutionaries, strictly selected, bound to absolute obedience towards superiors of the organization, ready for any sacrifice, severed from every link with the outside world, classless in the most emphatic sense of the term, knowing neither satisfaction nor moral obligation outside the good of their organization, is a specific creation of the Russian soil. . . . Lenin transferred this organization, with its peculiar methods of selection and work, its peculiar religious enthusiasm and its equally peculiar indifference to ordinary moral standards, into the Russian labour movement. Having conquered Russia with his organization of professional revolutionaries, he attempted to transfer the same methods to the west. The history of this attempt is the history of the Communist International.'[11]

The professional revolutionary was to prove a striking literary success in the West, but his material political influence there was limited—at least as long as he remained a communist. It was when he became, or found a direct imitator in, a nazi or a Palestinian terrorist, and when he was taken as the model for the Arab or Asian nationalist, whether of socialist convictions or not, that he had a real impact in west Europe and in Europe's colonies. Nechaev found no place in western social-democratic parties, which held to the view that a mass movement, a class cause, can no more pivot on the individual revolutionary than a pyramid can on its apex. He found a place, for a time, in the western communist parties, but he

---

[11] Borkenau, *op. cit.*, p. 26. Cf. Lenin's 1902 pamphlet, *What Is To Be Done?*

often moved on to other parties,[12] or, if he stayed in, he was quickly enough transformed by the rationalist, bourgeois atmosphere of the West from a religious fanatic into a party bureaucrat whose acts of heroism were of an ideological order.

'Better fewer but better', said Lenin, referring to the political purity that the smaller socialist party should have. The notion of ideological purity was nothing new to socialists at that time. As has been recalled, there was an official Marxist orthodoxy from the time of Engels's death in 1895, and within a few years Croce was complaining of Marxist dogmatism and Sorel of the 'clerical spirit' and 'pontifical authority' of social-democratic leadership. The terms of those early complaints are worth consulting,[13] for it is often thought that the Russian communists, or Stalin in particular, introduced scholasticism and arrogant *ex cathedra* judgment into socialist discussion. In reality, the Bolshevik contribution to the notion of political purity was different.

Nor was the idea new that a party must suffer fragmentation and undergo purges, at the cost of loss of membership, in order to retain political purity. Engels used to cite Hegel saying that a party showed it was fit to conquer by proving that it could withstand a split,[14] and he more than once reproved Lafargue and the French socialists for their 'opportunism', telling them that they must 'swim against the current' at moments when the rest of the working class was on the wrong course.[15] And it is well known how Marx made a virtue of necessity, consoling his few followers with the assurance that they were right, and scuttling an organization rather than see it fall into the hands of opponents. Marx and Engels conceived political purity as the duty to keep a point of view alive at a time of reflux, when there was no revolutionary opportunity, whereas when there seemed

---

[12] A typical case was Jacques Doriot; see G. D. Allardyce, 'The Political Transition of Jacques Doriot', in *The Journal of Contemporary History*, I, ii, p. 100.

[13] B. Croce, *Matérialisme historique et économie marxiste* (Paris, 1901), p. 180, in an essay dated 1897; G. Sorel, 'Les Polémiques pour l'interprétation du marxisme: Bernstein et Kautsky', in *Revue Internationale de la sociologie*, 1900.

[14] B. Tchaguine, *Le Développement du marxisme après la Commune de Paris*, (Paris, 1954), p. 19.

[15] F. Engels, Paul et Laura Lafargue, *Correspondance* (ed. Bottigelli, Paris, 1956, 1959).

to be a revolutionary situation or some historical urgency (as during the Commune), they would readily sink differences.

The Leninist conception of political purity, as it was put into practice in his own party and as it was forced on the western socialist parties (in the first place by way of the 21 conditions laid down for their admission to the Communist International), was original. It put loyalty to a changing *party* line above the traditional socialist notion of loyalty to a *class*, to an ethic, or to an ideal of revolutionary purity. A pure party for Lenin meant a perfectly tempered instrument that could be used for apparently contradictory tactical purposes because the user, the party leadership, had in mind a revolutionary strategy that required these manoeuvres. This conception was new to western socialists. They were familiar enough with the ebb and flow of the proletariat's revolutionary hopes, and had acquired from Marx a vague but firm conviction of the need to adapt political action to the 'ripeness' or maturity of the historical situation. Most of them, too, had lived through popular fronts, class collaboration in the defence of democracy (as during the Dreyfus case, in France), followed by phases of uncompromising proletarian hostility to the State and the employers (as in the great strikes of the early years of this century). But this alternation had been felt as an unsatisfactory oscillation, as a rising and falling of revolutionary hopes, and the inability of Marxism to clear up their confusion had been widely recognized. Thus the labour movement in the years just before the First World War was dividing into those that settled for the minimum programme of socialism, and they were the majority, and those who were prepared to hold, in season and out, to the maximum revolutionary programme. Lenin introduced the notion of a party that had to make no such choice, for its purity meant rigid discipline in the service of a theory about how the maximum could ultimately be attained through a series of zigzags.

This was an instrumentalist, or technological, meaning of purity, in the sense of fitness or aptitude, as may be seen by the following contrast. Hegel, Marx, Engels and the western socialists understood that a party was to be kept politically pure by purging or expelling, when needful and historically appropriate (that is, not in the face of the enemy or in a revolutionary situation), those of its members who were untrue to its ideal, or in disagreement with its ideology or foreign to its class. Lenin meant that his sort of party was to be purged both when it was on a left tack and when it was on a right tack, in the first case expelling those who lacked revolutionary purity or were 'opportunist', but in the second case expelling those who clung to an unseasonable revolutionism and declined to compromise. For what both had been untrue to was the technical fitness of the party to apply its historical strategy, its theory of revolution, in whatever way the concrete situation might require.

Western socialists had often gone through phases of self-examination about their revolutionary purity, as, for example, when they wondered whether they became tainted by Millerandism, by having a lawyer who claimed to be a socialist join a bourgeois government. Whatever side they had taken in such discussions, however, they were not prepared for a dogmatic theory of intermittent purity and of successive deviations, such as Bolshevism presented to them. For those who came to believe that Lenin possessed the revolutionary technology that required such an instrumentalist approach, it was acceptable intellectually—though emotionally, in political practice, it was soon to prove more than flesh and blood could stand, at least for those who identified themselves with their successive tactical stances. That is why eventually, in the conditions under which western socialism lived, the technique of fanaticism *à éclipse* could be practised only by a very small bureaucracy exercising authority over a changing and unstable party membership.

The professional revolutionary and the pure instrumentality of the small and repeatedly purged communist party are required by, and justified in, a science of revolution announced by Lenin. Even westerners who have made the most trenchant criticisms of Lenin have often conceded that he possessed this science. Thus, Borkenau said of *'Left-wing' Communism*, 'It is a handbook of revolutionary tactics and as such can sometimes be compared for force of argument, realism, directness, and convincing power, with Machiavelli's *Il Principe*. Here a great master of politics speaks. . . . Lenin knew perfectly the conditions of a successful social revolution.'[16] Max Eastman also praised Lenin as revolutionary 'engineer'. 'The most striking feature of Lenin's political tactics was the "policy of sharp turns". . . . Nothing like this had ever been seen before. . . . It contributed more than anything else to make his political power seem occult and almost magical. And yet it was the opposite of magic; it was the essence of scientific engineering introduced into the sphere

[16] Borkenau, *op. cit.*, pp. 191–2.

of politics. . . . That is the significance of the policy of sharp turns.
It is a proof that Lenin was in the full sense of the term a scientific
engineer. . . . Bolshevism is an unconscious, and therefore incomplete, substitution of a practical science of revolution for that revolutionary philosophy of the universe which Marx created.'[17]

The trouble is, as fifty years have shown, that this science not only
could not be transmitted to western socialists but could not even be
handed on to Lenin's successors, nor its propositions set out clearly.
Perhaps Lukacs is a better guide to the source of Lenin's opinions
when he says, 'The enrichment that Marxism owes to Lenin consists
simply—simply!—in the more intimate, more obvious, more meaningful linking up of isolated actions with the general destiny, the revolutionary destiny, of the whole working class'. He adds that this
linking up means 'treating each particular everyday problem in
concrete connection with the historico-social totality, considering it
as a component in the emancipation of the proletariat', and it is 'only
that linking up of isolated actions with a central core, which can be
found only by precise analysis of the historico-social whole, that
decides whether isolated actions are revolutionary or counter-
revolutionary'. Lukacs insists that for Lenin there 'is something
more important than isolated facts or tendencies, namely *the reality
of the general process*, the totality of the development of society'.[18]
The cumbersome language of the Hungarian philosopher conceals,
indeed, the kernel of Lenin's supposed science: each event is part
of a process that is not yet complete but of which Lenin knows the
end. It is because Lenin assumes that he knows the end of the story
that he can decree, with the vigorous certitude and the miserable
mock scientism of pamphlets like *'Left-wing' Communism*, who is 'too
far' left and who 'too far' right at any given moment, that he can
rule beyond appeal who is revolutionary and who counter-revolutionary.

This had always been the problem of the Marxist socialists. They
thought they had a general picture of the evolution of capitalism and
thus knew the future, but could not specify the timing of that evolution. And it was just the timing that mattered in judging whether a
political action was too far left or too far right. If the revolution is
for tomorrow, as Marx seems to have believed at the time of the

[17] M. Eastman, *Marx, Lenin, and the Science of Revolution* (London, 1926),
pp. 158, 168.
[18] G. Lukacs, *Lénine* (Paris, 1965), pp. 30, 38.

Communist Manifesto, then there is no need to reform or compromise, and all sorts of actions become needlessly opportunist; but if the revolution fades to some fairly remote, and at all events unspecifiable, future, then those same actions become reasonable, and another class of actions become reckless, even suicidal. The application of terms that socialists had debated for decades, such as 'realist', 'sectarian', 'opportunist', 'Blanquist', 'electoralist'—even terms such as 'terrorist'—depended on a view of how far ahead lay the consummation about which, as Marxists, they were generally agreed. Lenin brushed aside all such debate with the confident air of one who knows the exact course of the process of proletarian emancipation, and who can therefore fix precise meanings to all these terms and pronounce judgment accordingly. There is no need to criticize in any detail Lenin's confidence on that score; the facts have already done so, and some of them will be recalled later. Certainly Lenin's own prophecies, once he began to formulate them for western socialists, and those of his successors (neither more nor less), have been wrong with a quite unscientific frequency. This means that, in those cases, what they called 'infantile leftism' before the event was not so in fact, nor what they called 'opportunist rightism'. It is enough to recall the German Communist Party's use of such terms during the rise (in fact for some months after the installation!) of nazism.

The essence of Lenin's science is on one page of *'Left-wing' Communism* where he says, first, 'Communists should know that the future in any case belongs to them', and, then, 'Communists in all countries [must appreciate] the necessity of displaying the utmost flexibility in their tactics'.[19] Naturally, if we know that the present battle is to be decided in our favour in any case, our tactics can be arbitrary—first left, then right—and we shall always know who is 'condemned by history', namely those who oppose us, whether in the first case or the second.

Thus what western socialism discovered under the Leninist science of revolution, which was to govern brusque turns from one policy to its contrary, was dogmatic fideism. It led to arbitrary, unpredictable oscillation between two attitudes that, before the war, had been typified by Jaurès on the one side and Sorel on the other. Those men, and their followers, had put up reasoned arguments for their positions, for class collaboration and for proletarian revolutionism respectively. Bolshevism meant that one could be substituted for the

[19] *The Essentials of Lenin*, vol. 2 (London, 1947), p. 633.

other from one moment to the next with a brief justification which *always* consisted in a forecast about what was to happen in the near future ('we are on the eve of a new wave', 'the third period is about to begin', etc.). As an example of this science in application, one may take Zinoviev, at a time when he was Lenin's faithful mouthpiece, appearing before a meeting of communists in 1922 to 'explain' the difficult reversal of tactics from the ultra-revolutionism that had split the socialist parties in the previous three years to a new united front:

> The workers want unity. Not to take account of that state of mind would be to make sectarians of communists and to help the social-democrats. If we manage now to use that state of mind, we shall have both an intelligent communist party and a great mass movement. The indignation of the working class about splits in the movement is quite understandable. The effort towards unity is very often, almost always even, a revolutionary factor. The power of the working class resides in the fact that it groups millions. That's the power of numbers. It is quite understandable and justifiable that the working class should be against splits. But we could not always respect that sentiment, because the social-democrats were using it to the profit of the bourgeoisie. We had to make the split. Now, let's change roles: the splitters now will be the socialists and not us. . . . We are on the eve of a new surge of the working class.[20]

Apart from the *horrible détail* that in fact 1922 was the eve of the surge of fascism in Italy and of Tsankov's white terror in Bulgaria, this instance of scientific reversal of policies shows that as far as concerns the advancement of socialism's cause (as distinct from Russian interests) it is proposed without rhyme or reason. Because of a bad guess about the near future—what Lukacs calls relating events to the general process—words change meaning, roles are reversed, and a sentiment that was just now to the profit of the bourgeoisie becomes a revolutionary factor. In numerous other applications the Leninist technology, whether politically successful or not, never proved to have any rational or scientific foundation. It was this rational technology that was to explain the practice of brusque turns or fanaticism *à éclipse* and to justify the socialist use of the politically neutral professional revolutionary. And it was the combination of these three new Bolshevik concepts that divided the western labour movement.

It is not needful here to recount the story of that first division in detail. In any case, it would be mistaken to treat it as an original

[20] J. Humbert-Droz, *L'Oeil de Moscou à Paris* (Paris, 1964), p. 13.

schism that explains the persistence of a divided socialist movement since that day, in the way that the separation of Norway in 1905 explains, quite mechanically, the division of the Scandinavian peninsula since then. The events of 1919–20 were less an irreversible parting than the first application of the Leninist strategy in a phase of leftist tactics, as was seen when soon after—on the occasion of the third congress of the Communist International in June–July 1921— it was succeeded by the contrary phase of that strategy, the first 'united front'. These phases have gone on succeeding each other ever since, and so what matters is the political theory behind that alternation, rather than the peculiar circumstances of the first split. That political theory, Leninism, in its three original constituents of the professional revolutionary, intermittent fanaticism, and the technology of revolution, thereafter competed with the mainstream of socialism, first of all by drawing off from it adherents of certain types. Which types?

Communist-Socialist Competition

If we assume (and the assumption would not be entirely accurate) that at any given moment there are in each western country a certain number of people who, independent of the competition between the communist, socialist, and other smaller left-wing parties, are inclined to join, support, or vote for a movement answering the general description of leftist or socialist, then it will be seen that since 1919 these people have been divided, mainly, into supporters of communist parties and supporters of parties of the sort that could belong to the Second International; with a residue, in some instances substantial, supporting smaller extremist or splinter groups. The reason it is said that the assumption is not entirely accurate is that much evidence suggests that the number of people of left political opinions is not, in reality, independent of the competition between the communists and socialists; or, in other words, a united left movement would have a different size and membership from the sum of the divided left movement that has existed since 1919 as a result of the Bolshevik Revolution. However, it is not possible, for the time being, to quantify that statement more exactly.

It is possible, on the other hand, to specify some of the characteristics of the membership of the communist parties, and to show the effects that the separation of people of that sort had upon the socialist parties. One must bear in mind, however, that open competition between the two parties for the allegiance of leftists has not been possible for the whole of the last fifty years because one or both of them was, or were, illegal for part of that time. Of the major western communist parties, only the French has a more or less continuous history, and it was illegal from September 1939 to the Liberation (though it was making some of its biggest gains towards the end of that period in underground Resistance work). The German Communist Party was suppressed between 1933 and the end of the war, when it reappeared in the eastern part of the country as a Russian agency and in the western part of the country only briefly before being again suppressed. The Italian party was smashed by Mussolini's laws of exception, from 1926 to the liberation of Italy in 1943–4. The Spanish party existed legally inside Spain for barely three years in all. Even in democracies like the United States and Australia, the party has been banned for longer or shorter periods, while in some countries with less secure traditions of political freedom the communists (and often the socialists too) have been outlawed for longer than they have been allowed to operate publicly. Still, where there was competition between these two political forces it may be seen that communism tended to attract away from socialism the revolutionaries, the young, and certain social sub-classes, without, however, ever managing to find itself a stable clientele. These assertions are expanded in the following four sections.

Revolutionaries and Reformists: It would be wrong to imagine that, in every situation they have faced together since 1919, the western communists have been more revolutionary than the socialists, or even that, on the whole, they have been a revolutionary party at all. But the socialist parties have never been so in earnest since they lost their revolutionary members to the communists, while the communists have been or appeared to be so recurrently. The upshot has been that all those who wished to work for a political revolution to install socialism have found it increasingly difficult, and in the end impossible, to stay in western socialist parties, whereas there have been periods when the communist parties welcomed them. True enough, sooner or later the communist parties would take a brusque turn in the opposite direction and the revolutionaries would either have to submit (that is, give revolutionism the new and special meaning of unconditional attachment to a changing party line both in its revolutionary and non-revolutionary or anti-revolutionary moments), or be purged. When purged, such revolutionaries of course could not enter or return to the socialist parties (as sometimes happened with communist members, supporters, and voters who quit for the contrary reason, because they found the communists adventurously revolutionary). It they retained revolutionary aspirations at all, they joined one or other of the splinter groups, of which Trotskyism for a time was the largest, that have hovered between the socialist and communist parties ever since the split.

The result of this process has been a continual voiding of the socialist parties' revolutionary membership, so that simply because of the psychology of their supporters these parties would have undergone the shift to the right in their political ideas that is evident since 1919. Many other factors have contributed to that shift, which in any event has been to some extent a rational adjustment to changed social conditions; but it is clear, without adopting any particular psychological theory about 'the revolutionary personality', that there has occurred a *selection* of personalities such that the socialist parties have lost their former revolutionary wing.

They really did have that wing before the 1914 war, for the Bolsheviks did not introduce revolutionism to the West but only the special Leninist conception of it. There was much less hypocrisy than one might imagine when the western socialists of 1919–20 replied to the communists come to split their parties, 'We are revolutionists too!' The socialists before the war had indeed been moving towards integration into bourgeois democracy, and they had gone further along that road than their out-of-date ideology admitted; but they were still a pugnacious party in comparison with the socialists of fifty years later, because they had a revolutionary wing that was to be lopped off in 1919. In Italy, indeed, the revolutionary socialists, the 'maximalists', got control of the party from the reformists in 1912.

During the confrontation of French socialists and those who were to become the French communists, at Tours in 1920, Marcel Sembat answered the revolutionism of Moscow: 'It's not the first time we have prepared the revolution inside this party! When I entered the Chamber [of Deputies] I joined a group called at that time the Central Revolutionary Committee, and which was inspired by Vaillant. I assure you we spent a lot of time there talking about the revolution and even, often, we examined practical ways of preparing for it. Others, in the Parti Ouvrier Français, were preparing it too. By what strange error did you come to think that the

POF was just a party of vote-catchers? . . . we had a programme for the revolution too. And, heavens! the traditions that inspired our elders in that Central Revolutionary Committee were real conspiratorial traditions, too. But, damn it, we didn't tell the whole world the way you do in your Moscow conditions.' Succeeding him on the same platform, Léon Blum told the communists, 'Let me tell you that reformism—or more exactly revisionism, I like the word better— no longer exists in the party. . . . The doctrine of the party is a revolutionary doctrine. . . . For my part, I only know of one socialism in France to date, the one defined in our statutes, and it is a revolutionary socialism. . . . The dictatorship of the proletariat— we're in favour of it. There again, there is no disagreement in principle. We are so strongly in favour of it that the notion and the theory of dictatorship of the proletariat were included by us in a programme that was an electoral programme. So we are afraid neither of the word nor of the thing'.[21]

One may smile at this revolutionary oratory, and the advocates of acceptance of Moscow's 21 conditions who followed Sembat and Blum to the platform did not fail to point out that the record of the Second International parties scarcely corresponded to it. But the point is that even as oratory it passed from fashion in the western socialist parties soon after the communists drew off that section of socialists more inclined to be impressed by it. Moreover, when the pre-war socialists in France and perhaps even in Germany used such language, they did so with fewer mental reservations, with a less clear sense of hypocrisy, than was possible for communist demagogues exercising their party's monopoly over the revolutionary vocabulary forty and fifty years later. The socialist parties at that time contained and were keenly influenced by a revolutionary wing, and the loss of that wing after the defection of the communists explains much of their subsequent evolution. Much of the ageing, ossification, bureaucratization, and 'bourgeoisification' that overtook them from that time on, and which will be referred to below, was simply the consequence—or, rather, not the consequence but the fact itself—of the isolation of the radicals and the youth in the communist parties, leaving the conservatives in complete control of socialist machinery that previously they had managed only under the criticism of their own left wing.

Most of the western parties had been, before 1914, a parallelogram

[21] Annie Kriegel, *Le Congrès de Tours 1920* (Paris, 1964), pp. 28, 118, 127–8.

of forces where a revolutionary left had tugged against a conservative revisionist right to produce a centrist line that was, for all that, well to the left of anything known fifty years later. In German social-democracy, for example, there had been a left-right-centre triangle, and 'shifting tactical alliances among these forces had ensured that no single one of them would be completely dominant'; but once the left had moved to the German Communist Party this balance was destroyed, in favour of the conservatives. From then on, the Social-Democratic Party was a preponderant right faced with a small left-wing condemned to ineffectual opposition.[22]

The same thing looked like happening in Italy where, indeed, the reformists in charge of the party and of the unions would have dissolved socialism in a democratic radicalism had it not been for the accident of the Libyan war. Instead, something extraordinary occurred which prefigured part of the later history of European socialism. After a long crisis within the Italian Socialist Party, the reformists lost control to the maximalists at the Reggio Emilia congress in 1912. But this maximalism was not the familiar 'maximum programme' that the left in general was abandoning for a democratic 'minimum programme', for it bore characteristic fascist features, as, aided by hindsight, we may now see. The effective leader of the maximalist majority in the party was Benito Mussolini, and his demagogic extremism constituted a policy that we now know not to have been socialist at all: 'the absolute subordination of the workers' movement to the party, concentration of all powers in the central organs and eventually in the hands of a charismatic chief, creation among the masses of a state of revolutionary tension, abolition of the limits that had in the past contained social and political struggle, and willingness to accept all the risks of adventure'.[23] That this was not socialism was proven when Mussolini threw open the party to every type of malcontent and rebel, doubling its membership in the two years between the Reggio and Ancona congresses, drowning the old guard of socialists in a rabble of *sans-culottes*, and confounding the working class with the mob. Even though, by these means, the reformists were reduced to a minority inside the party, they continued to predominate among socialist electors and in the other working-class organizations, and they retained

[22] R. N. Hunt, *German Social Democracy 1918-1933* (New Haven, 1964), pp. 237-8.
[23] G. Arfè, *Storia del socialismo italiano 1892-1926* (Turin, 1965), p. 143.

this numerical superiority over maximalist and communist voters until 1924.

The French Socialist Party (SFIO), from the beginning of the century, had contained four main tendencies: the revisionists and Dreyfusards led by Jean Jaurès; the Marxists around Guesde; the Blanquists led by Vaillant; and an extremist wing, noted especially for its anti-militarism and anti-patriotism, led by Gustave Hervé. By the time of the Bolshevik Revolution, the French party was a left-right-centre triangle: a left wing around the Third International Committee of Loriot and Souvarine, a right wing associated with Renaudel and *La Vie Socialiste*, and, resultant of these forces, a dominant centrist majority, whose Reconstruction Committee ran the party. With the removal of the revolutionaries to the Communist Party—it was, in fact, the majority of socialists who joined that party at first, but only the revolutionaries stayed there, the rest returning to the SFIO—the party machine that had been constructed by Guesde remained solidly in the power of the conservatives.

That the isolation of the revolutionaries in the French socialist movement was, as just recalled, a two-step process was due to the fact that the 1920 division, in that as in many other parties, was not a single, clean surgical cut. It was complicated by socialist attachment to the notion of working-class unity, which led socialists to follow the majority wherever it went, not out of conformism but out of the conviction that socialism ceases to be itself when it is no longer a mass movement, the party of the greatest number. So in parties where the Third International's 21 conditions for admission were accepted only by a scissionist minority that hived off to form a communist party, that party did not at once get all the revolutionaries, many of whom preferred to stay with the majority and to attempt the experiment of acting as a left wing. Conversely, where the majority of the socialist party joined the Third International, as happened in France, many non-revolutionaries went along with the movement, scarcely taking seriously Moscow's 21 conditions. A cycle of purges, now of left sectarians, now of opportunists, was needed to convince all western leftists that the socialist parties no longer (and the communists never) put proletarian unity before the distinction between revolutionary and reformist doctrines.

This initial division was completed earliest in Germany, after events of great confusion and tragic import. By 1921 already, the Social-Democratic Party (SPD), now controlled by the conservatives, wrote the Görlitz Programme which in many ways foreshadowed the Bad Godesberg Programme of 1959. It renounced revolution and declared for democracy and gradualism. That the party could, so early and before the earth-shaking events of 1921–59, anticipate the programme it follows today shows that it was sufficient for the revolutionaries to hive off in the communist party for social-democracy to assume many of its present features. Similarly, though less strikingly, the electoral programme of the French Socialist Party of April 1919, which was endorsed by the right and the centre but rejected by the Committee for the Third International (that is, the revolutionaries who were to lead the movement towards communism), proved to be the SFIO's maximum programme for many years to come. In fact Léon Blum, who was the *rapporteur* for this programme in April 1919, was to implement some part of it while head of the government in 1936.

The ageing and taming of the socialist parties that resulted immediately from the departure of their revolutionary members initiated a vicious circle. As the Second International parties showed themselves less ambitious, less imaginative, and less inclined to promote thorough-going social change, the young and the radicals (later the unemployed) were driven more surely into the communist parties. And as these latter declared themselves more Bolshevik, in proportion as Stalin increased his control over them, the socialist parties reacted in horror towards the right and moved bodily across the political spectrum, losing on the left all they might gain on the right.[24]

As long as revolutionism retained its traditional western meanings, whether these were Marxist or Blanquist, it seemed possible for the socialist parties to encompass a revolutionary left wing and, at the cost of some incoherence, to widen their electoral base both towards the left and the right with the hope of eventually becoming a ruling party. In other words, political revolutionism as the extreme left socialists of before the 1914 war understood it, could fairly comfortably exist as a trend or tendency, often a powerful one, inside parties and movements that also contained consistently democratic, gradualist, and conservative wings. That co-existence scandalized non-political revolutionaries, the anarcho-syndicalists, but it was accepted by other socialists because they saw in it, first, the common form of all western political movements, which have a left and a right as naturally as a man has, and, second, the reflection of the

[24] Hunt, *op. cit.*, pp. 142–8, 245.

heterogeneity of the working masses. All of that ceases to be true once the revolutionaries adopt, as more efficacious, the Leninist notion of revolutionism, for this excludes constant cohabitation with conservative, democratic socialists, introduces the notion of a monolithic party without left and right, and, lastly, requires the communist party not to reflect the heterogeneity of the masses, in fact to cease to be a mass party whenever the party line indicates. Losing thereby the capacity to contain all those who take a revolutionary view of the way to socialism, the socialist parties would have been condemned to political opposition without hope of obtaining power in the name of the working class, even if the working class had not been shrinking in relative importance as a proportion of the western population.

Age: Partly because of the foregoing, the socialist parties lost many of their youthful adherents to communism, which has generally been a younger movement. (That is a good part of the explanation for its being a movement with a less stable membership, since the young grow old.) This was evident right from the Tours congress of the French socialists, where it appeared that the younger members (either in the sense of younger in years or of more recent entry to the party) were more inclined to favour adherence to the Third International. That fact came to be disputed, as one side argued that the youthfulness of its supporters was proof of its dynamism and its opponents that it was proof of its adventurousness and lack of political education. Yet it is certain that the French Communist Party has always been a younger party than the SFIO and it has been much more successful in running youth movements—though in the last few years its hold over some of them, in open revolt against an unchanging party leadership, was for a time unsure.

Not only is the French Communist Party membership young but, because of the policy of rapid promotion, its leadership is relatively young too. It is often recalled inside the party that Maurice Thorez entered the politbureau at 25 and Benoît Frachon at 30. The leadership aged somewhat after the war and in 1952 the youngest member of the politbureau was 40, but half its members were still in their forties. Forty also was the average age of communist deputies in 1946, making them the youngest of the major parliamentary groups. At the 1953 party conference the average age of delegates was barely 31; two-thirds were in the 25–35 age group and hardly any were over 45. This youthfulness has been a constant feature of communist militancy. In the United States party in 1925 (to choose from a different sample altogether), out of 43 communist leaders only one was over 50 and twenty-seven were under 40.[25] Communist electors, to return to France and to pass from membership to voting support, have also been younger than those of other parties. The percentage figures for 1952, according to a public opinion poll, were:

		Communist voters	Socialist· voters
Aged over 50	..	23	37
35 to 49	.. ..	35	33
18 to 34	.. ..	42	30

In Germany the corresponding facts are clearer still. Right from the beginning, the socialist youth bolted to the Communist Party (and to some extent to the Independent Socialist Party). The social-democratic youth movement, which had had 100,000 members in 1913, had shrunk to 36,000 in 1919. Though the war, with its hecatomb of youth, may explain that in part, the fact is that the SPD youth movement never had more than 50,000 or 60,000 members throughout the years of the Weimar Republic. Moreover, the party leadership was constantly bickering with its youth movement. There were more young people in the Communist Party (KPD), as the following percentage figures show:[26]

			1928		1930	
			SPD	KPD	SPD	KPD
Under 50	..	..	48	96	48	97
Over 50	..	..	52	4	52	3

It is only in recent years and in the absence of competition from a communist party that German social-democracy has been rejuvenated: the proportion of new members joining while aged under 40 years was 52 per cent in 1955 and 60 per cent in 1961.[27]

One might fairly suspect that the loss of the youth to the communist parties has partly caused (and then in turn been partly the effect of) the declining dynamism of the socialist movement as a party of protest. It is not inconsistent with that to recall that more demo-

---

[25] T. Draper, *American Communism and Soviet Russia* (New York, 1963), p. 201.
[26] Cf. Hunt, *op. cit.*, pp. 89–90.
[27] D. A. Chalmers, *The Social Democratic Party of Germany* (New Haven, 1964), p. 194.

cratically controlled parties (and the socialist party of a country has usually been more so than the communist party of that country) prefer older leaders, using length of service as a criterion for promotion.[28] The pre-1914 socialist movement and the socialist parties today are alike in venerating the veteran, from the top of the hierarchy to the bottom. In contrast to the youth cult in the French Communist Party, the SFIO's constitution requires five years membership in delegates to party congresses or to the national council, in members of the executive committee, in editors of the party newspaper, and in electoral candidates. Socialist candidates and deputies are regularly older than not only communists but the other parties' men too. In 1951, some 70 per cent of members of federal executive committees were over 40 and 30 per cent were over 50; only one committee in twelve had under-forties in a majority. Williams, who reproduces these figures,[29] comments:

> The consequence has been that the socialist appeal to youth, and in general to new elements outside its traditional ranks, has proved decidedly ineffective. Before 1939 the proportion of new members to old ones in any given year never fell below 15 per cent; since 1945 it has regularly been below 4 per cent. The socialist youth organization (in France as in other countries) has always been looked on with suspicion by the party leadership. In 1947, on account of its long-standing Trotskyist tendencies, it was deprived of its autonomy, and therewith of much of its appeal to youth. In 1953 the organization existed in only 45 out of the 90 French departments.

The contrast with the communists is, in the French case, so stark as to lead one to suspect deliberate discrimination against youth, an attitude that is not found in socialist parties that do not have to compete with a substantial communist party.

Social Class: The socialist movement in western countries before the First World War was a working-class movement led by intellectuals of bourgeois origin, staffed by militants of proletarian origin (which does not mean they were still proletarians), and supported predominantly by the urban proletariat. For example, the German social-democrats claimed in 1905–6 to have a working-class membership fluctuating around 94 per cent, though of the members of the Italian Socialist Party only 42 per cent were industrial workers because of the backwardness of Italian industrialization.

[28] Cf. M. Duverger, *Les Partis politiques* (Paris, 1951), pp. 188–97.
[29] P. Williams, *Politics in Postwar France* (London, 1954), p. 69.

Today, the socialist parties have a quite different composition and support, in some cases because they are very much bigger in absolute numbers than at the turn of the century. They are now national parties rather than class parties; or at least they want to establish themselves as such and indeed are much less dependent on the urban proletariat, especially the manual labour and factory worker, even if their following among agrarian sections of the population has not grown significantly. A moment's reflection suggests that in evolving thus these parties have followed the shift in western society generally, the decline in the proportion of both industrial and agricultural workers, and the large increase in the number of people working in clerical, technical, and service occupations. So no appeal is needed to the influence of the communist parties in order to explain this change. That is just as well, since the role of the communist parties in relation to the class structure of western societies, and to the class composition of the rival socialist parties in particular, has been extraordinarily complex, mercurial, and irrational.

The summary account of that role given by communists themselves is that the rise of their movement deprived the socialist parties of their authentically proletarian support, except for a treacherous working-class aristocracy, and offered the peasantry its first effective defence, so that the communist parties became *the* parties of the toiling masses while at the same time welcoming intellectuals and petty bourgeois from other sections who foresaw their ruination in the existing regime. It may be conceded that in one or two countries, and France would be a case, but then only for certain periods, this has been (when translated out of that question-begging terminology) a fair description of the source of communist support. But one must add that in other countries and at other times, the membership and support of communist parties has been totally different, and that the main feature of communism in the West has been the variety and instability of its clientele.

All such generalizations are hazardous, for the following reasons: the class and occupational composition (as far as there is any such thing; but we are assuming the class stratification on which socialists and communists would roughly agree) of western societies has changed radically in the past fifty years (and, in west Europe, is still evolving rapidly), in proportion as productivity per man has risen both in factories and on the land and as demand for technical and clerical skills has increased. Not only has the class structure of these countries been fluid, but the two major leftist parties have changed their ambitions in regard to representation of the proletariat. The socialists, as has been said, sought to reflect the changing social structure, primarily in order to retain or enlarge their electoral clientele. Instead of claiming to represent specifically the industrial proletariat, they became national parties with a more or less marked bias in favour of the 'wage-earner', *Arbeitnehmer, Schaffender,* employee, *producteur,* etc. The communists, on the other hand, have successively adopted contrasting attitudes to various classes, depending on which tactic of Leninist strategy was being followed at the time, depending on the sharp changes in Russian domestic policy under Stalin as far as concerned the class structure of Soviet society, and, lastly, depending on communist theories about the evolution of western countries. To complicate matters, the communists could be following different policies at the same time in different countries, with consequently contrasting membership drives. For example, in 1924–5 the communists were in a phase of proletarian purity in France, Germany, and east Europe, while practising a united front in the Anglo-Saxon countries and in China.

Writing in 1939, Borkenau could say, 'In China the Communist Party is a party of the peasants and the Red Army, in Spain it is a party of all classes except the urban proletariat, in Britain and U.S.A. it is mostly a party of young intellectuals. . . . Only in France and, to a certain extent, in Czechoslovakia, can the communists still be regarded as a real working class party with real influence on the proletarian masses'.[30] Throughout these variations in space and time, Marxist theory inclined the communists, as to a much lesser extent the socialists, to claim to be *par excellence* the working-class party. The desire to appear consistently what they were only occasionally, led to the suppression and falsification of relevant statistics; there exist no reliable figures on communist party membership in these terms for the past fifty years. Besides, it is in the nature of the case that the class affiliations of a political party are, on every theory except the mechanical pseudo-Marxist analysis of capitalist society into classes, extremely diverse. Then, too, one arrives at different results if one takes account of the supposed class of the card-carrying membership, or of the militants, or of the top leadership, or of the parliamentary representatives, or of the voters. There have been periods, as during the economic depres-

[30] Borkenau, *op. cit.*, p. 420.

sion of the early 1930s, when a western communist party had for members the unemployed and the peasants, for militants better-paid skilled workers currently in employment, for leaders full-time professional bureaucrats and intellectuals, for parliamentary deputies liberal-professionals, ex-militants and intellectuals, and for voters a mass whose class structure defied analysis and was, in any event, far from homogeneous. One will note, finally, the various class affiliations that may be ascribed arbitrarily to such *déclassés* as intellectuals, the unemployed, professional party bureaucrats, and politicians.

What is sure is that the communist parties have nowhere in the West and at no time since their inception been the representatives of the majority of the working class and of it only or mainly. Although the communist party is an organization of revolutionaries and not the expression of the 'trade union mentality' supposedly produced by capitalism in the workers, the communists still wish to represent the *avant-garde* of the working class, *avant-garde* being a suitably ambiguous term for a group that is at once in and not in a movement. Labouring for the 'real interests' of the working class, as opposed to its 'apparent interests' (that is, what it wants), they wish to include as large a number as possible of 'enlightened' workers, for Lenin had declared: 'Only one particular class— namely, urban workers, and in general factory workers, industrial workers—is capable of directing the whole mass of toilers and exploited.'

A constitution built on factory cells was introduced to ensure the communist parties this proletarian base. As a resolution of the fifth congress of the Communist International (1924) put it:

Social-democracy, busying itself solely with reformism within the framework of bourgeois democracy and especially with electoral and parliamentary jobs, is, consequently, organized into electoral districts. It has at its base the local section and it has as its principle of organization the place of residence. The CP, which leads the workers towards the revolutionary struggle to overthrow capitalism and conquer power, creates other forms of organization, for its main point of support is in the factories. The CP must have its base among the workers, in the factory and on the work site.

If this theory, which could have been announced by Antonio Gramsci himself and which certainly represents a last hangover inside communism of the tradition of Proudhon and Sorel, had been successfully implemented, the communist parties might have had an immense impact on western socialism, for this would have meant a new and revolutionary form of proletarian action, and it would have brought communists into direct collision not only with the socialist parties but with the trade unions. It was in part because of the conflict of the cells with the relevant trade union sections that the doctrine could not be applied in the West, where—unlike certain backward countries—the workers were not waiting around to discover their first experience of association. But there were more profound reasons for the failure of the communists to get anything more than a fraction of their own membership (let alone of the whole industrial working class) organized in cells at the place of work. The first is no doubt that they were never serious about it, for this doctrine leads straight to what Lenin denounced as 'economism' if not to anarcho-syndicalism, whereas the communists were in reality much nearer the 'political' obsession of the social-democrats than the passage cited from the fifth congress resolution suggests. Even more so were western workers, whose ambition, and achievement, was to feel less like workers and more like citizens, that is, to take less interest in what could be achieved directly at the place of work than in what was available through the market and through the indirect machinery of democracy. The trade union sections and various conventional or legislative creations such as employer-employee committees looked after the former, while it became clear that in the modern centralized economy even affairs that formerly could have been settled on the spot required indirect, political action.

Then, the workplace cells could never find application in various unstable trades or in many backward economies where, precisely, communist support was located most easily. Nor of course, could the workplace cells cater for isolated members—housewives, the self-employed, peasants, artisans, and intellectuals—who came to provide so much of the party membership to the detriment of its proletarian purity. Right from the start in 1924, accordingly, communists resisted the introduction of workplace cells[31] and have continued since to show a preference for organization by locality, just like any other modern party, despite the dogmatic insistence of party leaders. That preference is most marked at times of increased membership, which means that the communist party gets bigger the less proletarian it becomes. For example, in France when the Communist

[31] G. Walter, *Histoire du parti communiste français* (Paris, 1948), p. 171 ff. Cf. Draper, *op. cit.*, p. 193.

Party claimed its highest membership ever (over 800,000), there were 28,000 locality cells and only 8,000 workplace cells. In 1962 the same party had 7,688 local cells, 4,810 rural cells, and 4,534 workplace cells. In 1964 the latter were still the least numerous 'despite all the efforts of the party'.[32]

So the one project that could have meant a challenge to western socialism in its relation with the workers aborted. Still, the persistence of the factory cells, however shadowy and however submissive to higher echelons on which they have no reverse influence, has kept the communist parties of some countries, such as France and Italy, as closely in touch with the working class as any other party could claim to be.

In certain countries communism scored its biggest gains against the socialist movement in unstable or decaying occupations, like the marginal coal-mining areas of Britain or the waterfronts of Australia and some United States ports. Indeed, those toeholds were often the only ones obtained in those countries, exactly as the First International found its major support in Britain in the dying crafts and seldom in the characteristically capitalist large-scale industry of the day.[33] In the small United States Communist Party throughout the 1920s the bulk of the membership came from the 'relatively small-scale or distributive industries such as the needle and food trades'.[34] On the Continent, in the 1930s at least, the communist hold was in the smaller factories rather than in the bigger: 'The bigger the factory, the smaller the communist influence; in the industrial giants it is altogether insignificant'.[35]

Above all, the unemployed, when they existed in large numbers as during the 1930s, flocked to the communist parties just as they did to other extremist parties such as, in Germany, the National-Socialist Party. It has been estimated that in that country in 1932, just before its liquidation, the Communist Party consisted of three-fifths unemployed and one-fifth highly-paid skilled workers from the metal-working industries, and very little in between. Similar estimates for other countries are more hazardous in the absence of figures, but there is no doubt of the world-wide character of the alliance, in

[32] J. Fauvet, *Histoire du parti communiste français*, vol. 2 (Paris, 1965), p. 328.
[33] H. Collins and C. Abramsky, *Karl Marx and the British Labour Movement* (London, 1965), pp. 70–7.
[34] T. Draper, *The Roots of American Communism* (New York, 1963), p. 393; *American Communism and Soviet Russia*, p. 192.
[35] Borkenau, *op. cit.*, p. 363 for relevant statistics on the Ruhr.

communism during the 1930s, of the workless and the best-paid skilled workingmen, without, of course, the majority of either category ever being communist.

Another example of communist party membership being dominated by a transitional social category comparable to the unemployed is the American party, which for long was composed *almost entirely* of immigrants who did not speak English, mainly Finns and Slavs. They were organized in foreign-language sections, according to their language. English-speaking members were 7 per cent of the original 1919 party and, six years later, 10 per cent, of whom 8 per cent were in the Jewish section. When bolshevization led to the proscription of the foreign-language sections, immigrants left the party in large numbers. They were not replaced by native-born Americans until a new transitional category, the unemployed, arose in the 1930s.

As for the supposed class origin of the communist leadership, office-holders, and deputies in the West, this too has suffered wide variations as policies changed and as purges decimated those identified with a particular line of action now abandoned. Initially, communism in the West recruited a motley of classes under intellectual leadership. Thus, the first directing committee of the French Communist Party in December 1920 contained only four workers to twenty-eight intellectuals.[36] (The first Soviet Government contained four workers and eleven intellectuals.) Yet when the reaction set in against intellectuals in Russia, the French party was purged accordingly and, under the Barbé-Celor leadership, 70 per cent of the central committee were reputed working men. The Stalinist persecution of intellectuals, engineers, and eventually doctors, led to suspicion of the educated and the bourgeois in some western parties, with a consequent increase in working-class representation at the top. In Britain, the United States, and the English-speaking countries generally, the communist parties remained under the domination of intellectuals and ex-workers. One cannot stress too strongly, however, that one is no longer using precise sociological notions of class when one speaks of intellectuals and of ex-workers turned professional party officials.

The conclusion must be that the Bolshevik Revolution, through the national communist parties, did not have any decisive impact on the class composition of the western socialist movement. The communist parties would perhaps have wished to deprive the socialists

[36] D. Caute, *Communism and the French Intellectuals* (London, 1964), pp. 23–6.

of their proletarian base, except for the best-paid skilled workers whose class betrayal could be explained by Lenin's theory of the labour aristocracy. In reality, the socialist parties were not even trying to maintain a characteristically proletarian base. For instance, the proportion of workers in the German Social-Democratic Party fell from 94 per cent before the 1914 war to 54–57 per cent in 1955–61, without there being a rival communist party in existence at either date. It had claimed 80.5 per cent and 77 per cent in 1925–6 and 1930 respectively, when there *was* a communist party. And yet the communist parties were no more successful in obtaining, and much less successful in holding, a proletarian base: the percentage of factory workers in the German Communist Party fell steadily from 62.3 in 1928 to 20 or 22 in 1931.

This represents a failure for the communists only in terms of their own social theory. On a more up-to-date view of the nature of western societies, there is nothing surprising or discreditable in failure to establish a large and yet characteristically working-class party because it would be impossible. There is no one policy, nor even one type of policy, that expresses what all the industrial proletariat and no one else would want to see attempted in regard to the various problems that confront western nations, nor any objective set of interests, recognized or unconscious, apparent or 'real', that peculiarly characterizes the contemporary working class. In other words, the working class in those countries no doubt exists as a static category of economics, less surely of sociology, but it no longer exists (supposing it ever did) as a live political force or as the potential material for a major political movement. The socialist parties have, with varying degrees of frankness, adjusted to this situation. But the communist parties were bound by their outdated Marxist analysis to continue trying to pick up that globule of mercury, 'the real interests of the working class'. So it was inevitable that their impact should have been, in this respect, diffuse and ultimately irrelevant, and that their political career inside western societies should have been that of adventurers.

As has several times been noted, there is reason to give the French party special treatment in this respect as having, very imperfectly and far from consistently, come nearer than other parties to being what its statutes call it, 'the party of the working class of France'. Though the very top echelon of its leaders have been workers only by reminiscence (and for a period lived, Stalin-like, virtually without contact with workingmen), the level immediately below them is composed of *'fonctionnaires de la révolution'* of more recent working-class origin, and of men whose daily tasks keep them in touch with workers. At the level below that, the cadres are predominantly workers but all other social classes are well represented too.[37] At a 1964 congress 55.8 per cent of delegates were workers (with 27 per cent coming from the metal-workers, the aristocracy that makes up only 17 per cent of the French workers). However, that was after the party had shrunk considerably. In 1950, when it was almost twice as big, party leaders were complaining that worker representation (e.g. 37 per cent of federal committees) was too small.

The same dilution of worker strength whenever the party expands can be seen at the level below that, the level of the rank and file membership. Here workers are often in a minority, and even the party claimed only 40 per cent of members as working in private industry in 1959, compared with 47.5 per cent of cadres so employed at that date.[38] In the period of expansion of the communist ranks between 1937 and 1945, membership in industrial regions rose by only 50 per cent, whereas it rose 100 per cent in semi-industrial regions and 250 per cent in rural areas; party membership as a percentage of population was greatest in rural areas, a fact that has been plausibly connected with the strength of the Resistance *maquis* in those parts.

Passing to the base of this pyramid, the electors who vote communist, workers are in a minority in most elections, varying between 44 per cent in 1952 and 38 per cent in 1965, but touching 51 per cent according to one public opinion poll in the latter year. Naturally, one must add to these figures the percentage, which varies between 17 and 22, which is described as *sans profession*, these being, frequently, workers' wives. Incidentally, the poll that gave 44 per cent of communist voters as workers gave 25 per cent for the corresponding proportion among socialist voters; and it gave 64 per cent of communist voters as wage and salary earners, compared with 47 per cent of socialist voters.

Other researchers have sought to measure how much of the potential working-class vote goes to the Communist Party of France. There are large variations from year to year and from region to region, but the national average is between 40 and 50 per cent. It

[37] J. Fauvet, *op. cit.* pp. 333–40.
[38] Public sector workers in this survey were lumped in with civil servants.

fell as low as 36 per cent in 1958, when 19 per cent of the potential worker vote went to the SFIO, 15 per cent to the Gaullist UNR, and 30 per cent to other parties. In 1962, 38 per cent of workers voted for the PCF and 22 per cent for the SFIO and the breakaway PSU (United Socialist Party) combined. That meant that 40 per cent of electors classified as belonging to the working classes did not vote for the left at all. In the 1965 presidential elections, 45 per cent of workers voted for General de Gaulle and only 55 per cent for the single opposition candidate endorsed by both the communists and socialists (as well as by the extreme right).

There are parts of the country such as Paris (especially the working-class *arrondissements*), its 'Red Suburbs', and Marseille, where communists obtain 66 to 75 per cent of the worker vote when this is suitably defined, but it is no longer true (if it ever was) that 'outside Alsace-Lorraine, the great bulk of the industrial working class votes today for the Communist Party'.[39] Disagreements probably turn upon definition of the 'industrial working class' and 'potential worker vote', but if one gives working class the meaning it has in socialist discussion traditionally (say, manual workers in industry, mining, and transport, plus wives and people retired from these occupations), the French Communist Party seldom obtains the support of half of that class.

What makes it nevertheless the nation's largest party is the addition of the farmers' votes, which are regularly 13 to 15 per cent of its total support. Indeed, the reddest department of all France was Corrèze in 1951 and Creuse in 1956, predominantly agricultural regions where by far most peasants own their land. The phenomenon of peasant communism is interesting but not relevant to our theme, because there is a parallel growth in peasant socialism; the SFIO has been making similar gains, at the expense of the Radical Party, in rural regions.

Fluctuation of the Membership: We have seen that the communist parties attracted from socialism the revolutionaries, whom they regularly obliged to accept phases of anti-revolutionism as required by Leninist strategy; that they attracted in particular the young, and managed to stay young in average age of membership over long periods, even when total membership was declining sharply; that their total membership varied immensely; and that they frequently relied heavily for membership on transitional groups like the

[39] Williams, *op. cit.*, p. 54.

unemployed, students, immigrants, and refugees, and on occupations with a high labour turnover such as building. It would follow from any one of those facts, and *a fortiori* from their combination, that membership of communist parties has been and still is unstable in the extreme, unstable in the sense that the people who compose the communist parties this year are not the same individuals who composed them last year to the extent that that would be true of other parties and institutions. That is why we all know many more ex-communists than we know communists, and this has been the case in the West through all the variations of communism since 1920. That inconstancy in the human composition of these parties would be compatible with what has been claimed to exist in France in recent years, a 'constancy of communist temper in certain regions, professions and families',[40] if different individuals from those regions, professions, and families continued to make, in constant proportion, the brief experiment of communist affiliation. Since, however, the same author notes that communist support varies widely, depending on whether the party is currently promoting traditional socialist policies or revolutionary pro-Sovietism, and since he points out that the PCF remains France's youngest party and yet has lost half its membership in ten years, one must conclude that the constancy of its membership is quite relative. In France as elsewhere in the West, it has been seen, since the first united-front drive succeeded the first spell of ultra-revolutionism, that only a minority of western leftists would be capable of brusque turns, and that the people who follow one communist tack are not, for the most part, those who follow the next and contrary tack.[41]

This is the phenomenon known as 'fluctuation' or membership turnover, that has been constantly deplored in communist party litera-ture. It is something new in the western socialist movement, which always boasted, and still shows, a relative constancy in membership, and which has placed great emphasis on continuity in the service of the cause. Socialist parties and trade unions in countries known for political doggedness (Bagehot called it stupidity), such as Britain and Germany, and only to a somewhat lesser extent in countries of more mercurial political temper, such as France, have generally had

---

[40] Fauvet, *op. cit.*, p. 336.
[41] Draper, *American Communism*, p. 189, remarks, 'A much closer correlation existed between the party's fluctuation in membership and the party's political line than between the fluctuation and the economic situation'.

a solid core as big as half the membership that would pass a lifetime with the cause, though total membership might double in periods of crisis (such as the Liberation of France in 1944). It was that stability that enabled pre-1914 social-democracy in Germany to run ninety daily newspapers, to accumulate considerable property, and to manage an insurance business and numerous other enterprises that presupposed that socialism would continue to be 'a steady market'. It was that same stability that made that movement the subject of classic studies of bureaucracy, of the tendency towards oligarchy, and of ossification in political parties. To illustrate the constancy at the top of the old socialist parties, Roberto Michels noted the names of delegates to the 1893 congresses of the German, Italian, and French parties, and then asked how many of them were still active leaders in 1910, seventeen years later. He found that 30 per cent of the Germans were, 32 per cent of the Italians, and 13 per cent of the French. If that last figure seems small, it will emerge that western communist parties could seldom match it. The communist parties were to prove to be not only less consistently led than the old socialist movements, but less so even than the socialist parties of their day, which were exposed to the same acceleration of the pace of history.

For example, at the sixth congress of the Communist International in 1928, 65 per cent of delegates were attending their first such congress and only 7 per cent had been present at the second congress, held a scant eight years previously. Taking the names of office-holders appointed by the seven congresses of that organization, it emerges that no one, not a single man or woman, attended all seven nor even six of them. Only 1 per cent attended five congresses, 2 per cent attended four, and 6 per cent three. Some 73 per cent of names appear for one congress only, meaning that three-quarters of the leaders of world communism between 1919 and 1935 held their jobs only for the interval between two Comintern congresses.[42] Similarly, inside the national parties, delegates to even so lowly a function as an urban district congress were highly unstable. In Berlin, where in 1931 fluctuation was estimated at 40 per cent a year, 44 per cent of delegates to a local congress had been members less than a year and 66 per cent less than three years; only 14 per cent had been communists for over seven years. Borkenau comments, in reproducing these figures, 'They show . . . that there is a stratum of about 15

---

[42] Annie Kriegel, *Les Internationales ouvrières 1864–1943* (Paris, 1964), pp. 115, 122. The Stalinist purges hit the non-Russian communist leaders too.

per cent—of the delegates, not of the members—which has kept its faith in the party through all vicissitudes'.[43]

Turnover, or fluctuation, has been much greater among the rank and file. For the American party, Theodore Draper concludes, 'we may estimate, then, that about 100,000 people entered the party in the decade 1919–29, of whom only about 10,000 stayed in long enough to represent a basic membership'.[44] It continued to be true in the next few years that more than a third of new members of that party quit after a few months, while two-thirds had left inside five years. Similar fluctuation is evident in official communist statistics for that period relating to Britain, France, and Czechoslovakia, and even more notably for Germany, where a year such as 1930 saw around 100,000 members, or almost a third of the party, quit, while 143,000 newcomers joined. At the slowest rate of turnover, the big German party was losing three-quarters of its new members in seven years and was completely changed in membership in a decade, without much help from mortality (it was a young party). Borkenau drew the conclusion that there was a solid nucleus of at most 5 per cent of the membership of a communist party in the 1930s that was loyal through successive cycles of Leninist tactics, while the remaining 95 per cent was shifting sand. Actually, nucleus is not a good term for the stayers because they do not have any great influence over the party.

In times of economic slump . . . the big majority of the party members join and leave again within at most three years. In times of relatively good business . . . fluctuation is still extremely strong but not so strong as in years of slump. Only about one-fifth of the membership . . . changes within one or two years; the big changes occur when a party suffers some spectacular defeat. But within five to seven years the effects have been the same; practically the whole of the party membership, with the exception of the stable 5 per cent, have disappeared and been replaced by new members.[45]

Fluctuation inside the big western parties, those of France and Italy, has been no less extreme since the war, though statistics are harder to come by. The French party seldom reveals its actual membership, and the Italian party, which does, does not show how many leave and join each year. For France, we know that at the

[43] Borkenau, *op. cit.*, p. 370.
[44] Draper, *American Communism*, p. 189.
[45] Borkenau, *op. cit.*, p. 372.

Liberation membership was still under 400,000 and the party published the figures of 544,989 for 1945 and the all-time high of 804,229 for the year 1946. Thus membership doubled in two years. It fell constantly thereafter, and appears to have been back to under 400,000 (that is, the Liberation figure) by 1953 or 1954. Thus in a decade at the most a minimum of 400,000 people (or the equal of the total strength of the party at the beginning and end of that decade) had passed through the party; in truth, many more than that number did, for we are working with totals without knowing how they are made up. The decline continued until membership was, on a reliable estimate, 226,000 in 1959.[46] Since members are quitting as they grow older, and as the average age remains young, turnover must have been high in this shrinking number. Assuming that only 70 per cent of the cards distributed by the central treasury of the party to the federations are actually placed, the 1964 membership would be still under 300,000.

The Italian party, starting out with skeletal forces at the end of the war, had attained a membership of around 2.5 million by 1948 and claimed to hold it till 1956; thereafter a decline set in that was constant till 1963 when membership was put at 1,615,000. The same figure was claimed for 1965. Again it is clear from the bare totals that 900,000 party members, or well over a third, have left within a decade. In reality, that fraction could be leaving the party each year. One is entitled to make that guess by the figures given for the special 1966 membership-card drive launched before the end of 1965— the first time the party had sought to sign up next year's members this year. Naturally that drive was aimed at existing, 1965, members, so it is instructive that 933,177 cards were placed, for that is only 57.8 per cent of the 1965 membership. (For the Youth Federation, the corresponding percentage was only 43.3 per cent.) It would be rash to conclude that 42.2 per cent of the 1965 membership quit, to be almost replaced by a new draught of youth in 1966, but if accuracy is impossible the sense of the movement is plain.[47]

Thus the most recent facts suggest as strongly as those of the period 1920–4 that communism is a phase through which a large minority of western leftists pass but in which only a tiny fraction of that minority can make a spiritual home. It was not to be expected

---

[46] Fauvet, *op. cit.*, p. 364.
[47] Mario Cesarini, 'Il PCI nel 1965: un anno mediocre', in *Il Mondo*, 11 January 1966.

that Lenin's instrumentalist notion of a political party would accord with the western socialists' attitude to politics, that is, that any but an exceptional few could accept the brusque turn from one sort of policy to its contrary in the name of a science of revolution of which the rational basis never became apparent. Looked at in another way, it is precisely the fluctuation of communist party membership that explains the possibility of these brusque turns, in that only new-comers, with no acquaintance with the party's past, even its immediate past, could consent to do, say, and believe the opposite of what was being done, said, and believed in that party yesterday. Sarcasm about the dialectical versatility of communists is perhaps unwarranted except when addressed to the small number of ideological old-men-of-the-sea who perform these contortions, and of whom Maurice Thorez will long remain the champion. The bulk of communists only change their minds once, when they leave the party—shortly after joining it.

The Socialist Parties Today

We have seen what sort of leftists the communist parties separated off from the western socialist movement, and for how long. We could now try to draw the implications of what has been said by showing, succinctly, what the movement looks like as a result, taking it as an *organization*, or series of loosely connected organizations. What the socialist *ideology* is today, how socialist doctrine has shown the impact of communism, will be a later concern.

The world's largest socialist party, the British Labour Party, having on its left the smallest communist party of the industrialized world, has not been subject to any of the foregoing influences to any notable extent. On the contrary, it has influenced the British Communist Party, making it more moderate, less fanatical, and readier to colla-borate with non-communists at loggerheads with the Labour Party (such as Stafford Cripps's Socialist League and Fenner Brockway's ILP in the 1930s). The fact that the British Labour Party has not had to compete with native communism no doubt explains in part its earlier transformation into a non-class, national party. Indeed, it was just after the Bolshevik Revolution, in 1918, that the Labour Party revised its statutes, which till then had meant that its members were largely trade unionists, in such manner that non-workers could enter it through constituency parties. In that way, while echoing its original proletarian membership by speaking solicitously of 'workers by hand and brain' (that is, workers and non-workers), the Labour Party received the disbanding hosts of Liberalism. Already by 1932, Tawney could say, 'If variety of educational experience and economic condition among its active supporters be the test, it is . . . less of a class party than any other British party'. Since then, experience as a governing party and constant readiness, when it was not, to become so, have made it still less of a class party, while the enactment into law of much of its limited socialist ambitions during its period in office after the Second World War left it with little to distinguish it as a socialist party. Yet the curious thing is that the British Labour Party has been slower and more reluctant than other formerly socialist parties to part with the last shreds of its doctrine, whether as slogans or as velleities of action. The explanation would seem to be that, precisely because there is no sizable communist party in Britain, the Labour Party still has a militant left wing, composed of trade union leaders and intellectuals who elsewhere would be in the local communist party. It is still possible in the Labour Party to resist the non-socialist proposals of leaders like Gaitskell and Harold Wilson with doctrines that in other countries would be decried as so radical as to be 'pro-communist'. And of course socialist parties that rely on the support, financial, electoral, and other, of the trade unions (as the British party does, whereas, for example, the West German SPD does not), will always contain a radical left wing, not because trade unions are revolutionary but because if one is going to find the last hangover of proletarian socialism in the West today it will be in certain unions. The upshot is that while the British Labour Party has made the most successful adjustment to the new society of any of the major socialist parties, it can still appear to be further left than many Continental socialist parties—and the absence of local communist competition is the reason for both these facts. A comparison with the Australian Labor Party may illustrate the point. There, too, the absence of a substantial communist party means that the socialist party harbours many radicals who, in France or Italy, would join the communist party. They are numerous enough to ensure—once again with the backing of certain trade unions of importance to the Labor Party and boasting a tradition of proletarian radicalism—that the party does not surrender all its socialist slogans or all its old-fashioned socialist illusions. The difference, however, is that local communism is just so much more an active reality than in Britain for the accusation of pro-Sovietism, subversion, and anti-Catholicism to be taken more seriously when it is made by people with an interest to exaggerate those dangers. The consequence has been that the Australian Labor Party could be rent in two, with those taking the supposed communist menace seriously hiving off to form a Democratic Labor Party under Catholic leadership, leaving the Labor Party incapacitated. One might imagine, as a simple hypothesis, a situation where the Australian Communist Party was twice or three times its present size and influence, whereupon it would remain a negligible factor in the nation but would be large and respectable enough to attract to its ranks those who now, by remaining in the Labor Party, provide the pretext for its ruination; they are so few that their departure would still leave the Labor Party a potential governing party.

At the other extreme of communist influence on the socialist parties—to complete this reference to Anglo-Saxon countries where communism has never been a great force—is the case of the United States, where the Communist Party, while always small, was still large enough to contain all those attached to the old socialist ideals, while discrediting socialism in the eyes of others less blind to social change. The result was that the American Socialist Party simply disappeared. From a peak of one million votes in the 1912 elections, it declined till it can barely win a few thousand votes today.

The impact on the socialist parties of the loss of certain types of leftist to the communists has been much more visible, naturally, in continental Europe. In West Germany, for example, one has seen the disappearance of socialism as a political force, with the conversion of the SPD to a non-ideological electoral machine, and although this process has been completed only recently and under the highly peculiar conditions obtaining in divided Germany during the Cold War, one may nevertheless detect its beginnings from the earliest days of the Weimar Republic, that is, as soon as the communists had quit. As has been said already, the 1921 Görlitz Programme initiated the move away from nominally revolutionary socialism to gradualist reformism, thereby marking the surrender by German socialism of its pre-war pre-eminence as the great million-member model of world Marxism and as the backbone of the Second International. The party became, right from the start of the Weimar Republic, which indeed it helped to found and in which it shared governmental responsibility, a party of order rather than a party of protest, let alone a party of revolution. It gave the Republic a

President, three Chancellors, and the Government of Prussia which ruled over two-thirds of Germany's population. The party oligarchy left in control by the exodus of the revolutionaries to the Communist Party and, for a time, to the Independent Socialist Party (USPD), became older and even more solidly entrenched at the head of a party whose internal affairs were less and less democratic. It is fair to note, however, that every political party in Germany was becoming less democratic at the time, starting with the KPD, and the illiberal bureaucracy that ran the SPD was probably the least unresponsive management of any institution in the country. It has been seen that the KPD did not succeed in becoming a specifically and peculiarly working-class party, and that the SPD long retained as much working-class support as the communists; but it is also obvious that the Socialist Party had lost many members and millions of voters to the communists and, if it were to maintain its electoral clientele, it would have to replace them. It sought to do so on the right, but it could never win enough new support there (the fact is not surprising in a nation that was drifting towards backing the nazis) both to replace the extra workers it lost by trying to, and to pass the one-third barrier that had blocked its electoral progress. Unable to win more than 33 per cent of the votes, which, it is theoretically possible, a united socialist party could have done in the conditions of the Weimar Republic, the SPD gloomily settled down, as Hunt says, to the fate of 'a permanent minority party, a kind of parliamentary lobby for German labor'.

Perhaps the most notable change in the party was, rather than any decline in proletarian membership, the fact that the German workers who remained loyal to the SPD became increasingly 'petty bourgeois' in mentality, to use the polemical expression applied by Marxists to the first signs of the consumer mentality now general among western wage-earners. This evolution had many causes, some of them having nothing to do with the rise of the communist movement alongside the older socialist parties; but in Germany the shattering experience of the German Revolution and the loss of radicals to the communist and—be it noted—to the nazi parties must be mentioned as part of the explanation. Easier to measure than this change of spirit among the membership of the party is the transformation of the leadership into an unimaginative officialdom concerned primarily with their career in the party bureaucracy. Transformation is perhaps an improper term, since we know, thanks to Michels,[48] how far this process had gone well before the First World War, but it went to extraordinary lengths once the communists had left and had polarized (as the NSDAP did) elements liable to press for radical social change, such as the youth and the unemployed. For example, the plum jobs the party had to offer, the safe seats in the Reichstag, went increasingly to paid bureaucrats of the party. The KPD may have had no better a claim to be a working-class party but, at least, 58 per cent of the deputies it sent to the Reichstag in 1930 were workers, whereas only 2 per cent of SPD deputies were so, against 84 per cent who were full-time officials of the party. This might seem to be crass insolence on the part of a movement that claimed to represent German labour, but it must be recalled that the party's role was to serve as the passive instrument of the conservative leadership of the trade unions into which, exactly, German labour was organized. Only the exclusion of socialist radicals would ensure that it continued in that role, so from 1924 the executive was entrusted with the power to expel members from the party summarily. This weapon, which was given to party managements of various socialist parties from 1924 on, was justified in Germany, as elsewhere later, by the need to combat communist infiltration. Such infiltration took place, recurrently, but the weapon was mainly used to exclude non-communist socialists who wished to recall the conservative leaders to their supposed historical mission. The climax came in the SPD in 1931, when this weapon was used, in the face of the enemy, to exclude the whole left wing of the party, which then became the Socialist Workers' Party (SAP, Sozialistische Arbeiterpartei).

The transformation of the SPD from the time the communists quit to the close of the Weimar period has been summed up as *Verbonzung*, *Verkalkung*, and *Verbürgerlichung*, bossification, ossification, and bourgeoisification.[49] It became a middle-aged party without hope of gaining power and composed of workers who had adopted attitudes far removed from socialism. The treasurer of the SPD once explained an electoral setback during the Weimar Republic as due to the fact that there was much unemployment, inflation, and low wages, that is, the very conditions that would stimulate support for a radical party but would deprive a conservative party of order of

---

[48] Roberto Michels, *Zur Soziologie des Parteiwesens in der modernen Demokratie. Untersuchungen über oligarchischen Tendenzen des Gruppenlebens* (Leipzig, 1911).

[49] Hunt, *op. cit.*, pp. 241–8.

much of its working-class backing. It is not surprising, then, that the economic disaster of 1930 did not sweep the socialists into power, but a radical party. Nor is it surprising that the transformed SPD was helpless before the rise of that radical party, the national-socialists.

Re-emerging after the war, West German socialism at first found itself in competition with a local communist party. The suppression of the latter in 1952 made it possible for the SPD to draw, more frankly, the moral of its electoral defeat in 1953, held in the shadow of the Russian threat and the repression of the East Berlin workers' uprising, and of the first successes of the *Wirtschaftswunder*, the economic miracle of Ludwig Erhard. The conclusions it drew were not stated publicly and unequivocally until 1959 in Bad Godesberg, but their sense was clear from 1953. Fundamentally, they meant the liquidation of socialism in West Germany. The SPD became a democratic party with the slogan—once actually raised at a congress —of 'No more theory!' It required more than the disappearance of the competing communist party to complete this change; for example, the presence of a communist regime in the eastern half of the country and the means by which it was maintained there, made it politically impossible to promote, even demagogically and hypocritically, any Marxist policy in West Germany, especially after 1956. Thus it became urgent, in the peculiar conditions of West Germany, to give Marxist socialism a decent burial. But it had been dead long since. The SPD had begun, from the start of the Weimar Republic, to evolve towards a *Volkspartei*, which it finally avowed itself to be in 1959. The avowal, incidentally, appears to have had a liberating influence, removing from the party the dead hand of trade union domination, attracting a younger membership, and making possible a reversal of the oligarchical trend within the party.

In France, where the competition of communism and socialism has been constant since 1920, the impact of the division of the movement on the Socialist Party may be seen most clearly. It follows from the principles of that division that the SFIO has become a party of older people with a reduced working-class representation and a conservative conception of social change. 'It has left the impression of an ageing bourgeois party, sadly lacking in dynamic energy and continually buffeted by the attacks of more powerful rivals. Its shifting geographical and social basis is slowly bringing it to resemble the Radical Party of the Third Republic'.[50] In particular, it has

[50] Williams, *op. cit.*, p. 71.

become the lobby of the civil servants, notably the schoolteachers (it has been dominated by one for twenty years, in the person of Guy Mollet), with views about religion that extend over the narrow range between militant *laicité* and free-masonry. Like the SPD and other western socialist parties, it has tended to become an electoral machine seeking to broaden its clientele, but it has remained an extremely inefficient one because of the presence on its left of a powerful communist party. This has made it necessary for the SFIO to persist in certain rituals of working-class politics, which has prevented its expansion towards the right. However, since those rituals are so evidently insincere—electors on the right would attach more weight, for instance, to Guy Mollet's nationalist policy at Suez and in Algeria than to his party's faded Marxist incantations— the real difficulty hampering the extension of the SFIO's national base has been the issue of *laicité*, which has ruined every effort to found a French labour party down to that undertaken by Gaston Defferre in 1964–5. This in turn may result from the excessive reliance of the party on civil servants and schoolteachers among its membership, and especially among its militant adherents, for in France, these two groups are traditionally hostile to the Catholic Church. So one could argue that the French Socialist Party will become more efficient as an electoral machine in winning votes towards the right only when it broadens its base towards the left, winning from the Communist and Catholic parties workers and *salariés* less obsessed with the old-fashioned problems of secularity, *laicité*. Until then, the SFIO will remain a motley, representing proletarian interests in the industrial north of France, militant anti-communism in peasant areas, and anti-clericalism in the west of the country. The separation that occurred at Tours in 1920 is far from accounting alone for this decline of the French Socialist Party, but it does explain in large part the fact that the SFIO has not been able to make a more coherent, a more principled effort to adjust to changed circumstances.

The Internationals

Most of the socialist parties of before the First World War were, and most of them today still are, linked loosely in an international organization that dates from 1889, the Second, or Labour and Socialist, International. In 1912 this organization counted 3.37 million adherents around the globe and claimed to exercise an influence over 7.31 million co-operators, 10.84 million trade unionists, 11 to 12 million voters, and the readers of some 200 daily newspapers. In 1966 its secretary, Albert Carthy, claimed that it commanded the support of 70 million voters thanks to the membership of fifty national parties (the fiftieth, the Australian Labor Party, having joined only in that year).

No aspect of the socialist movement's organization was more bitterly criticized by the communists than its International, and on no point did the breakaway movement touched off by the Bolshevik Revolution seek to innovate more radically. Ironically, it is here that western socialism has been least disturbed by the communists, whose precept and practice the social-democratic parties simply ignored on this score for fifty years; and it is here, too, that communism registered one of its most obvious defeats. It accused the socialists of exaggerating national differences and thereby co-ordinating inadequately the various leftist movements around the world. In attempting to do otherwise, communism achieved for a time a substantial measure of co-ordination of movements subscribing to its cause, but that degree of international unity depended ultimately on a mixture of terrorism and appeal to the basest motives of subservience, so that as soon as there was relaxation of the central dictatorship, unity began to crumble. The collapse began first, naturally, in communist parties that had, with some Soviet assistance, gained power in their own countries, and thereby were able to match centralizing terrorism with armed resistance in defence of national independence. It soon spread to national communist parties that were, and seemed likely to remain indefinitely, in opposition, but could henceforth assert their doctrinal independence, relying if necessary on the authority of another communist State beside the Russian.

The Second International was formed only after the founding socialist parties had grown up independently of each other, so that when they came to consider the need for co-operation, they had to recognize their diversity and so they aimed no higher than at a loose co-ordination of their efforts. The International's small office, first in Brussels, where it returned after a spell in Zürich, was mainly used for exchange of information and for the organization of conferences which were the real instruments of unification. These congresses usually, said Sorel, 'set up commissions to draw up formulas that could reconcile the opinions of the various party chiefs; as a result of their work the various theses were reduced to abstractions divorced from real life, but the more easily accepted the more obscure they were'.[51]

The socialist parties of the day, for all that, had a theory of proletarian internationalism and they drew it not from the Mazzini-esque declarations of international fraternity that had inspired many adherents of the First International, but from Marx himself. That theory was that capitalism forced unity upon them, willy nilly, by creating similar conditions wherever it flourished. Guesde put it as well as any socialist orator, just after the 1904 Amsterdam congress:

> For us and for the immense majority of socialists represented in Amsterdam, socialism has its base in economic phenomena. It springs ready armed from capitalism, of which it is at one and the same time the culmination and the corrective. We are, to use the picturesque expression of one among us, the sons of the steam engine, that is of industrialism. The concentration of capital and the proletarianization of labour and so on, wherever they penetrate, engender the same ills and send their victims by millions into the same struggle to the death against the same enemy. There is room, on the self-same class basis, for unity not only of goals but of means and tactics whatever may be the diversity of governmental conditions. The International, not of words but of facts, of action, becomes, at the same time as a possibility, a necessity.

This limpid theory was accepted, as oratory, by French supporters of Jaurès and, as well as Guesde's Marxists, by the Russian revolutionaries, the British trade unionists, Belgian co-operators, and German social-democrats—that is, by a collection of groups whose differences not only of national character and local situation but of socialist doctrine and political aim precluded it from ever being translated into action. So the socialist parties of the day made an obeisance in the direction of international unity and then insisted so firmly on the peculiarity of their particular situation and problems that they were exempted from doctrinal agreement or practical co-ordination. That applied even to the famous resolution against war and to the cry, 'Insurrection rather than war!', because the socialist party of the nation most concerned, Imperial Germany, pointed out that it was so placed that, if it practised revolutionary defeatism, the only result would be that the country where socialism was strongest, Germany, would be subjugated to the one where it was weakest, Russia—an argument that we know would have appealed to Marx

[51] G. Sorel, 'Ultime Meditazione', in *Nuova Antologia*, 1928, p. 289.

because he used it. And the Germans, it will be remembered, were the backbone of the Second International at that time.

Thinking to draw the moral of the collapse of that International in 1914, when its member-parties collaborated in sending their adherents to fight each other for four years, the Bolsheviks organized a very different sort of International, the Third. The preamble to its statutes said: '. . . Communism must have a strongly centralized organization. The Communist International must, in fact and in deed, be a single communist party of the entire world. The parties working in the various countries are but its separate sections.' The fourth of those statutes declared: 'The supreme authority of the Communist International is the world congress of all the parties and organizations which belong to it. The world congress meets regularly once a year. The world congress alone is empowered to change the programme of the Communist International.' The ninth statute specified that the Executive Committee elected by the world congress 'issues instructions which are binding on all the parties and organizations belonging to the Communist International. The Executive Committee of the Communist International has the right to demand that parties belonging to the International shall expel groups or persons who offend against international discipline, and it also has the right to expel from the Communist International those parties which violate decisions of the world congress'.

These considerations were then translated into the 21 conditions for membership of the Communist International, particularly into the sixteenth condition, which added by way of explanation: 'The Communist International, working in conditions of acute civil war, must be far more centralized in its structure than was the Second International. Consideration must of course be given by the Communist International and its Executive Committee in all their activities to the varying conditions in which the individual parties have to fight and work, and they must take decisions of general validity only when such decisions are possible.' In that final reservation, as events were soon to prove, it was the Russian Bolsheviks who were making an obeisance in the direction of national differences before proceeding to enforce global policies that were more often than not quite irrelevant to conditions in the West—conditions of which, as they occasionally admitted, they were very ignorant.

How the Communist International worked in practice is not our theme, but it is to be noted that this centralized, military notion of world proletarian organization was so foreign to western socialism that even socialists who rallied to the Communist International simply did not take the statutes and conditions just quoted seriously. Accustomed to the internationalist sentiments of the Second International, which might seek to co-ordinate loosely but would never interfere in a national party's affairs, the first western communists reacted with surprise and resentment when they found that the Third International really intended that Moscow should intervene in national party life. Trotsky was soon complaining that 'fine words about discipline, liaison and so on are becoming empty conventions. Modigliani [a leading Italian communist] said that the connection with the International came down to sending occasional postcards with views of Italy'. And Frossard, a contemporary French communist, was later to confess, 'We could not manage to take the 21 conditions seriously', thinking in particular of the International's intervention in the French party's affairs. Western communists were to have even greater difficulty in taking those conditions seriously when it became plain that it was not a supposedly internationalist committee elected by a world congress that was interfering in their affairs but, quite simply, the Russian State. They discovered, as André Malraux said, that 'whereas we thought that in becoming less French we would become more human, in fact we only became more Russian'. With Stalin it was obvious, what was already to be seen with Lenin and Trotsky, that communist internationalism was Russian nationalism.

Ignoring these developments, the Second International sought to reconstitute itself after the war and the Bolshevik Revolution. It took four years, from 1919 to 1923, and the failure of the 'Two-and-a-half International', to reproduce the appearance of proletarian solidarity among the western socialist parties. It proved to be a more illusory appearance than before the war, precisely because the socialist parties had begun that integration into their various national political systems that was assisted by the loss of the revolutionaries and by the move towards the right. Before long the socialist parties of Britain, Belgium, Germany, Denmark, Czechoslovakia, and Sweden found themselves, to varying degrees and for different periods, accepting actual governmental responsibilities, while the French party had the experience of supporting a government. Naturally, therefore, they were inclined to be franker than before the war about defending national interests, and their international gatherings tended to become diplomatic conferences just like meetings of national authorities. Naturally, too, their international gatherings, notably those in Brussels in 1929 and in Paris in 1933, were no more successful than other diplomatic congresses in Europe in co-ordinating a common policy for the democracies in the face of fascism and nazism. The western socialist parties were divided on that issue much as the conservative parties were, and those of the countries where fascism came to power must share the responsibility for that fact, along with the other democratic forces of those lands. To find that dual failure—the inability of socialist parties to prevent fascism winning power at home, and the failure of the Second International to co-ordinate the general struggle against fascism—especially scandalous, as though socialist responsibilities were somehow more profoundly engaged in the affair than those of other democratic parties, is to betray that one is taking literally the outdated socialist ideology of that day. Western socialists were still, that is to say, talking of proletarian solidarity as though this was something that transcended national boundaries more readily than other causes, and they were still trying to explain fascism in Marxist terms, as a class phenomenon peculiar to a given 'phase' of capitalism. Those were two illusions. There is no special community of interests binding working people in various countries, except when those working people support liberal causes, in which case they have the common concern of liberals with a certain measure of international co-operation; even less is there any reason why a non-class political party that continues to brandish an outdated proletarian banner should prove particularly effective at organizing an internationalist cause. And of course fascism could not be accounted for as 'the terrorist dictatorship of the capitalists'. Thus the failure of socialist internationalism between 1922 and 1939 is to be deplored not in regard to some peculiar responsibility of the socialists, but in proportion to the numbers of western socialism's organized supporters; they were so many, and did so little.

That renewed collapse, after the less expected fiasco of 1914, cured western socialism of its internationalist illusions and no serious effort was made to revive the Second International as a political force. (Indeed, for a time, the Communist International having been disbanded by Stalin in 1943, the only socialist international in existence was the Fourth, demonstrating again that Trotskyism was the last refuge of several of socialism's discarded illusions.) The

Socialist International that was reconstituted at Frankfurt in 1951 is a small liaison force of no more importance than the international bureaux maintained by the western press and various other professions. Yet the age is precisely one of great international causes in the West, from the Common Market to UNESCO, and western socialists have played their role in all of these, sometimes a leading role. They have not done that, however, as socialists, since they could at any moment be replaced by politicians from other parties without loss to those internationalist causes. Indeed, in some countries such as Britain and Australia, the socialist parties have shown themselves more nationalist, in certain contexts, than parties of the right.

The communists were slower to abandon the hope of a particular proletarian aptitude for international collaboration. The Comintern being disbanded, the parties of the various countries maintained close contact, so that for a time they seemed to constitute an impressive global unity: 76 communist parties around the world with 32 million members, of which 13 parties (with 28 million members or 84 per cent of the total) were in power over 26 per cent of the earth's surface and 35 per cent of the world's population. Closer examination showed that the international scope of the movement was less extensive than it seemed. The 28 million members living in communist countries would not, of course, be free to join any other party, while four-fifths of the remaining four million were grouped in four big parties, the Italian, Indonesian, French, and Indian. Political adversity was to show that the membership of the Indian and Indonesian parties (the latter claimed to have 3.5 million members before its setback in 1965–6!) could melt as snow in the tropics, while the membership of the French and Italian parties steadily declined over the years. Notwithstanding these reservations, the communist movement would have remained a striking case of international co-operation if it had survived its own success and outlived the relaxation of Stalinist tyranny. This was not to be. Repeated open rebellion, sometimes successful as in Yugoslavia, sometimes tragically unsuccessful as in Hungary, marked the impossibility of enforcing unity upon nations under communist rule, until the diversity of interests between such nations had to be recognized throughout the east European camp. Concurrently, 'polycentrism' had to be allowed in the communist movement outside that region, while the Sino-Soviet rift removed the last foundation of the belief in a specifically Marxist internationalism. On all these fronts, the situation is still evolving rapidly fifty years after the Bolshevik Revolution, and there is no way of knowing how far disunity will ravage the communist movement; but it is already assured that communist internationalism has survived the trial of governmental responsibility no better than socialist internationalism.

The Bolsheviks failed, then, after a long and spectacular attempt, to change the thing they found most deplorable in the western socialism of 1914, its nationalism. Moreover, the way they went about trying to change it—namely, by seeking to pass off Russian nationalism as the common cause of the world proletariat—was so blatant that it never gave western socialists a bad conscience about their own retreat from internationalism. The new and viable internationalist causes arose, most promisingly after 1945, on grounds where socialism and Marxism had no relevance.

For all that, it must not be overlooked that in some particulars of great importance, the communists had a determining influence over western socialism's attitude to international questions. One example was colonialism.

Socialists and Colonialism

One is surprised today, in reading the socialists at the start of this century, to see their complacency on the question of European colonialism. Sorel, Bernstein, Jaurès, and their contemporaries had a faith in Europe's mission to bring the backward races up to civilization, and a tacit conviction of white superiority, that would be regarded as *ultra* in the conservative circles of 1967. Upon reflection, there is little reason to be surprised that the exponents of a doctrine of historical evolution from the 'Asiatic economy' via industrialism to communism, and the spokesmen of the urban proletariat, should be out of sympathy with the first stirrings of nationalist movements in which native bourgeois and peasants were to play the main roles. Yet a generation later, sympathy with such movements was to become one of the touchstones of leftism. In that change, the Bolsheviks had had a large part.

It is a change that could not have taken place without extensive adulteration of the Marxist doctrine of the socialist parties. The historicist theme of Marxism made it seem necessary that the colonial peoples must pass through the phase of capitalist industrialism before they could attain socialism, and capitalist industrialism then (and still today, almost as much) could come to those peoples only by European and American intervention. Socialists did not preach this comfortable doctrine only to members of other nations; Russia's most orthodox Marxists argued that their country too must pass that way.

H. van Kol declared at the Stuttgart congress of the Second International (1907) that European capitalism had a civilizing mission in the colonies, whose peoples were to be brought by imperialism to the next highest phase of culture, whereupon socialism would take over the work of guidance. Bernstein also thought that the advanced countries had a responsibility to develop their colonies as humanely as possible before setting them at liberty at some date far in the future. This view was the most popular among the rank and file of socialists, and it has remained common among western workers to this day. Jaurès carried it to the extent of disliking emergent nationalism, and even supported the maintenance of the Ottoman Empire, provided it were more tolerant of its Christian minorities.[52] There were many nuances in socialist opinion and socialists expressed themselves at their international congresses as being opposed to imperialism, but for reasons having to do with relations between Europeans rather than because they were particularly solicitous of colonies. What they would all without exception have found ludicrous was the notion that backward nations should arise and pass off their forced industralization as a form of socialism that gave them the right to lead the advanced West to a higher culture; that pretension was to become, after the Bolshevik Revolution, the essence of one species of 'Marxism'.

The colonial question first came up at a Socialist International congress in 1900, but it was seen exclusively in the perspective of European Great-Power rivalry, which socialists naturally deplored. From that date on, the question appeared regularly in socialist discussion, but only when one European Power clashed, or seemed liable to clash, with another in the quest for colonies, never when a colonial people resisted imperialism. The world-revolutionary import that Lenin read into the 1905 Russian Revolution was less evident to western socialists, and they largely ignored events that impressed Lenin such as the 1908 revolution in Persia and the overthrow of the Manchu dynasty in 1911. These things had little to do with the proletariat's cause, and so socialists felt they were outside their scope, though of course they were, on any given issue, opposed

[52] L. Hamon, 'Jaurès retrouvé', in *Preuves*, December 1965, p. 19.

to racialism, slavery, and oppression. Their ideas naturally evolved as the anti-imperialist struggle quickened, so that by 1912, when France established a protectorate over part of Morocco, Jaurès could exclaim: 'There is another force that is awakening. It is all those peoples of all races who have been inert till now or seemed so, who appeared to us, seen through the whirl of European agitation, to be wrapped in a winter-long sleep, and who now are waking up, claiming their rights, affirming their strength: races of Africa, races of Asia, Japan, China, India. . . . Yes, in our North Africa too there is a stirring that it would be quite imprudent to disdain or neglect'. As usual, Jaurès's golden oratory covered great vagueness, and passages such as the one quoted were no sign of a socialist theory of colonialism.

That theory was to come from Lenin and, after being one of the most influential ideas of the twentieth century, it was to prove as signal a misconception as the notion of proletarian internationalism.[53] Lenin's theory of imperialism as the relation between more advanced white races and backward coloured peoples was to make its Russian exponents no more successful in dealing with the latter, and specifically with the Chinese even when converted to communism, than other white nations had been. What was more, they were to show themselves far from proof against the temptation to practise imperialism to the advantage of their own supposed national interest, while their followers in the western communist parties were to acquire a record on the colonialist question that colonial leaders in European-dominated territories were to condemn as inadequately consistent. Today, indeed, we see the Chinese splitting the communist camp just as Russia did the socialist camp fifty years ago, and invoking very similar charges of bourgeoisification among a labour aristocracy

---

[53] D. K. Fieldhouse, ' "Imperialism": An Historiographical Revision', *Economic History Review* (London), 1961, pp. 187–209, summed up the extensive discussion of the Hobson–Lenin theory of imperialism, a discussion that benefited so greatly from the publication of A. K. Cairncross's *Home and Foreign Investment 1870–1913* (Cambridge, 1953). Fieldhouse concluded: '. . . it is clear that imperialism cannot be explained in simple terms of economic theory and the nature of finance capitalism [i.e. as the 'last stage of capitalism']. In its mature form it can best be described as a sociological phenomenon with roots in political facts; and it can properly be understood only in terms of the same social hysteria that has since given birth to other and more disastrous forms of aggressive nationalism.' Raymond Aron, *Paix et guerre entre les nations* (Paris, 1962, pp. 263–79) usefully summarizes the evidence that makes Lenin's theory appear 'purely arbitrary'.

that mouthed socialism while practising opportunism and drawing profits from imperialism.

Lenin at least foresaw the overwhelming importance the colonial question was to have in the twentieth century and, although he had a false theory of it, this was more than the socialists of the West could claim. Western socialism was to acquire an awareness on that issue, slowly and hesitatingly because of its increasing integration into national politics, but it was often uncomfortable and insincere in its anti-colonialist role, so that as a liquidator of European empires it has not much better a record than other western political forces such as conservatism or Gaullism. Those conservative forces, too, had learned from Lenin and were influenced by the agitation against imperialism that Bolshevism encouraged.

One should guard against exaggerating that contributing role of Bolshevism into an originating role, dating the liberation of the colonies and the rise of the Third World from 1917, for, as Lenin freely admitted, that process began with the century. Indeed, it would be more just to see matters the other way around, to take the Bolshevik Revolution as one incident in that process, as part of the emancipation of eastern nationalism from western dominance as much as it was a peasant-proletarian revolution against capitalism, rather than to take the continuing struggle of the Third World against the West as something unleashed by the Bolshevik Revolution. It was the fact that 1917 was both an anti-capitalist and an anti-western-imperialist uprising that has confused so many events since then. That 'over-determination' meant that bourgeois-nationalist and peasant movements in European possessions and protectorates, though aiming simply at replacing one non-socialist government by another no more socialist, could adopt Marxist language and find support among socialists and interested backing from Soviet Russia; while western socialists came to feel that they had to subordinate their socialist principles to their anti-colonialist convictions if they were not to be outflanked on the left by the communists.

It was outside of countries where the Second International had been represented before 1917, that is, in countries that had no significant industry and hence no socialist movement, that the Bolshevik Revolution was to have its greatest echo, and naturally that echo had little to do with the domestic anti-capitalist aspect of Bolshevism which interested western workers and intellectuals. In those non-industrialized, and hence dependent, countries the 1917 revolution had immense attraction for four reasons: it was a defiance of western Europe, an anti-imperialist act expressing racial, national, and colonial resentment; it suggested the efficacity of despotism in dealing with the problems of the twentieth century; it suggested that cultural progress was possible without any of those western liberal freedoms so much detested by the most influential social groups in pre-industrial societies; and it claimed to provide a spectacular short cut to economic and military power. Now none of these four had any connection with the socialist cause as this had been understood at least since Marx, that is to say with the emancipation of the working masses in a new culture that would remove the fetters that capitalism, in its mature development, had placed upon material progress and human betterment. Yet nationalist movements attracted by those four features of Bolshevism could claim socialist, even 'Marxist', credentials thanks to the duality of the 1917 revolution in Russia, and thereby they came to concern the western socialists.

The sources of this confusion lay ultimately in Tsarist Russia's own unique situation: a conglomerate of nationalities both European and Asiatic, where capitalism was represented largely by west European capital and technology, and where the subject nationalities (mostly peasants) were (or, at least, were thought by Russian socialists to be) the best allies of the small proletariat against the central power and its western capitalist supporters. But Lenin had other, theoretical, reasons for cultivating that confusion. Like all Marxists, he had to explain the fact that the standard of living of industrial workers in the capitalist countries had risen since the middle of the nineteenth century, whereas according to Marx it should have been falling. Actually, there is no Marxist explanation possible of that fact, which destroys at least the earlier and simpler historical *schema* of Marx and Engels. But Lenin introduced the saving hypothesis that western workers were preserved from ever-increasing misery by becoming the accomplices of their employers in the exploitation of the colonial peasantry. This theory, which also has no sound economic foundation,[54] fitted in happily with Lenin's explanation of

[54] As Borkenau noted in his conclusive critique of that theory (in the chapter 'Imperialism' in *Socialism, National or International*), Lenin had not 'ever taken the trouble to look up the international wages statistics' that were available in his day, for they would have sufficed to dispose of the notion of a

the failure of western socialism to become revolutionary or to rise above patriotism in 1914: the alliance of a treacherous labour aristocracy with the national bourgeoisie accounted, all at the same time, for 'social-patriotism', for the collapse of the Second International, for the unwillingness of western workers to revolt, for the rise in those workers' wages, and for the existence of European imperialism. Thus was suggested the objective of a counter-alliance of the revolutionary industrial proletariat of Europe with the peasantry of Russia and of the East and with the backward colonial countries generally. This conception had never occurred to western socialists.

It found expression in the statutes of the Third International: 'The Communist International breaks once and for all with the traditions of the Second International, for which in fact only white-skinned people existed. The task of the Communist International is to liberate the working people of the entire world. In its ranks, the white, the yellow and the black peoples—the working people of the whole world—are fraternally united'. Then the eighth of the conditions imposed on candidates for admission to that International stipulated:

A particularly clear and explicit attitude on the question of the colonies and the oppressed peoples is necessary for the parties in those countries where the bourgeoisie possesses colonies and oppresses other nations. Every party which wishes to join the Communist International is obliged to expose the tricks and dodges of 'its' imperialists in the colonies, to support every colonial liberation movement not merely in words but in deeds, to demand the expulsion of their own imperialists from these colonies, to inculcate among the workers of their own country a genuinely fraternal attitude to the working people of the colonies and the oppressed nations, and to carry on systematic agitation among the troops of their country against any oppression of the colonial peoples.

Those demands were made of western socialists at a time (the summer of 1920) when it seemed that the revolution might break out in

---

labour aristocracy being bribed with part of the super-profits earned in colonial markets. Nothing in the much more informative statistics that the economic historians have since made available lends any colour to that theory, either. Specially fortunate groups of workers ('labour aristocracy') who show little interest in socialism (who are 'bribed by the bourgeoisie', in Lenin's phrase) appeared most commonly in debtor countries, not in creditor countries (i.e. in the United States and the white Dominions, in Lenin's day), in which countries, of course, the imperialist nations of Europe had made by far most of their investments, rather than in their colonies of conquest.

western Europe. By the autumn of that year it was clear that this was not to be so, for some time at least, whereupon the proposal of an alliance between western workers and eastern nationalists was put before a Congress of Peoples of the East, called by the executive of the Third International in Baku and attended by 1,823 delegates from Russian Asia, Turkey, Persia, China, and India. That the Russian communists saw the alliance in terms of international power strategy and not as part of the socialist movement in favour of social and economic advance was clear from that first congress, at which 'the Russian comrades themselves excluded the small socialist groups of those countries when they came to criticize the great chiefs, the great feudal powers, the great Moslem leaders of whom [the Russians] had more need than of the proletarians of those countries for the struggle against England'.[55] That was still true, in Egypt for example, forty years later.

At first the communists of western colonialist countries found these conditions hard to accept. It is the French communists, mainly, that are in question, as the only large group of members of the Third International in a major imperialist country. The French-Algerian communists denounced the Comintern's call for a Moslem uprising in 1922 as 'dangerous folly', and they were to pass to extreme right movements when that uprising eventually occurred, in 1955. The French Communist Party was, as Manuilsky was still complaining in 1924, reluctant to proclaim the colonies' right to revolt and to independence, while that party was to continue to deny, for the next forty years, the wisdom of 'agitating among the troops of their country against any oppression of the colonial peoples', in the words of the Comintern. (A movement in favour of military disobedience during the Algerian war was condemned by the French communists, with the aid of a suitable quotation from Lenin.) In general the French communists' attitude to colonialism was to be far more opportunist than their principles would suggest, so that they must accept—as deputies forming part of the majority of the day or as members of the post-Liberation government—some of the responsibility for the 1947 Madagascar killings, for the start of the Indo-Chinese war, and for the opposition to the liberation of the North African countries. That was because the communists always put the tactical requirements of domestic politics before the general, theoretical line on colonialism, just as Russia was to subordinate its

[55] A. Kriegel, *Le Congrès de Tours*, p. 220.

support of anti-imperialism to broader strategic needs. However, it is not the implementation of communist anti-imperialist policy that concerns us but the effect of that policy on western socialists.

On that, G. D. H. Cole is explicit:

> I confess that, in those early days, my vision was in the main limited to the more advanced countries in which active Social-Democratic and Labour movements existed. . . . It must be borne in mind that when I became a socialist the Russian Revolution was still in the future and there had been almost no awakening of either socialism or even popular nationalism in the less developed countries. One envisaged the prospect of violent revolution in Russia, but hardly anywhere else—or, at all events, revolution outside Russia seemed altogether unlikely to take a socialist form. Apart from Russia, one still thought of socialism as essentially a movement of reaction against western capitalism, and of socialist policies in terms appropriate to the industrial societies of the West. Since then, mainly as a consequence of events in Russia, there has been a great social awakening in Asia and Africa and to some extent in Latin America; and in this awakening there has been a mingling of nationalist and socialist elements which has made it imperative both to re-make socialist thought in far more comprehensive world-wide terms and to revise earlier ideas about nationalism in its relation to socialism. It is now necessary to envisage the movement towards socialism as applying not only to highly industrialized societies accustomed to parliamentary government, but also to many and highly diverse societies which possess neither developed industries nor any tradition of parliamentary practice; and this makes the older conception of Social-Democracy clearly inadequate and even seriously misleading in relation to a great many countries now of importance in world affairs.[56]

Cole here faithfully reflects the confusion of western socialists on this issue, where they owe their awakening to the Bolshevik Revolution and to the political necessity to 'keep up with' the communists. He considers that it is a simple extension of socialist doctrine to incorporate into it ideas that are so distinct from it that they are shared with anti-colonialists of all sorts, such as American Presidents and French generals. Thus, when he says, 'But today it has become the plain duty of socialists of all countries to take their stand energetically on the side of popular nationalism in the colonial and semi-colonial countries and to give full support to the claims of the exploited peoples to self-determination and to the control of their own development', he forgets that for 'socialists of all countries' one could substitute 'Americans' or 'admirers of Mazzini who haven't read Marx'. Nor does he mention that western socialists have

[56] Cole, *op. cit.*, p. 8.

seldom carried their solicitude for the backward nations to the point of persuading their trade unions to abate opposition to immigration from those countries and to reduction of tariffs on 'cheap-labour' manufactures. However, he does note that 'the Asian socialists . . . are suspicious of the Socialist International'.

For all its limitations, the change in the western socialist attitude on these questions is to be ascribed to the Bolshevik Revolution and to the consistent teaching and inconsistent practice of the rival communist parties. Of course, almost everyone else in western society had meantime come around to anti-imperialist convictions, but they were not involved in the doctrinal confusion of the socialists who, learning their anti-colonialism from the communists, felt that there was indeed (as Cole says) something specifically 'socialist' or leftist about it. In other words, they subscribed to the change in the sense of *socialism*, a change that was initiated by Lenin, from its traditional meaning, 'the movement of proletarian liberation from capitalism's self-limiting restrictions', to the new meaning, 'the forced industrialization of hitherto dependent economies'. In turn that led to confusing socialism with the would-be efficacious illiberalism of nationalism in backward societies. This diminished emphasis on the libertarian motives of socialism was to contribute to the difficulties that western socialists had in what was, in actual practice, their real concern and occupation, adjustment to the post-capitalist society of the West. A political philosophy that had suggested emancipation and abundance came to be associated with dictatorship and penury.[57]

The Amputation of the Left

The western communist parties, although ostensibly revolutionary, have seldom paid much attention to revolution because their real concern has been to seize power, not in the State, but in other leftist parties. Their determination not to be outflanked on the left and their running warfare with the socialist parties on their right have occupied vastly more of their time than more general political affairs. These two considerations have alternated in importance, in accordance with the oscillation of Leninist strategy from left sectarianism to united-front co-operation and back again. The effect of that oscillation on communist party membership has already been re-

[57] For a longer and subtler analysis of the relations between western socialism and eastern nationalism see the section 'War and Revolution' in George Lichtheim, *Marxism* (revised ed., London, 1964), pp. 355–66.

ferred to; here, there will be question of its impact on the socialist movement, and first of all on the left of that movement.

The left of the socialist movement means all those forces that rejected integration into both capitalist and neo-capitalist society (in which bourgeois ideology still reigns), and claimed to be working instead for proletarian liberation and for the installation of a new culture that would take its origin in autonomous working-class institutions and ways of thinking. The negative aspect of this form of socialism was called left sectarianism, the repudiation of all who compromised in the least with bourgeois society as being as bad as the worst; that attitude was commonest among anarcho-syndicalists, but was recurrently adopted by the communists as well when on an ultra-left tack. The positive side of left socialism was expressed in actual independent proletarian institutions, conventions, and ideologies. Proletarian institutions seldom existed in more than embryonic form, in unions, syndicats, co-operatives, and soviets, but there was much discussion on the socialist left of further ventures in that direction 'after the revolution', notably in worker-managed factories, collective farms, and the like. Left socialism before the First World War claimed to be aiming, as well as at those institutions, at the abolition of the State, of money, and of the traditional family, and at the installation of an approximation to equality of incomes, internationalism, free love, federalism, workers' art, and a variety of other more or less connected and coherent revolutionary goals. Like all social programmes that have failed to materialize, this one looks in retrospect to be impossible, absurd, and rather embarrassing; certainly the communists and socialists of today are forgetful of, or hypocritical about, how this nineteenth-century ultra-left tradition bequeathed them a capital of morality, imagination, and generosity on which they have since lived like unproductive rentiers.

Left socialism was already in a numerical minority before the First World War, but its presence as the lively wing of socialism kept that movement infected with a spirit of revolutionary independence, and would no doubt have continued to do so. It was becoming clear, however, that the industrial working classes of west Europe, and even more so of America and Australasia, were unresponsive to the appeal to proletarian autonomy; they preferred citizenship and progressive material advance within bourgeois society. That preference was to become more marked as the moderate wing of socialism had more success in winning concessions, through trade union action, parliamentary representation, and influence over public opinion, that made bourgeois society more livable-in for working people. And by the time neo-capitalist society began to provide those working people with massive quantities of consumer durables at relatively falling prices, the issue was in no doubt: proletarian autonomy was a lost cause and the socialist left had no further role than one of criticism of the mass-consumption society. It was a declining force, then, but its annihilation was connected with the rise of the communist parties. Communism, indeed, was to become the graveyard of those ideas that had been most characteristic of socialism, because furthest to the left.

The first response to the Bolshevik Revolution was, against all expectation and to an extent that seems explicable today only in terms of an immense misunderstanding, the enthusiastic rallying to the Leninist cause of almost all the European socialist left, not excluding even numerous anarchists. Emerging from a long and senseless war to find that employers and the State had no intention of keeping the promises made during the war, but preferred to chasten the trade unions with armed force, many western workers were in a mood to take literally Bolshevik revolutionary slogans about soviets, proletarian supremacy, sexual liberty, etc. However, the details of that first rallying need not detain us because the process has been repeated often since: when on a left tack, communist demagogy has regularly succeeded in drawing off from the socialist movement much of the left extremist current, to the point of seriously debilitating in Italy and France the anarchist movement. But that communist leftism was a tactical or demagogic phase in the strategy of a party that had little intention or hope of carrying out a revolution, and which mostly resorted to extremist leftism in blind despair after the failure of a contrary, rightist tactical phase. So the welcome that incoming left socialists received would be of short duration, after which they would be subjected to an education in opportunism. One is bound to say that this education was intellectually of a high order: some of the most convincing and effective parts of communist doctrine, whether drawn from Marx, Lenin, or Gramsci, concern the futility and impracticality of the wilder social imaginings that attract so many young people to socialism and to revolt. To the extent that left socialism was utopian, communism has proven the most powerful antidote, far more effective than the external criticism of non-socialist adversaries. Yet left socialism was not entirely utopian, to the degree that it formulated the practice of some working people and certain proletarian institutions. Communism was still its most powerful opponent, but now for the reason that communism had stolen the name and prestige of socialism to cover the despotic industrialization and militarization of a backward economy, and thus was inevitably intolerant of anything so non-conformist, experimental, idealist, and independent as left socialism. Leftists who could not abide the uneasy and guilty conformism of the social-democratic parties, would find, after their new communist colleagues had dispensed with the left sectarian tactic, that they had joined a movement that, in their eyes and on their standards, was the most conservative and least enterprising of any known in the West at that day. So the communist parties functioned as a mill that swept in all the left socialists and turned them out either as disciplined communists, disillusioned and non-political ex-leftists, or unrepentant extremists attached to futile groupuscules such as the Trotskyists. (The third was usually a stage towards the second.)

Where left socialists were not drawn into the communist party, they were subjected to the keenest attacks of that party, which has never gladly suffered having any force to its left. They were, of course, liquidated speedily in Russia itself and in east Europe after the Russian occupation. The one country where they seemed to resist best the transformation of socialism by the modern economy and by the communist party was in Spain, where left socialism, from anarchism and anarcho-syndicalism to Trotskyism, represented a substantial force, until they were literally exterminated by the communists (and the forces of General Franco). Indeed, during the Spanish Civil War the international brigades and the Russians sometimes gave this task priority over the struggle against the rebellion. The anarchists, the POUM, and the Trotskyists, the left-wing socialists of Cabellero, the advocates of collectivization of the land, and, eventually, those who stood for any measure of social revolution in Spain, were systematically subjected to communist terrorism.[58]

Where the deliberate teaching and oppression of the communists did not serve to eradicate left socialism, their practice, both in Russia and in the West, served to discredit it. That is to say, where the

---

[58] Jose Periats, *Los Anarquistas en la crisis politica española* (Buenos Aires, 1964), pp. 353–70; F. Borkenau, *The Spanish Cockpit* (London, 1937).

communists, either early in Soviet history or recurrently since during brief leftist phases, tried to put into practice the ideas or the tactics of left socialism, they proved that many of them were unworkable, that others of them were hopelessly incompatible with the nationalist and industrialist ambitions that the Soviet State shares with all modern polities, and that others of them, finally, were at least incompatible with Soviet despotism, however much they might warrant further trial in more typical conditions. It would be too long a task to draw up a catalogue of all the many left-socialist illusions that have not weathered the first accession of socialists to complete revolutionary power; and if one did draw it up, there would be, naturally, disagreement about which of them Soviet experience had proved to be literally and absolutely utopian, which of them had been shown to be simply unsuitable to the present mood of economic and militarist nationalism in the civilized world, and which of them the Russians did not or could not or did not wish to give a real chance. But one can suggest cases, to illustrate each of those possibilities, about which there would be less dispute.

Among left-socialist illusions that stand disproven by the practical experience of the communist States are the notions that the ordinary worker can take over virtually any administrative, political, military, or productive task without special gifts, education, or training; that the people to do those jobs can be selected without offering them material incentives, without, that is, turning one's back on the ideal of literal equality of incomes; that this inevitable economic inequality need not lead to the emergence of a 'new class' of privileged people, though it might well be a more open ruling class than appears in other societies; and the idea that religious beliefs and conventional sexual morality would disappear quickly when no longer backed by the bourgeois State. Among the leftist ideals that socialists of most sorts have abandoned in the last fifty years as proven by communist experience to be out of tune with the industrial society, whether communist or western, may be numbered federalism, extensive decentralization of economic management, internationalism, democratization of the army and administration, and (whether all communists admit this yet or not) collective farming. Lastly, a minority of socialists would still maintain that, in conditions other than those of Russia under Stalin, more success would have attended leftist projects such as the abundant provision on a communal and perhaps non-monetary basis of many goods and services now available only to individual effective demand; or increased worker responsibility inside industry; or a serious effort to reduce social inequalities.

Western socialism was by no means unanimously in favour of all these notions before 1917, and to the extent that it is today almost unanimously against them, this has other causes besides Soviet experience. For example, western workers became less concerned with responsibility at their place of work, preferring what they could obtain in the free market and as citizens to what they could get as workers, and so socialism would have given up proposals for the bossless factory even if communist practice had not demonstrated its impossibility. For all that, Soviet practice—and in particular the numerous and glaring failures of Soviet society to cope with many modern problems and several enduring human needs—has been influential in curing western socialism of many of the generous illusions that used to flourish on its left wing. More recently, since the war, Soviet economic difficulties, when compared with the prosperity of most western nations, have led socialists in the latter countries to tone down, and even to abandon quietly, their former faith in centralized economic planning and in the beneficence of collectivization. At that point, of course, socialism is no longer being cured simply of its leftist illusions but of all it retains of characteristically socialist thinking.

The Guerrilla War on the Right

Given that western socialism was abandoning its sectarian leftism and its will to inaugurate an autonomous proletarian civilization, under the influence both of Soviet example and of the development of the western economy, it should have been better able to adjust to the new society created by democracy, by neo-capitalism, by the welfare State, and by socialism itself. Yet the tendency of communist activity was to impede that collaboration, to prevent western socialism drawing the conclusion from its own (and the communists') refusal to revolutionize society. In trying to paralyse socialism on its right, the communists were much less successful than in seeking to amputate its left, for they were up against a force of a very different magnitude. Leftism was, it has been recalled, a vestige of the vast dreams of the nineteenth century, and the whole current of contemporary history was flowing against it. Collaboration in bourgeois democracy, on the contrary, was a tendency in socialism before 1914 and one that seemed to gather strength each year. It was to gain momentum after the war, in proportion to the reforms secured in each country by the socialist (and other) parties and by the trade unions. So in this respect the most that communist influence could effect was to hamper, postpone, and complicate a process of adjustment, and then only in countries where communist influence was direct and consistent. That is to say, scarcely at all in Britain, the United States, or Scandinavia, but quite significantly, for varying periods, in Germany and the Latin countries. This influence will be examined under two heads: the impact of communism on the trade unions' gradual acceptance of the neo-capitalist economy, and then the influence of communism over the socialist parties' reconciliation with 'bourgeois' parliamentary democracy and in particular their participation in its defence from fascism.

The Unions and Communism: The trade unions were well advanced on the path towards integration before 1914 in all west European countries save France and Spain, where they remained (and this shows by contrast what is meant by 'integration') anarcho-syndicalist, that is, anti-capitalist, anti-State, anti-parliamentary, anti-militarist, unpatriotic, and dedicated to the abolition of the wages system and of the employing class.

In Germany, the trade unions carefully abstained from taking sides in the SPD controversy over revisionism, but that was only because of their distrust of every sort of socialist theory, rather than because there was any doubt about which side they were on.

Bernstein's rewriting of Marxism without dialectics, his demonstration that the middle class was not disappearing, his attempts to combine the Marxist theory of value with the new marginal utility approach, left the trade unionists completely cold. These matters, to them, were intellectual pastimes of no value for practical affairs. They felt that they *knew*, empirically, that the lot of the working class could be bettered by reformist activity within the existing order. After all, were not their unions doing it every day?[59]

Devoted to *Gegenwartsarbeit* (working for the present), the German unions were profoundly gradualist and reformist, and they had, as Schumpeter said, gone Marxist only by fraud. It was because they began to take control of the Social-Democratic Party, till it became their 'mindless instrument', that that party suffered the rightward drift that has been referred to.

[59] Peter Gay, *The Dilemma of Democratic Socialism* (New York, 1952), pp. 127–8.

Similarly in Britain. Although, surprisingly, there were among trade unionists syndicalist sympathies strong enough to complicate their relations with the Labour Party on the eve of the war, the trend was plainly towards integration. By 1910

their central function was less to serve as a means by which workers could regulate their own affairs as they wished, and more to negotiate with employers in laying down the terms and conditions under which work should be performed. This being so, the grounds for a defence of trade unionism had shifted. Previously the unions had been defended primarily on their right to freedom of association. If men wanted to combine they should be free to do so. Now it was increasingly argued that they were making a positive contribution to social welfare by joining with the employers in regulating industry so that order should prevail . . . it is beyond doubt that by 1910 the unions had become more closely integrated into the fabric of society. The proliferation of joint committees, conciliation boards, arbitration agreements, and procedures for avoiding disputes had brought their leaders into more frequent and formal relationships with the employers than ever before. And the state was taking an increasing interest in their affairs.[60]

Proof of that interest, and part cause of this process of integration, was the series of measures, demanded by the unions, that were enacted into law between 1906 and 1910.

That process was of course much less advanced in Italy, but there too the leaders of the Confederazione del Lavoro were reformists,[61] so much so that they called up a movement of revolutionary opposition in Turin which was to issue in the *consigli di fabbrica* immediately after the war.[62] However, this latter tendency had its home and origin in France, where the theory and the practice of an independent proletarian movement living outside the bourgeois world were carried to their extremes. There are various explanations for this late and hardy flowering of socialist ideals in French revolutionary syndicalism, but the main point (though the shrillness—and the superiority as theoreticians—of the revolutionaries hid the fact) is that the syndicalist majority was being reduced rapidly from 1910 onwards. Before that date was the 'period of heroism, of all or nothing, among the sons of the revolutionary nineteenth century become labourers and factory workers and imposing their ideas inside

[60] H. A. Clegg, A. Fox, and A. F. Thompson, *A History of British Trade Unions since 1889*, vol. 1 (Oxford, 1964), pp. 484–6.

[61] Franco Catalano, *Storia dei partiti politici italiani* (Turin, 1965), p. 278.

[62] Ezio Avigdor, 'Il movimento operaio torinese durante la prima guerra mondiale', in A. Caracciolo et al., *La Città futura* (Milan, 1959).

weak unions'.[63] After that date, the French working class began its belated entry into the twentieth century:

> Growing both in number and in the importance of its economic role, the working class enlarged its place within the nation and, increasingly, became integrated into it. The Great War . . . simply accelerated that normal evolution. Recognized as one of the components of the national community, praised for its participation in the victory of 1918, benefiting from new rights—more theoretical than real however—the working class of France became French, assumed its responsibilities, and, in order better to attain its own objectives, took account of the general interest of the country.[64]

Thus an adjustment that was in train elsewhere in Europe before the war gathered force in France only during the war, and, in particular, after the last and crushing defeat of revolutionary unionism in the wave of great strikes in 1920. From then on, with the revolutionaries in the minority and divorced from the CGT, the trade union federation, the course seemed clear for a development of the unions in France towards what we are calling for short 'integration', as in the rest of the western world.

This summary indicates the position of western trade unionism at the moment of the impact of the Bolshevik Revolution, at the end of the Great War. It was the unionists who made the first move to revive international co-operation after the war by founding the Amsterdam trade union international in July 1919, representing over 17 million workers in fourteen countries. That International addressed itself exclusively to the industrial workers of the economically advanced countries and it set out a programme of reforms which was, indeed, to inspire or at least prefigure the activities of western unionism for the next half-century. In brief, it took note of the transformation of capitalism in the first decades of the century, notably as a result of the war, and called for an increase in the workers' share of the goods and services produced and in their share in control over the processes of production. It was immediately denounced from Moscow as, in Zinoviev's words, 'the yellow trade union international that the agents of the bourgeoisie are trying to set up in Amsterdam'. During the second congress of the Communist

---

[63] J. Earle, ed., *Modern France: Problems of the Third and Fourth Republics* (Princeton, 1951), pp. 32–43. Cf. Daniel Halévy, *Essais sur le mouvement ouvrier en France* (Paris, 1901); Val Lorwin, *The French Labor Movement* (Harvard, 1954).

[64] Maurice Labi, *La Grande Division des travailleurs: Première scission de la CGT. 1914–21* (Paris, 1964), pp. 230–1.

International there was set up in Moscow the Profintern, or Red Trade Union International, while the famous 21 conditions laid down by that congress called upon adhering parties to 'pursue relentless and systematic propaganda inside trade unions, co-operatives and other working-class organizations' with the objective of winning the unions to communism, to a break with the Amsterdam International, and to affiliation with the Profintern. The Bolsheviks, then, had set out to split the trade union movement inside every country and at the international level. This schism was completed in France, for instance, by the last days of 1921, when the Unitary CGT split off from the CGT and allied itself with the Communist Party formed twelve months previously; and into that new revolutionary organization passed most of what remained of the French anarcho-syndicalists.

Neither the details of that great schism nor the subsequent and exceedingly complex history of the Profintern and its constituents need detain us, for in fact communist influence over western unionism was not exerted mainly through that channel. The reasons are these: first, many western trade unionists made a dogma (some still do) of political neutrality, of the refusal to favour consistently, much less to be subordinate to, any political party. So they could not openly accept subordination to the Comintern, nor to the Profintern which was always clearly the creature of the Comintern despite a pretence at independence, nor to the national communist parties. Yet the Russians could conceive of no other connection between a party and a union save the subordination of the latter to the former because their country has known no independent unions and scarcely any unions at all until 1917. Second, the Leninist strategy of alternation between left and right tactics was impossible at the trade union level without periodically liquidating independent 'red' unions and their Profintern. It was feasible to have separate 'red' unions, organized in Profintern, while the communists were on a left tack, when it was their job to compete with, divide, and discredit the 'yellow' unions. But once a united-front phase began, the communists' task was to work inside the regular unions, because it would be a mockery of unionism to pretend to have two parallel, separate unions working for similar objectives and appealing to an identical membership. A communist party can pretend to co-operate either with the leaders or with the rank-and-file of a socialist party, but a communist union cannot even pretend to co-operate with a non-communist union in exactly the same place and same industry without accepting to scuttle itself in the latter's favour. Thus separate communist unions have a broken history and have not been a major influence outside of special occupations such as the maritime and port industries, while the Profintern, after periodical eclipses, was liquidated at the height of the Popular Front period. The World Federation of Trade Unions, founded in 1945, is a less determined effort in the same direction, and has served only intermittent propaganda functions since the major western union confederations such as the Trades Union Congress and the Congress of Industrial Organizations left it.

Thus communist influence on western unions has been exercised from inside unions that were nominally non-political, or allied to some party other than the communist party, and which may have been, in either of those cases, explicitly hostile to communism. It is for that reason an affair of 'infiltration' (*noyautage*, white-anting), surreptitious influence or at least of hypocritical pretence in cases where (as in the French CGT today) communist domination of supposedly non-political unions was patent. Inevitably, then, the precise facts are hard to establish, especially in view of the natural hostility of employers (including the biggest employer, government) to unions during conflicts of material interest, a hostility that leads to taking advantage of the widespread suspicion of Soviet subversion by alleging communist 'domination' or, even more vaguely, 'influence' over unions when that might be impossible to prove. That is why Harold Laski said, 'Not since the emerging capitalist order gave birth to the trade unions, around the beginning of the nineteenth century, has anything influenced their habits of mind as profoundly as the Russian Revolution and the successful establishment of the Soviet state power. But it is far from easy to estimate how, and for what purposes, it has influenced them'.[65] At least, it is plain that we must separate the cases of countries where there was no important communist movement from those where, a substantial part of the workers being communist or voting communist, considerable communist influence inside the unions would be expected.

In the former group of countries, the integration of the labour unions into the economic system proceeded unhampered, and in fact it often proceeded too far. That is, union leaders sometimes took integration to mean subordination, and were ready to sacrifice even

[65] Harold Laski, *Trade Unions in the New Society* (London, 1950), pp. 5–6.

8

the unions' potential as a manpower cartel and as a pressure group, or, as is now said, as a 'countervailing power'. Subservience and political or monetary ambition (for which labour unionism has provided a rich field ever since it became legal) in those cases led to the unions' integration not merely into the economic system but into 'the Establishment'. The upshot has often been wild strikes by a rebellious rank-and-file, jurisdictional battles with rival and more aggressive unions, and, in numerous cases, the creation of opportunities for communist unionists whose rise to influence rested on their more combative notion of labour agitation. From this comes the widespread affirmation, and over a rather narrower field the proof, of communist influence inside unions out of all proportion to the number of communists in these countries. During the political and economic unrest of the first years of the Cold War it is certain that a militant minority of communists secured power beyond their due inside trade unions by being more active, zealous, and, by the very standards of labour unionism, 'better unionists' than the leaders in office. Barely 50,000 British communists, of whom probably no more than half actually worked in industry, came to prominence in a trade union movement of eight million members, while the disproportion between the number of communists and the number of workers whose affairs they influenced was even more stark in the United States at that time.

Acquaintance with communist ideology suggests what the motives of these communist infiltrators would be, but a knowledge of communist practice excludes the hypothesis favoured by many employers and officials, that their purpose was revolution. In the first fifteen years after the Bolshevik Revolution, during part of which time the Comintern leadership did hope and work for revolution in the West, communists failed to gain control of a single western trade union of any note or consequence. By the time—after the Second World War—that conditions for their rise to influence in some western unions had been created by bad leadership and undemocratic methods in the unions, the communists had long ceased to be a revolutionary force and had no aspiration or prospect of bringing about revolution in the English-speaking and Scandinavian democracies, which are substantially the countries here in question. In any case, their motives are less important than the circumstances that gave them power and the use they made of it. In regard to the latter, it is not clear that the influence of communists always led the unions into action inconsistent with trade union ideology. In many cases it led the unions, in defiance of their leaders, back to a militant interpretation of that ideology. The fact that this ideology had become out of date, and bore little relation to the responsibilities that unions actually assume in the modern economy, reflects on the movement as a whole. In other words, if western trade unions have not thought out a rationale of their real activities in today's world, but persist in a pretence of anti-capitalism, class war, pacifism, and internationalism, it is not surprising that communists should be able to pretend better and thus to win influence.

Harold Laski thought that the ground for such communist influence in the unions had been prepared by the spell cast by the Bolshevik Revolution over the workers. 'I am quite certain that, with all its blunders and mistakes, the Russian Revolution has helped to awaken from inertia, and from that helpless sense that he has no right to hope, a type of working man who, before its influence began to pervade the world, may have accepted a status of permanent inferiority akin to what was mostly imposed upon him during the Middle Ages. But the Russian Revolution is, among many other things, the symbol of a restless dynamic, which has made millions dissatisfied with their prospects and their status'.[66] And he went on to compare its effect with that of the discovery of America, of the French Revolutions of 1789 and 1848, and of the Second World War. Although these words were uttered in 1949 (incongruously, to an American audience), they could be applicable only to the years immediately after the Great War and again, after the palmy interval of the 1920s boom, to the black depression years. Even then, they refer to what has been called above the solacing function of the myth of the workers' paradise among western workers who had no intention of imitating Bolshevism. In the years after the Second World War, when communist influence in the unions became notable in countries having no big communist party, such illusions about Soviet Russia would not be common enough to assist the activities of western communists, however powerful those illusions then were among the peoples of Asia and Africa. Western communists had to rely on their own efforts, and on the errors of their opponents, to make their way inside the unions.

Those efforts included, as has become familiar, intrigue, lying, smear attacks, stacking of meetings, rigging of votes and the like,

[66] ibid. p. 38.

but it is less commonly admitted that such techniques were not exclusively communist but reflected the low tenor of dealings inside 'business unions' in the United States, and inside European unions that had lost all moral vigour and reformist (let alone revolutionary) zeal. If that were denied, it would have to be confessed that such methods could not have succeeded inside institutions that retained democratic controls; the proof being that they were tried elsewhere, in universities for example, and failed. Even then, they cannot explain much of the power communists won in the unions. Laski tells the other part of the story:

> Yet, when the last criticism has been made of the communists, I think it urgent to recognize that by far the largest part of their influence is due to their greater zeal, the continuity of their devotion to the purposes they seek to serve, and the faith they have in the over-all end to which they give so intense a devotion. At a branch meeting their record of attendance far surpasses that of non-communists. If there is a long, sometimes tiresome, agenda, they can be relied upon to endure it when others, wearied by the fatigue of endless petty detail, decide to go home. If there is an election for an official, they do not bring forward half a dozen candidates; they are careful to arrange their candidatures so that the maximum of votes for which they can hope are concentrated on a single person. They do not leave their members to find their way about trade union work by the light of nature. The communist in a trade union . . . knows that where grievance exists his business is to take the lead in exploiting it. He is constantly on the alert for the chance to discuss, to analyse, to explain.

In short, this amounts to taking union work seriously and to acting as though unionism were still intended for its original purposes; and if communist unionists had other aims in view, as well, in seeking to earn the repute of good unionists, one must note that they succeeded in encompassing those ulterior objectives much less often than in making their unions effective, by traditional unionist criteria.

Nor is there evidence that the usual communist procedure was to foment industrial disputes (though of course from the point of view of employers and consumers, all industrial disputes are needlessly fomented), so much as to take the lead of them when they arose, whether the official union leadership wanted them to arise or not. Moreover, using a mythopoeic technique that Sorel pointed to among the German labour leaders of the last century, the communists would link up one dispute with another in a coherent and dramatic legend about labour's heroic struggle against management victimization and exploitation. The creation of such explanatory legends is, in any social field, a path to influence and esteem. Laski concluded: 'I have read most of the tales of woe about communist infiltration into one or another of the unions. The main impression these tales make upon me is that they record the failure in leadership of men who have overwhelming majorities at their disposal and do not know how to bring their majorities into action. For the most part, I think that the explanation lies largely in the gap between the profession and practice of democracy in the habits of those leaders'.

Those reflections seem to cover even the cases where communist power in unions was used to support Soviet Russian foreign policy, though instances of successful ventures of this sort have been rare in countries where the communist party was small and without influence. Such an association, constructed by fraud, between unionism in those countries and communist causes of no concern or advantage to western workers, would have to be deplored on any theory of unionism—as would alliances between union leaders and reactionary groups in those same countries in witch hunts to 'clean the communists out of the labour movement' when the target was really the effective and principled use of labour's power, rather than its exploitation for personal gain and political advancement.

Ultimately the most important thing to say about communist influence over the unions is that it was nefarious, not in constituting some malevolent subversive force liable to threaten democracy (for it thrived only in undemocratic institutions), but rather in that it detained some unions in a traditional ideological stance of anti-capitalist hostility, blind to the changes in industrial society and deaf to the new requirements that economic management (e.g. national planning) and technological progress (e.g. automation) made of them. Of course, many unions have responded to those challenges, but not those where communist influence was dominant. It is in so far as communists earned praise from workers with outdated ideas as 'good unionists' that they did what harm they could, because it is precisely traditional ideas on unionism that have needed rethinking, whereas communist conceptions of labour-management relations are drawn from the world of 1848, 'modernized' with a reference to monopolies and imperialism.

This delaying effect of communist influence on the unions' adjustment to their new situation is naturally more evident in countries where communism was a major political force. Even there it must not be exaggerated. Communism and free trade unions were suppressed over much of Europe for a part of the fifty years since the Bolshevik Revolution, and where they did co-exist, communists were for many years very far from having great influence in the unions. It was only after the Second World War that communists gained virtual control of the major union confederations in France and Italy (the Conféderation Générale du Travail and the Confederazione generale del lavoro, respectively), and even then breakaway or opposition groups (Force Ouvrière, the Christian Workers, who have since dropped the confessional label, and numerous independent unions, in France; the Catholic Libera Confederazione generale italiana dei lavoratori and the social-democratic Federazione italiana del lavoro, in Italy) carried with them substantial sections of workers in explicit opposition to communism. Still, it seems that communist example can be effective without communist leadership, for the other organizations can be kept at a performance of dated working-class rituals by the fear of being outflanked on the left.

It is in France that this matter can be studied with the most continuity. The minority in favour of affiliation with the Comintern's trade union subsidiary quit the CGT and formed, in 1921–22, the CGT Unitaire. Rent by internecine strife (which is not surprising, since it drew off from the increasingly reformist CGT the remains of French anarcho-syndicalism as well as the communists), and reduced to subordination to the French Communist Party, the CGTU wasted itself in demagogic revolutionism and negativism, so that its membership declined from half a million in 1922 to 200,000 in 1935. Throughout that period it had no influence over the policies of the CGT. When the communists and SFIO formed the Popular Front, the CGTU returned to the CGT, but the Confederation was split once again into communists and socialists after the Hitler-Stalin pact in 1939. A *rapprochement* occurred at the trade union level, as at the political, during the Resistance, but this new unity lasted only from 1943 to 1947, for it collapsed when the communists adopted the Cold War tactics required by Moscow.

Between the wars, when the CGT was independent of communist influence, it followed a consistently 'realist', that is, reformist policy, seeking the integration of the workers into the economic system that it was helping to modify in their favour. Thus it participated in the International Labour Office and in the Conseil National Economique, while seeking to limit strikes, to increase wages by collective bargaining, to reduce working hours, and to improve working conditions. Its Workers' Education Centre pursued a characteristic task of intellectual and economic uplift, while in the matter of workers' control over the means of production, the CGT called for a moderate and vague measure of industrial democracy called 'social control'. Throughout the 1920s and 1930s its programme was so moderate as to draw criticism from the SFIO itself. André Philip wrote that the 'CGT seems to have abandoned more and more all militant attitudes and devotes itself above all to getting Parliament to pass laws favourable to workers', that is, acting as a pressure group for labour inside a system it had no design to change.[67] The minority inside the Confederation that called for a class policy and denounced participation in national institutions like the Conseil Economique was extremely small, raising only a few dozen votes in 1929 and a few hundred in 1933, against over 4,500 votes in each case. One sees again here the situation described above in regard to the socialist parties after they had lost their internal left opposition to communism. By 1936 the CGT, like trade union confederations in the other democracies, had so far entered into the system as to enjoy quasi-legislative powers in that it collaborated in fixing working conditions, and exercised responsibilities jointly with the State and the employers' organizations. Nevertheless, it clung to the figleaf of 'political neutrality' and showed the usual ideological lag in its oppositional vocabulary.

Communist infiltration of this integrationist force began, needless to say, with the Popular Front. After the short setback of the *drôle de guerre*, communist influence over the unions grew apace during the Resistance and at the Liberation, assisted by the fact that many anti-communist union leaders had gone over to Vichy. That influence was exercised with what all the parties admitted to be a striking sense of responsibility, particularly in the difficult days at the end of the war, when the presence of communists in the government and at the same time in the CGT unions was the main reason for the discipline and restraint shown by French workers in moderating wage demands and in boosting production. It was already clear, however, that this communist influence over the CGT could not be used for specifically communist political purposes, and that known communists (for the myth of political neutrality had to be respected) held their union posts because they were 'good unionists'. That

[67] A. Philip, *Trade unionisme et syndicalisme* (Paris, 1937).

became much plainer after the scission of 1947 when, the communists passing to the opposition, an anti-communist minority quit the CGT to form the CGT-Force Ouvrière: even though the bulk of workers who stayed with the CGT might be thought to be partial to the communists, they were not available for the series of agitations that the PCF launched as part of Moscow's Cold War strategy. 'The failure of the 1949 general strike when M. Moch was elected to the premiership, the party's inability in 1950 to stop arms arriving from America or troops leaving for Indo-China, the poor response to the anti-Eisenhower campaign in 1951, and the collapse of the protest strikes against M. Duclos' arrest in 1952, all show that the CGT is not available as a weapon of political pressure'.[68] This was amply confirmed by the events of the Algerian war and during the establishment of the Fifth Republic.

More remarkable than this inability of the communists to use what are too sinisterly called 'communist-dominated unions' for specifically communist purposes is the decline in the strength and pugnacity of the CGT, and for that matter of all French trade unions since the war, even on strictly professional issues of wages and working conditions. The weakening of French unionism, even in its role of countervailing power, is no doubt connected with its division into communist, socialist, Catholic (the last-named now being further divided into 'ex-Catholic' and 'still-Catholic') unions, and sundry autonomous organizations. While this division encourages a certain verbal competition in proletarian ritual, it makes agreement on action difficult, and disinclines any one group to risk losing its support by seeming adventurous. At the same time, all hesitate to proclaim their attachment to national institutions such as the planning authority, for fear of class-collaboration charges from the communists. In sum, the unions limit their own efficacy as agents of opposition while restricting their own influence as agents of collaboration. Hence the species of schizophrenia in which the French trade union movement lives and which was described by Goetz-Girey in these terms:

> With the exception of the Christian unions, the bulk of the trade union movement will not frankly rally to the [integrationist] tendency. It refuses to follow the unrealistic tradition of revolutionary syndicalism. It will not consent to defend the doctrine of integration, too 'moderate' and too tame. But in practice it comes close to a policy of integration. It

[68] Williams, op. cit., pp. 56–7.

is 'reformist-revolutionary'. It claims to be anti-capitalist and revolutionary; it collaborates with the State and the employers, while labour law is really evolving in the direction required by integrationist doctrines. Thus the trade union movement escapes neither the difficulties nor the remorse of reformism. It tries to overcome them by advancing projects for a planned economy: it really accepts integration and renounces a syndicalist system but it subordinates that integration to a prior *dépassement* of capitalism. It finds itself partly in agreement with others who are seeking to build a planned economy . . . .[69]

To a large extent, unions find themselves in this divided state of mind even in the absence of communist influence, for throughout Europe and Australasia there is a crisis of unionism that consists in this: the trade unions are pressing for a type of social and economic system that indeed is within view already, but in which they fear to lose their *raison d'être*. Traditional unionism (and the unions are still living on yesterday's ideas) was a twin to liberal capitalism, and so there is the question whether it could survive, any more than the untrammelled entrepreneur, in a planned economy, even if planning went no further than an 'incomes policy'. To get the sort of society it wants, it must collaborate with the State and with the managers of capital, but in doing so it surrenders its freedom of action. The further delineation of this crisis is not our concern, but it is clear that communism in the unions makes no contribution to its resolution, indeed complicates and clouds it. As a conservative force, communism has ruled out the search for an alternative system but denounces union collaboration in managing the present system, in the name of imaginary 'exploitation' and 'impoverishment'. And where the largest union confederation is tied to the communist party, as in France and Italy, the majority of the working class finds its leaders condemned to an oppositional proletarian demagogy that can never rally enough support—given the relative decline of manual labour as against service occupations—to exert a decisive political influence. 'The CGT talks in the name of the proletarians, whereas political power can be won only by a coalition of salary-earners'.[70] One is entitled to connect this impression of being old-fashioned and ineffective that French and Italian unions give, with the fact that union membership is far lower in those two countries than it is either in countries where unions have chosen to collaborate

[69] R. Goetz-Girey, *La Pensée syndicale française* (Paris, 1948), p. 157.
[70] A. Touraine, 'Situation du mouvement ouvrier', in *Arguments*, 1959, xii–xiii, p. 12.

in running the economy, as in Britain, Scandinavia, and West Germany, or in countries where the unions practise effective bargaining, as in the United States. Only about a quarter of French wage-earners are union members, despite the high rate of unionism in the civil service in France.

Another consequence of attachment to empty oppositional demagogy on the part of the major union confederation is that where conflicts of material interest arise (as they do even in the most integrated economy, given that integration is not subordination but a combination of collaboration and the exercise of countervailing power), it is possible for the State and for managers of capital to benefit from the division of the unions, and even to refuse to treat with those that are 'communist-dominated' on the ground that they are 'subversive'; admittedly, this Cold War tactic has lately passed from fashion.

Writing in 1959, Touraine described the situation of French trade unionism:

> Barred from taking an interest in 'structural reforms' by a revolutionary intransigence that is imposed by the political weakness of the Left and reinforced by communist dogmatism, the working-class movement is prohibited by that same revolutionary intransigence from undertaking an ideologically limited but efficacious strategy of wage claims. Rejected by the State and condemning it in turn, the working-class movement finds itself reduced, on the job, to an opposition-on-principle and to demonstrations of ideological firmness, of which the lack of practical results tires the workers. . . . The trade unions as a whole exert over political decisions, over the economic situation, and over organizational methods on the job, a control that is feeble or non-existent, not to be compared with the influence acquired by trade unionism in most of the major industrialized countries.[71]

In contrast stands the West German trade union movement, where the absence of communist influence is due not only, and perhaps not mainly, to the fact that the communist party is outlawed, but to the anti-communism of German workers mindful of the pre-1933 record of the KPD as well as of conditions in East Germany since the war. It is not only communist influence that is lacking, as compared with the French unions: the Catholic Church and the Social-Democratic Party, too, enjoy little power in the unions, and indeed there is a sort of tripartite truce, where none of these force seeks openly to challenge the unions' boast of being 'above party' for

[71] ibid. p. 14.

fear of encouraging the other two. As to the extent of their influence over union members, it is certain that social-democratic voters outnumber Christian-democratic voters, though the number of these latter is large; and, naturally, it was in the factories that the outlawed communists retained longest some organization and following.

The first consequence of this absence of open rivalry between socialist and communist parties is that the union movement is fairly united. It is dominated by the Deutsche Gewerkschaftsbund (DGB), with over six million members. There are smaller organizations, of which the main one is the autonomous clerical workers union, DAG, with 400,000 members; yet the DGB contains more clerks in its various industry federations than does the DAG. Naturally, there is a left and a right inside the DGB, typified respectively by the I.G. Metall and the I.G. Bau, the metalworkers' and building workers' unions. The contrast between the occasionally combative wage bargaining of the former and the optimistic adaptation to neo-capitalism of the latter has its explanation in their different economic situations, but does no more than represent the normal scatter of sentiment among workers in the absence of revolutionary demagogy. Yet, as far as one can generalize about that range of opinions, its average would be distinctly to the left (in the traditional sense, for example on such issues as nationalization) of the doctrines of the Social-Democratic Party. Whereas, a generation ago, the German unions were more conservative and gradualist than the party, today they seem more radical. 'The reasons for this are clear: the unions form the last major social force in which purely working-class interests find institutional expression. This is not to say that the DGB is a radical organization by any means, but simply that one must look within the large industrial unions to find the remnants of radicalism in Germany'.[72] But all that is meant by radicalism is that the DGB still represents a fairly well defined group, wage-earners, in contrast to the SPD which, as a non-class party, would presumably aim to represent employers as much as wage-earners.

As a united wage-earners' body, the DGB enjoys wealth and suffers bureaucratization both unknown to the small, weak, and divided labour movement of France and Italy. Its six million dues-payers, and the directors' fees collected by its representatives on the boards of coal and steel companies under the co-management

[72] Chalmers, *op. cit.*, p. 207.

arrangements, finance an elaborate organization. This is no longer
the framework of a whole subculture, as was the case before 1933
when the workers' associations fulfilled some functions now assumed
by the welfare State; but it still includes a bank that is reputed the
Federal Republic's fourth largest.

In what way is this material power used? It would be a mistake to
try to prove that the ideas of the DGB were more or less socialist or
more or less working-class than those of the French CGT; misunderstandings of this sort arise, for example, whenever American
unionists contrast their policies with those of European unions.
The real point is integration into whatever may be the ruling economic
ideology of the particular country. Here, there seems to be evidence
that the DGB, like the confederations in the United States, is more
at home with the liberal economics of the *freie Marktwirtschaft* than
the French CGT is with the planning of the Fourth and Fifth
Republics. Clinging to the shibboleths of the free enterprise system
(though of course economic realities in West Germany include more
state intervention than is commonly admitted), the German unions
can combine a scrupulous independence of the employers and a
fairly tough bargaining line, with the conviction that workers and
employers have a joint interest in economic expansion, increased
productivity, and stable prices. This amounts to a better integration
into the prevailing economic system than the attitude of those French
and Italian workers who are equally indisposed to combat and to
collaboration because they regard the existing system as fundamentally alien. It would be over-simplifying to trace that contrast
to the impact of communism on post-war French and Italian unions
at a time when communist influence was removed in West Germany.
But that circumstance is relevant—as may be deduced from the
violent criticism of West German unions by the East Germans,
and from the fact that the contrast becomes less sharp as French
and Italian communists abate their total opposition to economic
progress within the Common Market.

In the last two decades communists have been almost alone in
denying certain obvious facts about the situation of the western
working class and about the spirit in which it practises unionism.
Such facts, for example, as that the material conditions of working
people have improved vastly since the socialist ideology was cast and
that they still are improving; that employment, and security against
illness and family needs, are better assured; that the consumption

and the culture of workers are approaching (for good or ill) those of the middling economic brackets; that education, while still unequally available, is increasingly open to the least favoured; in short that the existing and continually evolving economic system is progressive rather than collapsing under the strain of 'contradictions' and, while it does contain tensions, these definitely do not include the paradox of deepening pauperization amid industrial plenty. The communists, moreover, have been the most reluctant to admit that the workers know all the above and approve it; that they are extremely responsive to the incentives, or temptations, of better pay, easier credit, and more consumer goods, and put these things well ahead of solidarity of any sort save aggressive nationalism; that they believe economic expansion and higher living standards to be the chief goals of the community, and feel that two or three good boom years will bring them more material advantage than any expropriation of supposed surplus-values; in short, that the workers have in their majority adopted the ideology of economic efficiency and see it best exemplified in the regulated market economy rather than in the fully collectivized and centrally-planned economy. Failing to base their policies on recognition of these facts, because that would entail radical revision of communist doctrine, western communists could have no influence over workers and their trade unions save a divisive or a negative influence, be it by way of destructive polemic or mystification and misinformation. Inevitably, then, they could play no role in furthering causes in which the workers were interested, and which are all reformist causes: a less unequal distribution of revenues, a reduction in the tendency of the education system to perpetuate existing social differences, systematic remedy of the negative concomitants of any rapid economic growth ('social costs'), and transfer of some influential economic decisions from the privacy of boardrooms to the publicity of representative bodies. If these causes are to be called 'socialist', it must be noted that they are espoused as well by various forces other than the socialist parties; nor is backing for them forthcoming only from workers.

Mistaken or dishonest about the workers' material situation, unperceptive of the change in working people's ideas about the economy, and unhelpful in the causes to which they, along with many non-workers, are attached, western communism's influence over the trade union movement—in a few countries and for only certain periods—has been retrograde but presumably transient.

Communism and Fascism: Attacking the right wing of the socialist movement in the shape of the unions that accepted the existing but evolving economic system, the communists also attacked it in the shape of the parliamentary socialist parties that consented to participate in, and when needful to help defend, 'bourgeois democracy'. Just as they regarded the union leaders as 'the last support of dying capitalism . . . the watchdogs of capital that bark furiously at anyone who approaches their master's lair . . . the last bourgeois barricade that the working class in revolt must storm in order to triumph',[73] and therefore as being 'more despicable even than the kings of the stock market and the sharks of capital', so too the communists regarded the socialists who practised and defended democracy as 'social patriots' and later 'social fascists', until they became, during the Cold War, 'the worst enemies of peace . . . the prime enemies of the working class . . . executioners in the service of the warmongers and imperialists'. As far as any rational explanation of this attitude is possible (that is, allowing that one might have to turn to psychology to account for the greater hatred that impotent revolutionaries feel for those that are nearest them in politics than for their avowed enemies), it stems from the Marxist prophecy of the inevitable collapse of capitalism. When the inevitable did not occur, that was held to be because of interference. When capitalism did not collapse, someone must have been propping it up, and that someone must by definition have been a non-capitalist, a renegade worker. Blame would attach to that action because social classes had been conceived as clearly defined and irreducibly opposed armies, so that when people disproved that view of classes by moving easily from one to another they could be described as traitors. This farrago of absurdity is tantamount to explaining Marx's errors in social science in terms of some people's wickedness.

There is no question but that the communists recurrently believed between 1917 and 1935 that the political system of western and central Europe was on the eve of dissolution, and that from that collapse the Left would emerge victorious without having to do anything actively revolutionary. Their confidence on that score looks in retrospect, even to communists, extraordinarily fatalistic; it entailed

<hr>

[73] *Compte rendu du Conseil International des syndicats* (1920–1), pp. 134–8. These amenities, signed by Lenin, Zinoviev, Bukharin, Radek, Bela Kun, Tomsky and others, were addressed to participants in a meeting of the International Federation of Trade Unions in London in November 1920.

a blindness to contrary evidence that one must re-create in imagination if one is to understand the harassment and vilification of the socialists by the communists of that day. It was in Italy that the communists were first proven definitively wrong, although it was many years before the error was admitted. On the eve of fascism's victory, the theorist of the Italian party, Antonio Gramsci, wrote: 'The proletariat becomes the dominant class and takes the lead of all the revolutionary forces of the country only when the collaborationist tendencies have been proved, patently and by experience of historical reality, to be incapable of resolving the political and economic crisis'.[74] This meant that there was nothing for communists to do while they awaited the inevitable triumph of communism except watch the socialists try, and fail, to defend democracy against fascism in collaboration with other democrats. For even trying to do so the socialists should, meanwhile, be denounced as among the most reactionary forces in the country because, added Gramsci, they were 'trying to hold Italian society together and even to avert that collapse that issued naturally from the ferment of corrosive acids inoculated into Italian society fifty years ago'.

By 1924 Gramsci admitted (but only in a letter to Togliatti and other communists, not yet in a public document) that this fatalism had been an error. 'In 1921–22 the party had this official conception: the coming of a fascist or military dictatorship was impossible—a conception very similar to the other one about the inevitable replacement of a fascist regime by a socialist one, similar because it too was based on the idea of a mechanical and automatic resistance of the working class to dictatorship without the need of political direction. At that time we undervalued the sullen and latent resistance of the industrial bourgeoisie to fascism and we did not consider that a social-democratic government was possible . . . this conception hamstrung our political action and led us into many mistakes'.

If these lessons had been made public and accepted by the Comintern, the course of events in Germany a decade later might have been different. But it is futile to think of that happening because it would have involved the communists in abandoning Marx's historical astronomy, their certitude of ultimate victory, which we have seen to be the basis of Lenin's 'science of revolution'. How hard that would be is shown by the fact that Gramsci himself retained the

[74] A. Gramsci, *L'Ordine Nuovo 1919–20* (Turin, 1954); Catalano, op. cit., pp. 292–3, 368–9.

'left-sectarian' attitude to co-operation with the socialists and other democrats well after fascism's final consolidation. Thus in October 1926, when Italian liberties had already been suppressed, Gramsci turned down flat a proposal from Nenni and Rosselli that the communists should, if not support, at least be neutral towards their 'republican concentration', a democratic front. Such collaboration was unthinkable, said Gramsci, shortly before disappearing into Mussolini's jails for the rest of his life, because 'we [communists] are working to make the proletariat the ruling class of a renovated Italian society', whereas 'the republican concentration is working to subordinate the proletariat to other social forms, which in practice can only be capitalism'.

It was not until the seventh Comintern congress in August 1935, after Gramsci's errors had been solemnly and disastrously repeated in Austria and Germany, that Dimitrov was to criticize the 'defects of many of our comrades, too attached to rigid schemes and lifeless formulas', of which one example was that fascist dictatorship 'would be necessarily and immediately replaced by dictatorship of the proletariat'. Another, he added, was to issue global judgments on social classes and parties without taking account of diverse tendencies within them, that is, to take all bourgeois as fascist and all socialists as social-fascists. Yet Dimitrov's admission was only tactical, too, and not the impossible revision of the basic communist conviction of the inevitable overthrow of capitalism.

The truth is—and this requires no speculation on what might have been if only etc. etc.—that at no time since 1917 were all the western institutions that Marxists too glibly lump together as 'capitalism and bourgeois democracy' in danger of collapsing, either for the reasons Marx had given or because of a revolution by the workers. Since that is so, the ultra-left tactics outlined by Lenin on the supposition that revolution was near were always and without exception mistaken. The proof is that no communist party has ever won and held power by those tactics, whereas every move by western workers to resort to violence or to the general strike has been ruthlessly and completely crushed. Revolutions have continued to be made by defeated national armies or imposed by victorious foreign armies (with the only partial exception of Titoist Yugoslavia). The industrial proletariat, the hero of Marxist-Leninist prophecies, has shown itself in all crucial situations to be, in the West, a divided and unarmed minority, partly attached to just that bourgeois democracy that was called in question, partly seduced by its fascist opponents, but only to a small extent inclined to support communists who put those two on the same footing. This, I have said, was plain in Italy by 1924, but Borkenau says it was obvious from the disastrous collapse of the German uprising of March 1921: 'At the time it seemed a tremendous lesson, of universal application, which would never now be forgotten. Everybody in the Comintern believed that never again would a similar experiment be attempted, and that the communist parties would now settle down and try to win over the majority of the workers'.[75] In reality, the only conclusion the communists could draw was that it was time to switch to the right without, however, withdrawing trust from the Leninist strategy, and meanwhile to denounce the traitors responsible for the failure of the left tack. Those traitors were firstly found inside the party itself, hence a purge at the top and a vast turnover of membership at the bottom, and secondly in the ranks of the socialist parties. Yet, just as the socialist leaders of 1914 had not betrayed the workers, as Lenin charged, but had loyally followed them into a war they largely approved, so the socialist leaders in the successive crises that communists called 'revolutionary situations' could not have taken the course the communists recommended without at once losing the support of the majority of western workers. The whole vocabulary of treachery that the communists developed so colourfully in their attacks on the socialists was devised only to hide the central fact that there was no objective revolutionary movement for the socialist leaders to be unfaithful to. And if there had been, the division of the labour movement that Lenin imposed, in the belief that victory was inevitable and imminent, would have been the best way to ensure its defeat. It was already foolhardy to attack the western social system in the name of the workers, but to divide the workers and condemn them to a war on two fronts was absurd. Events showed that the united working class would have been hard pressed to defend from fascism and from governments sympathetic to it the improvements in its situation won over the previous half-century. That defence became a lost cause in the absence of unity and with the refusal of help from outside the working class. In particular, the communists whom Lenin's lauded political realism sent into the battle were doomed to a monotonous succession of humiliations and

---

[75] Borkenau, *World Communism*, p. 218.

9

defeats once Leninist science required them to assail both the owners and managers of property *and* the social-democrats.

The main results of that mistaken policy were to terrify the western ruling classes and many of the middle classes with the spectre of revolution, and at the same time to provide them with a convenient model, in Bolshevism, for a counter-revolutionary force, which was fascism. The march of this counter-revolutionary imitator was then watched by the communists with a confident fatalism, while the socialists were denounced for seeking help to stand against it. This formulation is made without benefit of hindsight, for we can find the socialists forecasting that order of events, often with an uncanny precision, from the moment the Leninists sought to split their parties at the end of the Great War. Guesde, Blum, Longuet, and others gave warning of the 'veritable suicide' the socialist movement would be committing in the face of the adversary by dispersing its forces, and they sought to convince the communists that the western social fabric was of a very different solidity from the tissue that a few professional revolutionaries had torn apart in Russia. In particular, they dwelt on the immense powers of self-defence the modern State had against insurrectionary movements among unarmed workers. Paul Faure in 1920 listed the organizations that combined strike-breaking with voluntary police work, and from which numerous fascist-style bodies were to arise. He told the communists:

In the direction you are taking, you should know what forces of resistance and repression you will run into. All these organizations are getting ready to meet the working class and any possible uprising. They are getting ready not only with rifles—that period has passed—but, I repeat, with machine guns and gas. There is more than the police and the military to organize repression. You will also encounter the clever and systematic organization of strike breakers. You have seen fine gentlemen in white gloves driving the trams [during strikes]. Tomorrow you won't see that. They've got better than that now. . . . Take care. I warn you that there exists a powerful bourgeoisie and employing class such as has no precedent in history.[76]

The point to note is not simply that these facts were amply confirmed in the next twenty years at the expense of the communists, and of the workers when they were manoeuvred by communists as during the 1926 general strike in Britain, but that once they are seen to be true, the grounds for the communist attack upon the socialists

[76] Kriegel, *Le Congrès de Tours*, pp. 93–5.

disappear. The communist allegation was that proletarian revolution was possible in the West in this century and that the socialists were guilty of betraying it. Since it is not in fact possible, it is not treachery but common sense to make the best of the existing system and, in so far as it shows itself capable of reform, to defend it against fascism. Indeed, not only was aggressive revolutionary action by the proletariat impossible, but defensive action by the combined forces of the communists and socialists would probably have been inadequate to defeat fascism in those countries where it was victorious. It is the assumption of many critics of the western communists—for example Trotsky—that they sabotaged the fight against fascism and nazism and that if they had joined the popular fronts in time and sincerely, democracy could have been saved and, perhaps, a war avoided. There is slight support in the facts for the Marxist belief that the united workers would be all-powerful and that they were cast in the natural role of adversaries of fascism because fascism was 'capitalism in arms'.

On the contrary, industrial workers have been a diminishing minority in the West,[77] while the combined forces of socialism and

[77] Because of the growth of the tertiary sector, which now represents 63.1 per cent of the work force in the USA, 62 per cent in Canada, 60.1 per cent in Australia, 57 per cent in the United Kingdom, and 47.2 per cent in West Germany. 'Production workers' of all sorts, including those in the primary sector (farmers) and some in the tertiary sector (in building, for example), have been outnumbered by other occupations in the USA since 1957. Naturally, wage and salary earners in general may be (and are, when it suits leftist rhetoric) called 'workers', but they do not constitute the industrial proletariat. Nor do they constitute any other 'class', social force, or political group, or the raw material for any of those, but merely a static economic (possibly fiscal) classification. The expressions 'worker', 'labour', and 'proletariat' have throughout been used here in their traditional socialist meanings, which are clearest in Marx, for whom the working class was composed of the productive workers, those who participated in the creation of new material wealth and thereby created a 'surplus value' that was expropriated by the capitalists. Thus the workers, for the classics of socialism, meant the labour force of the 'secondary sector' of economists like Colin Clark and Jean Fourastié, plus some from the 'tertiary sector', namely the labourers in building, transport, and commerce. For the shrinkage of *this* working class in western economies, see, for example, Fourastié, *La Civilisation de 1975* (Paris, 1962), chapter 1; Robert Fossaert, *L'Avenir du Capitalisme* (Paris, 1961), chapters 7 and 9; and B. Mottez and others, 'Qu'est-ce que la classe ouvrière française?', in *Arguments* (Paris), 1959, xii-xiii. From being almost the whole of the non-rural active population at the time Marx wrote, this class has declined to a minority of the population in most advanced countries, despite the parallel and much faster shrinkage of the rural population. For instance, it was 30 per cent of the active population of the United States in 1960, and 33. per

communism were a political minority in countries that faced a fascist danger (winning in Germany 40.4 per cent and 37.6 per cent of the votes at the 1928 and 1930 elections). Only two popular fronts of any consequence were formed, in France and Spain, and they could not hold power alone (Blum governed with the Radicals, for instance), nor for very long. Moreover, the socialist parties were always divided within themselves over how to meet fascism. The SFIO, throughout the popular front period, was split into pacifists and resisters. The Second International split three ways over the issue: the 'revolutionaries' like Nenni and Spaak favoured violent opposition, but the British, Czech, Scandinavian, and Polish socialists wanted co-operation with the right and continued opposition to the communists, while in between the Austrian Adler and Blum spoke of socialism 'staying itself' by agreeing to join with communists on the limited ground of anti-fascism only when the communists suspended their attacks on the 'social-fascists'. More than that, many socialists

---

cent of the French population in 1954. In Britain in mid-1964 only 8.8 million out of a total in civil employment of 24.2 million were engaged in manufacturing industries, and 19 per cent of that 8·8 million were in fact doing clerical and administrative work (*Britain: An Official Handbook*, London, 1965, pp. 445–6); the addition of transport and building workers would not take the total much beyond a third of the active population, and, of course, an even smaller percentage of the total population. So when E. J. Hobsbawm says (*Le Monde Diplomatique*, Paris, October 1966, p. 12) that Britain is 'a country where the proletariat, even if one interprets this term in the strict sense to designate only manual workers, has long constituted the absolute majority of the population—about two-thirds at the present day', he is plainly using definitions different from those employed by the Ministry of Labour and the present writer. That happens. Indeed, exact delimitation of the 'working class' has given rise to Byzantine discussions, especially among Marxists, for whom the diminution of that class, instead of its increase, has posed insoluble theoretical problems. Hairsplitting apart, there is only one important misunderstanding to avoid: the confusion of worker with salary-earner. Obviously, because of the vast hypertrophy of the tertiary sector and the *fonctionnarisation* of the professions, almost all economically active people in the West today are salaried, the proportion varying from 65 per cent in France to 93 per cent in Britain. But of course at most about half employed persons (precisely 50.4 per cent in the USA in 1960 and 51.6 per cent in Australia in 1961, to cite two typical cases) do manual work. The virtually all-embracing category of salaried employees has much less sociological significance than the notion of the working class once had, and it has no political significance, i.e. it is not a dynamic concept representing any social force or movement. Labour parties (known by the neologism *partis travaillistes* precisely in order to avoid confusion with *partis ouvriers*), finding their electoral clientele in an amalgam of workers with various segments of salaried people, occasionally pretend otherwise.

were to prove to have fascist sympathies, both at the level of the leadership—from Mussolini and Doriot to Lagardelle and the other socialists that went over to Vichy—and at the level of the rank and file, which contributed to the millions of votes secured by the fascists and nazis. Then there is the point that much of the anti-fascist right in Europe was loth to co-operate with socialists and would certainly have refused to collaborate with a coalition of socialists and communists, so that what the anti-fascist alliance gained on its left it would have lost on its right. This, too, was clear from 1922 in Italy, where many who were not initially in favour of Mussolini felt forced into the arms of the fascists by the prospect of socialist entry into the government, while they would have regarded communist admission to the government as the prologue to a proletarian revolution. For the ecclesiastical authorities and for many owners of property, on the eve of fascist victory there was, in the phrase of the *Corriere della Sera*, 'only one disaster to fear: possible socialist collaboration'.[78] In sum, those who would include among the effects of communism the paralysis of an otherwise powerful united opposition to fascism, overlook the fact that fascism fed on the Bolshevik danger and would have prospered faster if the communists had joined the socialists.[79]

Nevertheless, instances can be adduced where the communists hampered the socialists in their struggle against fascism, or even gave positive assistance to fascists and nazis in the faith that *après le déluge, nous!* Leaving aside the period of open collaboration between communists and fascists from the Stalin-Hitler pact down to the invasion of Russia, this was true above all in the left sectarian phase between 1928 and 1934. The Comintern theory was, exactly as in Italy earlier, that by claiming that the fascist danger called for a democratic alliance against it, the socialists were spoiling a promising revolutionary situation, and were the sole obstacle to attracting all the workers to the revolutionary cause. So the first task was to liquidate the socialist leadership, if necessary with the help of

---

[78] Catalano, *op. cit.*, p. 290; cf. pp. 354–5.
[79] Speaking of the election of Hindenburg in 1925 by a margin over the Catholic candidate, Marx, that was smaller than the number of votes polled by the communist Thaelmann, Pierre Gaxotte, *Histoire de l'Allemagne*, vol. II, p. 407, says: 'If the communists had withdrawn their candidate, would Marx have been elected? This has been said. It is not certain: in all likelihood, Marx would have lost on the one side the votes that the communists brought him on the other side.'

fascists, whereafter the revolution could run its destined course, perhaps after a brief interlude of fascist rule. Therefore the French communists suspended the electoral tactics that had ensured that socialist, communist, and radical candidates withdrew in favour of the best-placed leftist in order to defeat the right, and thereby they reduced leftist representation considerably. This explicitly anti-socialist policy reached its climax in February 1934, shortly before being reversed, when communists joined with fascists in demonstrating against the Daladier government. It was carried to more extreme lengths in Germany and in Austria, where the communists consistently attacked socialists more than they did nazis, and 'attack' here means not merely verbal criticism but actual physical assault as well as co-operation with nazis in agitation against socialist administrations, as in the Prussian referendum. Exactly as in Italy a decade earlier, it was not sufficient for fascism to win and to begin the annihilation of the socialists for the communists to cease these attacks. Even in fascist jails, the socialists remained 'social-fascists' for the communists. The change came only when, in February 1934, Stalin saw the evident danger of a fascist Germany, France, and Italy combining in an attack on Soviet Russia. At that point, a brusque turn was made and preparations began for a popular front in countries where it was not already too late. In Spain, for example, the small (indeed insignificant) communist party ceased its opposition to socialist activity in support of the young republic—and began that systematic assault on the socialist left that has been referred to above.

In practice, communist attacks on the socialist parties did not cease with the introduction of a popular front. The communists were never (nor the socialists often, once they learned to distrust their occasional allies) sincere in these bids to repair working-class disunity. The organizational split was not healed, except at the trade union level where parallel red unions might be dissolved. The whole communist party machinery was kept intact, ready for another brusque turn into open opposition to the socialists. So it was during such alliances that the French, Spanish, and, to a lesser extent, Anglo-Saxon socialist parties suffered most from communist rivalry, by way of the infiltration of their cadres and associated unions, and by loss of members. Had not Lenin spoken of supporting reformists 'as the rope supports the hanged man'? And did not Zinoviev distinguish 'the united front from above'—that is, co-operation with socialist parties through their leaders—from the 'united front from below'—that is, the effort to woo followers away from those leaders by campaigns of denigration during periods of supposed co-operation? The socialists' experience of the dangers of cohabitation with communists will be as great an obstacle to the reconciliation of 'national communism' and social-democracy as their remembrance of wounds sustained in periods of frank rivalry.

The End of Socialist Theory

Whereas the Right in European politics has traditionally asserted that the State is an independent entity, indeed a sovereign one, embodying the principle of authority, the socialist Left has taken an instrumentalist view of the State. It was just the committee of management of the bourgeoise, a tool or means with no life of its own. Like other instruments, it could be used in a variety of ways depending on the will of the ruling class, whether this was an exploiting group of capitalists or the proletariat installed in its dictatorship. Or it could, if desired, not be used at all, whereupon, like an anatomical organ that had lost its function, it would 'wither away'. Meantime, most socialists felt that their political assignment was to get their hands on that instrument, either by 'seizing power' in the Blanquist fashion that became Lenin's, or by democratic election. By whatever means control of the instrument of the State was secured, it might then be used either to carry out a revolution from the top (and that is what the expression 'dictatorship of the proletariat' came to mean, though in Marx's mind it probably meant the very contrary), or to effect a series of reforms. It was more likely that those who 'seized power' would do the former, while elected socialists would do the latter; but it could be the other way about. The State, in sum, was a neutral instrument and could be applied to this purpose or that, if only the will were there, regardless of who controlled it or how they got hold of it.

Not all socialists shared these illusions, either because they rejected instrumentalism in general as poor logic (this was the case with Gramsci and Sorel), or because they had experience of a strong and progressive State (as Lassalle had of Bismarck's) whose independence of the capitalist would-be ruling classes was too evident to miss. Thus, the anarcho-syndicalists gave warning that the State could not be used and discarded at will, for 'power corrupted', and so the proletariat had to create its own new institutions, native to its class and derived from its way of living, which would replace the State. This was the libertarian tradition inside socialism that is found, however inconsistent with its context, in Marx as well as in Gramsci after he became a Leninist. From another point of view altogether, it was seen that Marx's experience of liberal Victorian England had led him to underestimate the independent power of the State as against either the capitalists (whom Marx thought doomed to run their system into the ground no matter what the State might try to do) or the proletariat. Conceding the State's prior independent existence, one could envisage a collaboration between it and the socialist movement.

For all the denunciations of this as state socialism, it is what happened. Instrumentalism having revealed itself an illusion, and libertarian socialism having died when spontaneous proletarian institutions wilted, the only extant form of socialism is state socialism, the alliance of the State that outlived capitalism with the socialist movement. Naturally, the partners have been mutually influenced by this alliance and neither has found the other a passive instrument. Everywhere that socialists have held or shared state power, the State has become, and has remained no matter who got power afterwards, a socialist State to a greater or lesser extent. Political forces in those countries may seek office in the name of liberalism, conservatism, or free enterprise, but they can exercise power only in socialist ways, not because 'we are all socialists now' but because the State certainly is. Similarly, socialism everywhere has been infected with habits of authority, privilege, inequality, restrictiveness, and arbitrariness, which are the habits of the State. Various national forms of socialism may be seen to differ, after the searing experience of power, less by their inherited socialist traditions than by the forms of the States they have allied themselves with. Where that State was, before their advent, oppressive and bureaucratic, as in Russia, ruling socialists have become so too. It was not simply that after 1917 autocracy was baptised 'revolution' (though that is all that has happened in 'African socialism', supposedly copied from Russia), for the autocracy was indeed revolutionized too; the effect was mutual. Where the State was traditionally unable to enforce its dogma of sovereignty over a pluralist society, as in England, socialists in office have had to respect opposition to their designs; where the State had a Jacobin cast, socialism seeking office or sharing it has adopted similar characters, as in France. In all cases, many of the doctrines of socialism were renounced in favour of efficient government as conceived in that country.

This mutual transformation of allied State and socialism has occurred largely since the Bolshevik Revolution. Before 1914 no continental socialist save a few French renegades who were promptly expelled had held a post in a Cabinet, and socialist votes were never necessary to adopt a budget. Only in Britain (where Labour participated in the Asquith majority), Australia, and New Zealand had socialists had a taste of political power. Since then, socialists in every country where a socialist movement existed already in 1917, save the United States, have had direct, though not always sole and exclusive, governing power. It is this that has changed the socialists as much as any single factor. Nor is it needful for them to be in office to adapt their ideology; it is enough to seek it.

There is much more that could be said, towards an understanding of the evolution of socialism, about its experience of power, but our concern here is with the impact of Russian state socialism on the movement in general. One respect in which the specifically governmental and oppressive form of Russian socialism since 1917 has impinged on the West concerns socialist theorizing. In Russia first and (because of its immensity and power) most acutely, socialism encountered the typical theoretical questions of governance, questions that it had hitherto ignored, such as those of economic planning, or had just denied existed, such as defence and international relations. Russian pioneering on both these subjects stimulated thinking among western socialists, but the solutions arrived at in Russia were so plainly incompatible with the conditions of political power in the West that they had little influence on the socialists. To take the example of economic planning, on which Marx had had nothing to say and succeeding socialists little more, Russia posed concretely problems that had been known theoretically since Barone and Pareto, and this set off the quest in the West for a 'socialist economics'. But the methods adopted in Russia to accumulate capital or to move labour from one task to another, to cite two examples, were clearly inapplicable in the West and, in any event, the results achieved were patently inferior to those of the regulated market economy. So Russia had less influence over socialist economic thought than had the techniques adopted or recommended to combat the Great Depression (notably Keynes's theories) and to undertake postwar reconstruction (notably in France).

In reckoning for the first time with questions of defence and international relations, socialists coming to responsibility after 1917 found that Russian example was no help to them in their difficulties of reconciling pacifist internationalism with national power (that is, of reconciling socialism and the State). Later they were to find that the international situation created by Russia's rise complicated their task immensely. Not that these problems were serious between the world wars. Socialists almost unanimously opposed intervention in Russia once the war against Imperial Germany had ended, and, fifteen years later, in general favoured an alliance with Soviet Russia against Hitler. It was only after the Russian expansion into east Europe after the Second World War, and the beginning of the Cold War, that western socialism, in Cole's words, found itself

caught in the toils of a cold war which turns it into the ally of American capitalism against the communist part of the world, and is thus both disabled by heavy spending on armaments from advancing further in the direction of social welfare and unable to struggle for socialism with its hands free, for fear of antagonizing American opinion . . . It dare not offend the Americans, for fear of being left to face the Soviet Union without their backing. It dare not do anything that might make the capitalism of its own countries inefficient, because it is not prepared to replace capitalism by a socialist economy. It dare not get on better relations with the communists, because it is afraid of falling under the domination of their stronger wills and greater zeal.[80]

What that supposed dilemma showed was simply how far western socialism in office had identified itself with the traditional interests of western States, to the detriment of its socialist principles, and yet how unimaginatively it approached the international power game. It required the example of government by the Right with a surer and more adventurous handling of national power, with which it was familiar and about which it had no complexes, to demonstrate, in Gaullism, that the socialists' dilemma was of their own making.

Socialism's failure to develop new thinking on such matters to replace the specifically socialist ideas it sacrificed to securing state power was part of the general euthanasia of socialist theory after the middle of the 1920s—that is, after the deaths of Lenin and Sorel, the imprisonment of Gramsci, and the first recantation of Lukacs. Russian state power was directly concerned in that, for the new autocracy killed enquiry at home as effectively as Tsarism had done, and forced this sterility upon all that part of the western socialist

[80] Cole, *op. cit.*, pp. 44, 47.

movement that fell under its domination in the western communist parties. True, the shock of 1917 had at first aroused an intense interest in Marxism in central and western Europe, and it is to that period that belong Lukacs's one work of merit and the beginning of the speculations that Gramsci was to continue in the timeless setting of Mussolini's jails. But the bolshevization of the western parties, and then the consolidation of a coarse and inane Stalinist orthodoxy, put an end to 'western Marxism,' and the western communist parties were soon as arid as Russia itself. Some interesting Marxist thought persisted, but only in the West and on the fringe of the parties, as with Karl Korsch and Maurice Merleau-Ponty. However, much of that work belongs with the periodic 'discoveries' and 'receptions' and 'revivals' of Marxism in France, Britain, and America, which are simply, as Lichtheim has observed, incidents in the incorporation of Marxism into those museums of ideas maintained by universities. Marxism had become academically respectable because safely dead.[81]

Numbed by the communist example of anti-intellectual rigidity, whereas communist competition might have been a stimulus to thinking, the socialist parties followed the easy course suggested by their electoral preoccupations and their integration into the western Establishment at one of the low points of western culture. They gave up socialist theory and put nothing in its stead, content with a pragmatic and incoherent adaptation to neo-capitalist democracy. The trade unions led the way by abandoning, indeed purging, all syndicalist thinking, while declining to reflect on their role in the society they said they wanted but shrank from contemplating; that is, they refused to have a theory of their own activity either as the basis of a new society or as an integral constituent of the present one. As for the socialist parties, their feeling was expressed by the member who exclaimed at a crucial meeting of the German social-democrats, 'No! No more theory!' His wish was realized by his party at Bad Godesberg in 1959, so that it can be said that 'as an idea, a philosophy and a social movement, socialism in Germany is no longer represented by a political party'.[82] But nor is it anywhere else in the West since about 1959, when the rehashing of Marxism went out of style in favour of a New Socialism that has nothing particularly new or socialist in it, and certainly contains no theory about the age we live in.

[81] G. Lichtheim, *op. cit.*, pp. 394–5.
[82] Chalmers, *op. cit.*, p. 228.

Socialism started with the vision of proletarian culture, a specifically socialist thought and art to set against those of the decadent bourgeois world. When they failed to develop spontaneously—and that was clear in west Europe by 1914, in Russia by 1924—socialists imagined that at least there was a natural and predestined alliance between the proletariat and the creators of culture. Art, enquiry, and socialism were all on the one side, the side of the revolution. It was this notion that brought many artists, scientists, and intellectuals to communism in the 1920s and created much of the elation of the days of the Popular Front and the Left Book Club. Of course, it was a greater illusion than the hope of a proletarian culture. A class, a nation, a race that does not produce its own culture is unlikely to make any sacrifice in order to remain the consumer of somebody else's culture. Thus the workers deserted art and enquiry, showed themselves unresponsive and censorious, and preferred the distractions provided in industrialized mass communications. That was true both in Soviet Russia and in the West, with the difference that socialism in total power in the former country matched its passion for such scientific enquiry as might appeal to readers of Jules Verne, with a militant vulgarity and ruthless obscurantism in every other department of culture. So, in the end, socialists in the West concluded that socialism had nothing to do with art or enquiry, any more than any other political force had, and it had no peculiar need of a doctrine or theoretical programme. If Russia seemed to suggest otherwise, with its vast enthusiasm for education and its undoubted successes in certain branches, that was only because socialism there had come to mean rapid industrialization, and the studies in question were those relevant to that end. The only special connection that persists between socialism and theory is that there is a theory about the failure of socialism, written from the Left, not so importantly in the recriminations of Trotsky and the ex-Marxists as in the work of Machajski, Nomad, Djilas, and the sociologists concerned with the bureaucracy.

Socialism's decline from a theory of proletarian culture to an allergy to all theory may be seen as a natural evolution. Borkenau thought so when he said that socialism before 1917 was *too* theoretical: 'being still a minority, denounced as revolutionary and dangerous, and debarred from ordinary participation in ordinary politics, the socialist movement was nearly everywhere forced into a negative, sterile and bitter opposition. It was this atmosphere that allowed doctrines to remain so important. . . .' He considered that on certain issues socialism before 1917 'lived in an atmosphere of unreality and irresponsibility'.[83] On that view, the retreat from theory and the abandonment of large visions of social regeneration would be simply the price socialism had paid for its active and effective integration into the polity, which in turn enabled it to make an extensive and characteristic contribution to the transformation of western society, especially since 1917. To that extent, it would be idle to regret the exchange of illusions for practical influence, even if the illusions were generous and if the practical influence were in fact wielded by a technocrat intelligentsia using the socialist electoral machines to give them a mass backing. And yet, while taking that hard-headed attitude to socialism's recent past, one would need, in taking thought for its future, to notice that the transition from utopian radicalism to more or less efficacious political professionalism entails the sacrifice not only of illusions but also of the socialist party's belief in itself as the party of theory,[84] the movement with a philosophy of history, and the ally of liberation of the human spirit. That would mean that socialism is no longer concerned to be the 'party of movement', the platform of social criticism, protest, and opposition, the creator of new social values. It is no longer these things at all in countries under communist rule and it is not specially so in the West, no more than some other parties. In other words, it is no longer Left.

[83] F. Borkenau, *Socialism, National or International* (London, 1942), pp. 123, 109.
[84] Jeanne Hirsch, a Swiss socialist, says (*Idéologie et Réalité*, Paris, 1958) that today 'socialism vegetates without an ideology, without fundamental justification, under a philosophical banner that almost no-one in its ranks is loyal to, of which indeed no-one knows the meaning any more, that no-one worries about, no-one thinks of'. Of the French party, Georges Lavau notes (*Le Monde Diplomatique*, October 1966, p. 11): 'They do not work any more in the socialist party, and the party has been incapable of serious reflection on any single one of the great problems that have dominated the last twenty years. . . . Not only has it not taken any interest but it has shown a dull hostility whenever such reflection claimed to be undertaken in the name of socialism. "Socialism" was the socialist party; it had nothing to learn.' As for the British Labour Party, E. J. Hobsbawm (*loc. cit.*), after noting the 'bankruptcy of all the ideologies born of moderate progressive democratic socialism' and the decline of Fabianism into 'a synonym for prudence and empiricism and a subject for academic theses', says that the party's ruling right wing has found it hard to 'elaborate a policy that might be distinguished from that of enlightened Liberals or even of Conservative technocrats'. Ignazio Silone, for the Italian party, and Günther Grass for the West German party, have advanced positive and reasoned apologies for the surrender of 'ideology', i.e. of political theory.

Nationalism and Imperialism

HUGH SETON-WATSON

THE November Revolution of 1917 took place during a European war which had arisen in large part as a result of conflicts between nationalisms. Lenin himself, as a revolutionary operating within a multi-national empire, had been deeply aware, for several years before the outbreak of the war, of the explosive quality of nationalism. In his exile in Switzerland during the first years of the war, he had studied the related problems of imperialism, of the conflicting interests of European capitalists and Asian masses, of western bureaucracies and nationalist movements overseas. Thus the fortunes of Russian Bolshevism, of the Soviet State, and of the Communist International, were from the beginning inextricably linked with the problems of nationalism and imperialism.

Under Lenin's leadership, the Bolsheviks proclaimed the principle of self-determination, including the right for all nations to secede, if they wished, from multi-national States. From its foundation, the Communist International set itself to fight imperialism, and to assist the struggle of colonial peoples for independence. The Comintern never accepted nationalism as an end: it always insisted on 'proletarian internationalism'. But it expressed its solidarity with victims of national oppression no less than of social exploitation. It held out hope of a future in which, when empires and colonies were abolished, and all nations were sovereign in their own countries, a new age of human brotherhood, based on the solidarity of the working classes of the world, would at last be possible. This combination of anti-imperialism and socialist internationalism, of national and social revolution, made a powerful appeal during the next decades to the new intellectual elites of the colonial and semi-colonial peoples. The appeal was not confined to those who became communist. To a far wider circle, the Soviet Union appeared a land of promise, and the October Revolution a source of inspiration.

Fifty years after the November Revolution, nationalism is as powerful a force as ever. Imperialism, by contrast, appears to have lost most of its importance. Yet appearances may be misleading.

Though most of the great colonial empires have dissolved, one retains substantially its old borders, even though its nature has undergone drastic changes: the very Russian Empire which Lenin had set himself to destroy. Moreover, it is arguable that the different forms of dependence of small States on great protectors, characteristic of the 1960s, constitute a different form of imperialism—'neocolonialism'.

It is the purpose of this essay to examine the phenomena of nationalism and imperialism, as they exist in the 1960s, in the light of the aims, hopes, and fears of 1917; to see how the development of nationalist and imperialist forces in the last fifty years has been affected by the events of November 1917; to examine briefly the theoretical diagnosis by Lenin and his disciples of these phenomena and its practical application in communist policies; and to see how both theory and practice have been affected by factors independent of communist control.

Nationalities and Empires in 1917

We may conveniently begin by a comparison of the state of nationalist and imperialist forces in 1917 and in the mid-1960s, and by brief references to the main features of the process by which the changes have come about.

At the time of the Bolshevik Revolution there were two multi-national empires in Europe—Austria-Hungary and Russia. The Habsburg monarchy was itself divided in two. In the Kingdom of Hungary the Hungarians formed very slightly less than half the population, and the other half was made up of Romanians, Slovaks, Germans, Croats, Serbs and others. In the other part of the monarchy, which may conveniently if inaccurately[1] be described as 'Austria', no single nation formed a majority, but Germans were the largest single group, the others including Czechs, Poles, Ukrainians, Croats, and Italians. In European Russia the Russians formed about half the population, the rest being made up of Ukrainians, Poles, White Russians, Tatars, and many small peoples in the Baltic provinces, the Volga valley, and the north Caucasus. A third large European State, the German Empire, had substantial national

---

[1] The official description of the non-Hungarian portion of the monarchy was 'The lands represented in the *Reichsrat*'. It was also sometimes called 'Cisleithania', the Leitha being the small river which formed the western boundary of Hungary in the direction of Vienna.

minorities—French in Alsace-Lorraine and Poles in Prussia. The Hungarian and Russian governments before the war had pursued a policy which may be described as 'official nationalism'. Their subjects were expected not only to obey the government and loyally serve the sovereign, but to merge themselves in the dominant nation: Romanians and Slovaks were expected to stop being Romanians and Slovaks and to become Hungarians, Ukrainians and Tatars to stop being Ukrainians and Tatars and to become Russians. The German government similarly sought to turn its Polish subjects into Germans. No such attempt was made by the Austrian government: Ukrainians, Czechs and Poles and other subjects were expected to be loyal to the Emperor (*kaisertreu*), but were not expected to become Germans. But though most of the Vienna statesmen had the virtues of tolerance and a supra-national outlook, they were too passive, too nostalgically conservative to enlist the positive support of their subjects. They proved unable to control the rising passions of the nationalities, which were directed as much against each other as against the central government.

A large part of the world in 1917 consisted of colonial empires. The two oldest of these, the Spanish and the Portuguese, had been reduced to a few sparsely populated territories of little economic or strategic value. The third oldest,[2] the Russian, had extended across Asia to the Pacific by the end of the seventeenth century, and had conquered Transcaucasia and Central Asia in the nineteenth. The largest empire, the British, was established essentially in the eighteenth and nineteenth centuries, and the second largest, the French, almost wholly in the nineteenth. Newcomers were the Belgians, who took over King Leopold's private capitalist concern in the Congo in 1906, and the Americans, who acquired the Philippines, Puerto Rico, and the Panama Canal Zone at the turn of the century.

There was a third category which may be described as 'semi-colonial' States. These remained nominally sovereign in international law, but were subject to repeated interference by the governments of the Great Powers, while their economic resources were the object of business enterprises controlled by citizens of these Powers. The largest single area of this kind was Latin America. British business

---

[2] It may, of course, be argued that the Russian Empire was older even than the Portuguese, since the expansion from the original territorial nucleus of Muscovy began in the fifteenth century.

was deeply entrenched in the Argentine, and to a lesser extent elsewhere. United States interference was most marked in the Caribbean area, and sometimes took the form of direct military action, as in Cuba and Mexico. A second area was the Ottoman Empire, for long subject to Russian, French, and British intervention, and in more recent times to German as well. The Ottoman Empire by 1917 had lost almost all its European territories, but in Asia and Africa it could also be regarded as a multi-national State. Its subjects were mostly Arabs and Turks, each of whose intellectual elites was beginning by this time to develop a separate national consciousness. Another 'semi-colonial' State was Persia, which had long been dominated, sometimes jointly and sometimes in rivalry, by Russia and Britain: the latest expression of this domination was the Anglo-Russian Convention of 1907. The greatest of the semi-colonial States was China. Russia had encroached on the periphery of the Chinese Empire in the late seventeenth century, but the period of large-scale interference began in the mid-nineteenth. The main interfering Powers were Britain, France, and Russia. Russia was the only Power which made large annexations, but Britain, France, and Germany took bases on Chinese territory, and all the main European Powers and the United States established privileges for their subjects in trade and investment. The privileged Powers were joined in the twentieth century by Japan, which through its annexation of Formosa and Korea became a colonial Power.

National States and the eclipse of Empires in 1967

Fifty years after the Bolshevik Revolution the general pattern is dramatically different, yet many of the same problems remain.

The multi-national empires in Europe were defeated within a year of the Bolshevik Revolution. Germany lost its French and Polish territories, and the the Habsburg Monarchy disintegrated. In the place of these two empires appeared a reconstituted Poland, an enlarged Romania, a small German-speaking Austria, a small, ethnically compact Hungary, a new State of Czechoslovakia, and a predominantly new State of Yugoslavia composed of the former Serbia and the South Slav provinces of the old Monarchy. The collapse of the Russian Empire was followed by large losses of territory in the west, but essentially the unity of European Russia was preserved under Bolshevik rule. Thus Poland acquired part of the long contested Russo-Polish borderlands, and three new

States of Estonia, Latvia, and Lithuania were established in the Baltic region; but the efforts of Ukrainian and Tatar nationalists to set up independent or autonomous governments were defeated. However, these changes, many of which were barely if at all affected by the Bolshevik Revolution, did not eliminate multi-national States. Four of the successor States to the Habsburg Monarchy had an undoubtedly multi-national character, though all four were ruled as national States. All four pursued policies of official nationalism essentially similar to those of Hungary from 1867 to 1918 and of Russia under Alexander III and Nicholas II. In Czechoslovakia and Yugoslavia the official nation formed substantially less than half the population, in Poland and Romania about two-thirds. These new 'official nationalisms' were no more capable than the old of enlisting the support of those subjects who did not belong to the official nationality. Conflicts between Czechs and Slovaks, Serbs and Croats, and the discontent of Hungarian, German, Macedonian, Ukrainian and other national minorities under Polish, Czech, Serbian, or Romanian rule, contributed largely to the state of insecurity in eastern Europe which enabled Hitler, first by diplomacy and then by arms, to conquer the whole region. Between 1939 and 1944 the foundations were laid for a vast new multi-national empire, in which the Germans would have been the master race, and perhaps an intermediate status of semi-autonomy would have been reserved for the 'allied' Hungarians, Romanians, Bulgarians, Slovaks, and Croats. This empire, however, never came into existence, as Hitler's Third Reich was destroyed in war. After 1945 the successor States of the pre-war period were restored. The one major difference from the 1919 settlement was Poland. Shifted physically westwards, by the loss of its eastern provinces to the Soviet Union and the acquisition of the Oder-Neisse frontier at the expense of Germany, it became an ethnically compact Polish State with only negligible national minorities. Czechoslovakia, Yugoslavia, and Romania remained multi-national States, but with the establishment of communist governments new policies were introduced, which can certainly not be regarded as a continuation of the 'official nationalism' of 1867–1939.

Today most of the great colonial empires have disappeared. The transfer by the British government of India, Pakistan, and Burma to the nationalist leaders was accomplished in an amiable atmosphere at the highest level on both sides, though it was followed by the massacre of half a million and the expulsion of twelve millions from their homes in the sub-continent, and by the assassination of most members of the first independent Burmese government. The British retreat in colonial Africa also began in an amiable spirit, though the experiences of Cyprus and Kenya had produced a more sour atmosphere by the end of the 1950s. The surrender of Indonesia by the Dutch was a more painful process, involving military operations and international pressure on the metropolitan government. The French showed much less willingness to retreat. The long Indochinese war began at the end of 1946, and twenty years later is still in progress, though some of the protagonists have changed. In French tropical Africa progress towards independence was smooth, and the pace was accelerated by the advent of General de Gaulle to power. The surrender of the Belgians in the Congo was sudden, and was followed by a general breakdown of public order. The Americans, who had promised independence to the Philippines already before the Second World War, carried out their promise in 1948. Of the maritime empires there remains the Portuguese, which lost Goa to an Indian invasion in December 1961 but is otherwise intact. The most striking exception to the general trend, however, is the survival as a territorial unit of the old Russian Empire. In the 1920s, Russia recovered the seceded Caucasian territories. In 1939–40 it added the Baltic provinces, most of the old Russo-Polish borderlands, and Bessarabia, and also acquired parts of Galicia and Bukovina which had never belonged to the Tsars. After the Second World War the Soviet Union made further annexations in Europe: parts of Finland, the north-eastern districts of East Prussia, and the formerly Czechoslovak province of Trans-Carpathian Ruthenia. In Central Asia all the territories conquered by the Tsars were retained, from the 1920s onwards, and the former client States of Bokhara and Khiva were annexed. In the Far East in 1945 the southern half of Sakhalin was recovered, and the Kurile islands and some other small Japanese islands were added. Thus territorially the 'Russia great and indivisible', which had been the ideal of the 'White' generals in the Civil War, is a fact. No secessions were permitted; no Asian nation was given the chance to 'prefer self-government to good government'.

Great changes have also occurred in the status of many of the States which in 1917 could be described as semi-colonial. The Ottoman Empire in Asia and Africa disintegrated. In Asia Minor its place was taken by an ethnically compact Turkish national State, which successfully established its independence and abolished the privileges enjoyed by foreign Powers, while the Arabic-speaking provinces were divided into mandated territories and placed under the rule of Britain and France. Iraq and Egypt were nominally independent States in the 1930s, but it was not until the 1950s that they emerged completely from British tutelage. Syria and Lebanon became independent States at the end of the Second World War. The two North African protectorates of France, Morocco and Tunisia, became independent in the mid-1950s. Algeria, which was juridically neither a protectorate nor a colony but a part of metropolitan France, achieved its independence in 1962 after eight years of bitter guerrilla warfare. Farther east, Persia attained a greater degree of national independence under Reza Shah in the 1920s and 1930s, but was occupied by British and Soviet forces in the Second World War. In the 1950s it remained heavily dependent on American economic aid. Finally, the greatest of all the formerly semi-colonial States, China, attained most of the substance of independence under Chiang Kai-shek in 1927, only to lose it as a result of Japanese conquest in the 1930s. After the Second World War came the Chinese Civil War, the triumph of the communists, and the reappearance of China as one of the world's real Great Powers.

Nevertheless, forms of semi-colonial status are still to be seen. The largest area is Latin America, in which political sovereignty coexists with extreme dependence on foreign economic power. Here British and European economic interests have been far surpassed by North American. The exception is Cuba, whose regime is not only independent of the United States but bitterly hostile to it. Another type of semi-colonial status is found in southern Africa. The Union of South Africa is an independent State, but within it the white minority dominates the black majority. A rather similar state of affairs has long existed in Rhodesia. This territory was nominally a British colony until its government repudiated British rule in 1965: in fact its indigenous white minority has been self-governing since the 1920s. Finally, yet another type of semi-colonial status is to be found in eastern Europe, whose communist governments depend in various and changing degrees on the Soviet Union. This category also comprises Mongolia, while the relationship of North Korea and North Vietnam to China and the Soviet Union has varied from time to time.

Nationalism and Imperialism in Bolshevik doctrine

The doctrine of nationalism derives from the doctrines of the eighteenth-century Enlightenment. Essentially, it is an application of the principle of popular sovereignty. In the French Revolution, a traditional monarchy and a semi-feudal ruling class had been overthrown by those who claimed to speak for the nation, but in practice corresponded more or less closely to the bourgeoisie. In the countries to the east and south of France the enemies could easily be identified: here too were traditional monarchies and more or less feudal ruling classes. It was less easy to identify the nation, in either its notional or its more precise form. In France everyone was a Frenchman, whether or not his normal language was French. There was no comparable consensus in the valleys of the Rhine and the Danube, though undoubtedly a strong national consciousness was to be found among the Dutch, the Castilians, the Poles, and the Scandinavian peoples. In France the bourgeoisie was strong, and this was also true in the Low Countries, the Rhineland, Lombardy, and Venice; but in the rest of Europe it was extremely feeble, if indeed it existed at all. During the Napoleonic decades, however, the doctrine of nationalism spread, and nationally-conscious elites became more numerous and influential throughout the continent. These two processes, intellectually distinct though connected and constantly interacting, developed further after 1815, despite the efforts of Metternich and others to restore the old order. In 1848 nationalism convulsed central Europe. Small nations, whose names were hardly known to Frenchmen or Englishmen, demanded equal rights with old and respectable nations. There had taken place, to quote the words used a century later by E. H. Carr, a 'shift from the conception of individual self-determination as a corollary of democracy . . . to the conception of nationality as an objective right of nations to independent statehood'.

The multiplication of national claims, the conflicts between insurgent nationalists, and the exploitation of these quarrels by the counter-revolutionary monarchies, raised serious theoretical and practical problems for the political leaders of the Left in Europe, including Marx and Engels. The founders of 'scientific socialism' shared the sympathy, then virtually universal in the democratic camp, for four nations: Germans, Italians, Poles, and Hungarians. They also shared the general belief of democrats in the virtues of centralized government and in the reactionary nature of local and provincial autonomies. The French Revolution, by crushing the revolt of Vendée, was continuing the work of Louis XIV and Colbert: its work was carried on by Napoleon and taken up by liberals and socialists in western and central Europe in the nineteenth century. Marx and Engels also preferred large to small nations, as these were more likely to produce large and viable economic units, suitable for modern industrial production. Finally, Marx and Engels, who, like most Europeans of the Left (Bakunin was the most distinguished exception), regarded Russia as the most serious danger to all political progress in Europe, favoured those nations which were most anti-Russian (Poles, Hungarians, with even a kind thought or two for the Romanians), but felt little if any sympathy for those small Slav peoples which looked to Russia for support against Turks or Habsburgs.

These attitudes of Marx and Engels were on the whole accepted by Lenin. Even the anti-Russian trend was not objectionable, because those Russians who took up the cause of small Slav nations were the politicians of the Right and Centre whom all Russian Marxists considered as enemies second only to the Tsar and his bureaucrats. However, the national problem was extremely complex within the Russian Empire itself, and was likely to grow more rather than less important as the Ukrainians, Tatars, Balts and other nations of the Empire acquired more complex social structures and more active national elites.

Lenin's attitude to the national question was not unlike his attitude to the peasant question. Non-Russian nationalists and Russian peasants alike had essentially 'petty-bourgeois' outlooks and ambitions. Both were objects of distrust and contempt to Marxists, but both were enemies of the existing regime which the Bolsheviks sought to overthrow, and both represented a tremendous revolutionary potential to be exploited.

Lenin devoted particular attention to the national problem when he was living in exile in Galicia shortly before the First World War. In 1913 he asked the young Georgian Bolshevik Joseph Djugashvili to prepare a study on the subject, with special reference to the ideas of the Austrian socialists, Otto Bauer and Karl Renner, which were then much discussed. Under the title *Marxism and the National Question*, by J. V. Stalin, this work, translated into dozens of languages, has become known to millions throughout the world.

Stalin laid down that a nation must have four characteristics: a common language, a common territory, a common economic life, and a common psychological make-up. No group which did not possess all four of these characteristics was a nation. After fifty years this does not seem a very helpful definition. The last of the four points is so vague as to be useless: it presumably covers all the complex historical factors, including religion, which help to form a nation. The first three points are admittedly important, but they are not sufficient in themselves, while the fourth amounts to no more than a verbal formula. However, Stalin was not primarily concerned with historical analysis or political definition. His task was to fight two opponents, the Jewish *Bund* and the Austrian socialists. The *Bund* had aroused Lenin's hostility in 1903 with its claim that it should form something like a distinct party within the Russian Social Democratic Workers' Party (RSDRP), its claim to be the 'sole representative of the Jewish proletariat in whatever part of Russia it lives and whatever language it speaks'. Now by Stalin's reasoning the Jews could not claim to be a nation at all. His definition included no mention of religion, and it insisted on a common territory, which Jews lacked. Stalin also took issue, at the express wish of Lenin, with the Austrian socialists. They had proposed, for the Habsburg territories, a solution which they called 'national autonomy', designed to combine the political centralization necessary in a modern State with a cultural variety assuring cultural rights to each citizen, wherever he might live. Each nationality was to have its own cultural authority, with its own finances, operating throughout the State, and the individual was to have the right to decide for himself what was his nationality, and to which cultural organization he was to belong. This scheme would have been especially attractive to those nations which were geographically scattered: the Jews, the Armenians, and the Tatars in the Russian Empire. But to Lenin it recalled the claims of the *Bund* in the RSDRP. Such claims were particularly objectionable within the party, which must be highly centralized, but they were equally objectionable within the State.

Stalin's article rejected cultural autonomy of the Austrian socialist type, but considered the possibility of territorial autonomy within the State. This would be less disruptive, as it would be available only to geographically compact nations, and it would in any case be countered by the centralization of the party, in which no division on national lines was to be permitted. In the same year 1913 the Bolshevik party adopted a resolution, after a conference held at Poronin in Galicia, in which it accepted 'the right of the oppressed nations of the Tsarist monarchy to self-determination, that is, to secession and the formation of an independent State'. It was however to be the task of the party to decide the desirability of the exercise of this right 'from the point of view of the whole social development and of the interests of the class struggle of the proletariat for socialism'.

The Russian Empire had national problems similar to those of the Habsburg Monarchy and the Balkans. It also had colonial problems, similar to those of the western empires. Central Asia, with its Moslem peoples speaking Turkic languages, had been acquired and was being ruled by the Russians in much the same way as Algeria by the French or Egypt by the British. During his exile in Switzerland in the First World War Lenin developed his study of national and colonial problems. In his April 1916 *Theses on the Socialist Revolution and the Right of Nations to Self-Determination*, he distinguished between three types of State. First were the leading capitalist countries of western Europe and the United States. Second were the States of eastern Europe, where 'the twentieth century has especially developed bourgeois-democratic national movements and sharpened the national struggle'. Russia in Europe of course belonged to this group. Third were 'semi-colonial countries like China, Persia, and Turkey, and all colonies', where 'bourgeois-democratic movements are either only just beginning or far from finished'.

At this same time Lenin was working on what, fifty years later, is still probably his best-known work, *Imperialism as the Highest Stage of Capitalism*. It was written in the autumn of 1916 in Zürich and published in Petrograd in May 1917. It is assumed that readers are familiar with the contents of this easily accessible classic. Here only a few points should be noted in passing.

Lenin was concerned to understand the nature of his enemy, to discredit him with propaganda, and to find allies against him. The enemy was capitalism. His studies, based largely on the researches of Hilferding, the theories of Kautsky and Luxemburg, and the brilliant journalism of Hobson, convinced him of the indissoluble connection between capitalism, imperialism, and war. The imperialism of the last half-century, which had partitioned Africa among the

European Powers and reduced the nominally independent States of Asia and Latin America to economic vassalage, was the result of the evolution of capitalism itself, of the growth of monopolies and the increasingly frantic search for more profitable areas for investment and for markets. This evolution made inevitable not only the subjection of weak States but great wars between the great States. These horrors would continue until capitalism itself was destroyed. The fight against capitalism, imperialism, and war was indivisible. The interests of the working class, of the oppressed nations, and of all peace-loving humanity, were inextricably linked.

That Lenin should have held these views is not surprising: a good deal of evidence pointed in this direction, and so did his political needs. It was the genius of Lenin as a political pamphleteer and a man of action that made his work so powerful an influence. But after fifty years it is almost as important to note two things which he did not say, and would probably not have said, but which his disciples have deduced from his arguments. The first is that because rivalry between capitalist governments leads to wars of conquest, there can be no wars of conquest between governments that are not capitalist, or even that there can be no dangerous conflicts between States that do not have capitalist governments. The second false deduction has been that acts of conquest committed before the age of imperialism are somehow morally more respectable than conquests in the age of imperialism, and therefore that their results should be regarded as morally justifiable and not in need of reversal. This reasoning is thought to be applicable to the maritime provinces acquired by Russia under the Treaty of Peking of 1860.

One other aspect of Lenin's theory of imperialism deserves a few words, namely the effect of imperialism on the metropolitan nation. Lenin believed that the prosperity of the colonizing nations depended on their colonies. If they lost their empires, the capitalists of Britain or other imperialist States would be ruined, the whole structure of their economies would collapse, and the revolution would be greatly facilitated. This was the view of communists from this time onwards. They were firmly convinced that they could best strike at British capitalism through its colonies or its semi-colonial domination, for example by undermining British interests in China. Communist efforts in this direction were not very successful, though they certainly frightened the British and other capitalists. But when the time came, and the colonial empires were lost, the prosperity of the metropolitan capitalist economies was greater than ever. The case of Holland after the loss of Indonesia is perhaps even more impressive than the case of Britain after the loss of India.

Connected with this was the doctrine of earlier writers that there was a privileged upper stratum in the British working class whose interests differed from those of the proletarian mass. In later years, communist writers built up a whole theory of the corruption of the labour aristocracy which shared in the profits of imperialism, and therefore abandoned the class struggle in favour of 'opportunism', or indeed simply betrayed the labour movement (whose leadership it captured) to the capitalists. Obviously there has always been a good deal of truth in this sort of argument. Both before and since the development of large-scale capitalist industry, there have been elites of skilled and better-paid workers. The profits of empire, from the slave trade onwards, have enriched others besides capitalists, and there have been industries whose workers did especially well out of the colonies. It is also true that there have been and are identifiable under-privileged categories in the western working classes: immigrants in the United States in the first part of this century, and Negroes in the North at the present time, are classic examples. But the doctrine of the labour aristocracy was elevated by Lenin's disciples into a dogma. It served indeed as an alibi for the failures of communist parties in many advanced industrial societies. It was assumed that all workers would normally support the revolutionary party—that is, the communists. If in fact they did not do this, but supported moderate social-democratic parties, then the only possible explanation must be that their leaders had been bought by the capitalists, and they themselves deluded by the prosperity obtained through the exploitation of colonial labour. This over-simplified and incomplete explanation has been widely accepted for decades, both by communists and by non-communist nationalists in colonial countries.

The problems of nationalism and imperialism have played a major part in the history both of the Soviet Union and of the world communist movement. We shall not attempt to summarize this long and complex story. Instead we shall take a number of examples from four main types of situation, and see how communists have dealt with them. We shall illustrate each of them by examples taken from different periods and regions, but we shall try to keep in mind essentially the comparison between 1917 and 1967. We shall conclude with some observations on the effect of the November Revolution on nationalism and imperialism and of these forces both on communist government policies, and on communist movements in search of power, and shall briefly consider the prospects for their further mutual interaction.

The first type of situation we shall consider is the operation of nationalism within a State ruled by a communist party. Here we shall be mainly concerned with the Soviet Union in its first years and in recent times, but some features of the intervening decades will need mention, and the case of modern Yugoslavia also deserves some attention.

The second is the attitude of communists to national conflicts within a European non-communist State, or to conflicts inspired by nationalism between such States.

The third type of situation is the relationship between 'socialist States', that is, between states ruled by communist parties.

The fourth is the attitude of communists to nationalist and anti-imperialist movements outside Europe. This large theme may be divided into three sections: colonial nationalism in the strict sense, movements for independence in semi-colonial countries, and the relations of independent new States with each other and with other Powers.

Nationalism within communist States

The disintegration of the goverment structure, which proceeded at an increasing pace after the March Revolution of 1917, affected both Russians and non-Russians, but in the case of the latter the social and political claims of the disaffected classes and parties inevitably took a nationalist form. This was true of workers as well as of peasants and intelligentsia, and not only Populists (Socialist-Revolutionaries or SRs) but even some Marxists were affected. During 1917 the Bolsheviks encouraged the process. They had committed themselves to the principle of self-determination as early as 1913, and the revolutionary potential of anti-Russian nationalism was a force of which Lenin was determined to make full use against his rivals. German military conquests also played their part in the 'national question' in Russia. At the time of the November Revolution the Germans held large territories in the west of the empire.

By the Treaty of Brest-Litovsk Lenin had to abandon all Poland and all the Baltic provinces, and to recognize an independent Ukrainian State which became a vassal of Germany. In the south, three Transcaucasian republics—Georgia, Armenia, and Azerbaidjan—declared their independence. It was not until the defeat of Germany by the western Powers at the end of 1918 that it became possible to reconsider the relationship between Russians and non-Russians.

The Bolsheviks were committed to self-determination. But in each case the practical question arose, who was to exercise the right of self-determination. If there were a conflict between a workers' movement, led by communists, demanding union with Soviet Russia, and a 'bourgeois nationalist' movement demanding separation, what were the Bolsheviks to do? How could it be decided which group had the greater support? Ought communists in any case to acknowledge the standards of 'bourgeois democracy', and accept the will of a mere numerical majority? Lenin did not do this in the case of the Constituent Assembly in Russia in January 1918. Should the wishes of bourgeois Balts or Ukrainians have greater weight than those of petty-bourgeois Russian SRs? In practice, the Bolsheviks tried in every case to keep the non-Russians within Soviet Russia. Their action was rationalized by identifying the true interests of each nation with those of its working class (or, in the case of completely agrarian nations, of the future working class which would one day come into being), and the interests of the working class with the policies of the leadership of the Bolshevik Party. And when such rationalizations became difficult, there was still the powerful argument that Soviet Russia stood for the cause of international socialist revolution, which was far more important than the interests of any single nation, however democratically expressed, which might stand in its way. Nations whose aims objectively served the capitalist Powers must be overruled, just as Marx had once argued that nations whose aims objectively served Tsarist Russia must be overruled. In all cases therefore the Bolsheviks sought to keep the non-Russians united with Soviet Russia. But Lenin was a realist, and where he saw that the forces against him were too great, he abandoned the attempt.

The independence of Finland and of Poland had long been accepted in principle by the whole Russian left, including the Bolsheviks. When a civil war broke out in Finland in 1918, the Bolsheviks wished to help the Finnish Reds, who would have remained closely associated with Soviet Russia, but they were unable to do so. In the case of Poland, the old problem of the eastern borderlands, from Lithuania to the Ukraine, which for three hundred years had been the main single source of conflict between Russians and Poles, still remained to be solved. After the war of 1920 a compromise was reached. Poland was left with large territories in which the majority of the population was not Polish. One might say that the eighteenth and nineteenth century partitions of Poland between Russia, Austria, and Prussia had been replaced by a partition of the Ukraine between Poland and Soviet Russia. The Bolsheviks did not like this, but it was a price worth paying. During their greatest military successes in the war of 1920, they attempted to set up a Polish communist government in the Polish city of Bialystok. Led by the Polish-born head of the *Cheka*, Feliks Dzerzhinsky, it could have been expected to bring Poland completely into line with Soviet Russia. But when the tide of war turned once more, it was abandoned, and Western White Russia and Western Ukraine were abandoned too.

The three Baltic peoples (Lithuanians, Latvians, and Estonians), were also able to secede, and to set up small independent States of their own. British naval power in the Baltic, and Polish military power (backed by the French) on land, provided a balance of forces which remained favourable to them for nearly two decades. Lenin accepted the facts. This meant a serious sacrifice, for the working class of Riga, a brave and stubborn minority of the Latvian people, had certainly desired union with Soviet Russia. The three Transcaucasian peoples (Georgians, Azerbaidjanis, and Armenians) were less fortunate. The essential difference between the Baltic and Transcaucasia was that in the latter case there was no powerful neighbour well disposed to the Transcaucasian peoples. The only other neighbour besides Russia was Turkey, whose leaders and people were hostile to Armenia and indifferent to Georgia and Azerbaidjan. The working class of Baku was more fortunate than that of Riga. Largely composed of Russian and Armenian workers surrounded by a rural population of Moslem Azeri Turks, it naturally preferred Soviet Russian rule. Rebellious Baku was liberated by a Soviet Russian invasion, and the Azeris were subjected once more to Russian rule. Georgia had a social-democratic government supported by its workers and peasants, but this did not save it from Soviet Russian invasion. As a result of successful military operations in 1920 and 1921, Soviet Russia recovered the oil of Baku and the manganese ore of Georgia.

Though these peripheral territories were lost for shorter or longer periods, the great mass of European and Asiatic Russia was retained, together with its numerous non-Russian peoples. Ukrainian independence was short-lived. After the collapse of the German-sponsored regime at the end of 1918, Ukrainian nationalists, Russian counter-revolutionaries, Polish invaders, and Bolsheviks succeeded each other, but it was the Bolsheviks who won. The Bolshevik Ukrainian government, some of whose members had small right to call themselves Ukrainians, nevertheless granted the Ukrainian people some cultural liberties which they had never enjoyed before. At least their administration was in Ukrainian hands, and the Ukrainian language was used in public business. Ukrainians who disliked communist rule had no more and no less reason to complain than Russians of similar views. They did not suffer discrimination as Ukrainians: on the contrary, it was the Russian minority in their midst who had some ground to feel that they were being forcibly 'Ukrainianized'.

Another people who had acquired a strong national consciousness, and had made substantial economic and political progress in the last decades of the Russian Empire, were the Tatars. These had in fact been the first of all the Moslem peoples of the world to accept modern European social and political ideas. By 1917 they possessed a considerable secular intellectual elite, devoted to modern democracy, including so revolutionary a concept for Moslems as the emancipation of women. Their greatest strength was in the Volga valley, especially in the city and province of Kazan. They were, however, a scattered people, lacking a single large area of compact population, but found in substantial numbers in the eastern and south-eastern parts of European Russia and in Central Asia. For this reason, neither territorial autonomy nor an independent State made much sense to them: far more attractive was the Austrian socialists' notion of cultural autonomy which Lenin and Stalin had denounced. In 1917 the Tatars put forward ideas of this sort at a congress of the Moslems of Russia. These ideas were rejected by the other Moslem peoples, who lived in compact territories in Central Asia or the Caucasus region, held traditionalist Moslem ideas, and had a distrust for the commercially and intellectually talented Tatars which recalls the attitude of east European peasants to Jews. In the Russian

Civil War the homeland of the Tatars was ravaged by both armies. When it was over, however, some Tatar intellectuals were recruited to the service of the Bolshevik regime. Intellectually more developed than their fellow-Moslems, they were more accessible to Marxist ideas. To some extent they became the bearers of communism among the Russian Moslems. However, their relationship to communism and Islam was ambivalent. The outstanding Tatar communist, Sultan-Galiev, thought in terms of an independent Moslem anti-imperialist, anti-European revolutionary force. In a sense he was a forerunner of 'Titoism', of modern anti-colonialism and even of 'positive neutralism'. Though hostile to the imperialist enemies of Soviet Russia, he was also suspicious of Russian power even when it was revolutionary. When he was found to be in treasonable correspondence with non-communist Moslem nationalists, he was removed from his post in the Commissariat of Nationalities, where he had been the chief assistant of the Commissar, Stalin himself. However, there was at this stage no mass repression of Tatars. In comparison with the Imperial regime the Tatars had made the same sort of material and cultural gains as the Ukrainians.

The situation was different in Central Asia. The peoples of Turkestan were far more backward. Their outlook was that of traditional Islam, their leaders were tribal chiefs or *ulema*. Only the first beginnings of a secular modernist intellectual elite had appeared before 1917, largely as a result of Tatar influence. The breakdown of the Imperial regime led to movements among the Moslems, but these took a simple anti-Russian form, based on religious rather than national consciousness. The local Russian population reacted savagely. The city of Tashkent contained a substantial number of Russians, minor bureaucrats and railwaymen for the most part. Apart from this there was a large population of Russian and Ukrainian peasant settlers in some parts of Central Asia. The rapid Russian colonization in the last decades before 1914 had bitterly antagonized the Asians, and had much to do with the bloody rising of 1916, which had been bloodily suppressed. The November Revolution of 1917 was nominally accepted by the Russians of Tashkent. But in fact the main purpose of the new authority, which set itself up there in the name of the Bolshevik government, was not to organize a socialist revolution in Turkestan but to suppress the nationalist movement among the Moslems. The forces which supported the Tashkent government were essentially 'poor whites', and they showed the same hostility to the aspirations of the native people as other similar communities have shown (for example, the *pieds noirs* in Algeria or the European miners in the Rhodesian Copper Belt). They succeeded in destroying the Moslem nationalist movements and celebrated their victory with brutal reprisals. When Lenin and his colleagues heard the truth they were sincerely horrified, but it took many years to undo the results.

Fifty years later the situation, as viewed by Soviet spokesmen, has undergone a fundamental change. In the place of the 'bourgeois nations' and half-developed embryos of nations that had struggled with each other after the collapse of the empire of the Tsars, is a community of fully grown 'socialist nations' living in friendship with each other now that national oppression and bourgeois nationalism have been liquidated. 'The solution of the national question', the second (1961) programme of the Soviet Communist Party (CPSU) states, is one of the greatest achievements of socialism . . . with reciprocal fraternal assistance, primarily from the great Russian people,[3] all the Soviet non-Russian republics have set up their own modern industries, trained their own national working class and intelligentsia, and developed a culture that is national in form and socialist in content. . . . The union and consolidation of equal peoples on a voluntary basis in a single multi-national state— The Union of Soviet Socialist Republics—their close cooperation in state, economic, and cultural development, their fraternal friendship and flourishing economy and culture, constitute the most important results of the national policy of Lenin.

The transformation of the economic and social life of the people of the Soviet Union, and the tremendous quantitative and qualitative progress at all levels of education are facts, and the non-Russians have shared in them. But the bland assertion that the 'union' of these peoples was 'on a voluntary basis' is contrary to the facts of history. Essentially, the arguments for keeping the non-Russian

---

[3] The adjective 'great', usually prefixed to the words 'Russian people' in Soviet pronouncements, has a moral rhetorical element in it. It should not be confused with the phrase 'Great Russian people'. The adjective 'Great Russian' is purely descriptive: it refers to those who speak what in English is called the Russian language, and was formerly used in Russian to distinguish the Russian, or 'Great Russian', language from 'Little Russian' (Ukrainian) and 'White Russian' (Belorussian). In Russian, 'Great Russian' is a single word (*velikorusskii*), while 'the great Russian people' is three words (*velikii russkii narod*).

peoples within the Soviet Union—and they are by no means contemptible arguments—are the direct antithesis of the argument which sums up the conventional wisdom of the United Nations in the 1960s—that 'self-government is better than good government'. The peoples of the Soviet Union have never been allowed to decide for themselves whether they would prefer to choose self-government. Instead, the blessings of good government, Leninist style, have been showered on them. That they have much to be thankful for, is certain; that they are grateful, is possible; that the only publications which appear in their homelands extol the Soviet regime with unbounded enthusiasm, proves nothing at all.

The Soviet Union consists of fifteen Soviet Socialist Republics (SSRs).[4] The Union is often described as a federation. This is however a dubious description, for the essential characteristic of federal government, the sharing of power between the central and regional governments, is missing. The republican governments are in no sense coordinate with the central government: they are in every sense subordinate to it. All that can be said is that the Constitution provides for devolution of powers, for decentralization. This has taken place in some respects, but the real importance of this decentralization is limited by the fact that the organization of the Communist Party of the Soviet Union, which has always controlled the governmental structure, is highly centralized. Some of the SSRs themselves contain subordinate units which are supposed to correspond to the territories of specific nations. The Russian Soviet Federal Socialist Republic (RSFSR) contains sixteen Autonomous Soviet Socialist Republics (ASSRs), the Georgian SSR has two ASSRs, and the Uzbek and Azerbaidjan SSRs each have one ASSR. It is worth noting that in only three of the sixteen ASSRs in the RSFSR does the nation which gives its name to the ASSR have an absolute majority of the population, and in four a relative majority; while in nine ASSRs Russians outnumber the titular nation, and in five of these there is an absolute majority of Russians over all

---

[4] The original Soviet Union, formed in 1923, consisted of four republics (Russian, Ukrainian, White Russian, and Transcaucasian). The Transcaucasian later split into three; five republics were set up in Central Asia in the 1930s; three Baltic republics and a Moldavian SSR (formerly Romanian Bessarabia) were added in 1940; and in 1940 a Karelian SSR was made up of formerly Finnish and Russian territories, but in July 1956 its status was reduced to that of ASSR (see below).

other national groups.[5] The Russians also have a relative majority in one other SSR, the Kazakh, where they form nearly 43 per cent of the population and the Kazakhs themselves only 30 per cent.

Some nationalities are scattered throughout the Union in comparatively small communities. The Armenians form a compact majority in their own SSR (88 per cent of its population), but 44 per cent of the Armenians in the Soviet Union live outside the Armenian SSR. There were almost five million Tatars in the Soviet Union at the time of the 1959 census, but only a little more than a quarter of these (1,345,000) lived in the Tatar ASSR, of whose population only 47 per cent were Tatars. The remaining three quarters were divided between the Central Asian SSRs, the Bashkir ASSR, and the officially Russian provinces of the RSFSR. The Jews in 1959 numbered 2,267,814 and were scattered all over the Union, the largest group being in the Ukraine. They had no compact territory of their own.[6]

In the half century of Soviet rule the fate of the non-Russians has varied in accordance with the general trends of Moscow's policy. National resentments were strongest, and repression of national aspirations most severe, in the periods of greatest crisis, in which the sufferings of the Russians too were most intense—the collectivization of agriculture and first five-year plan (1928–32), the great purge (1936–9), and the Second World War and its immediate aftermath. A special case of repression was the deportation of whole nations from their homelands on the grounds that they had assisted the German invaders: the Crimean Tatars, the Caucasian Chechens, the Kalmyks, and some other smaller groups suffered this fate. Such action by a capitalist government would of course have been unthinkable. Probably the proportion of Burmese who actively assisted the Japanese invaders was not smaller than the proportion of Chechens who assisted the Germans. The British government in 1945 did not consider deporting the whole population of Burma to Arctic Canada. Yet the deportations carried out in the community

---

[5] The Daghestanis (themselves a number of distinct peoples), the Tuvins, and the Chuvash have absolute majorities; the Kabardins, Ossetins, Tatars, and Yakuts relative majorities. Russians form an absolute majority in the Buryat Mongolian, Kalmyk, Karelian, Mordvin, and Udmurt ASSRs, and a relative majority in the Bashkir, Komi, Mari, and Chechen-Ingush ASSRs.

[6] The project of creating a special Jewish region in Biro-Bidjan in eastern Siberia was never carried out. This 'Jewish autonomous province' still nominally exists, but in 1959 it contained only 14,269 Jews (8.8 per cent of its population).

of fraternal socialist nations have been barely noticed by those representatives of world opinion who most eagerly unmask the crimes of imperialism. In the period of Khrushchev's ascendancy the situation of all non-Russian peoples greatly improved, perhaps even relatively more than that of the Russians. Khrushchev openly expressed his disapproval of the deportations, and most of the peoples concerned returned to their homes, though in depleted numbers.[7]

It is not possible to discuss here the fate of all the major peoples of the Soviet Union. We will content ourselves with some brief remarks about the most numerous nation, the Ukrainians, and will consider at somewhat greater length the situation of Central Asia.

The Ukrainians suffered exceptionally severely in the period of collectivization and in the great purge. During these years a minority of the Ukrainian people remained under Polish rule, bitterly hostile both to the Poles and to the Soviet Union. The region in which Ukrainian national consciousness was most developed, in which a compact population of all social classes firmly and indisputably regarded itself as a distinct Ukrainian nation, was Eastern Galicia, which had not been under the same rule as Russia since the early Middle Ages. In September 1939 this territory, together with the whole eastern half of Poland, was incorporated in the Soviet Union as a result of the Ribbentrop-Molotov pact, or Fifth Partition of Poland. The Galicians were extremely hostile to the Soviet regime. Less than two years later, when the German armies invaded the Soviet Union, they were welcomed by the Galicians, and to a lesser but still considerable extent by the people of the rest of the Ukraine. There were German experts, chiefly in the Ministry for Occupied Territories headed by the nazi ideologist Alfred Rosenberg, who sympathized with Ukrainian nationalism. They were however over-ridden by Hitler himself, who preferred a policy of exploitation and virtual enslavement of all Soviet subjects. Thus the reconquest of the Ukraine, including Galicia, by the Soviet armies in 1944–5 met with comparatively little active resistance from the population. However, the restored Soviet regime treated its liberated subjects with extreme severity. There were widespread arrests and deporta-

---

[7] The Chechens numbered 418,756 in 1959. In 1926 their number was 318,500, in 1939 407,600. If the rate of increase of 1926–39 (not a high rate, because it included the years of collectivization and the purge) had been continued between 1939 and 1959, the population in 1959 would have been over 580,000. A large part of this deficit of more than 150,000 (about 35 per cent) must be due to the casualties resulting from the deportations.

tions, the collectivization of agriculture in Galicia was rapidly enforced, and special attention was paid to the suppression of traces of 'bourgeois nationalism' in Ukrainian literature. The man directly responsible for these policies was N. S. Khrushchev, who was in control of the Ukraine from 1938 to 1950.[8] However, it is possible that in practice Khrushchev sought to mitigate the impact of official policies, to protect his Ukrainian subjects from the full severity of the measures dictated by Stalin and Kaganovich.[9] Certainly, when Khrushchev himself attained the first place in the Soviet Union after Stalin's death, he made great efforts to flatter Ukrainian national feeling. In 1954 the third centenary of the reunion of Eastern Ukraine with Russia[10] was celebrated with much publicity, and the Ukrainians were given a special place in the brotherhood of Soviet nations: if the Russians were the eldest brother, the Ukrainians were the second brother. In the following years Khrushchev also brought a number of Ukrainian communists into high positions in the central government. In his last years in power, however, this trend was reversed, and this may have continued under his successors.

It is exceptionally difficult to estimate the attitude of the Ukrainians to the Soviet regime, and the extent to which the Ukraine is administered by Ukrainians. The prevalence of Ukrainian names among lists of office-holders does not prove much. Many bearers of Ukrainian names are in fact Russians, just as many citizens of southern England bearing such names as Mackenzie or O'Brien have ceased to be more than nominal Scots or Irishmen. The modern history of the Ukraine is full of evidence of fanatical anti-Russian nationalism among Ukrainians. On the other hand, the similarity of the languages and cultures of the two nations, the effects of centuries of a common religion, are equally obvious facts. Russian culture is attractive to Ukrainians, just as English culture has been

---

[8] Most of the time as party secretary, part of the time as prime minister, and part of the time as both.

[9] Kaganovich, a Russian Jew born in the Ukraine, was for many years responsible for Ukrainian affairs. He was also Khrushchev's patron in the early decisive years of his political career. Kaganovich is generally considered to have stood for extremist policies. Khrushchev broke with him in 1957, when he was one of the 'anti-party group' expelled from the central committee of the CPSU.

[10] The significance of the Treaty of Pereyaslavl of 1654—whether it was an alliance between two equal States, or the acceptance by the Ukrainians east of the Dnieper of the sovereignty of Moscow—has long been, and still is, a matter of controversy among historians.

attractive to Scots or Irishmen (especially to Protestants among them). Undoubtedly millions of Ukrainians have become assimilated in the last fifty years. Whether assimilation and acceptance of a common fatherland, or national resistance and a passion for ultimate independence, is the predominant trend, especially among the younger generation in the Ukraine, it is not possible for a foreign observer to say, and it is doubtful whether either the Soviet government or the Ukrainian people themselves know the answer.

Soviet official discussion of Central Asia understandably emphasizes the industrial and educational progress which has been attained under Soviet rule. There is no doubt that the Moslem peoples of Soviet Central Asia enjoy a far higher standard of living, and far greater opportunities of education, than the neighbouring peoples of Turkey, Iran, Afghanistan, and Pakistan. Some qualifications have to be made. Central Asia has been obliged to concentrate on cotton production, to the neglect of cereal crops. This makes sense from the point of view of the overall needs of the Soviet economy, just as the specialization of Egyptian agricultural effort in cotton in the years of British occupation made sense from the point of view of the overall economic needs of the sterling area. Food crops have been relatively neglected in Soviet Central Asia, which is dependent for its supplies on the Ukraine and Siberia. Independent Central Asian republics would probably not have made the same economic choices. Even the communist leaders of the Central Asian SSRs have often shown reluctance to implement Moscow's economic decisions, and have expressed the view that Central Asia is not getting a fair economic return for the contribution it makes to the Soviet economy. Moscow has repeatedly denounced Central Asian communist politicians for opposition to its cotton policies, sometimes coupling this with the ominous accusation of 'bourgeois nationalism'. Nevertheless, Central Asian economic progress is a fact, and the region now has a substantial manufacturing industry, including other branches besides textiles. Again, educational progress must be qualified by the observation that the large Russian community in Central Asia has better opportunities, especially in higher education, than the Asian communities, and that in the remoter rural districts schools still leave more to be desired than the generalizations of Soviet propaganda would suggest. Yet the fact of tremendous progress is undeniable.

The extent to which Central Asia is ruled by Asians is more doubtful. The apparatus of the communist party, which controls government, is largely in Russian hands. The top posts are held by Asians, but the posts immediately below have Russian incumbents. The first secretaries of the republican central committees and of the provincial party committees are as a rule Asians, but they are usually assisted by a Russian second secretary. The heads of departments of republican central committees tend to be Russians. Similarly, Asian Prime Ministers have a Russian Deputy Prime Minister, and Asian ministers have Russian deputy ministers or departmental directors. The evidence suggests that it is the Russians in the nominally subordinate positions who hold the real power. The administrative changes introduced by Khrushchev and repealed by his successors, including the short-lived establishment of a Central Asian Bureau of the CPSU, do not seem to have affected this basic relationship.

Russian political control is also accompanied by a broader pattern of Russification. Immigration of Russian settlers, begun under the Imperial regime, has continued. Khrushchev's plans for the development of the 'virgin lands' in Kazakhstan accelerated it. In 1959 Russians outnumbered Kazakhs in the Kazakh SSR, and in the Kirgiz SSR they formed as much as 30 per cent of the population. In all the other Central Asian republics more than 10 per cent were Russians, and the proportion is increasing. The use of Russian as the state language is inevitable and unobjectionable, but the introduction of the Cyrillic alphabet for the Turkic or Iranian languages of the region, and the imposition of very large numbers of Russian words on their vocabularies, seem to go beyond normal administrative or economic needs. Particularly striking has been the systematic interference in the Asians' literature and history. Traditional poetry which could be claimed to have 'nationalistic' features has been denounced and withdrawn from publication. The conquest of Central Asia by the armies of the Tsars has been retrospectively justified as a progressive phenomenon, since it not only preserved the area from the danger of coming under the control of the British Empire, but had the positive merits of expediting the social evolution of its inhabitants from feudalism to socialism, bypassing capitalism, and of bringing them into contact with the advanced culture of the 'great Russian people'. This argument is fundamentally the argument for justification of all colonial empires: the conquest of

Asiatic or African lands by the British brought their peoples into contact with the advanced culture of the British people. But Soviet spokesmen have further arguments to justify Russian conquests. 'Russia, in spite of the reactionary regime of Nicholas I, was at the same time the Russia of Belinsky, Herzen, Dobrolyubov, Chernyshevsky, the Russia of revolutionary democrats.'[11] One day the Russian revolutionary movement was to have its Lenin, Lenin was to lead the November Revolution, a working class was to appear in Central Asia, and this working class was to have the benefits of socialism bestowed on it. Therefore conquest by Nicholas I or Alexander II was a sort of gift of progress by post-dated cheque. On the other hand, England was only the England of Palmerston, not the England of Robert Owen or the Chartists or Charles Dickens. The English working class was destined to become corrupted by its labour aristocracy, bought by the profits of colonialism, whereas the Russian working class was 'the most revolutionary working class in history'. These extraordinary arguments, a kind of quasi-Marxist Victorianism that puts Kipling or President McKinley in the shade, became official Soviet doctrine in the 1950s and have not been repudiated.

The question remains whether the peoples of Central Asia have national consciousness and potential nationalist aspirations. At the time of the November Revolution of 1917 the concept of the nation barely existed in Central Asia. What did exist was a consciousness of being profoundly different from Russians, a consciousness that Russian rule was foreign. But the consciousness was based not on the idea of a nation but on the fact of the religious community of Islam. Only a few intellectuals, possessing a modern secular education and influenced by the democratic nationalist movement of the Volga Tatars, had begun to think of themselves as belonging to a Turkestan nation. This notion might perhaps have become popular, as the idea of a Ukrainian nation, conceived by intellectuals, became popular among the people of the Ukraine in the nineteenth century, if its bearers had had time and opportunity to spread it. But this they did not have, and it must be stated that a single Turkestan national consciousness was never formed.

The Bolsheviks were opposed in principle to Islam as a religion, and to any form of Panislamic or Panturkic political movement.

---

[11] Quoted from the Soviet Kazakh historian E. B. Bekmakhanov, *Prisoedinenie Kazakhstana k Rossii* (Moscow, 1957), p. 115.

They felt the need to replace these dangerous ideas by some other focus of loyalty which could attract the Central Asians without threatening the Soviet Union. The answer they found was to encourage the formation of a number of distinct nations, based on the factor which had historically been the main formative element in national consciousness in European Russia and central Europe, the regions which Lenin and Stalin had studied—the factor of language. The existing spoken dialects were to be developed into distinct literary languages, and those who spoke each of these languages were to be made into separate nations: Kazakhs, Kirgiz, Turkmens, Uzbeks, and Kara-Kalpaks. The Tadjiks, speaking a dialect of Persian, were to be elevated into a Tadjik nation, distinct from the Persian nation. Undoubtedly this policy was designed to break up the Central Asian Moslem community: in this sense it is legitimate to describe it as a policy of 'divide and rule'. But it is incorrect to say that it aimed to disrupt the Turkestan nation: no such nation existed. At first the policy was completely doctrinaire and artificial, but after four decades it appears to have achieved considerable success. Modern Uzbek, Turkmen, Kirgiz, and Kazakh nations, perhaps even a Kara-Kalpak nation, have come into existence, complete with their own educated elites and more modern social and professional structures. The great unanswered question remains: against whom will the national aspirations of these newly-created nations be turned? Will the modern secular nationalism of five or six small nations prove more dangerous than the earlier, probably exaggerated, danger of old-fashioned Panislamism? Will the creatures turn against their creators?

The greatest success in the treatment of national conflicts in a country ruled by communists was attained not in the Soviet Union but in Yugoslavia. The first Yugoslav State, from 1918 to 1941, was torn by national hatreds, of which the most serious was between Serbs and Croats, two nations with a common language but different religion and different cultural history. The attempt of King Alexander's dictatorship to impose a 'Yugoslav' official nationalism was a failure. It was opposed by the vast majority of Croats, and its original purpose was distorted by Serbian nationalist politicians who talked of Yugoslav patriotism but in practice required the submission of the Croats and other non-Serbs to Serbian domination. When Yugoslavia was destroyed by German invasion in 1941, a Croatian puppet State[12] was set up under a Croatian fascist dictator, and Serbian citizens of this state were persecuted. Serbian armed resistance was met with massacres of Serbs and Jews by Croatian fascist bands, and these provoked counter-massacres of Croats and Moslems by Serbian nationalist bands.[13] Tens of thousands perished in this fratricidal war while the occupying armies of Germans and Italians encouraged the bloody work.

The communists alone set themselves deliberately against the tide. They declared that Croats and Serbs were brother nations, and must fight together, without national discrimination, against the invaders and against the fascists among their own compatriots. At first this argument had few supporters. But the communists set a fine example, by their heroism in guerrilla warfare against superior odds, and by their genuinely non-discriminatory treatment of the population in those territories which they liberated from the enemy. Their achievements contrasted even more strikingly with the tragic and sordid picture of massacre and counter-massacre, destruction and counter-destruction of houses and property, which were all that the Croatian Ustashas and Serbian Chetniks could offer. After two years of these horrors more and more people in both nations came round to their point of view. With the triumph of the communists in the war came the triumph of their nationality policy, and it ensured the survival, in a different form, of the Yugoslav State.

The Constitution of the new Yugoslavia set up six republics, following the model of the sixteen SSRs of the Soviet Union.[14] As in the Soviet case, the Constitution was unitary, not genuinely federal, the republics subordinate, not coordinate. But the essential difference from the Soviet Union was that there was no one nation which in strength, material progress, and numbers overshadowed all others, as the Russians did in the USSR. The Serbs were the most

---

[12] Its official name was Independent State of Croatia. The unprecedented insertion of the adjective 'independent' into its title was eloquent proof that the State in fact lacked any independence.

[13] The people of Bosnia, one of the main provinces of Yugoslavia, had one language but three religions. The Catholics and Orthodox had names for their nationality—Croat and Serb—and indeed what separated them in the 1940s was much less a religious than a secular national consciousness. But the Moslems, who were neither Croats nor Serbs, had no name other than the name of their religion. Thus 'Moslem' came to be accepted, in this special Bosnian context, as a nationality.

[14] There were sixteen SSRs at the time of the acceptance of the Yugoslav Constitution, as the Karelian SSR still existed. See above, p. 153.

numerous single nation but the Croats and Slovenes, together
with the smaller Macedonian, Montenegrin, and Moslem groups,
counterbalanced them. Differences in economic and cultural level
were small compared to those dividing the Russians from the Asian
nations of the Soviet Union. There were desperately poor areas
and prosperous areas inhabited by both Croats and Serbs, though as
a nation the Slovenes had a much higher and the Macedonians a
much lower standard of living than the average for the country.
In the last decades there have been disagreements between the republics, largely concerned with the unwillingness of the richer areas to
pay for economic development in the poorer, and this has inevitably
caused nationalist grumbling. But the evidence seems to show
clearly that the common Yugoslav State is accepted by its citizens,
and that among the younger generation a Yugoslav national consciousness coexists with the earlier Serbian, Croatian, or other
national consciousnesses. To anyone who recalls the depth of national hatred that prevailed a generation earlier, this cannot fail
to appear a magnificent achievement, and a large share of the credit
must undoubtedly go to the Yugoslav communist leaders.

Communism and nationalism in Europe

The peace settlement of 1919 satisfied many of the national aspirations which were frustrated under the old order, but it denied others.
The new States, allegedly based on the national principle, contained
large minorities, or even majorities, of nations other than the leading
nation in the State. New 'official nationalisms' replaced the old,
and a new group of 'oppressed nationalities' appeared—Germans,
Hungarians, and Macedonians from the first, soon followed by
Croats and Slovaks. It was among the defeated nations, with large
communities of their compatriots transferred to foreign rule, that
communism had the greatest support, while those small nations which
emerged as clients of the victorious western Powers were able to a
large extent to appease social and political discontents by displaying
national gains. It was therefore natural that both the Communist
International and the Russian Communist Party should take a
sympathetic interest in the German, Hungarian, Macedonian,
Ukrainian, and White Russian minorities under foreign rule, and
that they should show special antipathy to the Polish, Czechoslovak,
Romanian, and Yugoslav States.

The policies of local communist parties, of the Comintern, and of the Soviet government, in central and eastern Europe have been frequently and variously affected by the numerous national conflicts which have at different times simmered, erupted, subsided, and exploded anew within this region. Here we shall consider only three important cases—Transylvania, Macedonia, and the relations between Poles and Germans since 1945.

Transylvania was not so much a country with a majority nation (Romanians) and a minority nation (Hungarians) as a homeland of two nations, which each regarded as its own. The political leaders in Bucarest and Budapest were determined to include the whole country in the Romanian or Hungarian State. This was bound to make one nation or the other feel a stranger in its own home. Yet neither nation was prepared to treat the other as its equal, and without this it was impossible to maintain the peculiar character of Transylvanian culture in the face of the small-power imperialism of the rulers of Bucarest or Budapest. The Romanians of Transylvania were well aware of the differences between themselves and the Romanians of the Old Kingdom; they were constantly grumbling about the Bucarest politicians, yet they insisted that their Hungarian fellow-Transylvanians must submit to them as masters. The Hungarians were no less implacable. Their upper classes resented the loss of power to people whom they had hardly ceased to regard as their serfs, and their peasants met with indifference or hostility from the Romanian peasants. Inevitably all classes of Hungarians looked to Budapest. As for the German minority, a privileged community of burghers and prosperous peasants established since the thirteenth century, who had made great contributions to Transylvanian culture, they tended simply to support the authorities in order to preserve their privileges: after 1918 this meant supporting Bucarest. In short, if ever there had been a hope that the sense of a certain common Transylvanian culture would crystallize into a Transylvanian national identity, the political attitudes of the 1920s destroyed it.

Those persons in Transylvania who were attracted to communism tended naturally to wish to join either a Hungarian or a Romanian communist party. The Comintern took the view that communist parties should be organized according to existing state frontiers. Therefore Hungarian communists in Transylvania should belong to the Romanian Communist Party. This principle proved difficult to apply in practice. The Comintern's attitude was dictated in any case by administrative convenience, not by any preference for the Romanian over the Hungarian national cause. In fact the prestige of the Hungarians stood higher in Moscow than that of the Romanians. The Hungarian Soviet Republic of 1919 had been destroyed, but still Hungary had at least had a communist government for several months, and its greatest success had been won by appealing to Hungarian nationalism. The Romanians on the other hand had taken Bessarabia, which the Soviet leaders persisted in regarding as Russian territory, and whose loss they never recognized.[15] The Comintern therefore showed marked hostility to Romania, and the Romanian Communist Party was obliged to proclaim, for the territory of the Romanian State, Lenin's principle of the right of the nationalities to self-determination including secession. This policy had the advantage of attracting to the party some hundreds of members of the non-Romanian third of the population, but the much greater disadvantage of repelling the Romanian two-thirds. In the late 1930s the Comintern's policy changed. With the introduction of the Popular Front tactic at its seventh congress in 1935, emphasis was laid on unity of anti-fascist forces within each State, and on resistance by all States threatened by Hitler's Germany. National irredentisms which threatened this overall aim were discouraged, though the Comintern never specifically committed itself to formal approval of the frontiers created by the 1918–20 peace treaties. With the German-Soviet pact of 1939 the emphasis again changed. Resistance to the nazis was discouraged, as the enemies of the nazis were also the enemies of the Soviet Union. When Germany and Italy imposed a partition of Transylvania, with the northern half being returned to Hungary, the Romanian communists were not allowed to call for resistance. When Hitler attacked the Soviet Union in 1941, both Romania and Hungary were his allies: the Soviet leaders therefore saw no reason to prefer the one to the other. When Romania abandoned Hitler in August 1944, but Hungary remained loyal to him (despite Horthy's pathetically incompetent attempt to break loose), the Soviet government came down on the

---

[15] This inflexible attitude still lacks explanation. Lenin was perfectly willing to accept the Treaty of Riga, which gave to Poland large territories which on both ethnic and historical grounds could be regarded as Russian (or at least as Ukrainian or White Russian), but neither he nor his successors would accept the loss of Bessarabia, where both the ethnic and the historical arguments were unquestionably on the Romanian side.

Romanian side. Romanian troops reoccupied Transylvania, and its restoration was officially confirmed in the peace treaties of 1946. The communist regime in Romania at first strongly emphasized its opposition to all forms of national discrimination. Complete equality was promised to the Hungarians of Transylvania. Two universities were established in the historic capital of Cluj (Kolozsvár), one Romanian and one Hungarian. The area with the largest compact Hungarian population, the Székely district in the south-east corner, was made into a special Hungarian Autonomous Region, modelled on the ASSRs of the Soviet Union. The government publicly discouraged any form of anti-Hungarian nationalism. One of the main charges against the leading Romanian communist Lucreţiu Pǎtrǎşcanu, who was purged from the party in 1948, was that he had been guilty of Romanian chauvinism. However, in the 1950s the emphasis gradually changed. In 1960 the Hungarian university of Cluj was merged with the Romanian university, and the Hungarian Autonomous Region abolished. At the present time the Romanian communists categorically declare that Romania is not a multi-national State but a Romanian national State, the Romanian Socialist Republic. In 1944 the old order, with its fanatically nationalist bureaucrats and bourgeois, had been replaced by a party which professed proletarian internationalism. Now, more than twenty years later, the Romanian communists have adopted nationalism, or perhaps nationalism has taken over the Romanian Communist Party.

Macedonia, which formed part of the Ottoman Empire until 1912, was inhabited by an even larger variety of national groups than Transylvania. The largest single group were Slavs, but their allegiance was uncertain. Some considered themselves Serbs, a much larger number considered themselves Bulgarians. The dialects spoken in the province were closer to the Bulgarian than to the Serbian language. The majority of Slavs knew only that they were Christian, not Moslem, and Slav, not Greek. In the last years of Ottoman rule an organization was created called the Internal Macedonian Revolutionary Organisation (IMRO). It was pledged to create an independent Macedonia, but its members were in fact divided between those who simply wished to annex Macedonia to Bulgaria and those who wished for a separate Macedonian State, possibly to be included in a federation of Balkan States.

As a result of the Balkan Wars of 1912–13, Macedonia was partitioned between Serbia and Greece. In the First World War the Bulgarian army occupied the Serbian portion, but in 1918 this was returned to Serbia, which had now become Yugoslavia. Many pro-Bulgarian Macedonians went to live in exile in Bulgaria, where they became a turbulent element in internal politics. Within Yugoslavia IMRO reappeared, and its terrorist activities were directed essentially in support of Bulgarian aims. In Bulgaria the communist party was comparatively strong, though it did not obtain power. In the Comintern the Bulgarians had greater revolutionary prestige than any other Balkan people. With its general hostility to the 1918–19 peace treaties it was to be expected that the Comintern would show rather more sympathy for the Bulgarian than for the Yugoslav cause, and in 1920 it approved the establishment of a liaison organization between the communist parties of the region, known as the Balkan Communist Federation. Its general line was solidarity of the workers and the peoples of the Balkans, but within this framework it urged that attention should be paid to the Macedonian problem. This attitude pleased the Bulgarian party but aroused no enthusiasm in the Yugoslav or Greek parties. The Bulgarian communists were bitter enemies of the right-wing Macedonian exiles, but they had their own Macedonian following, and they believed, like all Bulgarians, that Macedonia had been incorporated against its people's will in Serbia. The Yugoslav and Greek communists were most unwilling to support the cause of Macedonia against their own States, as this exposed them to the accusation of treason. In 1924 the Balkan Communist Federation came out openly in favour of a Macedonian republic within a federation of independent Balkan republics, and IMRO gave this declaration its support. Within three months, however, the leader of IMRO, Todor Alexandrov, was murdered, and the organization came under fascist control. The communists set up a Macedonian organization of their own, the so-called United IMRO, but it had little support within Macedonia. In all the Balkan countries at the end of the 1920s the communists were fiercely suppressed by the governments, and had little popular support.

The change came with the adoption of the Popular Front by the Comintern in 1935. As in the case of Transylvania, less emphasis was placed on the injustice of the 1918–19 peace settlement, less encouragement given to irredentism. In Yugoslavia communism made rapid progress among the intellectual youth, who detested fascism and opposed German and Italian aims. These new communists were determined to defend Yugoslavia, though they genuinely opposed the Yugoslav government's repressive policies in Macedonia. The German-Soviet pact of 1939 brought another change. The Communists were required to oppose Anglo-French policies, and the Popular Front slogan of a common struggle of the Balkan peoples against German imperialism lost its urgency. The German occupation of Yugoslavia in 1941 brought a new period of Bulgarian rule in Macedonia. The attitude of the Comintern and the Soviet government was at first uncertain. Even after the Germans had attacked the Soviet Union, the Soviet leaders hesitated between support of the Yugoslav and Bulgarian points of view, and between the rival claims of the Yugoslav and Bulgarian communist parties for the allegiance of Macedonian communists.

The issue was decided by the Yugoslav communists. Tito's resistance movement not only held out heroically in central Yugoslavia against the Germans and their auxiliaries, but extended its authority into Macedonia. By 1943 there were Macedonian partisan bands acknowledging Tito's authority, and direct contact had been established with the communist resistance movements in Albania and Greece. By comparison, the achievements of the Bulgarian communist resistance movement were trivial. The Soviet leaders had to recognize Yugoslav authority over that part of Macedonia which had been Yugoslav before 1941, and when the war ended Tito was in effective control of the whole province. The new Yugoslav State, moreover, had a solution for the national conflicts that had bedevilled the region for half a century. Its official doctrine was that the Macedonians were neither Serbs nor Bulgarians, but a separate Slav nation, and Macedonia became one of the six constituent republics of the new Yugoslavia. In the years since then this policy seems to have produced good results. From the Macedonian dialects an official Macedonian literary language has been artificially created, and Macedonian national identity is becoming a reality. Macedonia has also benefited from large-scale economic investments by the central government: the more advanced regions of Slovenia, Croatia, and Serbia have paid, if with some grumbling, for the development of this long-neglected province. Nevertheless Macedonia remains a potential source of international tension owing to the existence of substantial numbers of Macedonian

Slavs in northern Greece and in south-western Bulgaria. These territories are regarded by the Macedonian politicians in Yugoslavia as unredeemed Macedonian lands. At the same time the numerous Macedonians, originating from Yugoslav territory but living for many years past in Bulgaria, as well as the compact Macedonian population of the Pirin region, form an anti-Yugoslav faction in Bulgaria. These problems occasionally influence the relations between the three States and between the three communist parties.

Thus the role of the communist parties in the development of the Macedonian problem, as of the Transylvanian, has been largely influenced by the general trend of international politics and by the interests of the Soviet Union. Nevertheless both problems have now reached a stage in which local factors are decisive. In Transylvania the triumph of the most numerous nationality of the region seems assured: nationalism has made itself felt through the communist party. In Macedonia a more complex solution has been found. In the south, Greek nationalism has triumphed: Greek refugees, expelled from Turkey in the 1920s and resettled in Macedonia, have submerged the Slav population, reducing it to a rather small minority. In the north, both Serbian and Bulgarian nationalism have failed, and the best answer to the problem appears to be the encouragement of a distinct Macedonian nationality.

The European national problem whose treatment at the end of the Second World War had the most far-reaching consequences for communism was the German problem. When the war ended the Germans were almost universally hated. This was a factor of which both communist and other parties and governments had to take account. The Soviet government decided to exploit it in the interests of communism as it understood them. Having reconquered the eastern provinces of Poland, the eastern borderlands which for centuries had been the main object of Polish-Russian hostility, Stalin offered the Poles compensation in the form of the German provinces east of the Oder and Western Neisse rivers, reserving for the Soviet Union only the north-eastern part of East Prussia with the city of Königsberg, which he renamed Kaliningrad. At the same time he encouraged the government of Czechoslovakia to expel the three million Germans who had lived for many centuries in Bohemia and Moravia. As a result of these decisions, some twelve million Germans lost their homes. Of these, roughly two million perished in the process, and ten million found a refuge in the rest of Germany. The fate of Germany itself became in the post-war years the main subject of increasingly embittered discussions between the Soviet government and its former major allies. When no agreed settlement could be found, Germany was in fact divided into two States. Fifty million Germans live in the Federal Republic, which became an independent State allied with the western Powers. Fewer than twenty million Germans live in the German Democratic Republic, ruled by a dictatorship of the Socialist Unity Party, led by German communists imported from the Soviet Union, imposed and maintained by Soviet military power. Thus, by a strange historical irony, the nineteenth-century partition of Poland between Russia, Prussia, and Austria was replaced by a partition of half of Germany between the Soviet Union and Poland, and a division of the whole of Germany into a western and a Soviet sphere of interest. The sufferings of the uprooted Germans, which were a consequence of the still more cruel treatment by Germans of Poles and Czechs, created new resentment among Germans against Poles and Czechs, and still greater fears among Poles and Czechs of ultimate German attempts at revenge. These fears provided convincing arguments for a close alliance of both Poland and Czechoslovakia with the Soviet Union. It is likely that any free government in either country would have eagerly sought Soviet friendship after 1945. The freely elected multi-party Czechoslovak government of 1945–8 certainly did this. However, Stalin believed in leaving nothing to chance which he could himself determine, and he imposed governments of subservient communists in both countries. Yet when the Stalinist regime in Poland came to an end, and Gomulka's government obtained full sovereignty, Poland's alliance with the Soviet Union was strengthened.

The essence of the situation now is that the Polish and Czechoslovak governments need a German bogey. For twenty years both governments have poured forth a stream of nationalist hatred against Germans. Lip service has been paid to the reformed and democratic character of the East German government, but the Federal Republic is represented as the heir to Hitler. No credit is given for any of its achievements, for any evidence of democratic principles or practice. Every statement by an ex-nazi or a fanatical expellee from the formerly German provinces of Poland or Czechoslovakia is given publicity, and is used to show that Western Germany is dominated by 'revanchists'. Fear and hatred of Germany, being almost the only sentiments shared by the communist parties with a large number of their subjects, are exploited to the full. Essentially, the Polish government needs the Germans as the German nazis had needed the Jews, as a scapegoat against which to concentrate all discontent. Its task has been made easier by the unwillingness of the Federal German government to accept the Oder-Neisse frontier. The West German leaders argue that if they are eventually to surrender their theoretical claim to these lands, based on the fact that they had never been given to Poland by an international treaty, but only temporarily placed under Polish administration until the peace conference should decide their fate, then they should receive some concession in return. But the truth is that the last thing the Polish government would do is to pay a price for German recognition of the frontier. On the contrary, it needs an unrecognized frontier in order to be able to show its subjects that the Germans are incurably revanchist. The government which would gain from German recognition of the frontier would be the German government, not the Polish.

The policy of maximising hatred of Germans has been pursued not only by the Polish and Czech communists, but also by the Soviet government. In particular, great use has been made in international propaganda of the bogey of the eventual nuclear armament of Germany. One must doubt whether the Soviet government, well aware of the disparity of force between the Soviet Union and Germany, and of the extent to which German military policy is controlled by its NATO allies, has any serious fears in regard to Germany. But the Soviet people, which remembers the horrors of the Second World War, and the cruelty of the German invaders both to the civilian population and to Soviet prisoners of war, can be impressed by this argument. It is also useful for exploiting differences between the nations allied in NATO.

The German problem is the clearest example of systematic long-term exploitation by communists of national hatreds, a policy which is in flagrant contradiction with the principles of Marxism, and which goes against the long tradition of international solidarity that is an inseparable part of 'scientific socialism'. The contradiction is officially explained away by the arguments that the security of the Soviet Union and its allies is the first condition for the progress of world socialism; that the Federal Republic is an instrument of the imperialists, especially of the United States; that the United States aggressors are the true heirs of Hitler; and that the absence on their part of hatred of Germans as such is proved by the friendly relations which exist with the German Democratic Republic. But the facts do not support these arguments.

It seems possible that at the present time anti-German propaganda is a diminishing asset at least in Poland. When the Polish Catholic bishops invited the German bishops to the celebration of the millennium of the Polish Catholic Church in 1966, the Polish government unloosed a tremendous campaign against them, and Gomulka publicly committed himself to the view that for a Pole to forgive the Germans was treasonable. Yet the campaign was singularly ineffective. Not only did huge Polish crowds attend the Catholic festivities, despite government efforts to divert them to rival celebrations of their own, but they publicly declared their agreement with the Catholic hierarchy's advocacy of forgiveness.

Relations between communist States

If modern wars are caused by imperialism, and imperialism is a product of capitalism in its last phase, then it seems reasonable to assume that within regions where capitalism has been abolished, the causes of war would disappear. At least between socialist States there could be no conflicts of interest sufficiently serious to threaten peace.

It became possible to test this theory against reality when a number of east European States came under communist rule at the end of the Second World War.

In the case of Yugoslavia there can hardly be any disagreement as to what happened. The Yugoslav communists had created, during four years of armed resistance, a powerful army and an effective, if somewhat primitive, apparatus of civil government. By the autumn of 1944 they controlled most of the central mountainous core of the country. In October their forces entered Belgrade, the national capital, together with the Soviet army advancing from Bulgaria.[16] In the following months the German forces in western Yugoslavia

---

[16] The liberating force also included units of the Bulgarian army, which changed sides in the war after the armistice of September 1944. Farther north, units of the Romanian army, which had similarly changed sides at the end of August 1944, took part in the liberation of Czechoslovakia by the Soviet army.

were driven back by the combined efforts of Yugoslav regular army units, Yugoslav guerrilla forces, and the Soviet army. As the Germans abandoned the cities and provinces of the plains, the Yugoslav communists' civil government took over. In all this process of liberation the role of the Soviet forces was marginal: essentially, the Yugoslav communists freed their own country.

In the other countries of the region, the Soviet army was the decisive factor. In Poland the embryonic civil government created by the national resistance movement, which was not led by communists, was broken up partly by the German destruction of Warsaw, with the tacit complicity of the Soviet military command, in the autumn of 1944, and partly by military operations and mass arrests by the Soviet military occupation which replaced the German. In its place was established a rival government composed of Polish communists partly brought in from the Soviet Union and partly recruited locally. In Romania and Bulgaria the existing machinery of government, manned by officials of conservative, and in many cases fascist, outlook, was ordered to co-operate with the Soviet authorities. This co-operation was insincere on both sides, and the political and security experts attached to the Soviet military command used various methods to purge officials and to replace them with communists, many of whom, as in the Polish case, were former nationals who had been living in exile in the Soviet Union and had returned with the Soviet army.[17] In Czechoslovakia and Hungary civil government virtually collapsed in the last stages of the war, and the Soviet authorities helped to create a new government machine, in which communists held many powerful positions. Once the war was over, and government was beginning to function more normally, they proceeded to the next step. By various methods of purge, black-

---

[17] Many of these were survivors from two stages of persecution—the first from right-wing dictatorships in their own countries, the second from the Soviet security police in the great purge of 1936–9. The Polish Communist Party was even formally dissolved in 1938, and revived under a new name, with a largely new membership, in German-occupied Poland and on Soviet territory, in 1942, as the Polish Workers' Party (PPR). In the purge many Polish and Yugoslav communists perished, and there were also Hungarian, Romanian, and Bulgarian casualties. Survivors had little cause to love the Soviet regime: they lacked the innocent enthusiasm of the communist who had fought heroically in the underground, inspired by love of Stalin and his country. At the same time they well knew the importance of obedience to the 'teacher of genius of all progressive humanity', and they had learned the techniques of promotion in their career by denunciation of their comrades as foreign agents, spies, and saboteurs.

mail, or outright intimidation, the non-communist parties, which at first had been encouraged to co-operate with the communists in 'democratic coalitions', were deprived of political influence, and all power passed to the communist parties. This stage was essentially achieved in Poland, Romania, and Bulgaria before the end of 1945, though some resistance continued for another two years or more. In Hungary the decisive period was the spring of 1947. Czechoslovakia, where the communists seized power in February 1948, was the only country in which local communist forces made a considerable effort from their own resources. Even in this case, it is arguable that Soviet intervention, between 1945 and 1948, was decisive: in the other four countries its decisive role is indisputable. The third stage came with large-scale purges within the communist parties, in the years 1949–51. The occasion for the purges was the breach between the Soviet Union and Yugoslavia, and the alleged danger of 'nationalism' within the parties. The purges all show a common pattern, and it was clear that both the mechanism of terror and the *mise en scène* of public trial were closely copied from the Soviet model of 1936–9. Nevertheless, there were significant differences in the results. The purges were far heavier in Czechoslovakia and Hungary than in Poland, Romania, and Bulgaria, and the treatment of the victims was undoubtedly more humane in Poland than elsewhere. On the other hand the extreme degree of subjection of Poland to the Soviet Union was symbolized by the appointment of a Soviet marshal, Konstantin Rokossovsky, as Polish Minister of Defence, with a seat in the Polish politbureau.

These events can be regarded as a process of imperialism, consisting of the conquest and subjugation of six nations, all of which had previously enjoyed periods of independence,[18] by the Soviet empire. Military domination, ideological intolerance, and totalitarian power appear its outstanding features. But this is not how communist spokesmen describe it. In their view the process of establishment of 'socialism', which inevitably required the use of force, was the work of the 'peoples' themselves, assisted by 'brotherly aid' from the Soviet Union. Once 'socialist' governments were established in this way, however, the struggle was by no means over.

[18] Five nations (Poles, Czechs, Hungarians, Romanians, Bulgarians) undoubtedly enjoyed independent status after the First World War. Whether the sixth nation, the Slovaks, enjoyed independence under the first Czechoslovak Republic (1918–38) or the Slovak State (1938–44), or both, is a matter for argument.

Economic and social policies had to be put into effect, and the continued resistance of the old ruling classes, and of persons whose mentality had been formed under the old regime, had to be crushed. Sufferings and hardships in the following years were due partly to 'mistakes' on the part of inexperienced leaders and mainly to the opposition of former capitalists, or the intrigues of foreign capitalist governments and their agents, or simply to the 'remnants of capitalism in the consciousness of people': they were not in any way due to any imperialistic quality in Soviet policy.

Soviet domination included an economic element. Hungary and Romania were obliged to pay heavy reparations, besides paying for the costs of the Soviet armies of occupation, and both countries also suffered further huge losses from unofficial requisitions and plunder. The Soviet authorities also took over German property in both countries. Not only was 'German property' made to cover a surprisingly large number of enterprises, but the Soviet authorities refused to accept liabilities to third persons arising from them, while insisting on the payment of debts to themselves. From these confiscated German assets were later formed Soviet-Romanian and Soviet-Hungarian joint companies, which allowed the Soviet government to interfere massively in the oil, bauxite, and timber industries and in air and sea transportation. The Soviet government also used its overwhelming military and political position to impose unfavourable prices for goods exported from east European countries to the Soviet Union and to extract high prices for Soviet goods sold to them. An especially bad case was the Soviet-Polish trade agreement which imposed a very low price for Polish coal at a time when coal was in short supply all over Europe, and an independent Polish government would have been able to do extremely good business with the West, and thus to facilitate substantially the desperately difficult task of reconstructing its ravaged economy. All these measures must seem to an impartial observer to add up to 'economic exploitation' by the Soviet Union of dependent States. However, because the exploiting government was not capitalist, the policies could not, by definition, be regarded as 'imperialist'. Furthermore, it was argued that the peoples which had been liberated from fascism by the heroic Soviet army had an obligation to compensate their liberator for all that it had suffered. That there was some force in this argument, many east European democrats were willing to admit. But the argument was insufferably overworked. The propaganda machines of the Soviet Union and the communist governments of eastern Europe invariably referred to trade transactions between the USSR and neighbour countries as generous disinterested aid. In this they were acting on the well-established totalitarian model. In Soviet labour camps inscriptions expressed the inmates' joy at their happy new life and gratitude to their gaolers, and German concentration camps bore the legend *Arbeit macht frei*.

The problems of relations between communist-ruled States were dramatically raised in the summer of 1948 by the conflict between the Soviet Union and Yugoslavia. Various practical issues were involved, such as Yugoslav disappointment at lukewarm Soviet support for their claim to Trieste, Soviet support for a type of Balkan federation which did not appeal to the Yugoslavs, Yugoslav resentment at the efforts of the Soviet security services to enlist members of the Yugoslav Communist Party as their agents, and Yugoslav opposition to Soviet economic demands. But the essential cause of the conflict was simpler. The Yugoslav communists had created their own army and their own civil government, and the first loyalty of their officers and bureaucrats was to Marshal Tito and the Yugoslav leaders. They had learned to admire the Soviet Union, indeed they felt it to some extent to be their own 'socialist fatherland'. But they did not expect to be asked to sacrifice their socialist homeland to distant socialist Russia. This situation was unacceptable to Stalin. He not only insisted that for all communists, everywhere, the interests of the Soviet Union must come before all, but he believed it necessary that all communist parties, and still more all communist-ruled States, should be directed by persons whom he had chosen, and who owed their careers to him. In a sense, Tito had been so chosen, when he was selected in Moscow in 1937, in the early stages of the great purge, to go back to Yugoslavia and reorganize the underground communist party. But the events of 1941–5, his own political and military abilities, and the contact with his own brave and loyal people had transformed him from an obscure Comintern agent into a powerful national leader. Stalin must dimly have understood this, yet he drew the wrong conclusions. The alliance of an independent State, communist yet not controlled by him; consistent support for Soviet foreign policy all over the world; and the friendship of men who had proved themselves in a hard school—these things Stalin already had if he would choose to accept them. But they were not enough for him. He believed that men whom he did not command would act against him. He made his prophecy self-fulfilling. He caused his revived Comintern (the Cominform or Communist Information Bureau, composed of the east European and the French and Italian communist parties) to excommunicate the Yugoslav party. He expected that Yugoslav communists would overthrow Tito and bring their country back into the Soviet fold; but this did not happen. He did not dare to invade Yugoslavia with his army, and the very independence of the state machine which had brought down Stalin's wrath enabled Tito to survive. The Yugoslav affair seemed to the rest of the world an unsuccessful thrust by Soviet imperialism. In the Soviet view, however, since it did not fit the categories laid down by Lenin, it was not imperialism. The only possible explanation was that Tito and his friends were traitors to socialism, bourgeois nationalists, and conscious or unconscious agents of capitalism.

After the death of Stalin the relationship between the Soviet Union and the east European States changed. First, the communist governments were encouraged by the Soviet leaders to rule their subjects more mildly. The biggest change was in Hungary, where Imre Nagy, appointed Prime Minister in June 1953, released many political prisoners and paid more attention to the needs of the peasants and of consumers. The removal of Nagy in April 1955 did not lead to a reversal of this policy. In the summer of 1955 Khrushchev visited Tito in Belgrade. Though he did not specifically repudiate Stalin's treatment of the Yugoslavs, his actions were clear evidence of his desire for better relations. At the twentieth congress of the CPSU in February 1956 came the denunciation of Stalin, and the attribution of the worst features of the Soviet past to the 'cult of personality'. This phrase was ritually used in the following years to explain away unpleasant facts. The un-Marxist use of Stalin as a scapegoat, in order to avoid the necessity of looking for more profound causes of degeneration within the political and social arrangements of the Soviet regime, was firmly if mildly rejected by the Italian communist leader Palmiro Togliatti already in July 1956. But the impact of even this half-sincere half-repentance in eastern Europe was enormous.

Already in 1953 the combination of accumulated economic discontent with the first communist reforms had produced disorders among the working class. In May Czech workers rioted in Plzen, and for some hours took over the whole city. On 17 June a rising of workers on a far larger scale broke out in East Berlin and other industrial centres of Eastern Germany. In 1956 the combination of popular resentment with official concessions produced similar effects. At the end of June the Polish industrial centre of Poznan was taken over by the city's workers, and in the summer months at meetings of the Petöfi Club in Budapest, a centre of Hungarian writers and other intellectuals, fierce criticism of the government was expressed.

All these outbreaks were essentially the result of discontent with internal conditions: the aim of the protests and rebellions was reform at home rather than any change in foreign relations. However, when the Poznan rebels were brought to trial, a clear divergence appeared between the Polish and Soviet communist leaders. The Polish leaders admitted that the workers had had legitimate grievances, treated the rebels leniently, and promised reforms. The Soviet communists declared that the Poznan rebellion was the work of foreign imperialist agents. Within the Polish party the desire for internal reform increasingly fused with traditional Polish hostility to Russian domination. A majority in the party demanded that Wladyslaw Gomulka, the leading victim of the anti-nationalist purge of 1949, should be appointed first secretary of the party, and that the Russian marshal Rokossovsky should be removed from the politbureau. The existing first secretary, Edward Ochab, supported the demand. When a group of Soviet leaders, headed by Khrushchev, visited Warsaw in mid-October 1956, they found not only a large majority of the Polish communist leaders, but the mass of party members, the Warsaw working class, the army and police and Polish public opinion united in opposition to them. Khrushchev decided to yield. A compromise was achieved. Rokossovsky returned to Russia, Soviet advisers were withdrawn from the Polish government services, most of Poland's economic grievances (including the compulsory sale of Polish coal to the Soviet Union at artificially low prices) were remedied, and the Polish communists were allowed to shape their own policies at their own pace. In return, the Russians were assured that the communists would maintain their one-party dictatorship over Poland. Subsequent events showed that Khrushchev acted wisely from the point of view of Soviet interests. In the following ten years the Polish government has gradually become more dictatorial, revoking many of the concessions which Gomulka had made to the people in the stormy days of October 1956. In foreign policy Poland remains the most loyal of all the Soviet Union's allies. If Stalin had given Tito what Khrushchev gave Gomulka, there would have been no breach between Moscow and Belgrade. Polish-Soviet relations since 1956, in short, are an example of successful Soviet statesmanship, of the abandonment of imperialism, and come nearer than any other example to the model of what 'relations between socialist states' ought to be.

In Hungary, too, the demand in 1956 was for internal reform, not for a change in foreign relations. A first success was won when the hated boss of the communist party, Mátyás Rákosi, was removed. But his successor, Ernö Gerö, lacked the statesmanship shown by Edward Ochab. As demands increased, he lost his nerve, and ordered the police to fire on the demonstrators. When the crowds resisted, and soldiers in uniform helped them, he appealed for Russian military aid. Within a few days the crisis had developed into a Hungarian-Russian war. Imre Nagy, the reforming communist leader who became Prime Minister, was at first unable and then even unwilling to prevent the abolition of the communist party dictatorship. His government turned into a multi-party coalition, and he asked that Hungary be allowed to secede from the alliance with the Soviet Union and adopt the kind of neutral status assured to Austria. Probably the prospect of the re-establishment of 'bourgeois democracy' in a country which had once belonged to the 'socialist camp' was at least as objectionable to the Soviet leaders as the loss of a rather minor strategic position in central Europe. Both, however, were unacceptable. Hostilities, which had been suspended for a few days' uneasy truce, were resumed. The Soviet task was facilitated by the preoccupation of the western governments with the Port Said expedition and of the United Nations with the denunciation of Anglo-French imperialism. Hungary was quickly reconquered, and experienced its third counter-revolution in a little over a hundred years. Like the Habsburgs in 1849 and the followers of Horthy in 1919, the restored communists exacted a bloody vengeance. However, in the view of the devoted Leninist, these events did not add up to imperialism. Imre Nagy had betrayed Hungary to agents of capitalism. Far from being instruments of Soviet imperialism, the Soviet soldiers had saved the Hungarian people from the horrors of capitalism and restored it to the socialist camp.

Neither in Hungary nor elsewhere (with the possible exception of Eastern Germany) was the old system of Soviet domination restored. In the following years the east European States have gradually ceased to be satellites of the Soviet Union, and have become comparatively independent. All have communist party dictatorships, never freely chosen by their own peoples, but all are ruled by their own nationals, and their policies show considerable variety. Their origins as creations of the Soviet invaders remain historical facts, but today the force which keeps them in being is local native force, not Soviet force. This change is due to a slow reassertion of national feeling within the communist parties, influenced by popular feeling outside the party. This national feeling has been enabled to assert itself partly by the genuinely more liberal policies of Khrushchev (themselves largely the result of pressure from the Soviet public), and partly by the Soviet leaders' need to pay a price for the support of the east European communist leaders in their conflict with China.

The most striking case of independence within the 'socialist camp' is Romania. The Romanian communist leaders have shown the patience and obstinacy which have always been the most outstanding features of their nation in its long and tragic history. In the economic field they made remarkable progress in the late 1950s, successfully exploiting the natural riches of the country and the intelligence and industry of its people. The pressure of the Council for Mutual Economic Aid (Comecon), which in its search for a better distribution of economic effort within the socialist camp tended to stabilize the existing divisions between the more industrial and more agricultural economies, was increasingly resented by the Romanians, whose industry, though starting from a relatively low level, had made rapid progress. In 1962 Romania flatly rejected Comecon advice. In the years since then it has achieved a greater degree of independence in foreign policy than any other east European communist-ruled State has yet attained. It has adopted a neutral attitude between the Soviet Union and China, it has taken its own line at the United Nations, and it has established good cultural and economic relations with western countries.

An unmistakably nationalist trend is visible in Romanian political life, and this nationalism has an unmistakably anti-Russian flavour. For this there are two special reasons. One is resentment at the loss of Bessarabia. This territory, which should correctly be described as Eastern Moldavia, having been a part of Moldavia for centuries, was annexed by Russia in 1812, recovered by Romania in 1918, re-annexed by the Soviet Union in 1940 and renamed the Moldavian Soviet Socialist Republic. The second and more important reason is resentment at the policy of Russification which had been forced on Romanians since 1944. Ever since their emergence as a modern nation, the Romanians have treasured their Latin language and their cultural links with France and Italy. To destroy these links was a special aim of the Soviet leaders after 1944, and the Romanian communists were obliged to carry out their wishes. French and Italian culture were derided, their Romanian exponents persecuted, and Romanians were forced to learn Russian, and to express admiration not only for Soviet socialism but for Russia past and present. In the worst period of Stalinism the Romanians, who shared with the other peoples of eastern Europe the common sufferings of totalitarian rule, were subjected to the additional miseries of Russification, a direct onslaught on their own language and cultural identity. The accumulated bitterness which this provoked accounts for the fact that, when the conflict of economic interest led the party leaders to oppose Soviet policy, anti-Russian feeling became more explicit than elsewhere in eastern Europe. In the early 1960s the Soviet government was obliged to accept the fact of a more independent Romania. Its policies of economic and cultural domination, whether or not they deserved to be called imperialist, had certainly failed.

The 'socialist' country with which the Soviet Union has had the best relations in the 1960s is Cuba. The main reason for this is no doubt the fact that there has never been any possibility of any direct exercise of Soviet power over Cuba. The process by which Cuba entered the socialist camp is of course unique. Not only was Fidel Castro accepted, despite his poor ideological qualifications, but he was allowed to take over the Cuban Communist Party. The Soviet government has shown quite extraordinary generosity and patience in its dealings with Cuba. Admittedly its experiments with ballistic installations were not a success, but the economic aid it has given to Cuba seems to have been quite expensive. In this case at least it cannot be said that there has been any Soviet imperialism: if there has been exploitation, it has been exploitation of the Soviet Union by Cuba.

Far the most important relationship between communist countries has of course been that between the Soviet Union and China. The Soviet-Chinese conflict, which became obvious to careful observers in 1959, and has grown steadily more bitter during the 1960s, has many causes. The events of 1927[19] left a legacy of distrust of the Soviet leaders among leading Chinese communists. Mao Tse-tung's experiences with Stalin in the 1930s and 1940s deepened the distrust. In the 1950s the Soviet government gave communist China little economic help, at least in comparison with Chinese needs and Soviet resources. In the last years of the decade this disparity became still more odious when the Soviet government began to grant large-scale aid to non-socialist Asian countries. The general Asian policy of the Soviet Union became increasingly distasteful to the Chinese. Moscow would give no real support to Chinese attempts to recover Formosa, or even the off-shore islands, and it refused to supply China with nuclear weapons. In its attempts to improve relations with the United States it paid no attention to Chinese needs. Worst of all, it refused to support Chinese demands on India, and gradually moved towards support of India against China. As Peking's hostility became more uninhibited in its expression, the Chinese began to make it clear that they regarded the Soviet Union as an imperialist Power, the heir to Imperial Russia. They made it clear that the unequal treaties imposed on China in the nineteenth century, some of which were still in force, included the Treaty of Peking of 1860, by which the Russian Empire had acquired not only the whole lower course and the mouth of the river Amur, but also the long maritime strip of territory south of the Amur, on the southern extremity of which the port of Vladivostok was built. There was also increasing evidence of friction between the two Powers in Central Asia, and a possibility of conflicting boundary claims in Turkestan.

These economic, strategic, and territorial conflicts are the stuff of which traditional Great Power conflicts have long been made. They are perhaps not 'imperialist' if the strictest interpretation of Lenin's doctrine is maintained, because neither government can be said to be controlled by finance-capital. But their disagreements look remarkably like the sort of disagreements which occurred between Great Powers in the era in which Lenin wrote his *Imperialism*. Certainly there is no evidence that the nature of their relations has been affected for the better by the fact that both claim to be socialist. Rather the contrary. The conflict has in fact an ideological

---

[19] See below, p. 187.

dimension which makes it still more serious. Even in Stalin's lifetime, Chinese spokesmen attributed to Mao Tse-tung a status as prophet and embodiment of Marxism-Leninism which was clearly unacceptable to the Soviet party. When Stalin died, Mao did not trouble to conceal his belief in his superiority to any living communist. In 1958 the Chinese party made the astonishing claim that, by its adoption of the institution of the People's Commune, it was so rapidly accelerating its advance towards the achievement of communism that it would reach it within a few years, by implication sooner than the Soviet Union. This pretension was later allowed to lapse, but as the dispute between the two Powers grew more open and more bitter, the denunciation of the Soviet leaders as 'modern revisionists' who had betrayed Leninism, and of their country as an ally of American imperialism, took on a markedly nationalist, if not indeed racialist tone.

Whether the ideological, economic, or strategic-political causes of the conflict are the earlier, or the more fundamental, is a matter of opinion, and cannot be demonstrated. But it seems permissible to conclude that they have been fused into an overall consuming hatred on both sides. Indeed, it may be argued that conflicts between communist States are in fact likely to become more serious than conflicts between capitalist States, simply because all disagreements tend to acquire an ideological character, and all conflicts to turn into total conflicts.

Communism, Imperialism, and New States

The Communist International devoted increasing attention from the 1920s onwards to the struggles of colonial and semi-colonial peoples against imperialism. The influence of communists in strictly colonial situations, where an Asian or African people was directly ruled by a European Power, has been small, though it was greater in Asia between the wars than in Africa after the Second World War. In semi-colonial situations communists have been a much more significant factor. Important cases were Turkey and China in the 1920s, and there have been successes in Latin America since the Second World War. Since the 1950s a third type of situation has become far more important. The main effort of communist parties and communist governments, in connection with what they regard as the world-wide struggle against imperialism, has been concerned with the 'new States' that have arisen in Asia and Africa since the disintegration of the old empires.

The first colonial territory in which communists made themselves felt was the Netherlands East Indies. Indonesian communism was derived from Dutch socialism, and its founder was a Dutchman named Hendrik Sneevliet. He was responsible for the co-operation between the communists and the Javanese nationalist movement Sarekat Islam. This body, originally anti-Chinese and concerned with rather narrow commercial and religious interests, grew into a moderately anti-Dutch and democratic mass movement. In 1918 the local Communist Party entered Sarekat Islam as a body, while retaining its own ideology and its allegiance to the international communist movement. But the two organizations were divided by too serious differences to remain united: in October 1921 the communists seceded. They continued in the following years to preach both class struggle and nationalist resistance to the Dutch, and in 1926 they led an armed rising in Java, and in early 1927 another in Sumatra. The Dutch government repressed the revolts and broke up the organization of the party. However, communism continued to appeal to the Javanese intelligentsia. During the Japanese occupation from 1942 to 1945 communists were active in the underground resistance movement, and in independent Indonesia after 1950 they emerged as one of the leading parties.

In India Marxism appealed to the radical intelligentsia, especially in Bengal, in the years immediately after the First World War. One Indian Marxist, M. N. Roy, was for some years a leading figure in Comintern affairs, in Mexico and China. The British Communist Party was the main channel by which communist ideas and organization spread in India. During the 1920s the communists built up a substantial following among the intellectual youth and in some trade unions, though they remained a small group in relation to the nationalist movement as a whole. In the late 1930s the Popular Front strategy and the idea of a world-wide struggle against fascism made communism very attractive to young Indians. The communists, however, lost support when, acting on directives from the Soviet government after Hitler's invasion of the Soviet Union, they urged co-operation in the British war effort, at a time when Congress, and Gandhi himself, were calling on the British to quit India, and carrying out civil disobedience.

In Indochina communism was introduced by French communists, and by Vietnamese who had lived in France. Outstanding among the latter was Nguyen Ai Quoc, who later became known as Ho Chi Minh. Communists were involved in a rising against the French in 1930. During the Second World War Vietnamese communists played a leading part in the resistance to the Japanese. Before French authority was temporarily restored in 1945, communism had become a powerful force.

Essentially the appeal of communism in colonies in Asia was to the intelligentsia, above all to students and university graduates. The centres in which these men learned to become communists were the metropolitan capitals—London, Paris, and Amsterdam. In addition to Asians, some Negro intellectuals from both the British and the French West Indies became converted to communism in western capitals, and a very small number of Africans were influenced to some extent. Apart from the three western metropolitan cities, Berlin was also an important centre as the headquarters of the League against Imperialism, founded at a conference in Brussels in February 1927. Many non-communist radical nationalists as well as communists were involved in the League's activities, which were essentially propagandist. Among them were Jawaharlal Nehru and Muhammad Hatta, who became Vice-President of independent Indonesia after 1950.

After the Second World War, as the numbers of the politically conscious intelligentsia in Africa rapidly increased, and as more Africans came to study in London, in Paris, and in American cities, they too became acquainted with Marxism, and some became communists. However, the influence of communism was even smaller in the African nationalist movements than it had been in Asian movements between the wars. Perhaps the main reason was that the metropolitan governments offered so much less resistance, and used much less severe methods of repression, than had been the case in Asia. The struggle evoked less bitterness, and there was less need for revolutionary methods or revolutionary mystique. In the Arab world, too, communist influence was small. Here of course there was plenty of bitterness, especially in Algeria. But communism in Algeria was essentially a French movement, based on the large resident French working class and free professions. The French communists' attitude was ambivalent: they supported revolutionary action directed against the French ruling class, but disliked efforts to remove Algeria from the political and cultural orbit of France. In the National Liberation Front which led the Algerian Moslems to victory, communist influence was minimal, though a quasi-Marxist ideology was widespread.

In the semi-colonial countries communism was more successful, for the peoples of these countries were politically and culturally more developed, and had a stronger national feeling, than the peoples of the colonies. Yet communism suffered from an insoluble contradiction. The leaders of the nationalist movements in these countries came from the upper social strata—army officers, bureaucrats, merchants, and landowners. They wished to end foreign domination of their countries, but they certainly did not wish for social revolution: even land reform and labour legislation were unacceptable to them. Any communist movement must fight these upper classes. Yet the hostility of the nationalist movements, led by these classes, to the western imperialist Powers who were unfriendly towards the Soviet Union, made them valuable allies for Soviet policy. The Soviet government therefore supported such movements, and the Comintern provided ideological justification, in Marxist-Leninist terms, for Soviet policy. It was hoped that the communists would be able to increase their strength during the national struggle, and eventually take control of it.

Soviet support for Kemalist Turkey proved advantageous to both parties, but the Turkish communists paid the bill. Kemal suppressed them pitilessly, and for the next forty years communism was negligible in Turkey, even among the intelligentsia. In Persia there was slightly more support, and this was encouraged by temporary Soviet occupation of the Caspian province of Ghilan in 1921. The Persian communists were however repressed by the military dictator Reza Khan, who later proclaimed himself Shah. Modelling himself to some extent on Kemal, he combined ruthless repression with internal reforms, and maintained good relations with the Soviet Union. While he was in charge, communism made no progress. When he was overthrown by the joint Anglo-Soviet invasion in 1941, the Persian communists got a new lease of life in the zone of Soviet occupation. But the international balance of power was unfavourable to the Soviet Union in this region after the war, Soviet troops were withdrawn from northern Persia, and the communists were repressed by the new Shah, Muhammed Reza. Distrust of Russia as an imperialist neighbour, derived from Persian experience of the Tsars but reinforced by Soviet action in Persian Azerbaidjan in 1945-6, limited the communists' opportunities. Their party failed to make use for its own ends of the upsurge of anti-western nationalism in 1951-3 under Mossadeq, and was once more repressed after Mossadeq had been overthrown. Nevertheless the Persian communists (Tudeh or Masses' Party) remained a force to be reckoned with.

By far the most important of the semi-colonial countries between the wars was China. Here Marxism made a rapid and profound appeal to a section of the intelligentsia, which was reinforced by the blow to Chinese hopes and claims inflicted by the western Powers at the time of the Versailles peace conference. It appeared to combine a mastery of western scientific thought with implacable hostility to the western capitalist system which had bullied China for so long. It offered Chinese intellectuals the fruits of western science together with the emotional satisfaction of hating the West. It promised victory over the West by the use of western intellectual strength. A group of Chinese intellectuals formed the Communist Party of China in 1921, and soon obtained a nucleus of mass support in the working class of Shanghai and among the workers on the Chinese railways.

Meanwhile the Comintern had established relations with the Kuomintang, the non-communist radical nationalist movement, founded by Sun Yat-sen and based on the southern city of Canton. In August 1922 the Dutch communist Sneevliet, who appeared as the emissary of the Comintern under the name of Maring, persuaded the Chinese communists to adopt towards the Kuomintang the same tactics that the Indonesian communists, on his advice, had adopted towards Sarekat Islam: to enter it as a group while retaining their own ideology and organization. The Kuomintang accepted this Trojan horse. During the next years, communists obtained considerable influence within the Chinese nationalist movement. They were trained as army officers, and rose within the Kuomintang party hierarchy. Their influence spread in the trade unions and the peasant associations. Nevertheless, communists and nationalists distrusted each other. When Sun Yat-sen died, his successor, General Chiang Kai-shek, was definitely hostile to the communists. Soviet advisers had difficulty in overcoming the bitter conflicts which broke out between the two groups. The crisis was temporarily postponed by the decision that the nationalist armies, including the communists, should march northwards to the Yangtse valley in 1926. The march was successful, but it was followed by the final breach between Kuomintang and communists, marked by the massacre of communist workers in Shanghai.

The Chinese communist tragedy of 1927 was the occasion for the last phase of the struggle of Trotsky against Stalin in Russia, and it has been the subject of a vast controversial literature. Whether, if the Comintern and the Soviet government had been led by Lenin and Trotsky at the height of their powers, a communist revolution could have been successful in China; whether bold revolutionary mass action among workers and peasants could have destroyed the Kuomintang and the war lords, and defied all intervention by the Great Powers, no one will ever be able to say with certainty. What is certain is that the directives sent to the Chinese communists by the Comintern—that is, by Stalin—were woefully unrealistic, that they denied them the means either of trying revolution or of defending themselves against Kuomintang attack. It is equally certain that the basic reason for Stalin's failure was his inability to choose between a social revolution against the Chinese ruling classes and a nationalist movement which was hostile to the Soviet Union's enemy Britain. By trying to please both revolutionaries and nationalists, by trying to solve real conflicts with verbal slogans, he lost on both counts. The Chinese communists suffered terrible casualties, but they were not destroyed: the remnant never forgave the Soviet leaders, and the consequences were seen in the relations between the two communist parties thirty years later. As for the Kuomintang, they turned completely against the Soviet Union, which they believed had treated them with complete dishonesty: instead, they came to terms with the western imperialist Powers, cleverly using the communist bogey to raise their price.

The appearance of the first 'new States' in Asia after the Second World War did not impress Stalin. In the official Soviet view these States were no more than fictions. The British Empire was continuing under a new name; Nehru was a mere agent of British imperialism, U Nu of Burma little if any better. One is tempted to guess that Stalin took seriously the talk about the British Commonwealth of Nations, that he saw their future in the same way as his wartime acquaintance and admirer, Lord Beaverbrook. Of his contemptuous hostility there can be no doubt. As for Indonesia, the Soviet Union strongly supported the nationalists' cause against the Dutch at the United Nations, but when independence came, it too was dismissed as a fraud. Clearly Sukarno was no agent of the Dutch, but he and his friends had merely changed masters by accepting the protection of the United States. The general communist line in these years was revolution against the new regimes. In 1948 there were communist armed rebellions in independent India, Burma, the Philippines, as well as in half-independent Indonesia and colonial Malaya. The communist-led revolutionary movement in Indochina was of course of much earlier origin: it was a result of wartime resistance to the Japanese and post-war conflict between French and Vietnamese, in neither of which external communist influences had played more than a subsidiary part.

The events of the next few years hardly confirmed Stalin's view, but he does not appear to have changed it. The attitude of India to the Korean war, and the deteriorating relations between independent Indonesia and the West, seem to have passed almost unnoticed in the Soviet Union. The Chinese, however, were more perceptive. The Peking government courted Nehru's India, and began to assume, with great propaganda success, a posture of ideological moderation and of sympathy for every variety of Asian nationalism that was directed against 'the imperialists'. This attitude was the counterpart in foreign relations to the strategy which the Chinese communists were then pursuing in internal politics. This was a new version of the old Comintern strategy of 'united front from below'. The communists claimed to be leading a broad front of social forces which included not only workers and peasants but also a large part of the bourgeoisie. They even claimed that they represented the interests of the capitalists. The criterion was to be neither class nor ideology, but solely willingness to join an 'anti-imperialist', that is to say, an anti-American and anti-west European movement. Those who were willing, counted as the 'national bourgeoisie'.

Even after Stalin's death the Soviet leaders paid little attention to these issues: the reason was probably their absorption in the internal struggle for power, and to a lesser extent their preoccupation with the problems arising out of the 'new course' in eastern Europe and the complexities of the German problem. The potentialities of Asian non-communist nationalism were however strikingly demonstrated by the Bandung Conference of April 1955, at which Chou

En-lai was the outstanding personality. In the next months Khrushchev gave a high priority to Asian and Middle Eastern affairs. In
the autumn came the loans to Egypt for the purchase of armaments
and the visit of Khrushchev and Bulganin to India and Burma.
In 1956 the loudly proclaimed threats of Khrushchev to use Soviet
rockets against the Anglo-French aggressors in the conflict with
Egypt (he was himself engaged in conquering and repressing Hungary at the time) greatly increased Soviet prestige in Asia. A year
later it rose still further when Soviet spokesmen proclaimed their
intention to defend Syria against a non-existent danger of Turkish
aggression. In these years economic aid from the Soviet Union, and
from the more advanced east European communist countries, made
its appearance. Soviet and Chinese policies appeared to be in harmony. It was not until 1959 that public disagreements between them
about relations with Asian nationalist movements appeared.

In these years there was much discussion in communist publications, especially in the Soviet Union, of the role of the 'national
bourgeoisie'. The category was never satisfactorily defined. 'Bourgeoisie' in communist literature is a confusing word. At times it
simply means the business class, at others it includes the two other
middle classes—the government servants, or civil and military
bureaucracy, and the unofficial professional classes or intelligentsia.
Soviet writers have always appeared to be confused about the role
of these three distinct groups in the social and political life of Asian
countries, and even in the earlier history of their own Russia.
In most of these cases the business class has played a very limited
role in politics: even when it has provided funds to political movements, it has not necessarily controlled, or even clearly understood,
their actions. The bureaucracy, in colonial regimes and in conservative regimes of semi-colonial countries, was the politically dominant
force. In colonies its higher ranks were mainly filled by Europeans,
but among those indigenous officials who rose to high positions there
were also persons of nationalist, and even some of radical anti-
imperialist outlook. The intelligentsia was the social group from
which the most active political leaders came. In the struggle for
independence the intelligentsia played an outstanding part. After
independence, many members of the intelligentsia became ruling
politicians or bureaucrats. The bureaucracy changed its character:
instead of being an inert force carrying out the will of the colonial
Power, or of a semi-colonial regime dependent on foreigners, it was

the most active force for change, but its effectiveness was limited by the fact that it was composed of a mixture of former active nationalists from the radical intelligentsia with professional trained bureaucrats of the old regime. This was especially the case in India, where before independence the relationship between Indian members of the Indian Civil Service and Indian nationalists had been a strange mixture of mutual respect, toleration, and distrust, and where after independence many members of the ICS remained in office.

Soviet writings on Asian nationalism seldom distinguish between these groups, and if the experts in such periodicals as *Sovetskoe Vostokovedenie* did not make them clear it is likely that the communist party officials and policy-makers who relied on them did not understand either. Sometimes they mentioned the 'national intelligentsia' as a separate category, sometimes they included it in the 'national bourgeoisie'. Published communist discussions about the national bourgeoisie in the narrower sense, confined to the business class, did not succeed in differentiating it in any significant way. The attempt to divide the Indian business class into big, medium, and small, according to the arbitrary income categories of over 100,000 rupees, 10,000 to 100,000, and under 10,000, and to equate these three groups with significantly different political attitudes, brought no enlightenment. Some big capitalists in the Philippines were found to be objectively progressive because they were anti-American, although neither their business practices nor their treatment of their workers could be commended. It is not unfair to sum up these discussions by saying that the communist experts were looking for a category of capitalists who could be induced to support anti-American action in Asia, and ended up by concluding that the most promising capitalist opponents of America would be those capitalists who were anti-American.

During these years a certain amount of communist theory about the new States was formulated. There was one group of States which considered themselves independent, but maintained alliances with the United States or its European allies (in CENTO and SEATO). These States were not independent at all. To ally oneself with the United States automatically meant the loss of independence. The independence of such countries as Pakistan, Thailand, or Iran, was purely fictitious. A second group were States which were allied with neither the western nor the communist States. These possessed 'political independence', but they had not yet achieved 'economic independence'. Western business enterprises still functioned on their territory, and in many cases had enormous wealth and power, and trade was principally with the West. To this group belonged, around 1960, India, Indonesia, Burma, Egypt, and the larger and more advanced republics of Latin America. They would attain 'economic independence' when western businesses had been taken over by the State, and when their trade was principally with the socialist camp. Soviet writers gave faint praise to the state capitalism of India. Soviet aid and advice should help the Indian government to develop its state sector at the expense of both Indian and foreign private capital. However, the claims of the governments of new States that they were building socialism must be vigorously denied. They were building state capitalism, in the interests of the bureaucrats and other elements of the national bourgeoisie. Socialism could be built only by the working class, after a socialist revolution. This might be brought about by 'parliamentary means', without using violence to seize power, as in Czechoslovakia in 1948, but it must be followed by a dictatorship of the proletariat, wielded by a Marxist-Leninist party. This was clearly stated in the Moscow Declaration of the communist parties of November 1957.

These discussions and theoretical formulations have not been able to overcome the inherent contradiction between the two aims of strengthening bourgeois nationalism against western imperialism and of promoting the violent overthrow of bourgeois nationalist governments by communist-led revolution. The issues of 1927 in China are still alive. They were recalled in the article by Yu Chao-li in *Red Flag* of 1 April 1959, strongly criticizing Soviet policy towards new States, in the form of an attack on the Egyptian and Iraqi governments,which were then repressing their communist parties. These governments were compared with that of Chiang Kai-shek in 1927, and the parallel between Stalin's support of Chiang in 1927 and Soviet support of Nasser and Kassem in 1959 was clearly present in the writer's mind, though he did not make it explicit. The conflict between the Soviet and Chinese communists, which became acute at the end of the 1950s, had, as we have seen, many other causes. But the problem of relations with the new States played a large part in the polemics of the following years. The essence of the disagreement in this field was not a question of theoretical strategy: it was Chinese jealousy of Soviet support to India. However, there were genuine differences. The Chinese essentially stood for 'united front from below,' while the Soviet government was in practice much closer to a 'united front from above'. The Chinese were willing to assist traditionalist governments in Morocco and Yemen, and actively to help the struggle for independence of the Algerian FLN, which was neither led nor infiltrated by communists. But they were not willing to support in power a bourgeois nationalist government which kept communists out, or even repressed them. They also insisted on the need for the use of force to obtain power, and attributed far more importance than the Russians to the role of guerrilla warfare.

During the 1960s the centre of interest has passed from Asia to Africa. The first African new State, Ghana, appeared at the start to offer unpromising ground for communist action, as its relations with its former rulers and with the West in general were good. The same was true of the French African States which received independence in 1959, with the single exception of Guinea. The quarrel between Sekou Touré and General de Gaulle, brought about by inflexible attitudes and preoccupation with prestige on both sides, gave the Soviet Union and its allies opportunities. The situation was transformed by the events in the Congo in 1960. The continuing anarchy and tribal warfare, the activities of the United Nations forces and the white mercenaries, the accusations and counter-accusations enormously increased the volume of race hatred. In the first instance, the attempts of the Soviet Union to interfere in the Congo were unsuccessful, but the atmosphere was favourable to its long-term aims. The political climate in which the next stages of decolonization took place in British Africa, especially in East Africa, was marked by widespread distrust and hatred. In these years the conflicts in South Africa rapidly grew more bitter, there were serious rebellions on Portuguese territory, and the Rhodesian crisis proved insoluble.

During these years the Soviet government encouraged its academic experts to study Africa, and made efforts to train specialists in African political affairs. These efforts were reflected in the specialized Soviet press, and to some extent in communist publications in other countries. The chief exponent was I. I. Potekhin, a Soviet specialist on modern Africa who was at the same time an academic and a political figure. His writings are extremely interesting, as one can see in them the honest but confused attempt of a Marxist-Leninist to explain African reality, as well as to recommend tactics for communist action. Potekhin admitted that 'bourgeois nations, (as defined in the Stalin article of 1913) did not exist in Africa. Frontiers had been drawn arbitrarily by European colonial rulers, cutting across tribal and linguistic boundaries. Consequently the new States had been faced with some difficult frontier disputes and with tribal irredentism which recalled the national irredentism of modern Balkan history. For example, the Ewe people were divided between Ghana and Togoland, the Bakongo between the two Congo republics and Angola, and the Somalis between Somalia, Ethiopia, and Kenya. Following the teaching of Lenin and Stalin, itself a result of the historical experience of European Russia and eastern Europe, Potekhin attributed to language a leading role in the formation of national consciousness. He argued that European colonial rulers had artificially increased the number of languages in Africa, in order to play off groups against each other and to prevent the formation of a modern national consciousness. He claimed that a fairly small number of widely spoken languages could be developed, by the elimination of dialects, into standardized literary languages for large countries, and that this would help the formation of large nations. For example, from the various Nilotic languages spoken by peoples inhabiting the Sudan, Congo, Uganda, and Kenya, a single Nilotic language might be created. 'It is by no means out of the question that in favourable conditions the Nilotics may be able to form themselves into a single people'. It is interesting to note that the aim which he attributed to the European colonizers was precisely that of the Soviet rulers in Central Asia: they had fostered multiplicity of basically similar Turkic dialects, elevating them into separate languages. The policy which Potekhin advocated for African language groups was that which the Soviet rulers of Central Asia had rejected: they had opposed the development of a single Turkestan language, which might have provided the foundation of a single Turkestan national consciousness. The long-term prospects of political exploitation by communists of African languages might indeed seem bright.

Potekhin also had interesting things to say about African class structures. In tropical Africa the predominant form of society was neither feudal nor capitalist, but tribal. The national bourgeoisie consisted only of very small capitalists. For the system of land tenure found in much of Africa, Potekhin used the word *obshchina*, employed in Russian historical literature for the traditional

Russian peasant commune, which had bulked so large in the controversies of the 1880s between Russian Marxists and Populists. The Russian Marxists had then insisted that the commune must disappear as capitalism advanced in the countryside, and that only after the advent of capitalism could a socialist revolution take place. The Populists claimed that the commune, if controlled by socialists, could be made the instrument of a socialist society. Potekhin, in an article published in January 1962, adopted essentially the Populist position. The colonial Powers, he argued, had sought to replace communal tenure by private ownership of land, and the rising national bourgeoisie in the new States was also in favour of private ownership. However, 'for the absolute majority of the peasantry the adoption of private ownership of land means in the immediate future the loss of their land and final ruin. The most progressive representatives of African society express themselves in favour of maintaining the commune, regarding it as one of the means which can facilitate the transition to socialism'. For some time Soviet writers had accepted the possibility of a society moving directly from feudalism to socialism, bypassing capitalism: now Potekhin was advocating a jump from tribalism to socialism, bypassing feudalism as well. The only possible instrument to bring such a change about would of course be a disciplined communist elite, to be formed from the same source as the Russian communist elite was formed sixty years earlier, the intelligentsia and skilled workers. Potekhin and other Soviet writers always stressed the need for leadership by 'the working class', by which was of course meant the communist party. But in tropical Africa a working class was virtually non-existent. A promising partial exception was the Sudan, where already under British rule a small nucleus had been formed around a trade union movement, composed essentially of railwaymen, clerks, and students, in which communists were dominant. In the independent Sudan the communist party played a part much larger than its numbers alone would suggest.

There is however one country in Africa where a real African industrial working class exists, the Republic of South Africa. The periodical published by its exiles in London, *The African Communist*, adopted a more orthodox Marxist line than Potekhin. An article in 1962 by N. Numade argued that even before the advent of the Europeans, African tribal societies had begun to dissolve, and class differentiation had begun. 'Colonialism hastened and completed this process. It shattered and disrupted, once and for all, our tribal economy and its institutions'. It was an illusion 'that tribal institutions and relations are suitable for, or can be adapted to the needs of, a complicated, changing and advanced economy'. It might of course be argued that Numade was right about South Africa, but that Potekhin was right about the tropical countries. But Numade maintained that his view was valid throughout Africa. His article was largely a reply to the statement of Julius Nyerere that 'with rare exceptions, the idea of class is something entirely foreign to Africa'. The Soviet leaders wished to avoid the necessity of sharp dogmatic pronouncements. Potekhin and others had refused to accept at its own valuation the 'African socialism' professed by various African leaders. They insisted that the only 'scientific socialism' was Marxism-Leninism. However, they did not wish to offend these men by insulting polemics: they preferred to use them for the purposes of revolution. But the uncompromising attitude expressed by Numade was bound to appeal to many sophisticated members of the African radical intelligentsia, and the competition of the Chinese communists, with their claim to be more revolutionary and to be better Marxist-Leninists than the Soviet leaders, was bound to strengthen it.

In 1960 the Soviet leaders introduced the formula of the 'State of national democracy'. This was held out as a model for 'progressive forces' in Asia, Africa, and Latin America. It was to be a regime intermediate between a regime of the national bourgeoisie (such as India) and a regime of people's democracy (such as the east European countries after 1948). There were four main points that were to differentiate the national-democratic from the national-bourgeois State. Its economic links with the socialist camp must be more important than with the West, and the influence of western business interests in its economy must be greatly reduced or eliminated. Its foreign policy must not be neutral, but must support the policies of the socialist camp. It must carry out a number of radical social reforms, especially a land reform of the type earlier adopted by communist governments. Finally, the working class—that is, the communist party—must enjoy complete liberty of action, and must exercise a considerable measure of real power, whether or not the communist party were formally represented in the government. This concept was first formulated in the Moscow Declaration of the twelve ruling communist parties in December 1960, and was elaborated in the Soviet press in the following months. Cuba was cited as the best example of a State of national democracy, and those States which were noted as moving in this direction were Indonesia, Ghana, Guinea, and Mali.

The State of national democracy did not prove satisfactory either in theory or in practice. Cuba developed too fast. It became in fact a 'people's democracy', and its attractiveness to non-communists correspondingly diminished. On the other hand some of the new States, while pursuing internal and foreign policies which were in principle acceptable to the Soviet leaders, became embarrassing by their insistence on promoting revolutionary action abroad on their own, without any tutelage by communists. Indeed the same years which saw the development of communist polycentrism, with Moscow and Peking as major centres and with the Cuban and Italian parties virtually independent, also saw the establishment of centres of revolution in other countries: Egypt, Algeria, Ghana, and Indonesia were the most important, but Guinea, Mali, and Tanzania might perhaps be included. All were centres for revolutionary movements directed not only against hostile neighbour countries (this is of course a traditional feature of statecraft for centuries past), but also against distant lands. The motivation of the help given to such activities was not conventional state interest, but ideological principle. The enemies were also the enemies of the communists, and the immediate aims of the actions were more or less acceptable to the Soviet government. However, the ideologies (Panafricanism, Nasakom, or New Emerging Forces) were distinct from Marxism-Leninism, and the recklessness and inexperience of the operators were liable to involve the Soviet government in embarrassing situations which it could not control. This proliferation of revolution-mongering looked as if it would be a growing menace not only to the imperialists but to the socialist camp as well, and indeed to world peace. However, in 1965 and 1966 the regimes of Ben Bella in Algeria, Sukarno in Indonesia, and Nkrumah in Ghana were overthrown. Nasser in Egypt remains, but he has his troubles. The Soviet government seems eager to strengthen him. Egyptian communists are urged to join his party and influence it from within, but not to attack it, and Soviet diplomacy makes strenuous efforts to bring Egypt into close cooperation with Syria, in which since the *coup d'état* of February 1966 the communists have become an important factor. The success of this policy remains doubtful.

It recalls Sneevliet–Maring's policy of communist infiltration of Sarekat Islam and Kuomintang. The basic contradiction between international political aims and internal revolutionary aims remains essentially unresolved.

Fifty years after

Any objective assessment of the impact of the Bolshevik Revolution is made more difficult by the messianic claims and apocalyptic style which mark most Soviet writing on the subject. Lenin's seizure of power in Petrograd was the Great October Socialist Revolution, introducing the fourth decisive stage in human history, the age of socialism, dividing the history of the human race in two by an event more significant than the birth of Christ. This great event was the work of the Russian working class, 'the most revolutionary working class' in history, and of the greatest human genius in history, V. I. Lenin. Yet, however great the merits of the Russian workers and of Lenin, the great event was no mere achievement by a handful of men. It was an ineluctable necessity, the culmination of historical processes transcending human will. Thereafter, the tempo of human progress had rapidly accelerated. Exploitation of man by man had disappeared in the Soviet Union. Led by the CPSU, whose 'general line' was always scientifically correct (though most of its leaders were either saboteurs, traitors, and agents of capitalism, or instruments of a 'cult of personality' which had its origin, not in any defect of the system, but in the personal character of one man), the Soviet Union achieved material and spiritual heights hitherto unknown. The different peoples of the Soviet Union were transformed into socialist nations, united with each other in brotherly love. Not a trace of imperialist sin was to be found in the Soviet Union's relations with other States. Inspired exclusively by love of peace and justice, the Soviet Union repulsed the attacks and the threats of the imperialists and offered a radiant example to all the nations of the world.

Any external comment is bound to be sacrilegious. It is not pleasant to find oneself in a position where one cannot speak, even in praise, without defiling a sacred shrine. It would be so much more pleasant if one could discuss these matters in normal language with Soviet colleagues. The Revolution of November 1917 was, after all, one of the greatest events in history, and its greatness does not need to be proved by dressing it up in apocalyptic verbiage.

Yet unfortunately, this is the state of affairs produced by Soviet propaganda. Any one outside the shrine, who uses his independent judgment, must be prepared to face the consequent odium.

It cannot seriously be maintained that the communists have made any original contribution to the diagnosis and analysis of nationalism. Stalin's famous article, which reflected Lenin's thought, tells us very little. It is true that many nations are communities which share a language, a territory, economic interests, and a common psychological make-up. The fourth characteristic of course requires further analysis; as stated, it explains nothing. The other three are usually, but certainly not always, present. The complicated historical process of the formation of national consciousness, and the roles of religion and of the state machine, of which an enormous variety of examples are available to the historian, or even to the day-to-day observer of modern politics, were ignored. Yet the Stalin article was for several decades held up as the ultimate expression of wisdom on the subject. Since Stalin's reputation has been deflated, it has been less emphasized, but it has not been abandoned, as it is well known that Lenin himself was concerned with its formulation. Official communist theory about nationalism still owes much to Stalin, is still, one might say, weighed down by the mental fetters he imposed. It was interesting to see, in the writings of the late Professor Potekhin on Africa, the efforts of an intelligent and enquiring mind to free itself from this *damnosa hereditas*.

The contribution of communists to the practical handling of nationalist problems has been little more original than their contribution to theory. The first errors were due to inexperience, but after some decades communists showed themselves skilful in the manipulation of nationalist ambitions. Yet this is no new contribution to human happiness or world peace: essentially the communists are using the same skills formerly displayed by imperial diplomacy, showing themselves in their Balkan and Danubian enterprises to be worthy pupils of Aehrenthal or Izvolsky.

One should perhaps take more seriously the claim to have created new 'socialist nations' in the Soviet Union, especially in Asia. The manipulation of the languages of the Central Asian peoples, in order to create distinct nations among the large amorphous Moslem mass of Turki speech, was a substantial achievement. Yet even this was less original than it appears at first sight. The Russian Orthodox Bishop N. I. Ilminsky (1822–91), the friend of

K. P. Pobedonostsev, used the same techniques in his dealings with the small Finno-Ugrian peoples of the Volga valley. Admittedly, he did not do so well, but he did not have the whole power of a modern totalitarian State behind him.

As for the claim that the peoples of the Soviet Union are now socialist nations, different in kind from bourgeois nations, this is yet another example of the arbitrary treatment by the Bolsheviks of the time factor. After 1905 Lenin believed that a long interval would be required between the bourgeois revolution (which still had to be accomplished in Russia) and the socialist revolution. This long interval would be necessary, in order that the polarization of peasant society between a rural bourgeoisie and a rural proletariat should be completed, and the necessary ally of the urban working class should be available. But in 1917, seeing his practical opportunity, he suddenly announced that the time for the socialist revolution had come. The social-economic processes were ignored, the struggle for power was on. Again, in the 1920s both Lenin and Stalin had declared that a long period would be required before a socialist government could create socialism in backward Russia. But after a few years of forced collectivization of peasants and mobilization of labour for industry and construction, Stalin decided that socialism had been achieved. What existed in the Soviet Union *was* socialism: the 1936 Constitution proclaimed it. Similarly the Kazakhs, Kirgiz, Turkmens, Kara-Kalpaks, and Tadjiks, who in the 1920s had not been any sort of nation, bourgeois or feudal or whatever, were declared in the 1940s to be socialist nations. This may perhaps be called the Humpty-Dumpty principle of social development[20]: it does not appear to have much to do with Marxist-Leninist science.

That Lenin's *Imperialism* contains true and penetrating comments on the type of conquest of weak nations by strong States, and of rivalry between strong States for the domination of weak nations, which characterized international relations at the end of the nineteenth and the beginning of the twentieth century, it would be absurd to deny. Even if Lenin obtained most of his facts and arguments from earlier writers, his pamphlet remains a brilliant achievement. But too much has been claimed for his theory. If there were no more to imperialism than Lenin saw, then it would have sufficed

---

[20] 'When I use a word,' Humpty Dumpty said in rather a scornful tone, 'it means just what I choose it to mean—neither more nor less.'

to remove the causes he identified in order to abolish the phenomenon itself. Certainly there is no finance-capitalism to be found within any of the States which have had communist governments since the 1950s. Yet the relations between these States have frequently been marked by attempts to impose or to resist domination, and by rivalry for control over third parties. As for the relations between Russians and non-Russians within the Soviet Union, it remains a matter for argument whether the imperial and colonial relationships have been abolished. There is of course no doubt that the material conditions of the Central Asian peoples have improved immensely by comparison with those of fifty years ago. This may however prove only that the Soviet Russian empire has conferred benefits on its subjects, not that it has ceased to be an empire.

But if the Leninists have not revolutionized the understanding of nationalism or imperialism, and have not removed either of these persistent causes of international conflict, this does not mean that the Bolshevik Revolution has not affected the operation of these forces. It has in fact affected them in two ways.

Firstly, it has profoundly affected the balance of power in the world to the advantage of nationalist forces in Asia, Africa, and Latin America. The Bolshevik Revolution removed from the European colonialist community the huge territory of Russia. For many years Russia remained weak, after all that it had suffered; but gradually the old resources were revived and new resources were added, and an enormous military and industrial Power emerged, vowed to implacable hostility towards the colonial Powers. This fact would have been a source of encouragement to nationalist movements in the colonies and in semi-colonial countries even if it had not been reinforced by the emotional impact of the Soviet myth, by the belief in the Soviet Union as a promised land of social and national equality—a belief accepted, as we have seen, by many members of the Asian and African intelligentsias who were not communists. Admittedly, other protectors also appeared, who at first seemed to offer more to some Asian nationalists than did the Soviet Union. The hopes of Arab nationalists in the 1930s were placed in Hitler's Germany and Mussolini's Italy, and the Burmese and Javanese nationalists owed their successes to the support of Japanese imperialism. But with the destruction of Hitler, the Soviet Union remained the main champion. All who showed themselves to be irreconcilable enemies of the European colonial Powers, and of their new protector the United States, were welcomed by the Soviet leaders, whether they had previously been democrats or nazis or exponents of the Greater East Asia Co-Prosperity Sphere. For a time the United States, whose comparatively modest imperial efforts in the Philippines and the Caribbean were outweighed by its long tradition of anti-colonialist rhetoric, proved attractive as a patron. But the Soviet leaders and communist parties for two decades were fairly successful in outbidding the United States with the Afro-Asian and Latin American nationalists, until they themselves began to be outbidden by the Chinese.

Soviet might and Soviet hostility to the West have indeed been an inspiration to many nationalists. Many who were never Leninists were nevertheless attracted by the Soviet myth, by the mixture of truth and fiction about the new society and the new brotherhood of nations. The very fact that western spokesmen so fiercely denounced the Soviet system, seemed the best proof that the communists were telling the truth. It was in London and Paris that Asians and Africans were converted to communism: the insults of Battersea landladies were perhaps more potent than the blandishments of the Communist Party of Great Britain.

Now, in the late 1960s, things are changing. African students have met with insults in Soviet and Balkan cities. Asian and African governments have found Soviet diplomats and engineers less different from their 'imperialist' counterparts than they had expected. Chinese denunciations of the Soviet Union as an accomplice of the United States have had some effect. Perhaps most important, it is becoming clear to all that the situation in the sub-tropical and tropical zones of the world is too complex to be explained by ritual hate campaigns against northern or southern white men. Soviet diplomacy can not keep out of conflicts between Asian States, in which white capitalist governments are marginally or not at all involved. Areas of bitter race hatred have appeared in which the white race is not a factor. The conflicts between Arabs and Negroes in the Sudan, between Indians and Negroes in Guyana, and between Malays and Chinese throughout the eastern archipelagoes of Asia, can not be solved by denouncing western imperialism, and can not be ignored by communists.

In Yugoslavia between 1941 and 1945 the communists bravely faced the national problem. At the risk of derision and hostility, they opposed all national hatred and preached fraternal unity against a common enemy. The facts proved them right, and the derision turned to acceptance of their leadership. Communists in the 1960s face a similar challenge in South Africa. Their aim of a common struggle by all races against a common enemy is treated with scorn by white and black racialists alike. The prospects of their struggle are most uncertain. But at least the South African communists have a policy about racialism: most communist parties, and the leaders of the Soviet Union itself, seem to be struggling fitfully against a tide that is sweeping them away.

The second main influence of communism on the problem of imperialism has been its impact on the peoples of the former metropolitan countries. Here the influence, direct and indirect, of Lenin's *Imperialism* and of the propaganda derived from it, has been enormous. A potted version of Lenin's views, themselves a potted version of those of Hobson, Hilferding, and others, has become part of the conventional wisdom of western capitalist society. But it would not have had this success if there had not existed, in western society, exceptionally favourable intellectual conditions for its acceptance. Lenin's views were received in a climate of guilt about the colonial past, which under their influence has grown into a widespread mood of inverted racialism and national masochism. This mood is especially prevalent in Britain today but is also to be found to a lesser extent in other European countries and in North America. This phenomenon has not yet been sufficiently studied by historians and sociologists, and this is no place to attempt the task. Yet something must be said at this point, and the case of Britain deserves most attention.

In Britain at the end of the nineteenth century the dominant attitude to colonial empire was complacent pride. The subject peoples were regarded with varying shades of contempt, condescension, and pity. The motives of the colonizers ranged from commercial enterprise through old-fashioned military patriotism to Christian missionary zeal. Opposition to empire, compounded of Little-England isolationism and social radicalism, existed, but was a minority trend. It was strengthened by the disillusionments of the Boer War, and still more by the First World War, in which Europeans had hardly set a shining example of civilization to lesser breeds without the law. It was most widespread in the unofficial educated class, among writers, academics, journalists, and part of the clergy, both dissenters and Church of England. It had religious roots which extended beyond the conscious membership of the churches. The tendency of the unbelieving intelligentsia to seek fulfilment of its unconscious religious needs through political passions is to some extent a common feature of the history of modern European nations. In the British case, one might perhaps say that guilt about colonialism is a secularization of the sense of sin, itself a feature more marked in Protestant than in Catholic communities.

In Britain the guilt complex was not confined to the intelligentsia: it spread to politicians, then to government officials, and in more recent times even to the business class. In France a similar feeling appeared at about the same time as in Britain among the intelligentsia: the different climate of Catholicism and anti-clericalism, and the persistent effects of the mythology of 1789, 1848, and 1871, gave it a different flavour, but it was a comparable phenomenon. It spread quickly to the politicians, of whom many belonged to the intelligentsia. But for many decades the government officials and army officers, in France and in the colonies, were insulated against it, indeed to some extent are still insulated even in the mid-1960s. The explanation of the difference between Britain and France may be that the sense of guilt has deeper religious roots in Britain, or that the intellectual, bureaucratic, and military elites are much more closely interwoven in Britain than they have been in France since 1789, or perhaps especially since the cleavage of the Dreyfus Affair years. In the United States the intelligentsia has been strongly infected, but the government machine and business world are still resistant, except perhaps the north-eastern elite. The intoxication of world power is still potent, and the comfortable belief that colonialist guilt is something that other nations have, of which Americans are innocent, is still widespread.

One of the most fascinating open questions today is whether these phenomena will in time affect Soviet society.

It is tempting to correlate the arrogant imperialist self-confidence of late Victorian Britain with the rise of the new business class, which by this time had established itself securely in the elite. Soviet society of the 1940s and 1950s was marked by the rise of a new class which showed many of the characteristics of the late Victorians, including an intolerant puritanism in private morals, a taste for ponderous architecture, philistinism in literature and the arts, and a bullying condescension towards other nations and other cultures. It remains to be seen whether self-confidence will give place to self-doubt.

Certainly there is a strong tradition of self-doubt in the Russian intelligentsia, and there have been indications in recent years that the tradition has not died out among the intellectual elite in the narrowest sense—among writers and students. But it should not be forgotten that the self-doubt of the old Russian intelligentsia could be expressed in the comparatively free conditions of the Imperial regime, and that it was sustained by the repeated defeats and failures of Russia as a Great Power between 1815 and 1917. In Britain and France too, there has been freedom of speech and thought in the last three quarters of a century, and both have been, at least for several decades, declining Powers. Neither condition applies to the Soviet Union in the 1960s. Though weaker than the United States and aware of the growing Chinese challenge, it is still a giant world Power, and virtually no public criticism of official social or political institutions, policies, or attitudes is permitted.

One essential factor in the change of western attitudes to colonialism was pressure by the colonial peoples themselves. This is something which may possibly emerge in the Soviet Union. Under the unbroken surface of self-righteous public incantations, of dithyrambs to the brotherhood of socialist nations, who can tell what forces may be stirring? It is of course possible that the new social elites of the Central Asian peoples, created by decades of industrialization and education, are united in passionate gratitude to the Russian elder brother who conferred these benefits on them. In the absence of freedom of speech, one can only speculate, on the basis of the experience of other empires. This experience shows clearly that the good deeds of imperial rulers have brought them no more gratitude than their evil deeds. Slovaks benefited from Hungarian schools and universities, Indians from British, Vietnamese and Algerians from French; but these graduates became, not happy exponents of imperial policy, but leaders of their peoples in the struggle for independence. Always hitherto, the higher standard of living and wider intellectual perspectives available to the elites of subject peoples have increased, not diminished, their irritation at foreign tutelage. It may be that 'socialist nations' are free from such reactions. It may be, but we do not know it, and the Soviet leaders do not know it. Meanwhile a new Great Power is arising on the borders of Soviet Central Asia, and independent Moslem States (Iran, Afghanistan, and Pakistan) are becoming involved in the three-cornered relationship between Russia, China, and India. The perspectives before the

Central Asian peoples are bound to grow more complicated. It is at least possible that by the end of the twentieth century students of the process of the decline and fall of empires may be able to base their theories on a wealth of data from the experience of the Soviet Union, data unforeseen by Lenin or Stalin.

Power without Influence
The Impact on Non-Communist Economic Policy

PETER WILES

WHAT the Russian Revolution showed to the rest of the world is that there is a road of economic development that is different from the one which was taken by the first countries to become industrialized. In this sense Moscow's policy was a harbinger. But it was not a prototype. For if we consider them in detail, Soviet economic policies have had amazingly little influence on *government action* in non-communist countries. The Red Army has occupied many countries and imposed these detailed policies along with the rest of the social and political system; but that is not 'influence'. Some communist parties have seized power without Soviet help, or at least without much of it—Yugoslavia, China, North Vietnam, Cuba. But while that is certainly influence it is not influence on non-communists. For the same reason the lucubrations of western Marxists may be dismissed, unless they influenced government action, which they almost never did.

If these independent communist regimes later turned to their own courses, they still began as rather crude imitators, swallowing the detailed policies with the general doctrine hook, line, and sinker.[1] But a non-communist government would be expected to pick and choose among the economic policies that the USSR exemplified, just as it would pick and choose among the parts of the ideology, or of the political, social, and military policies. Just which economic policies, then, have been imitated, and by whom, is the question to which this essay is addressed.

---

[1] Of all communist countries only Cuba *began* with a few deviations, notably the syndicalist management of state farms, which were also rather numerous by communist standards for the immediate aftermath of revolution. This reflects the fact that Castro did not really become a communist until about 1960 (compare also sec. XIII below). There was, however, slavish and disastrous imitation of Soviet industrial management and investment policy, principally because of Che Guevara, now removed.

In a general way all 'socialism' has received a tremendous fillip from the Bolshevik Revolution—whether that much disputed word means state planning, the nationalization of property, the levelling of incomes, the substitution of public advantage and indeed of altruism for private profit, or the liquidation of imperialism. These, be it noted, are the five possible economic meanings of 'socialism' in this essay; and each aim can be, and has been in some measure by some system or other, achieved without the other four. The point is not that many people knew anything precise about the USSR, or tried to imitate it; it is that things coming vaguely under these five headings were known now to exist. The whole complex had been shown to be possible in general terms, so all kinds of socialist, many very anti-communist, took heart.

We must even allow great effects on systems other than socialist. Keynesian fiscal and monetary policy, for instance, owes nothing at all to Marxist theory or Soviet practice, and has been ridiculed and condemned in Moscow. But its world-wide adoption, in the teeth of strong opposition, was doubtless helped by the competition of the Soviet system. For the claim was correct that the USSR had abolished unemployment, if this term be confined to that caused by deflation, the slumps in the trade cycle. Unemployment due to over-population, and more recently technological unemployment, have not been abolished at all; but they have not been publicized. What people *think* about the USSR matters most in this connection. If we wish, as practical communists, to imitate, we must eventually stop mere thinking and find out. But if we wish to instal our own brand of socialism, or simply to compete by some other kind of reform, we shall never face this painful necessity. Ignorance may be a greater stimulus.

The same must be said of many practices, good or bad, much older than the Keynesian economics. Protectionism, trade unionism, state welfare—all were practised or organized long before 1917. The first is without direct application to a Soviet-type economy, which uses no tariffs.[2] The second has been utterly denatured, and turned from collective bargaining to the administration of welfare and the encouragement of productivity. Only the social services even look the same under capitalism and communism. Yet surely

---

[2] It has them, but they are functionless appendices. Protectionism is implicit in the foreign trade plan, which consists of direct orders to import and export just so much.

all three are stronger today because of Soviet economic competition.

Perhaps above all we owe to this competition our new-found interest in economic growth. This again is no monopoly of socialism or communism, and in a secular view both Sweden and Japan present more attractive examples. But it was the USSR that made the noise and got the publicity—and indeed that showed more single-minded devotion, though no more success. It was not so much the mere existence of 'socialism' as the successful growth of a 'socialist' economy that turned others' attention to growth.

But if in these respects, socialist and non-socialist alike, the non-communist world has moved very far since, and because of, 1917, it is still extremely difficult to prove direct imitation in any detail. This chapter, then, must be a dull and negative one; though heaven knows the negativity at least is no fault of the writer's. For I entered upon this subject with no conscious bias, and am neither pleased nor displeased, merely surprised, by the result. I wanted to prove no specific generalization and would just as willingly have traced great Soviet influence all over the world. Why not?—after all the Sovietologist lives off it.

It cannot be sufficiently emphasized, however obvious it may be, that the presence or absence of imitation is to be proved only by an intimate study of non-communist countries. The intrusion of the Sovietologist into this preserve is a foolhardy act. His excuse is that at least he knows what it is that has to be imitated; his weakness is that he must learn the history of the country concerned from scratch. Too many of the discussions of Soviet influence[3] have been limited to Soviet recommendations, and/or to theoretical exercises upon the consequences of adopting them. Such studies have of course their value, but they are rather easy to write and never get down to brass tacks. The further step must eventually be taken of finding out what actually happened, and why, in countries and periods allegedly open to this influence. It is normally very difficult indeed

---

[3] Oleg Hoeffding in *Ost-Europa Wirtschaft*, 1958, iii; Werner Klatt in Alec Nove and Jane Degras, eds., *Soviet Planning* (Oxford, 1964); Peter Knirsch, 'Der Ostblock und die Entwicklungsländer', *Vierteljahresberichte der Friedrich Ebert Stiftung*, December 1965; Alex Inkeles in *Ost-Europa*, 1958, xii; W. K. in *Ost-Europa Wirtschaft*, 1959, iv; Stephen Clarkson, 'L'Analyse Soviétique des Problèmes Indiens du Sous-Développement' (doctoral thesis, Fondation Nationale des Sciences Politiques, Paris, 1964).

to prove or disprove such allegations, particularly when, as is to be expected, the influenced wish to conceal the truth.

It is as well to insist on this point, if only in my own self-defence, lest I be accused of pedantic niggling or anti-Soviet propaganda. The attribution of literary influence or of cheating in examinations has become a careful science. Scholars in these fields do not lightly say that A influenced B unless they know that B read A, or spoke to A, or said he was influenced by A (preferably in a context where it was embarrassing to admit it), or demonstrably could not have got the idea from C, or copied A word for word, or can be shown to be utterly incapable of independent thought and action, indeed without common sense.

It is far different when we discuss communism. Its friends and enemies alike see communist influence under every bed. All caution, all the rules of evidence, all ordinary meanings of the word 'influence', are thrown to the winds. If some Tory politician or Latin caudillo uses the word 'planning' he must have got it from Lenin. Never mind whether he ever read Lenin or not, or what the word 'planning' meant to him[4] or to Lenin, or if he ever spoke to a communist, or even if he *says* he got it from a nineteenth-century politician in his own country: he is all part of the 'Soviet Impact on the Western World'.

Mr E. H. Carr's influential book of that title (1947) simply cannot be avoided in a sceptical account of this matter. The chapters on the 'Economic Impact' and the 'Social Impact' are marked by an extraordinary paucity of reference to, indeed of knowledge of, the allegedly impacted countries. This paucity stands in sharp contrast to the breadth and depth of knowledge, other than economic, displayed about Marxism and the USSR. The treatment of Keynes is a good example. His extremely explicit disavowal of Soviet influence is very honestly quoted, but called 'rash'; it is immediately followed by these sentences:

. . . Nevertheless, even if it were demonstrated—as I think it can be— that Lord Keynes reached his own conclusions by different routes and quite independently of anything that happened in Russia, it would be still true to say that the main positions of 'Keynesian economics' had already

---

[4] An excellent case is the first Mexican six-year plan (sec. V). Soviet influence, undoubtedly present in Mexico in 1933, was responsible only for its name. The thing is an ordinary Mexican party platform, a collection of promises without definite goals or detailed co-ordination. Cf. Robert J. Shafer, *Mexico* (Syracuse, 1966), pp. 43–5.

been established in Soviet economic policies, and that Lord Keynes's doctrines found such ready acceptance in Great Britain and elsewhere partly because the ground had already been prepared in the minds of his contemporaries by contemplation of the planned economy of the Soviet Union.

The cardinal positions of the Keynesian economic revolution may be summarized as follows:

(a) that resources left unused owing to individual abstinence from consumption do not necessarily, or by any automatic process, find their way into 'investment', i.e. the creation of productive capital.

(b) that abstinence of the well-to-do from consumption, far from being an unconditional blessing, may be less useful to the community than their spending, and that the classical argument which justifies inequality of wealth as an impetus to investment thus disappears. (Lord Keynes at one time looked forward with satisfaction to 'the euthanasia of the *rentier*'.)

(c) that, even in default of a sufficient volume of individual savings and investment, investment can still be maintained at the requisite level by 'communal saving through the agency of the state', i.e. through fiscal policy.

(d) that this 'communal saving', together with its counterpart the 'comprehensive socialization of investment', i.e. the treatment of investment not as an automatic product of private savings in search of profit, but as a decision of public policy, is the condition of full employment.

It would not be difficult to show that these principles had been applied in the Soviet Union and accepted as the basis of Soviet planning before they were worked out in the form of economic theory by Lord Keynes (pp. 34–5).

Points (a) and (b) add up to a complete refutation of what is known as Say's Law of Markets. They are to this day disputed by Marxists, whose confused attitude to the operation of Say's Law under capitalism had already been documented when Mr Carr went to print.[5] Moreover Say's Law *does* operate, automatically, in a command economy, so that points (a) and (b) do not hold for it. On the other hand in points (c) and (d) the macro-economic policies that Keynes recommended for a market economy (control of the *general* volume of investment) are incorrectly equated to the micro-economic policies of the Soviet command economy (determination of every investment project, without too much concern for the volume). None of Keynes's four principles, then, was applied or accepted or implicitly anticipated in the USSR, and none was derived from it. We have, however, already expressed our agreement with Mr Carr that the acceptance of Keynes was eased by the Bolshevik Revolution.

Then Soviet peace-time planning is said (pp. 36, 38) to 'provide

[5] Cf. Joan Robinson, *An Essay on Marxian Economics* (London, 1942).

so many precedents for British practice during the second world war'. But precedents are not influence: in fact British planners during the Second World War were copying their predecessors in the First,[6] and were unaware of these undoubted Soviet precedents. More is the pity, of course: they would genuinely have benefited from such knowledge, and their ignorance is to be condemned. But they *were* ignorant, so there was no impact. Indeed, we may turn the tables: rationing and high liquor taxation are called the *inventions* of Soviet planners. But the latter is as old as the Tsars, and the first was used in Britain and—above all—Germany during the First World War! It is in fact the Soviet impact on Mr Carr, not on the Western World, that this book describes.

The attribution or denial of economic influence, then, is no light task. One must be very familiar with the economic history of the two countries concerned, indeed with that of the world, and with both Marxist and western economic theory.[7]

There is, furthermore, little room for generalization. While this is obvious when we study the Soviet impact on advanced western nations, it is no whit less true elsewhere. Poor countries differ profoundly from each other. The differences between Ghana and Guinea, let alone Ghana and India, are quite as great as those between Britain and France. It would be on a jejune and abstract level indeed that a scholar could speak of the effects of the Reformation, or indeed the Russian Revolution, on 'western Europe'. To suppose that 'underdeveloped countries' or even 'West Africa' are easier to cram into a generalization is a relic of imperialism— or communism! However little we like it, there is no substitute here for brass tacks, that is, for the historical and personal ambience. This unspecialized essay has barely scratched the surface.

In what follows we examine, in chronological order,

> the effect of 'War Communism' on world opinion;
> the New Deal in the United States;
> the Mexican collective farms;

---

[6] Cf. my 'Pre-war and Wartime Controls', in G. D. N. Worswick and P. H. Ady, eds., *The British Economy 1945–51* (Oxford, 1953).

[7] One must, for instance, know what a price index is, and why Stalin suppressed his retail price index in 1931. Not (Carr, p. 41) because it was 'meaningless in a planned economy', but because it was all too meaningful—it 'meant' that real wages were falling. Since about 1949 the USSR has again published a retail price index, and its use in planning never ceased.

German bilateralism;
the first British Labour government;
the second Indian Five-Year Plan;
Ghanaian economic policy under Nkrumah;
Sekou Touré's Soviet episode;
the example of Stalin's forced labour camps;
the general Soviet influence on the end of colonies;
the Algerian nationalizations of 1962–3.

Our general conclusion is that only Mexico, Guinea, and India provide even a shadow of direct, detailed imitation.

II. The Models Offered to the Outside World

But first we must specify what it is that has to be imitated—and concurrently what the Russians think it is.

In the forgotten first seven months of Soviet power (November 1917–June 1918), and again during the years of the New Economic Policy (NEP), 1921–8, the Soviet system did not differ widely from what we have below called Indian planning, in deference to the largest nation that practises it. The 'commanding heights' only were nationalized: banks, railways, heavy industry, foreign trade, etc. The rest of the economy was in private hands. Agriculture was in the hands of millions of private peasants, and many similar small-scale enterprises existed in trade and handicrafts. Larger enterprises were still nominally capitalist, but were subject to audit (usually mistranslated 'control'): by the workers in the enterprise in 1917–18, by the trade unions and the Communist Party during the NEP. Planning, in the sense of direct government intervention, was confined to investment projects financed by budgetary funds. Even the nationalized enterprises functioned on the free market.

The first seven months were followed by civil war. In the brief mad period of so-called War Communism, the Bolsheviks attempted totally to communize not only production but also consumption, the choice of jobs, and family life. The nation was to be run without money or accounts of any kind, as one family. When all this failed completely, Full Communism was relegated to the far future, and it was retrospectively pretended that 1918–21 had been a war economy. This was quite untrue, both in intention and in fact. But anyhow in both succeeding periods, the NEP and the Plan Era, it was recognized that the USSR was in for a long pull.

Medium-term ideals remained essentially the same after 1921, and were grouped together under the name 'socialism'. As fleshed out by the experience of the Plan Era, they included:

(i) The means of production must be socialized, that is, brought under the direct ownership and control of the workers' State. And not, be it noted, of any old State. Ownership or control by a bourgeois State is not socialism at all, but 'state capitalism'. This is not wholly unprogressive, but it is no substitute for the proletarian revolution, and it does not in any way obviate its necessity. As to the form of this socialization, the 'State' must eventually yield to 'society'. That is, planning must become persuasive not coercive, and involve the whole population in active consent (which is the Soviet definition of democracy). Meanwhile, until the State withers away, it and not any semi-independent trustee must own the means of production. The top managers are Ministers of State and sit in the Cabinet.

(ii) Objects of consumption are not on the whole to be socialized, though there is a strong prejudice against large objects of private consumption like cars and town houses. Such things go, of course, with great private wealth, whereas under socialism all substantial advances in consumption should be as communal as possible. Thus townspeople should live in high blocks of flats and use public transport; a laundry in the basement of a big building is fine but a private washing machine is rather bad; collective tours are good but private travel is questionable, etc. etc.

(iii) In the special case of agriculture the millions of small traditionally minded peasants will not immediately accept state control. They must therefore be persuaded to pool their work and property locally, in small voluntary co-operative farms. In fact Stalin's collectivization was extremely forcible and bloody, in sharp contrast to the Mexican collectivization (below). This item, then, has been a very lively skeleton in the cupboard.

(iv) Artisan production and petty trade shall also be co-operative. In fact, however, Stalin simply destroyed artisan production and left no substitute: contrast the Indian second five-year plan, below.

(v) The national plan shall embrace not only long-term investment but also every detail of current operation. It will dictate wholly, by central command, the operation of socialized enterprises (i); it will strongly influence the actions of co-operative enterprises (iii); and it will work on private individuals as consumers, small farmers, and workers by ordinary market means. For this latter end, money is retained.

(vi) It follows that in contrast to 'War Communism', labour must essentially function in a free market, even though production is tightly planned. Therefore enterprises bid against each other for labour, and higher wages must be paid for scarce skills or to induce people to work in unpleasant places or at unpleasant jobs. Similarly, consumer goods are sold against money, and the consumer is not planned in any detail either. So prices are varied in order to persuade him to buy whatever happens, under (v), to have been produced. The difference between cost and price is the celebrated variable turnover tax, the main source of budgetary revenue.

(vii) Incomes shall vary only as much as base unregenerate human nature requires for minimal incentives. All shall work, at things defined as useful by the State. This will be easy, since it is the workers' own State. Basically, even under Stalin, who despised egalitarianism, incomes were never so unjustly distributed as under capitalism.

(viii) No income shall be drawn from ownership of the means of production, except in a very modified sense by peasants. These must, if private, enjoy in essence management, not property rights, and over holdings of approximately equal worth. If in co-operatives or collectives, they will enjoy no unearned income at all, except in the (mostly unrecognized, but very important) sense that a fortunately-placed collective farm is more productive, or has lower transport costs, than a less productive one. No-one may employ the labour of another, since that would be exploitation.

(ix) As to sheer productivity, the USSR must catch up with and surpass the USA. Moreover, it must do so without much borrowing abroad, which would reduce it to semi-colonial status.

(x) The essential means to economic growth, other than socialism as defined above, is priority investment in heavy industry. Such a disequilibrium is impossible under capitalism, which is hampered by the laws of market profitability, but it is a most progressive force under socialism. We shall examine the logic of this item when we come to deal with India.

Being unselfcritical to an almost absurd degree, the Soviet communists until recently pursued a large number of other policies which to outsiders seem highly characteristic of them, but which they themselves hardly recognize. Among these we may mention first, as minor curiosities, a preference for metal-working over other types of heavy industry, and for canals and railways over roads. We have not space for such details, so I shall simply state my personal but considered opinion that these are both romantic hangovers, the one from the Petersburg metal-workers who were the leading working-class supporters of the revolution, the other from Saint-Simon. They have no other visible rationale.

Larger items of policy have been the hostility to services of most kinds, notably shops. This is derived from a false nineteenth-century definition of services as unproductive, which Marx perpetuated, not knowing that his words would one day become holy writ. Then, too, there was until recently a deep suspicion of foreign trade—not shared by smaller communist countries. Only since 1964 have these quirks of policy been admitted and discussed. I have found no imitation of them at all by non-communists.

But perhaps the largest item, only half understood by the communists, has been the command economy itself (item v above). Not only do they not use the phrase 'command economy'; they have no periphrasis for it. For them it is an integral part of planning; that a planner should use market mechanisms has until recently been quite inadmissible. Hence on Soviet lips the word 'planning' has been the only word for enormously disparate things, ranging from the Indian investment-and-foreign-exchange planning through the French 'concertation of expectations' to their own detailed lists of output and input orders.

Cognate with this muddled attitude to the command economy has been a muddled attitude to the 'law of value'. Marx himself wrote before the resource allocation problem was recognized by anyone. Consequently he saw in the market mechanism only chaos, and could not even imagine that in respect of resource allocation a centralized command economy would be worse. From that day to this, the question of resource allocation under planning has been continuously confused in the USSR. It is indeed no easy problem, but the adherence to Marxism has made it quite insoluble. For the labour theory of value excludes land and capital as scarce resources to be considered, the acceptance of the command economy excludes consumer's sovereignty, and the nineteenth-century confusion between margins and averages is the *comble de malheur*.

III. The Impact of 'War Communism'

In the period of so-called War Communism, when the Bolsheviks tried to communize everything, as we have seen, there was very great foreign interest in the details of their economic system. This kind of interest was taken mainly by capitalists and right-wing economists in Europe and the United States, for in that period the rest of the world still slumbered. The communist parties that grew up everywhere in the wake of the Russian Revolution were a political phenomenon; their members did not on the whole care about the details of the economic structure of a far country. The social-democrats found little to defend or admire.

The catastrophe of War Communism, and its end in a bloodily suppressed counter-revolution, were grist to the mill of right-wing, free-market propaganda. Moreover such propaganda was perfectly justified on the results of the Soviet experiment up to 1921. The cause of socialism and planning was set back many years. The great counter-attack of von Hayek and von Mises,[8] which had immense influence, took place, it is true, in the thirties. But its picture of the USSR was a War Communism picture, and was indeed based on Brutskus's rather good book on that period.[9] Very small knowledge was shown by the authors of this symposium about the NEP or the first five-year plan (FYP).

Indeed, after this early burst of interest few economists bothered their heads about the USSR. Western economics was turned inwards on the problems of imperfect competition and unemployment. Communism still appealed through the emotions, not the intellect. The non-Soviet communist was a dedicated revolutionary, a harbinger of the new man, a spy, a *guru* for certain intellectuals. Neither he nor his opponents nor anyone else really tried to find out the facts about Soviet reality. Indeed the Iron Curtain was already coming down, with himself outside it. Too much curiosity would have been a breach of discipline. His professional opponents were interested, like him, only in propaganda points. Governments also were uninterested in imitating something that had gone so badly (though the German Intelligence services and the German government had an interest and trained many excellent Sovietologists).

Yet the NEP was not a full retreat to capitalism, and Soviet economic performance under it was most creditable. Moreover the

---

[8] Notably in F. A. von Hayek, ed., *Collectivist Economic Planning* (London, 1935). For a brief description of the effect of Soviet events on western academic economics cf. my essay in N. Spulber, ed., *Study of the Soviet Economy* (Indiana University Press, 1961).

[9] B. D. Brutskus, *Economic Planning in Soviet Russia* (London, 1934).

people were fairly contented, especially the peasants, and found the system a natural one—as they have not found the Plan Era. But nobody thought so at the time. The outside world was ignorant, and saw only the abandonment of 'socialism' in 1921. Communists were ashamed, and saw only the same thing. The NEP was strictly a temporary expedient, not to be recommended. It is only, perhaps, since 1965 that Soviet writers have dared to find in the NEP some of the virtues that Sovietologists have for some time attributed to it.[10] It is now permissible to preach the NEP system in underdeveloped countries.

IV. Roosevelt and the Russians

The early years of the New Deal[11] were a period of extreme effervescence. In a society whose ancient and surprisingly homogeneous myths had been destroyed by the Stock Exchange crash, nearly every conceivable view found a hearing. The public and in part also the Presidential ear was bent by funny-money men,[12] back-to-the-landers,[13] fascists,[14] technocrats (discussed below), opponents of big business and perfectors of competition (Louis Brandeis), socialists (Norman Thomas), extreme left-wing protectionists,[15] and above all communists. From its base among the east European immigration of New York City, the Communist Party spread out among the young intelligentsia of the country. In particular the tremendous influx of ideas men and additional bureaucrats brought many crypto-communists and fellow-travellers into Washington posts. It would be needlessly controversial in this context to name names, but I at any rate incline to estimate high the number of such people, and to accept most of the later 'witnesses' as factual, even though hysterical and too well paid.

Like most aristocrats when confronted with economics, President Roosevelt was entirely unprejudiced. It was certainly not within his power to abolish capitalism, but he would listen to everybody and

---

[10] E. A. Utkin, *Problemy Planirovaniya v Slaborazvitykh Stranakh* (Moscow, 1965); V. Kazakevich in *Aziya i Afrika Segodnya*, 1966, i. I owe these and many other quotations to my pupil Mr Ian Jeffries. Stephen Clarkson, *op. cit.*, found no recommendation of the NEP up to 1963 (p. 289).

[11] I have leaned heavily on Arthur Schlesinger's *The Age of Roosevelt*, vol. III (Cambridge, Mass., 1950).

[12] Principally Marriner Eccles, Lauchlin Currie, and, on a brief visit, Keynes.

[13] M. L. Wilson, and to some extent Mrs Eleanor Roosevelt and Henry Wallace.

[14] None in the Presidential entourage. But cf. Father Coughlin and Huey Long.

[15] David C. Coyle, in his *Brass Tacks* (Washington, 1936).

anybody, and it is highly germane to our subject to ask what proposals and advice he in fact received. He received, in brief, no communist advice at all, though infiltration was certainly strong enough to make it possible. Nor was this unnatural: the communists were far too busy with taking up covert positions, with espionage and propaganda. They knew that capitalism was on its last legs; it neither could nor should be shored up.

This is indeed the general attitude of communists and Marxists towards countries in which the proletarian revolution has not yet happened. It is not merely that the USSR refuses to give advice and treats the whole situation as hopeless: resident communists do the same. They seek not influence but power. On the level of agitation the strikes, wage claims, demands for price freezes etc., may bring in members, but hardly add up to a policy. On the level of propaganda, prophecies of doom and assertions of governmental impotence inspire the orthodox but are even less like a policy. Moreover such a policy as could be extracted from the pronouncements and actions of a western communist party would not resemble at all that of the Soviet government for its own economy. It is not meant to; it is not *in pari materia;* its object is to make a revolution, not to defend one. For these reasons western Marxism scarcely figures in our account.

Nevertheless the blankness and crudity of Stalinist rejection need not have put off enquiry into Soviet methods. The fact however remains that there was none. Seemingly no influential American thought anything could be copied with advantage, and very few bothered to find out in the first place. South of the border another President was, as we shall see, more interested.

Planners there were a-plenty, with a bent for centralization, big socialized business, co-ordination, mass production, etc. etc. But they seem to have all derived from the native stream of Technocracy, that has its origin in Thorstein Veblen. Time and again we meet his phrase 'production for use not profit'; his belief that the problem of production was already solved; his consequent stress on distribution; his hostility to financiers rather than capitalists as a whole; his rejection of class warfare; and of course his total ignorance of both resource allocation and public administration—but this at least he shared with the communists.

Of the many native Technocrats[16] one stands out as having had

---

[16] Let us mention *honoris causa* Alfred Bingham and Charles Beard.

both an actual plan and the ear of the President. Mordecai Ezekiel[17] came to this subject from the administration of the new agricultural price su ports. His scheme was that an association in each basic industry should draw up a production plan for the next few years, assuming full use of capacity. These plans should then be checked and revised against each other, and finally the government should promise to buy the planned outputs if private buyers failed. But since the goods would thus in any case be produced the purchases of each sector of the economy, made in order to produce, would support every other sector, and in the result the government would not have to buy anything. Since Ezekiel did not recommend a budget deficit, his scheme would have worked only through its effects on the speculative feelings of businessmen.

The scheme would have been extremely complicated—very much more so than for agricultural products which are much less numerous and much more standardized. But it bears a very striking resemblance indeed to the planning system that Jean Monnet successfully established in France after the war. It was also far and away simpler than what was then being administered by much less competent people in the USSR. Notably, too, it relied on the profit motive: it was hardly anti-capitalist at all. It was, however, still too left-wing to stand much chance.

V. *Cárdenas's Collective Farms*

Meanwhile, south of the border a great leader, combining the characteristics and influence of F. D. Roosevelt, W. J. Bryan, and Norman Thomas, was doing even stranger things. The collective ejidos of Mexico[18] were a better instance of communist influence. 'The word ejido', says Simpson (*Problemas*, p. 11), 'is derived from the Latin, *exire*, exitum, which means way out. In Spain, originally, the term was applied to uncultivated lands owned collectively and situated outside rural communities. In Mexico in our times the word

[17] Schlesinger, *op. cit.*, pp. 216–18; Mordecai Ezekiel, *$2500 a Year* (New York, 1936), and *Jobs for All* (New York, 1939).
[18] Cf. Nathan Whetton, *Rural Mexico* (Chicago, 1948), ch. 10; Victor Alba, *Ideas Sociales Contemporáneas en México* (Mexico City, 1960); E. N. Simpson, *The Ejido* (Chapel Hill, 1937), chs. 24–6; idem in *Problemas Agrícolas e Industriales de México*, IV, 4; C. Senior in ibid. VIII, 2; H. F. Infield and Koka Freier, *People in Ejidos* (London, 1956); Rodolfo Stavenhagen, 'La Réforme Agraire et les Classes Sociales Rurales au Mexique', in *Cahiers Internationaux de Sociologie*, vol. 24; William C. Townsend, *Lázaro Cárdenas* (Ann Arbor, 1952); Shafer, *op. cit.*

is used to refer to all types of land devolved or conceded to agricultural communities that come under the Agrarian Reforms initiated in 1915. By extension the word also indicates the communities'.

The *collective* ejidos were formed by President Cárdenas in and after 1936. They bear very striking resemblances to the Soviet collective farms (kolkhozy) in administrative detail, though the differences are still more striking; and Cárdenas came after Stalin, and eventually (1955) received the Stalin Prize. It is my own opinion that there was in fact enough Soviet influence, by way of free imitation, to justify our saying at least that 1936 in Mexico would not have happened without 1928 in the USSR. For the Soviet influence there speak the mere dates: there was little such talk in Mexico until Cárdenas became President in 1934; indeed the only body to advocate collective ejidos before then seems to have been precisely the Mexican Communist Party.[19] And here we meet for the first time communism in an underdeveloped country. In Latin America particularly the communist parties have always been undisciplined: Stalinism meant little to them, fellow-travellers had scandalously much influence inside them. But indeed, all over the underdeveloped world the communist party has been more constructively inclined than in the economically advanced countries. Whatever Stalin said, it has always seemed to the communist on the spot that his government was not an ordinary capitalist government, and that reform and revolution were not antithetical. No doubt, then, Cárdenas took his views in this matter from local communists; but this does not at all imply that he took them from Moscow.

Now from the fall of Calles until 1940 Cárdenas was very much the sole boss of his country. No examination of Soviet or any other influence can avoid the question of his personality. President Cárdenas was—and is—entirely his own man: *un original* on the grand scale. Professing large but confused ideas, generous to a fault, honourable and dictatorial, he is nevertheless consistent in a few *idées maîtresses*. One of these is the goodness and reliability of the average Mexican, another is to soak the rich and give to the poor, and a third—irrelevant to our theme—is anti-clericalism. In all three cases he alarmed sober people by putting his ideas into practice. Never officially a socialist, he is best thought of as a very

---

[19] Alba, *op. cit.*, pp. 317, 320. However Stavenhagen (*op. cit.*, p. 156) speaks of a little spontaneous collectivization before 1936, without giving any details. Cf. also Townsend, *op. cit.*, p. 157.

left-wing populist, in the *norte-americano* sense of that word. With the exception of foreign oil companies, the Catholic hierarchy, and his political opponents, he has usually been in favour of everybody and everything. In particular, at his inauguration he was mildly pro-communist, just as Calles meant him to be. The Communist Party continued to be tolerated, a six-year plan was drawn up to coincide with the dates of his presidency, he gave commissions to the eminent pro-communist mural painters, whose works so greatly embellish modern Mexico. Then Calles denounced him for going too far to the left, and was exiled in June 1935. The collective ejidos were formed one year later. But of party discipline or exact imitation, we obviously cannot accuse the man who protected Trotsky (December 1936), initiated workers' control on the railways, condemned Stalin's invasion of Finland, adopted a refugee Russian Baptist as his second son, and distributed Protestant Bibles to his army.

Even so mild an attribution of Soviet influence will seem shocking to Mexicans for more than one reason. They may object, first, that the Mexican Revolution antedated the Russian by seven years (a fact tirelessly repeated in Mexico)—but it had no fixed ideology and certainly no-one asked for *collective* ejidos. Even the great radical leader Zapata wanted private peasant farms. Secondly, the ejido as such is a traditional pre-Conquest institution, never totally destroyed—but it was at no time a kolkhoz. In the traditional ejido pasture land was grazed in common, while crop land was indeed inalienable and subject to periodical redistribution, but it was always tilled on an individual family basis. There were no Aztec kolkhozy; the pre-Conquest *calpulli*, to which reference is constantly made, was exactly as we have described the traditional ejido.[20] The most we can say is that for loose thinkers there is little difference between a primitive calpulli and a mechanized kolkhoz, since they do not know what either is anyway. Now this was a period of conscious reversion to pre-Conquest culture (most visible in the celebrated murals), and for a whole generation of intellectuals the Conquest and Spain represented both feudalism and capitalism, while the Aztecs stood for primitive socialism. So class war and the deepening of socialism in the 1930s meant a reversion to Aztec from Spanish norms. The communists supported this whole-heartedly; many of the pro-Aztec muralists were communist party members or fellow-travellers, and the Soviet ambassador named his

[20] Simpson, *op. cit.*, pp. 4–6.

son Cuauhtemoc, after the hero who had succeeded Montezuma and resisted Cortes. (Incidentally, this is also Cárdenas's own son's first name.)

So illusions about Aztec land tenure may have played a part. There is indeed, thirdly, a Spanish tradition of collective farming and fishing which is strongly reminiscent of the kolkhoz. But although this was of course known in Mexico, the only agrarian principles that Spain in fact transplanted to the New World were those of the private peasant farm and of the latifundio, with or without slaves. The Mexican Revolution constituted the overthrow of the latter by the former, with the traditional ejido a *tertius non gaudens*. The revolutionary leaders had accepted the traditional ejido as a transitional device for leading the poor Indian towards a peasant capitalism of which he would one day be capable.[21] There was no collectivism among the Spanish colonists.

So the origins of the collective ejido must be sought elsewhere. I incline to think that the Soviet example and the practical necessities of the Laguna region in October 1936 brought about this modification of the traditional ejido. Of these two, immediate circumstances perhaps spoke louder. Faced with perpetual strikes in a defined region, with a land reform law long on the books but hardly implemented, with an irrigation system that dictated large-scale management, and with the pre-existence of the traditional ejido, what could a left-wing President do? If the latifundia were to be expropriated *here*, there would have to be either state or collective farms. But the Mexican Revolution was radical-democratic, and based on land hunger. It would never have tolerated state farms. Moreover, the traditional ejidos already existed in the Laguna region. It was almost inevitable that they should be burdened with these new duties.

They have fulfilled them badly, and the collective ejidos may be said to have failed, after a not unpromising start. They are lapsing into bankruptcy, population loss, and creeping individualism. The ones Cárdenas subsequently founded among the primitive peoples of Yucatán have fared even worse. Subsequent presidents have stood far to the right of him on this as on most other issues— not least because of the evident failure of many of his policies even by 1940. But that is not our subject. Rather must we consider the

---

[21] The Russian specialist will think of the *mir*, not the kolkhoz, and will note that Mexican governments until Cárdenas wanted to liberate the peasant from the *mir*, not to keep him there, as did Russian governments until Stolypin.

degree of the ejido's resemblance, when founded, to the kolkhoz. The list of similarities and dissimilarities is of importance to us, however technical, in that it illustrates Soviet influence as opposed to Soviet power. If imitation occurs in an entirely independent but left-wing country, this is the kind of untidy detailed picture it ought to present. So:

(i) the ejido pays no rent to its members, but for a very different reason: whether collective or traditional, it was founded on land confiscated from non-members, so rent would be unnatural; but the land of a kolkhoz is what its members have contributed, so rent would be very natural indeed, and has been paid in other communist countries;

(ii) both institutions are nominally democratic. Only some ejidos were genuinely democratic, depending on the personalities, whereas the kolkhoz is simply a party dictatorship over the Soviet peasant;

(iii) in both the foreman or brigadier is a key figure. If he can get his gang to work all is well, but usually he can't;

(iv) there are large and very distracting private plots, on which members prefer to work. Only in the kolkhoz these plots were a concession, made after collectivization; while the ejidatarios already had private plots as members of their traditional ejidos, and these lands were never brought into the scheme. They also hire themselves out as wage labourers, notably to the owners of the latifundia, who were permitted to retain 150 ha. each;

(v) as members, ejidatarios and kolkhozniki cannot be hired or fired. They are there, and that is that. Only at least the ejidatario can leave without permission.

On the other hand there are sharp differences:

(a) though it was conceived 'on high', and corresponded to no local tradition, the collective ejido was welcomed by the peons. If they have not succeeded in making it work, they certainly did not fight against its imposition or sabotage it;

(b) the collective ejido originated in an act of confiscation (with some compensation) of *other* people's land; the kolkhoz was disguised confiscation of the members' own land;

(c) the kolkhoz pays only a 'dividend'; that is, it allots accounting units for work done, and settles the value of the unit on the basis of the annual accounting. The ejido pays a wage and a bonus—a system to which the kolkhoz is now going over;

(d) there are trade unions to protect the lower-paid ejidatarios against their own managements. Nothing so dangerous has ever been permitted among kolkhozniki;

(e) the ejido possesses its own machinery and is proud of it. But Stalin had to take away nearly all moveable machinery from the kolkhoz for fear of sabotage;

(f) both institutions, being weak, had to rely on some outside force. The Banco Ejidal was more than a bank: it was interfering and corrupt. But the Soviet Communist Party was very much worse, and carried detailed interference to a fantastic degree.

The collective ejido must not be thought of as important. It employs about 3 per cent of the agricultural labour force, while members of both kinds of ejido account for 42 per cent. Works by Mexicans on this subject are very hard to find, though Mexico has many and competent social scientists. Local interest is by now absolutely minimal. The interested parties seem to be American sociologists and stray Sovietologists.

VI. Schacht and Bilateralism

There was a great innovation in the principles of capitalist international trade in 1931 and in 1934, when H. H. G. Schacht, the President of Germany's Reichsbank, introduced exchange control and bilateral bargaining. Such things had been by no means unknown 130 or more years earlier, in the Mercantilist era; but they had hardly been practised since, even in the First World War. Schacht's new methods were widely imitated by all sorts of countries.[22] But was he not perhaps himself imitating the USSR?

Hardly. For a start, bilateralism was not then, and had never been, a principle of Soviet foreign trade. There was and is no conceivable reason why a Soviet-type economy should achieve an approximate balance of imports and exports with any country that has a convertible currency. A Soviet-type economy is, in international trade, simply a very large firm; and just like a firm it would be insane to balance its physical sales and purchases with each client. Bilateralism was Schacht's invention, not Stalin's; it was a prerequisite of the nazi, not the Soviet, system.

---

[22] Cf. K. Mandelbaum in *The Economics of Full Employment* (Institute of Statistics, Oxford, 1944); Wiles, *Communist International Economics* (New York, 1967), ch. 11.

Basically, in the latter system, exports paid for imports, but short-term debts and credits did of course pile up. These were all held in foreign currency. Both legally and in administrative practice, the sole importer and exporter was the Ministry of Foreign Trade. An enterprise or shop requiring imports of its own volition would have had to exchange rubles for foreign currency at the bank, but the ministry did nothing of the sort. It simply spent, according to plan, the foreign currency it had earned. Its ruble transactions were conducted separately from its foreign exchange transactions. It paid rubles for exports, and received rubles for imports. It did not matter much whether these sums balanced, or whether the ruble figures for each import and export corresponded to the foreign currency figure multiplied by the rate of exchange. Indeed, they did not. Inflation rendered the rate of exchange ludicrously too low, but who cared, when there were no exchanges? Moreover—and the point is a separate one—imports were on the whole priced lower in rubles than exports, so that the ministry paid more rubles for exports than it received for imports, even though the sums in foreign currency balanced. But again, who cared?—it was only rubles, and the treasury willingly made up the difference.

Owing to the State Bank's (Gosbank's) foreign exchange monopoly, no foreigner could hold rubles, and therefore no foreigners could suddenly present the Gosbank with a claim for gold. Debts to foreigners were expressed in foreign currency—and paid punctiliously, by the way, in goods or gold or foreign currency according to the Soviet foreign-trade plan. The Gosbank and the Ministry of Foreign Trade held balances abroad, and these of course were instantly convertible—but that was the foreigner's business. If his system required him to hold large reserves of international liquidity and be at the mercy of foreign creditors, so much the worse for him.

We cannot therefore speak of Soviet exchange control. The ruble is an entirely internal currency, whereas exchange control implies a few exchanges. The nazi system on the other hand was a non-revolutionary modification of existing practice. Foreigners could still hold marks and convert them, and German importers still had to convert marks into foreign currency. Only now both parties had to have the Reichsbank's permission. In particular the foreigner was normally allowed to buy only German goods, not gold or foreign currency. As to the German exporter, he was compelled to surrender his foreign exchange to the Bank. This, then, was a very different system from the Soviet. The initiative still lay with the German entrepreneur or individual, and the essential act remained one of exchanging marks into foreign currency—albeit only at the discretion of the Reichsbank. If the Bank had a qualified foreign exchange monopoly the Ministry of Foreign Trade had no sort of export-import monopoly. On the contrary, it sold and bought nothing at all.

The nazi and Soviet systems resembled each other only in their 'non-commercial' transactions. These, in Soviet parlance, are 'invisible' transactions other than the transport of goods. They are the responsibility of the bank, not the ministry. Thus tourists and diplomats do buy rubles with foreign money; and residents are able, before going abroad, to buy foreign money with rubles. The unfortunate foreigner and the lucky resident both use the ludicrous official rate of exchange. The resident is of course subject to exchange control, and this puts him on a par with the resident of nazi Germany. But it is in my opinion unthinkable that an item so trivial in Soviet and even German circumstances should have inspired Schacht to imitate Lenin and Stalin.

As to politics, nazi bilateralism was directed at the small countries of east Europe. The diplomatic situation was such that the Reichsbank could prevent, say, a Romanian exporter to Germany from converting his marks into francs or pounds, and compel him to convert it instead into German exports. That is, not only the resident but also the non-resident was denied convertibility. Hence the celebrated exchange of 'wheat for aspirin'. This increased employment in Germany, while, *mutatis mutandis*, a similar inconvertibility of the leus increased employment in Romania. In conditions of unemployment and lack of confidence in the exchange value of currency, neither the wheat nor the aspirin would otherwise have been traded at all—and so they would not have been produced. Romania may have got the worst of the commodity exchange,[23] but additional aspirin, and the employment generated by producing the wheat, are better than nothing at all. As to Germany, it was enabled to use its francs and pounds for purposes nearer to its heart than the honourable treatment of Romanian exporters. By

---

[23] Though much evidence speaks to the contrary. In particular its terms of trade were better with Germany than with Britain; i.e. Schacht had to bribe Romania. Cf. Wiles, *Communist International Economics*, ch. 10.

bilateralism it was able to create inflationary finance which first went abroad to buy Romanian wheat and then came back to spend itself harmlessly on the export of aspirins; but at no point caused a drain of gold. If Romania had been granted multilateral privileges it would of course have demanded gold for its wheat, and so the Germans would not have dared to create the finance in the first place.

Bilateralism was forced upon the USSR in Soviet-German trade by Schacht! Later, when Britain and France imitated Schacht, they also enforced bilateralism in trade with the USSR, which continued to trade multilaterally where it could. Only after the war did it willingly accept this system and make it its own. Why it did so is another and a complicated story. I present elsewhere[24] reasons to believe that the whole thing was an intellectual error, even in trade with other communist countries.

VII. *The British Labour Government* (*1945–50*)

'Bliss', as Wordsworth put it in a similar context, 'was it in that dawn to be alive'. For here was a peaceful, democratic take-over by an experienced socialist party with an unshakeable parliamentary majority. What did it do, and did Soviet experience guide it? Hostile to native communists, the Labour Party was not hostile to the USSR. The Cold War had not yet broken out and the wartime alliance had engendered friendly feelings, so imitation would not have been disastrous to the government's political standing.

The government's idea of nationalization bore at least some resemblances to the Soviet idea. It was monopolistic not competitive, it was to take the given industry at least part way out of the market. To this we must add the faint beginnings of a command economy, even in the non-nationalized sector: certain output targets were set, in physical or monetary terms, and even certain targets for the employment of labour. But these resemblances were largely due to chance. Thus Soviet nationalization was essentially enterprise by enterprise, not industry by industry; and the first hierarchy of command ran rather by territory than by industries defined according to what they produced. For it was the local authorities that did the actual job of nationalization. Even at the height of Stalin's centralism

---

[24] Wiles, *Political Economy of Communism* (Oxford, 1962), ch. 8.

there were strong traces of this territorial principle[25]; but the Labour government nationalized, and tried to run from one centre, all the municipal gas works! De-municipalization was indeed a quite important and unpopular side-effect.

In any case British nationalization had a very long British tradition behind it—in the public ownership of docks, London transport, etc. In this tradition the owner was a public trustee, most carefully separated from the government and not even open to control by Parliamentary question. Until the 1960s this tradition, established by Conservatives and Liberals, was fairly well maintained by Labour, and even today it is not worn out. The Russian tradition, on the contrary, was that gross railway revenues[26] and current expenses, not merely net profits, flowed through the budget, while the minister responsible sat in the Tsar's cabinet. Interrupted by Lenin, this tradition was fully restored by Stalin, who would not easily have understood Herbert Morrison's notion of a nationalized industry as a public trust independent of—Stalin.

As to the elements of command in the government's first two *Economic Surveys*,[27] they were simply a carry-over from the war—and the British war economy of 1939–45 was mainly a copy of what had been done in 1916–18. In particular, had Soviet experience been attended to, there would have been less emphasis on *employment* targets. The USSR had never succeeded in fulfilling these, and is extremely chary of publishing them. But its difficulties were reproduced with comical fidelity and maximum publicity in the United Kingdom. After the complete failure to fulfil the 1947 and 1948 plans, nothing more was heard of physical planning in Britain.

In other respects there was scarcely any resemblance at all. Neither Stalin's deliberate wage differentiation nor the all-out equality of War Communism marked the Labour government's income policy—which was in any case wholly un-communist in permitting unearned income from the means of production. In this matter the trade unions determined policy—a thing no communist leader has ever permitted. None of the quirks of Soviet investment policy reappears. There was no emphasis on heavy industry, but great emphasis on exports; rail was hardly favoured over road.

[25] Later (1957) Khrushchev foolishly made it the only administrative principle.
[26] The same applied to the post office, but so it does in all countries. As original royal property, the post office antedates all modern controversy over public ownership, and its status is always anomalous.
[27] HMSO, Cmd. 7046, 7344. Cf. my *Political Economy of Communism*, p. 74.

It would not be too imaginative, however, to detect Leninist influence in two places. One is the idea of 'capturing the commanding heights'. The *choice* of things to nationalize—coal, iron and steel, railways, the central bank, gas, electricity, much of road transport—resembles strongly Lenin's choice in 1917 (*not* the wholesale nationalization of 1918). The very phrase 'commanding heights' was much used. Just what it meant to the Labour Party is unclear. To Lenin it seems to have meant that he would be able to place an embargo on the services of these industries to capitalists who disagreed with him; it was a political measure.

Such a thought may not have been absent from the minds of the Labour government; but they also felt that nationalization would facilitate *planning*. This is the second probable point of influence. For the Soviet government was the first in the world to plan its economy, whatever sense we give to the word 'plan', and thus set a most pregnant example.

But what, it may be asked, of all the pre-war Marxists, some of whom were very influential in the Labour Party of 1945? West European communism, like that of the United States, is of little relevance to this study. Such considerable economists as Maurice Dobb and Charles Bettelheim have never been consulted by their governments,[28] have never sat on tribunals or commissions, and have seen few or none of the students they influenced go on into high places. And this must be taken as a critical comment on the governments and societies in which they live.

But Dobb was not in the Labour Party: he doubtless helped to encourage the wave of 1930s Marxism in Labour circles, but that is another matter. The prime instances, at top level, of this Labour Marxism were Harold Laski and John Strachey. Laski was chairman of the National Executive in 1945, and Strachey became Minister of Food in the Cabinet.

Laski[29] was never as pro-communist as Strachey in the thirties, nor as anti-communist as the latter became. At bottom he was just a very radical Labour man, in the British tradition. But onto this he did graft the Marxist doctrine of inevitable class war, which he felt

---

[28] Though Bettelheim may have influenced India; see below.
[29] Of the immense corpus of his writings I have selected: *Law and Justice in Soviet Russia* (London, 1935); *Reflections on the Revolution of Our Time* (London, 1943); *Marx and To-day* (Fabian Pamphlet, London, 1943); *Faith, Reason and Civilisation* (London, 1944).

to be the empirical lesson of history: the rich—though he used the phrase 'relations of production' he only meant the rich—would not yield to the poor without violence. For the rest he was a democrat, a non-conformist, and a constitutionalist. It is difficult to detect in him any other element of Marxism, from the dialectic to the kolkhoz.

Like any very left-wing man he found it difficult to see, let alone condemn, communist crimes and follies until very late. But he did in fact condemn very many of them, vigorously and often, after an undue lapse of time. In other words he remained a thorough British empiricist. His *Law and Justice in Soviet Russia* is a particularly interesting example. Laughably incorrect about Vyshinsky, tragically blind about the purges and the Ogpu, it remains a solidly factual pamphlet about the ordinary actions of the lower courts; and is literally the only work I have read in preparing this contribution that seeks in the USSR detailed practical lessons for non-communist countries.

Appropriately, the pamphlet concerns the law, a field much nearer to Laski's speciality than economics. He was a 100 per cent non-economist, and spoke of our subject only in the most superficial and inaccurate way. He was also rather moderate, asking in 1943 for the nationalization of the 'commanding heights' only. His preoccupation with these heights was characteristically Leninist, that is, political. But he was not actually a revolutionary. Rather he shared the constant preoccupation of the post-MacDonald leaders of his party: will the bourgeoisie offer no violence after we have, by constitutional means, got our majority? He rather thought they would, and so may be described as a violent anti-counter-revolutionary—a much milder sort of thing.

Why, then, it may be asked, does Laski figure in these pages? The answer is, in default of better instances, and to show how things really were. Let those who see greater communist influence upon the Labour Party and upon the management of the British economy name a more plausible channel for it.

Strachey's pro-communist period covered the Popular Front.[30] His activity—he was never formally a member of the British Communist Party—was directed towards converting the Labour Party,

---

[30] See his *What We Saw in Russia* (with Aneurin Bevan and George Strauss), (London, 1931); *The Coming Struggle for Power* (London, 1932); *What Are We to Do?* (London, 1938); *A Programme for Progress* (London, 1940); *The Just Society* (Labour Party pamphlet, 1951); *The Strangled Cry* (London, 1962).

particularly its rank and file, to communism. The Popular Front policy was what would today be called revisionist, and though an orthodox communist by the doctrinal standards of the thirties, Strachey was always a half-hearted revolutionary. Pre-revolutionary collaboration was his speciality, and he certainly believed that a Popular Front government would bring about genuine improvements. He also seems to have believed from the very first in a peaceful transition to socialism—in common with the later Engels but not with Lenin. The show trials and the pact with Hitler brought this ardent fellow-travelling to an end. In 1940 he published one of the first Marxist attempts to grapple with Keynes, whose policy he admitted to be effective but thought would promote socialism. By 1945 there remained of his Marxism only the admirable habit of deep and serious thought, the search for *general* and *coherent* views. Even in respect of nationalization he now occupied a position in the middle of the Labour spectrum.

It is of particular interest that though he wrote with enduring brilliance on the relation of Marx to Keynes in 1940, and held an economic position in the 1945 Cabinet, Strachey was not really an economist and took no particular interest in the Soviet economy or the problems of central planning. As a practical economist he was, in the Tanganyika ground-nuts affair, a disaster: even an ex-Marxist, it seems, should not be allowed near a farm. His short pamphlet on the Soviet economy (*What We Saw in Russia*, above) is slight, inexpert, and naive: today it interests only a student of its author(s), not of its subject. His longer works say almost nothing about the Soviet economy, but he assures us[31]—and from so honest a man even an *ex parte* statement may be accepted—that he never believed the USSR was a utopia, only that everything else was worse.

'Everything else was worse'. It is impossible to overstress this element in all fellow-travelling. In the advanced capitalist countries before Keynes, one needed sharp eyes and a clear head indeed to perceive that everything else was not, after all, worse. The advance of fascism and the extent of unemployment were terrible beyond measure. The countervailing Soviet horrors of collectivization and the Great Purge were hardly known, and were also very remote and peculiar. Self-deceit was easy, guilt for one's own personal comforts

[31] *The Strangled Cry*, p. 188.

obligatory, and rejection of one's own world honourable. But exactly these conditions, that imposed the fellow-travelling attitude of mind, precluded the accurate knowledge of the USSR that was its enemy. It was not in such soil that practical, detailed imitation was likely to grow.

Thus those who did expect detailed imitations of Soviet policy from the new Labour government were doubly wrong. First, it was overwhelmingly non-Marxist, and had fairly successful traditions of its own, in municipal ownership, the London Passenger Transport Board, the war-time controls, etc. Second, even its quasi-Marxist members were without the particular beliefs or interests that would have set them copying the USSR.

VIII. Mahalanobis and Investment Policy

Of the incidents we have chosen to discuss, the most certain case of direct and detailed Soviet influence was the formulation of the second Indian five-year plan. Indian planning had many origins. I list them in approximate order of importance:[32]

(i) the *New-Statesman*-type socialism of Nehru;

(ii) the war-time and post-war reconstruction planning of the British Raj. As so often, the British Raj imitated British domestic techniques but stood slightly to their left, and took account of Indian circumstances, notably in respect of 'village uplift';

(iii) the vague general feeling that the USSR was a good thing, particularly because it had a plan;

(iv) Gandhist economics, hostile to market forces and free trade, but also to big industry and centralization.

I almost hesitate to mention Gandhism in this context, since it is not even clear that it was a positive influence on planning at all. It would seem that a plan that was not for centralization, and not for industrialization, would be a mere theoretical construct; logically it gives us no difficulty but psychologically we know that 'there ain't no sich animal'. For the rest it is clear that the actual details of the first Indian FYP (1950) were British, derived from either (i) or (ii) above. It was, to be precise, a plan for allocating government investment funds and foreign exchange. There was no direction of labour, practically no command system for current outputs, very

---

[32] I follow here A. H. Hanson's invaluable *The Process of Planning* (Oxford, 1966). Clarkson, *op. cit.*, is an immense and systematic quarry for Soviet opinions on India.

little nationalization, and only a moderate emphasis on equality. The word 'socialism' was not used. The Indian government stood to the right of the British in all respects but one; it did set up a five-year plan, instead of confining itself to one year at a time.

In autumn 1954 P. C. Mahalanobis, Director of the Institute of Statistics in Calcutta, became Nehru's economic adviser, and the latter plumped openly for the 'socialistic picture of society' which had always been his personal preference. The content of this socialism, now official Congress policy for the first time, is presumably to be seen from what Mahalanobis did to the second FYP. There was a little, but only a very little, about the collectivization of agriculture, which was in any case to be voluntary. A note of urgency was indeed struck on the need to equalize incomes, and it was promised that the highest incomes would be reduced as well as the lowest raised. But there was little that was anti-capitalist in the method chosen: new taxation did not hit income at all, let alone unearned income. This, on the contrary, was the moment when Mr Nicholas Kaldor sold the Indian government his expenditure tax. Whatever may be said for or against this fiscal contraption, and however progressive its tariff, it is not socialistic. Nationalization also received very scant emphasis, all things considered. Nor was command to be substituted for the market on any great scale.[33]

The truth is that Mahalanobis's interests had hitherto been statistical (he was, most significantly, by origin a physicist), not economic or institutional. The aspect of Soviet experience that appealed to him was the relationships of magnitude between heavy and light industry. He was it is true very anti-western,[34] but has not to my knowledge exercised much influence over income distribution, village uplift, and other aspects of economic policy. He was never a member of the communist party. His doubtful gift to his country was an econometrical growth model, in which the parameters were set at unrealistic levels so as to justify a very great deal of investment in heavy industry.

Others more competent than I have criticized the values of these

---

[33] Direct orders are from time to time given by the government to Indian nationalized industry, but not in a Soviet way. Such orders are crisis measures, not a normal part of planning. Fulfilment of them brings, of course, no bonus to management.

[34] Cf. his article 'Industrialization: the Key to the Consolidation of Independence', in *Sovremenny Vostok* (Moscow), December 1958.

parameters and the consistency of the model.[35] What concerns us here is that it was a Soviet model, developed by one G. A. Feldman in 1928.[36] Feldman had been a minor member of that galaxy of mathematical economists which the USSR produced during the NEP era. Stalin liquidated him, we do not know exactly why—for being Jewish, perhaps, or for using mathematics, or indeed for thinking at all. Yet when we say Mahalanobis used the Feldman model, or a Soviet model at all, we still have to prove that he did not develop it independently. There is much evidence, however, that he did just that. Feldman was resuscitated by Evsey Domar, whose essay originally appeared in 1957.[37] But Mahalanobis took the essential step at least as early as 1953.[38] He had visited Moscow in March 1952, it is true, but his original article shows no trace of influence from that visit. What he says about the intellectual origins of this earlier model is:

In recent years I have had occasion to come into contact with the work on national income and also with some of the problems of economic planning in India. I am not an economist; . . .

In a lecture delivered at the National Institute of Sciences of India on 4 October 1952, I used a model to represent economic growth as a first approximation. According to this model, the ratio of net investment to net national income at factor cost in any period of time is taken to be a constant α. Secondly, in any time period the increment of income divided by the investment is also supposed to be a constant depicted by β. On these assumptions, the rate of growth of the economy is given by $\alpha\beta$. If we suppose that the population of the country increases at the constant rate ρ then the rate of growth per capita income is given by $\alpha\beta - \rho$.

When I was studying about this model, I did not know that considerable work had been done on models of the same type by Harrod, Domar and others because I was not familiar with economic literature. Now that I have come to know about the previous work I wish to acknowledge their priority.

[35] M. Bronfenbrenner in *Economic Development and Cultural Change* (Chicago, 1960). Other sources quoted by Hanson, *op. cit.*

[36] *Planovoe Khozyaistvo*, 1928, xi; translated in N. Spulber, ed., *Foundations of Soviet Strategy for Economic Growth* (Indiana University Press, 1964). The mere notion of priority for heavy industry is of course as old as Imperial Germany and Imperial Russia.

[37] Evsey Domar, *Essays in the Theory of Economic Growth* (New York, 1957), ch. 9.

[38] In his institute's journal *Sankhya* (Calcutta), September 1953.

He mentions the USA but not the USSR. He can lay a very good claim to have independently invented the Harrod/Domar model. However, his September 1953 model goes further: it distinguishes first- and second-order investment [39]—the basic feature of Feldman's Marxist model. In making this distinction, Mahalanobis acknowledges Marx's own priority, but shows no acquaintance with Soviet work.

In winter 1953 the French Marxist economist Charles Bettelheim visited Calcutta, and a strong and direct Marxist influence became apparent. In 1954 Indian planners visited Moscow. In November 1954 Nehru inaugurated the Calcutta Institute's planning division, which was visited by R. M. Goodwin of Cambridge, the Norwegian left social-democrat and mathematical economist Ragnar Frisch, the doyen of Polish economists and member of the Polish central committee Oskar Lange, Professor Bettelheim again, and four Russians. There emerged the famous Draft Plan Frame,[40] which under Nehru's influence determined the second FYP. The Draft Plan Frame also incorporated the Feldman model, with priority for second-order investment.

As we see from Table 1, Mahalanobis's draft was severely cut before the plan became official. Even so it was nothing like fulfilled. One of the most Soviet things about the draft was the size itself of total investment. In our excitement over the finer issues we should not forget this obvious point.

If behind the parameters lay the growth model, behind the model lay the economic theory. This too was profoundly Soviet. It holds that (a) the 'take-off into self-sustaining growth'[41] is impossible without self-sufficiency in the production of modern machines; (b) capital-intensive processes are better than labour-intensive ones, whatever the relative scarcity of labour and capital; (c) people can be forced to save large amounts; (d) people can be forcibly mobilized to work. It also holds that these doctrines cohere, indeed form an interdependent system.

---

[39] First-order investment is the construction of, say, looms, and issues in consumption goods. Second-order investment is the construction of, say, machine-tools, which can be used to make either looms or more machine-tools. Cf. my *Political Economy of Communism*, ch. 15.

[40] *Sankhya*, December 1955; D. Degtyar in *Kommunist* (Moscow), 1956, iv, p. 79.

[41] The phrase is W. W. Rostow's, but the theory is extremely un-Rostovian. Cf. his *Stages of Economic Growth* (Cambridge, 1961).

Now for (a) there is no evidence at all. Clearly a given nation might more economically use its savings to finance its own exports to swap against foreign machinery. Whether this was more or less profitable than producing the machinery at home depends on ad hoc calculation alone. The foreign-trade solution is of course no less heroic, no less demanding of national effort, than the autarkic one. It is merely more or less efficient according to the circumstances the individual country happens to be in. It was judged *more* efficient by the Soviet authorities under the NEP *and the first five-year plan*— a historical fact that the dogmatists of autarky like to forget. As to (b), it virtually contradicts (a), since machine-building is not a capital-intensive industry. Machines, on the contrary, are among the most hand-made of all industrial products. But in any case if capital is concentrated upon particular projects of an extremely modern character, others will have to go short; no economy can be more capital-intensive overall than its overall capital supply permits. (Incidentally, if this is a Soviet doctrine it is certainly not a Chinese one, and China's communism is presumably more relevant to Indian conditions.) Against (c) there is no logical or theoretical objection; it only needs to be repeated that it has no necessary connection with (a) or (b). For the quantity saved is one thing, but the exact uses of this quantity are an entirely separate question. Similarly (d) is unobjectionable in a particular, non-Soviet form: we discuss it at length in sec. *XI*. One must ask, however, about both these latter policies, whether the Indian political system is compatible with them—a question Mahalanobis, who is not a communist, considered beyond his purview.

However, it is less our task to criticize Soviet-type policies than to see whether they were applied. In this case they were certainly applied, by a conscious imitation. And India stands as an example of very many countries, very many development plans in the newly liberated nations. '*In general*', says Mr Jeffries, '*the strategy of Soviet development has been more popular with the underdeveloped countries than the institutions associated with the model*'. It was particularly popular in the late fifties and early sixties, before its faults became obvious.

Where other things are not equal, and space is lacking, it would be dangerous to examine the second FYP closely for its effect on economic performance. As primarily a plan for investment outlays it must be pronounced a shocking failure:

TABLE 1

India: Central and State Governments
Five-yearly Investment Targets and Achievements (Rs crores)

	Planned in 1952	Achieved 1951–5	Planned in 1956	Achieved 1956–60
Prices of 1951	2,069	2,013	—	—
Prices of 1956	—	2,356	4,800	3,700

But as a period of sheer achievement it was only a little worse than the first FYP: real income per head rose at about 2.0 per cent a year in the earlier period, and at about 1.6 per cent in the later. It is true that this, the most important of all targets, was overfulfilled in the first FYP and underfulfilled in the second. But even so we must remember the gross inaccuracy of national income figures, and the better harvests of the earlier period. Soviet-type thinking had proved itself unrealistic, but then there had not been Soviet-type institutions. Nor is it certain that some kinds of unrealism are bad in a planner. For instance a more realistic investment plan might not have raised investment by so much. It might even be rather a disgrace that the investment target of the first FYP—as given final shape after the plan period had begun—was so nearly fulfilled.[42]

It is easy in any case to exaggerate the Soviet-type bias of the investment priorities in the second Indian FYP. It is impossible to describe as a move towards communism an investment policy that favours village and small industry more than any other branch, even heavy industry;[43] and that gives rather high priority also to housing:

---

[42] The figures in this paragraph are from Hanson, *op. cit.*, pp. 110, 114, 134, 162, 170.

[43] Mahalanobis allocated 30.3 per cent of government investment to power, mining, large and medium industry, as opposed to the 17.4 per cent achieved in the first FYP. But he nearly trebled the allocation to village and small industry.

TABLE 2

Indian Government Investment: the breakdown

	(i)	(ii)		(iii)
	1951–5 achieved	1956–60 plan		(iii) as % of (i)
		Mahalanobis 1955	Official 1956	
Total (Rs crores 1956 prices) ..	2,356	5,600	4,800	204
In percentages:				
Agriculture	10.2 ⎫		7.1 ⎧	142
Community development ..	4.9 ⎬	17.1	4.7 ⎨	197
Irrigation and flood control ..	17.0 ⎭		10.1 ⎩	121
Power	11.1	8.9	8.9	162
Mining, large and medium industry	6.3	21.4	14.4	467
Village and small industry ..	1.3	3.6	4.1	636
Railways	11.4 ⎫		18.8 ⎧	343
Roads	5.5 ⎬	16.1	5.1 ⎨	188
Other transport and communications	6.7 ⎭		5.0 ⎩	152
Education	7.0 ⎫		6.4 ⎧	186
Health	5.9 ⎪		5.7 ⎪	197
Housing	2.1 ⎬	32.9	2.5 ⎨	245
Other social services	7.6 ⎪		5.1 ⎪	137
Miscellaneous	3.0 ⎭		2.1 ⎩	143
TOTAL	100.0	100.0	100.0	204

In the third Indian FYP Soviet-type influence has been much more moderate. But in any case the second FYP is a *locus classicus* for the dangers of attributing influence. The emphasis on heavy industry was Mahalanobis's own. He *may* have got the idea from Moscow in 1952 (where he met Bettelheim)[44]; but if so it was surely his independent conclusion in the main. He *was* reinforced in his

[44] Source: I was there myself.

attitude by sundry communist economists, and his influence on Nehru is nowhere disputed. But he did not pursue a communist policy, and he showed a lively and sensible concern for just that sector that Stalin wantonly destroyed, rating it even above heavy industry.

IX. *The Economic Content of Afro-Marxism*

Ghanaian economic policy under Nkrumah, on the other hand, was a classic example of empty phrase-making. The Osagyefo span his theories, making himself out a great Marxist on a level with Khrushchev and Mao, but also mixing in his early western training as an epistemologist and throwing in for good measure a justification of his foreign policy by means of symbolic logic.[45] But although many ignorant and alarmed people thought he was a communist this is not true at all. His epistemology, to begin with trivialities, is profoundly un-Marxist. His one-party system was of a different and more attractive kind than the communist, since it was supposed to embrace most of the adult population and to allow discussion. He was also wise enough to reject class war and collectivization.

'Seek ye First the Political Kingdom', said the Osagyefo. He certainly meant it. To turn from Ghanaian politics to Ghanaian economics is to walk out of the Kremlin and find yourself in Great George Street. Indeed the word Kremlin fits only inasmuch as Flagstaff House was an immense paranoiac fortress, equipped with Soviet security devices: the security system as a whole was the most communist thing in the country. In contrast the whole atmosphere of the learned economic journal[46] and of the principal state paper[47] is western and sedate. If a Polish economist (Professor Jan Drewnowski, educated at the London School of Economics) edited the journal and headed the economics department at the university, we do not know exactly what advice he gave. In any case he understandably made less of a splash than Mahalanobis in India, for he was not a native. A professor from Budapest (Josef Bognar, a Smallholder

---

[45] Kwame Nkrumah, *Consciencism* (Oxford, 1964). For the hollowness and instability of Nkrumah's ideology cf. Tibor Szamuely, *The Spectator*, 11 March 1966. D. G. MacRae takes a contrary view in *Government and Opposition* (London), I, iv, 1966. The authorship of *Consciencism* is much disputed. But at least it remains well within the circle of intellectual interests to be expected of a professor of philosophy turned dictator; and it surely reflects his views.

[46] *The Economic Bulletin of Ghana*, quarterly.

[47] *Economic Survey*, annual.

Party man who had made his peace with the regime) even contrived to write an article on plan *implementation* machinery without implying that there should be a command economy. But the implementation of plans is exactly where communism is strong and capitalism is weak. There seem, again, to have been no communist economists in the Planning Commission. But as this goes to press surprising revelations continue to trickle out, and it may yet transpire that really influential people were at work in the Soviet embassy. The same Professor Bognar, for instance, wrote a confidential report on the seven-year plan.

At the very least the problems with which the published literature concerns itself are standard western problems: inflation, the market for capital, over-expansion of the public sector, the budget deficit, the balance of payments crisis, the minimum wage. Not only did Ghana lack an east European Mahalanobis; it lacked a Ghanaian one. Indeed a Ghanaian at that time in high office has suggested to me that Nkrumah deliberately imported very moderate communists in order to have the appearance without the reality.

It is true that Nkrumah's 1961 visit to the communist bloc was a turning point.[48] Returning, he scrapped his own second five-year plan (1959–60—1963–4) and substituted a seven-year plan (1963–4—1969–70). But this document is by no means at all a Soviet-type plan. Technically its sole advance over the second FYP is that it is not just a 'shopping list' but a macro-economically integrated affair. In other words the latest *western* techniques were used.

In early 1963, for instance, the Central Bureau of Statistics wrote, and in July the Osagyefo (notionally) presented to the National Assembly a report that said, inter alia:

> The greater proportion of the [foreign exchange] reserves was utilized in the establishment of an economic and social infra-structure which ranks as one of the best in the developing countries. The present level of infra-structure is now capable of supporting a level of production and distribution far above the present. The time has now come for the Government to lay more emphasis on investment in directly productive projects. This point was stressed last year and it formed the basic policy of Government during the budget. Unfortunately, preliminary results indicate that the relative share of Government expenditure in directly productive projects has not risen as much as one would expect. It should be emphasized once

[48] Cf. W. Birmingham, L. Neustadt, and E. N. Omaboe, eds., *A Study of Contemporary Ghana*, vol. I, *The Economy of Ghana* (London, 1966), ch. 18. Though written under Nkrumah for the Ghanaian Academy of Sciences, and politically discreet, this is a work of serious and independent scholarship.

more that the productive capacity of the country and also the rate of growth which will be attained in the coming years will depend upon the proportion of the national resources devoted to investment in agriculture and industry. Investment in social services like health and education should be made to keep pace with other investments in the directly productive sectors. Unless this balance is maintained the economy will be saddled with a high standard of social services without the generation of sufficient economic activity to support it. This problem has been realized by the National Planning Commission and it is emphasized throughout the chapters of the draft of the Seven-year Development Plan.

The management of the various industrial and agricultural projects which will be established during the plan period should also be carefully considered. It is not the policy of the government to establish factories for the sake of national prestige. On the other hand it is expected that these factories should make worthwhile contributions to the domestic product. It is necessary during the initial period for these factories to be protected against unfair competition from outside. It should be noted, however, that the factories are expected after the gestation period to be operated on commercial lines and to be able to stand competition from outside. . . .

The Government's socialist policy makes provision for the existence of a private sector of the economy. It is expected, however, that the activities in the private sector should be consistent with the general policy which the Government lay down for the nation. The economic and social climate was somehow confused during part of 1961 and 1962. This, unfortunately, contributed to the absence of a high rate of economic activity in 1962. This slight misunderstanding has now been removed and the way is now clear for renewed activity in the private sector of the economy.

There was, of course, no command economy and no agricultural collectivization.[49] Even the seven-year plan was simply an 'Indian' plan, concerned with state investment and foreign exchange. But any lingering doubts about the government's non-communist attitude can be set at rest by its investment allocations. (See table 3 on page 242.)

Other figures, seemingly incompatible with table 3, show a more pronounced shift:

	Ghanaian Government Investment (%)	
	Agriculture and Industry	*Social Services and Infrastructure*
First FYP ..	11.2	88.8
Second FYP ..	20.3	79.7
Seven YP ..	37.3	62.7

Source: W. Birmingham et al., *op. cit.*, p. 455.

[49] There were a few state farms on virgin land; they failed.

TABLE 3

Ghanaian Central Government Capital Expenditure (%)

	1960–1	1961–2	1962–3	1963–4
General services..	10.7	10.4	14.4	8.9
Roads and waterways..	5.8	5.9	3.1	7.6
Other community services	3.9	3.6	4.0	10.0
Social services	18.1	15.5	20.4	16.1
Agriculture and non-mineral resources	3.8	4.9	7.2	8.5
Fuel and power	14.3	15.3	17.0	18.7
Other material resources, manufacturing and construction	20.0	21.2	9.6	19.7
Transport, storage, and communications	16.8	15.9	12.7	9.7
Other economic services	2.1	2.1	11.2	0.4
Transfer to local government ..	4.5	5.1	0.4	0.4
Total (£G mn.)	46.9	62.7	52.9	50.3

Source, *Economic Survey 1964*, pp. 120–1.

But these proportions still fall far short of typical communist ones, and agriculture is put quite on a par with industry.

If we take the economy as a whole, including private investment, the picture is unaltered. Thus gross domestic fixed capital formation moved, from before to after independence, as follows (%):

	1955	1964
Buildings	51.9	46.6
Other construction works ..	23.1	26.7
Transport equipment	11.5	11.2
Machinery and other equipment..	13.5	15.5

Source, ibid., p. 20.

The intervening years show about the same figures. Nkrumah had become Leader of Government Business in 1951. Ghana became independent in March 1957.

This to my mind sensible investment pattern recalls a passage from the Osagyefo's own autobiography:

> The problem of unemployment in rural areas must be solved by creating industries in the rural areas. . . . The concentration of labour in industrial areas and modern factories requires large capital investment countries cannot bear. . . . Transport by rail, by road, and by civil aviation will be given high priority. . . . [It is] our desire to start industrialization of our country at the same time as we increase the productivity of our agriculture.[50]

Actually, however, what Nkrumah invested in was the development of the State, not the economy; dignity and security, not wealth. We have already drawn attention to the exceedingly costly fortification of the Presidential residence. Professor MacRae puts it well:

> Development investment is not really separate or different from prestige investment—statues, conference halls, luxury dwellings—from the viewpoint of political rhetoric. The show of steel and concrete is part of the political propaganda of our time—as are shipping and airlines, embassies and motor-roads. Communication by finding Rome brick, and leaving it marble, served Augustus and Mussolini alike. It was not unlikely that it could serve Nkrumahism by communicating the same messages.

All communist countries have exhibited a similar syndrome, of course, but it has much older origins. The aggrandisement of the nation, coupled of course with the name of its monarch, by some act of useless investment, explains Pérez Jiménez as well as Mussolini, Henry VIII as well as Augustus; it goes back at least to Ozymandias. It has, indeed, motivated such comparatively democratic rulers as Kubitschek, and is largely a matter of the ruler's individual character.

It seems that despite his frankly ridiculous 'Consciencism', Nkrumah did not move from his early economic views, or more accurately that he never had any economic views. His attitude to Marxism resembled strongly, *mutatis mutandis*, that of Lord Melbourne to Christianity: it was all right so long as it did not interfere with private life. Here, then, was an allegedly Marxist dictatorship with no Soviet, indeed no Marxist, influence on the economy at all. Nkrumah was using the vocabulary alone, and for political ends, mainly to keep his own rabble-rousers happy. None

[50] Kwame Nkrumah, *I Speak for Freedom* (New York, 1961), pp. 53, 157. The authorship of this work too has been disputed, but it is again inconceivable that it should not represent Nkrumah's views.

of his party ideologues ever received executive power.[51] It would have been pointless to ask in Flagstaff House whether the socialist model was that of Britain in 1946, Yugoslavia or the USSR, or some original one; because no-one there could have defined these models. In fact the economy just ran on as it had under British rule, with much more government expenditure and corruption, and rather more nationalization. The east European advisers did not in fact interfere, but if they had wanted to what levers could they have grasped? For Nkrumah did not easily accept advice. My Ghanaian informant saw him be insultingly inattentive and abrupt with his Ghanaian ministers. It was not in his nature to listen to anyone. Nor must he be denied credit for simple common sense. It is true that he ran through his country's foreign exchange reserves and started many very wasteful projects. But these are the faults of economic *il*literacy. Economic *semi*-literacy might have brought about unacceptable institutional changes, like those in Guinea. Again economic performance under Nkrumah was not a disaster. Figures of very doubtful reliability put the annual growth of national income per head as follows:[52]

1890–1911	1.8%
1911–1950	1.5%
1950–1955	0.4%
1955–1960	3.3%
1960–1964	−1.0%?

The principal determinants of growth in any short period are the cocoa harvest and the cocoa price—both outside Ghanaian control. That the last disastrous four years should have coincided with Nkrumah's swing to Marxist *talk* is the purest coincidence. Moreover we must make allowances for the passage of time in the USSR. What actually would have been Soviet advice to Nkrumah in, say, 1964? We have strong evidence that it would not have been anything like so crude a stereotyped repetition of Soviet experience as was recommended to India in 1956. There must have been by the later date a very considerable gap between the publicly printed professions of Soviet advisers and the counsel they in fact gave. Innumerable quotations[53] demonstrate a slow drift towards less

---

[51] I owe information on this and many other points to Mr Emil Rado of Glasgow University.
[52] W. Birmingham et al., *op. cit.*, pp. 18–19, 413; my own rough calculations.
[53] Supplied to me by Mr Jeffries. Cf. also Clarkson, *op. cit.*

dogmatic and Soviet-centred thinking, at least on the short-run problems of underdeveloped countries. The ultimate goal for them is still to reproduce the Soviet institutional model, but they may pick their way.

In particular we saw that the NEP is now held up—surely rightly—as worth imitating. But in the NEP, too, investment was concentrated on heavy industry, and in every year since 1925 inclusive heavy industrial output grew faster. So recommending the NEP is one thing and recommending a new investment pattern is another. By coincidence, Mr V. Kondratev mentions Ghana in this context. Conditions in Ghana impose

the necessity of a three-stage process of industrialization. The first stage presupposes the building up in the country of the production of consumer goods and building materials and also ensuring the output of valuable types of raw materials. . . . The second stage is marked by the transition to the creation of such branches as ferrous and non-ferrous metallurgy, the production of chemical products, fertilizers, and synthetic fibres. The creation of machine engineering and a number of other branches of modern technical industry is the mainstay of the third stage of industrialization.[54]

If such things were being said in public in 1965 they were probably being said privately in 1963. I am in no doubt, all the same, that Soviet influence in this field was minimal, so un-communist was the style of Ghanaian economics; but it is at least interesting to reflect that we hardly know any more what it would have been.

It may be thought—indeed I have been told—that the foregoing account is insufficiently serious, and therefore not scholarly. But if 'scholarly' must mean 'serious' then it may also mean 'untrue'. The unfortunate Ghanaian people *were* living through a sort of tragic light opera. In economics, frivolity, corruption, and waste *were* the keynotes. As to ideology, MacRae indeed proves that in African history and current foreign policy Nkrumahism showed a certain stability, and brought up propositions that could be understood and affirmed or denied. It is very true that it was not an evil ideology. Indeed it was less inherently mischievous and aggressive than communism, itself not the most evil of ideologies. But there are also ontological, ethical, artistic, and economic questions, with which communism and even nazism also dealt—indeed dealt well enough to hold water for a decade or more. And here it would be flattery to describe Nkrumah's structure as a house of cards. When the situation

[54] *Mirovaya Ekonomika i Mezhdunarodnie Otnosheniya*, 1965, v.

satirises itself, satire becomes simply the good historian's *wie es eigentlich gewesen*. And in the presence of such instability, *all* foreign influence is shown to be impossible—which is what we are asked to consider.

X. The case of Guinea

A far better example of Soviet influence, while it lasted, was shown by Guinea.[55] When Sekou Touré decided in September 1958 to vote against the inclusion of his country in the new Union Française, the French State (but not all private Frenchmen) withdrew not merely its personnel but the very telephones on their desks. It even dismantled the light fittings. It also boycotted Guinea's bananas. Many private capitalists took out all the capital they could.

There were at the time about fifty native graduates in this country of about two and a half million people. As so often, French colonization had penetrated to far lower social levels than British. If the British Empire was 'outdoor relief for the aristocracy', then the French Empire was outdoor relief for one and all. So Guinea lost at one blow most of its upper, upper middle, and lower middle classes. It was put into a more desperate position than ever were Cuba or Algeria, and the story of its Soviet period is the story of its search for a country that would help it with electricians and midwives. This is what 'aid' principally meant. Development was of course expected, but even stagnation would have been a feat.

Touré, the absolute master of his country, had originated in the trade union movement and been under the sway of the French communist Confédération Générale du Travail. It appears that the CGT even sent him on a short, secret course to Czechoslovakia. His own Parti Démocratique Guinéen is often too glibly compared to a communist party. It has many resemblances, especially in being a monopoly party. But it is in fact of the 'African' or 'directly mobilizing', type: nearly everyone belongs, discussion is very free, and it does not profess communism or class war. Nkrumah's party was also of this type, as we saw, and he has always had a great influence on Touré.

Touré also tried to dominate religion—80–85 per cent of the population is Moslem. He founded a communist-seeming 'front', the

[55] Jean Lacouture, *Cinq Hommes et la France* (Paris, 1961); Elliot J. Berg, in *Quarterly Journal of Economics*, 1964; Jacques Miandre, in *Esprit*, 1963, x. I am also greatly indebted to the Chatham House press library.

Moslem Cultural Union. This met in Conakry on 22–24 September 1959. There exists a PDG document[56] showing that this too is a modernizing or mobilizing organization. The document condemns Panislamism, reactionary superstitions and habits, and most marabouts (preachers). It is clearly written by non-Moslems with a purely functional attitude to religion. It specifically praises Soviet Moslem policy, but adds the Pakistani and Ceylonese examples. It fails entirely to reflect the usual Soviet hostility to religion as such, and is clearly pretty tolerant. Later, when he turned round, Touré began to refer to himself as Ismail Sekou Touré. There seems, however, to have been nothing specifically Islamic about his economic policies.

Beginning, then, as a fellow-traveller with the French Communist Party, he had moved by the time of his declaration of independence to a strongly Afro-Marxist position, very close to that of Nkrumah. But with one vital difference: the erstwhile trade union boss, though economically illiterate, was no mere phraseur. Faced with the virtually complete withdrawal of educated men, he asked around for aid. Fearful of offending the French, the NATO Powers other than West Germany kept out, and the USSR came to the rescue. With the help of Czechoslovakia and East Germany, it provided technicians, trade, and aid. But did it have influence?

It is beyond the slightest question that Touré was at all times his own man. But he had many communist advisers—of whom the largest contingent was French, for the French CP had not abandoned its tutelary, 'colonialist' role. Also he was himself a Marxist. So how many Soviet institutions and policies did he copy? The answer seems to be that he was 'in spirit' founding a Soviet-type economy, but he copied very little exactly. For his Soviet period lasted only three years (January 1959–December 1961), and the objective circumstances of his country were utterly different.

First, of course, came state security: as elsewhere in the world, so also in Africa the prime consideration of a serious government. Czechoslovakia delivered arms already in March 1959, before Touré even had an ambassador in Moscow—an interesting confirmation of the priority of his Czechoslovak connection. East German civilian aid had been agreed on already in November 1958, and Nkrumah made a large and immediate contribution from Ghana's still considerable currency reserve in the same month. Thereafter,

[56] Vincent Monteil, *L'Islam Noir* (Paris, 1964), pp. 318–22.

however, the Ghana-Guinea union effectually took a back seat, and the main aid was communist.

Next after the security measures, foreign and domestic trade were in large part nationalized—simultaneously, and into the same corporations. In the USSR foreign trade had been one of Lenin's 'commanding heights', and had been nationalized long before domestic trade. But then Guinea imports so very many consumer goods, and private capitalism had conducted both kinds of trade under the one roof. So what Touré did was a perfectly logical extension of what Lenin did. On the other hand it was a fairly obvious left-wing measure, requiring no foreign precedents. It was also a terrible disaster. When in October 1963 Touré returned trade to the private sector, he excused his previous aberration by saying that the communist countries, on whom Guinea had been utterly dependent, had refused to trade with private business.[57] I strongly suspect that this is untrue. Such a refusal is very unlikely indeed, and Touré's interest in alleging it *ex post facto* is overwhelming.

A much more convincing instance of Soviet influence was the monetary reform. At the time of the break with France, Guinea shared with the rest of Francophone Africa the franc CFA, over which it had no powers. In January 1959 it agreed with the Banque de France to introduce its own separate currency and central bank, but to accept the French franc as the sole reserve currency, and to keep its own franc convertible. But Soviet influence grew during the year, and eventually the notes and coins were printed and minted, it seems, in Czechoslovakia in October 1959. But they were not issued then.

Touré visited Washington, London, Bonn, and Moscow about this time, and gave pleasure in Bonn and offence in Moscow by leaving out East Berlin. He had been there in February, and the aid was coming in anyway, but West German aid, his only western aid, was at least in part contingent on the non-recognition of Ulbricht. However, Touré's speeches on this tour, though stressing his independence, were far more pro-Moscow than pro-Washington.

In March 1960 came a yet further turn to the left. East Germany was recognized, a Soviet long-term credit agreement was completed, a planning ministry was formed, and the new currency was at last issued, on very Soviet terms. The new franc was 'based on gold' but had no role in foreign trade (cf. sec. VI above); that is, it was

[57] *Commerce du Levant* (Beirut), 19 October 1963.

not in principle convertible but in practice subject to restraint; it was in principle inconvertible. This measure effectively expropriated foreign traders, and even technicians, whose remittances and imports for personal consumption were seriously curtailed.

To complete the monetary story, a very Soviet-type banking system was introduced in June 1961. In addition to the single big bank of issue and deposit, catering for the ordinary needs of business, there were to be only specialized banks for foreign trade and investment.

Great caution, however, was shown in nationalizing industry and mines—and here Lenin provides a good Marxist precedent if common sense did not give us a better. In February 1961 a power failure embarrassed Touré at a reception for a Chinese delegation, and in a typical fit of rage he nationalized electricity and water undertakings. His real object came out more clearly in the instant deportation of the French technicians. Diamond and gold mining was nationalized in March, but the really important capitalist enterprises in bauxite and iron ore, the pillars of the whole economy, were left alone. They even very greatly increased their output during the Soviet period, thus at least keeping down Guinea's foreign debt while everything else went wrong.

Agriculture was host to a modest number of communist experiments: a Soviet state farm, some Chinese advice on rice, and above all some Chinese-style labour-intensive projects under the title of 'human investment'. None of this prevented a fearful decline in production. French planters, however, were not expropriated.

Finally we must re-emphasize that in all new countries security and propaganda are a major industry. While Nkrumah, as we saw, made a paranoid Kremlin of Flagstaff House, Touré at least moved freely among his people. But he did set up a powerful wireless station and a big printing press, and import the Czechoslovak arms mentioned above. These things were in fact the show pieces of communist aid.

But what really happened was that everything stopped functioning. The USSR delivered two snowploughs, and East Germany three million screwdrivers—more than one per head, and possibly more than one per screw. Cement—there is always such a proverbial cement shipment in every foreign aid story—hardened in the rain on the quay of the wrong port. 'Tchèque' came to mean 'technically inferior'. Communist technicians could not speak French. Lifts stopped, cars broke down and could not even be cannibalized. The powerful wireless station developed trouble owing to the iron ore on which its foundations stood. The big printing press clanked but intermittently, and so was grossly uneconomic. Lavatory pans, without seats or plumbing, stood in fields. Mobile bridges were lost, and discovered later under rusting machinery. Russian miners were arrested for stealing diamonds. A Chinese cigarette factory stood empty because the country could not import tobacco. Poles complained of the humidity and heat, and Guineans complained of the Poles. The West German slaughter-house stood empty, because the cattle were all being smuggled out to earn 'real' money. Everything French seemed better, though a proud people did not regret its decision to be free and poor.

Much of this was *dans la nature des choses*, and much of it was Touré's own fault. It is not, for instance, denied that three million screwdrivers had been duly ordered; and everybody steals diamonds. After what France had left undone (a more practical education for the elite, an education of any sort for the rest), and done (its sudden withdrawal), things were bound to go very badly. Any country trying to fill its place at short notice, and under the general authority of the irascible dictator and his fifty graduates, would have failed.

But the snowploughs had *not* been ordered, and the cattle were smuggled out (as was much else) because of the inconvertible currency, and the East Germans did not have to commit themselves to actually running the biggest nationalized trade corporation. Above all the western mining concerns did indeed shine like a good deed in a naughty world. Some fair part—though less than half—of the communists' disaster was in fact due to their own technical inefficiency and the bad advice they gave at high levels.

Several different events brought Guinea's Soviet episode to an end. In October 1960 the United States finally understood that Touré was indeed independent, and signed its first aid agreement. By August 1961 the Soviet ambassador with the brilliant reputation (Daniel Solod), at whose advent the chanceries of NATO had trembled, was no longer being admitted to the presence.[58] In November he was held responsible for some communist student riots—who knows, perhaps he was innocent?—and on 16 December he left, at Touré's request. No-one saw him off. For good measure, in July 1962 the Algerian war stopped: the France that every Guinean, not least Touré, loved and hated and admired was no longer a pariah.

[58] *New York Herald Tribune*, 29 December 1961.

It is beyond our purview to describe the de-Sovietization of the Guinean economy. Enough to say that it has gone a very long way indeed: wholesale, foreign, and retail trade have for the most part reverted to the private sector, along with diamond mining; there has been another monetary reform; much of the Chinese-type 'human investment' has been abandoned; exchanges with the West and particularly with France have much increased, at communist expense. But official gratitude remains for what the communists did, and 'African Socialism' remains as official, and as undefined, as ever. The promising Mr Solod has been replaced by someone less brilliant, communist aid still flows, and Touré's foreign policy is still anti-western, if no longer pro-anything. Perhaps most importantly, he made, at least for a time, his peace with the right-wing M. Houphouet-Boigny of the Ivory Coast. For let us remember that France and the USSR are very far away, and whatever the head-lines say the policy of an African State towards the major Powers preoccupies it no more than policy towards its neighbours.

The temptation must be avoided of generalizing from this rout of communist economics. Where all economic systems would have failed badly, it failed very badly. If it was helped by the political set-up, it had everything else against it: the rash and innumerate dictator, the proud and idle people, the humidity, the heat, the extreme under-development, the linguistic barrier, the nostalgia for France . . . anyone who reads this tale with feelings of superiority deserves to be instantly deported as a development economist to Conakry. A simpler and a better lesson is: economics is a bread-and-butter issue. Things have to work.

XI. *Foreign imitations of the penal labour system*

There has been much talk about the influence of the Soviet forced labour system. In an exceedingly general way, Stalin's ruthlessness with the vested interests of his subjects, especially his poorer sub-jects, has impressed many non-communists. I would not deny that all kinds of people talk tough, and a few even act tough, because Stalin did so. Indeed, the same Mr Carr whom I have so severely criticized above has a most convincing passage (*op. cit.*, pp. 48–63) on the Bolshevik impact on western labour policy. The powerful independent trade union, imposing cost-push and restrictive practices, is a threat to every economic system alike. It would have been impossible to curb in the West—in so far as it has been curbed—had there existed genuine, free unionism in the USSR. Such a phenomenon would indeed have had an impact. But it was not so. Lenin and Stalin wholly emasculated the unions, turning them first into economic planning organs and then into welfare organs. They have never been permitted to develop their own policy, and when, in periods of comparative liberalism such as the NEP or the present day, they give signs of so doing, their policy is recognizably western. In other words, Lenin and Stalin did not crudely suppress some creative third way. There was, of course, none to suppress: free unions are an integral part of capitalism, and stand or fall with it.

So the influence of the Soviet example has been that non-communist governments have faced no ideological competition in this field. Soviet unions are the least free. Strikes, though legal, are in fact always punished by the police. The wage-freeze is perpetual. These very well known facts have given the rest of the world room to manoeuvre. Eventually, sporadically, it has turned upon its unions and brought them within measure to heel. There has been a lag here: compare the union-favouring policies of Roosevelt, Cárdenas, and Léon Blum in the thirties. But there is scarcely a country in the world today that encourages unfettered unionism. We may say with great confidence that this is a natural development, needing no Bolshevik Revolution to blaze the trail. But had that revolution not pretended to be pro-labour, or had it found some better way, it would have inhibited the march of events. Its influence was, in the upshot, permissive.

In rather less degree Stalin's policies on the *individual* employment contract have had the same impact: there is nothing new for us to imitate, so we may go ahead. I say in less degree, because communism had gone very far out on a limb here, and had to retreat towards the western norm. Stakhanovism, universal piecework, fines for bad work, prison for persistently arriving late, the abolition of labour exchanges: these things were an obviously pathological caricature of the capitalist attitude. They influenced no-one while they were practised, and Stalin's successors have abandoned them. In keeping with our scepticism about influence and our respect for most people's common sense, we need not seek for any deep reverse western influence on the USSR at this point.

To turn to penal labour itself, Stalin has not been imitated directly or even anything like it. Thus from time to time Indian economists, in their pardonable desperation, speak of forced labour as something that must probably come. But it has not come; on the contrary, it has practically disappeared in the USSR. Today only China in all the world practises forced labour, and even there it is done mainly by the very extensive direction of free labour to jobs and places. Prison labour is not a large factor.

Stalin did indeed surprise the world by re-introducing large-scale forced labour, and it worked well enough to satisfy at least him. But in face of an almost complete blank in the non-communist world, we need hardly here pursue this matter. It is perhaps worth while to set the system in its particular place among the forms of human slavery. Drawing on my own unpublished studies, I am prepared to assert that:

> very few were arrested and falsely condemned because the em-
> ployers of forced labour needed more of it; rather were the
> millions of arrests due to security paranoia or draconian laws;
> the forced labour camps were a natural extension of the early
> communist penology, which rightly held that prisoners should
> work;
> they were also the necessary resultant of the combination of
> millions of able-bodied prisoners and ambitious growth plans;
> the system often showed a paper profit, counting the guards'
> wages as a cost of production;
> but on the most cold-blooded reckoning it was a terrible economic
> waste, since it grossly misemployed expensive skills and
> shortened working lives by cold and starvation;
> the cold northern areas it was used to develop would have been
> better left unexploited.

But neither this precedent, nor that of Negro slavery in America and Arabia, nor that of British and French penal transportation, seems to have had the slightest influence on any non-communist government. There has indeed been one kind of forced labour in the modern world: the colonial corvée, particularly practised in the Congo and Angola. The corvée takes a very unskilled labourer, and transports him a short distance for a limited time to perform some gang work. He may then return home. He may originally have been selected by the village headman, even perhaps democratically or on some principle of natural justice from among many eligibles.

In other words he is a labour conscript just as others are soldier conscripts. The system is often of extreme brutality, but it has in principle very much to recommend it in very poor countries. This essentially colonialist device far antedates even the birth of Stalin, and has clearly no connection at all with his *penal* system.[59] It has not been abandoned in independent Africa, nor, doubtless, should it be. But it has much diminished.

Stalin's system was penal. To forced labour it added terror. It is not surprising that less totalitarian rulers have been neither willing nor able to imitate it. On a strict economic reckoning there is no doubt at all that they are very fortunate. For it would have been better for Stalin too if he had been unable to waste his country's scarce resources by setting trained engineers to hew wood in the frozen north, and die in their prime.

Stalin practised also a milder kind of forced labour: he exiled people to defined areas, where they would find what work they could, and he forbade collective farmers to leave the farms on which they had been born. The exile was penal (mostly an extra-judicial security measure), and the *adscriptio glebae* of the peasant was a measure of convenience. Both practices were of Tsarist origin, and both had ample colonial precedents from before Stalin's birth. Administrative exile continues to be a common practice in many ex-colonies to-day, based on the tradition of the previous regime. South Africa has the best developed system for keeping the tribal peasant on his reserve—and this too owes nothing to Soviet example.

Thus there is forced labour a-plenty in the world, but less than there used to be. Democracy, Freedom, and the Century of the Common Man are not *utterly* meaningless terms, even in underdeveloped countries. Moreover, only communists ever went to the USSR for a model, and of these only the Chinese continue in the game. The opinion of Professor S. Swianiewicz that 'Soviet experience has shown that such hardships are conducive to a drift towards slavery—and this may ultimately lead to a disaster on a world scale', seems to be wholly without foundation.[60]

---

[59] Though there was a Tsarist corvée, which has survived in the little-known obligation on rural residents to perform a few days of public work every year, at the expense mostly of their farm, if any, but on the orders of the local authority.

[60] In a book nonetheless full of important insights and original factual material, *Forced Labour and Economic Development* (Oxford University Press, 1959).

XII. The Example of Soviet anti-imperialist tactics

Lastly we make a more general enquiry: how many other countries have adopted the Soviet economic weapons against imperialism? These weapons are debt repudiation, and autarky, especially in heavy industry and arms. The main point to grasp is that non-communist regimes are almost all less violent and hostile than Soviet Russia was. It has been possible for India to forgive the depredations of the East India Company, the suppression of the Mutiny, the humiliation of Amritsar. In comparison Russia had suffered virtually no injury from imperialism—certainly much less than Russia itself had inflicted under that heading. But the Bolshevik government was Marxist before it was Russian. Class antagonisms were supposed to be irreconcilable, and foreign capital was all part of the single, world-wide class enemy.

There has always been opposition to imperialism, and we can certainly attribute no general originality to the Bolsheviks here. Nevertheless the flat repudiation of foreign debt on principle was a *novum* in the world of 1917. Innumerable weak and disorderly governments had defaulted right through the nineteenth century, but Lenin did not merely default. Again, the Boxers (China, 1900) had been far more violent towards foreign nationals; but that, and not debt repudiation, was their *raison d'être*. They aimed to wipe out missionaries and foreign teachers in the name of the old Chinese culture, where Lenin was an internationalist and wanted to admit many kinds of foreign teacher.

When it comes to the confiscation of foreign capital as such, on vaguely left-wing or progressive grounds, only Mexico has a tenuous claim to priority. We reviewed in sec. V above, and rejected, the Mexican claim to have collectivized agriculture independently. But the much more general claim to have anticipated the Bolshevik Revolution as a whole is by no means nonsensical. The period 1910–17 brought deep social changes that were never reversed, but have rather continued to roll forward. If they can mostly be described as Populist—in the American and not the Russian sense—they nevertheless contain many elements that must be called socialist. As concerns foreign capital, Mexico took extremely mild measures of expropriation already in May 1917. The government revoked certain rights of foreign landowners to the subsoil, without compensation. That the measures were so mild was doubtless due to the threat of United States intervention, easier to bring about in Mexico than in Russia. Mexico was at the time nearly at war with the United States.

Whether or not this partial exception be admitted, Lenin was certainly the first to apply the *Marxist* theory of imperialism. In fact he intended to do so very mildly, and initially repudiated only the Tsarist state debt. It was the Civil War, which began in the summer of 1918, that forced the Bolsheviks to confiscate foreign enterprise capital, in that they nationalized the whole economy. During the NEP years they tried to get foreign enterprise capital back, but on the whole failed, since their compensation offers were derisorily low.

But the moderation of Lenin's intentions is a much less lively memory than the fact of his 100 per cent repudiation, *and the fact that he got away with it.* There is little doubt that subsequent debt repudiators have him to thank for their immunity. The wonder is that so few have taken advantage of it. For in fact the only real imitators have been other communist countries—and not all of them. There have been quarrels over the Argentine railways and the Suez canal, but outside the communist world actual repudiation is very rare. Default, of course, is common—and in the modern world the USSR often finds itself on the wrong end of it! Both Albania and Indonesia have defaulted on large sums of Soviet aid.

Along with the failure to repudiate debt goes the failure to cut off current economic relations. The trade of underdeveloped countries and ex-colonies with the West, if not always specifically with their ex-masters, increases year by year. They also continue to borrow from them extensively, being limited only by their capacity to repay.

While this is contrary to Soviet precept, it is not, as we saw in sec. VIII, contrary to the practice of the NEP and the first five-year plan, when trade grew faster than the national income, and there was even considerable foreign borrowing. In this period Stalin 'imported to be autarkic'; that is, he stocked up the foreign machinery which later enabled him to dispense with foreign machinery. This advice many poor countries have taken, though we have seen that in many cases it may be bad advice. The Soviet period of real autarky began in about 1932. It may be said that it still continues, but is little imitated. Poor countries import in order to grow, not to be autarkic. Indeed, even the east European communists have behaved very differently. Autarky, then, is not as universal a communist practice as we tend to think.

But in one respect there has been imitation: the ex-colonies do try to confine their imports to the products of heavy industry. Since imports are among the few things an administratively backward country can control, its import policy will reflect its general development policy. I personally find this very sensible.

XIII. The genuine Titoism of Ben Bella

So much, then, for instances of imitating or of failing to imitate the USSR. But Algeria is perhaps the clearest case of the direct and conscious, yet selective, importation of a foreign model of socialism. However, the model is Yugoslav! The vigorous growth of Titoist institutions in Algeria,[61] at most ten years after their perfection in their country of origin, stands in striking contrast to the total failure of any non-communist country to adopt Stalinist institutions, after nearly forty years. It is related of an ignorant examination candidate in biology that, faced with a question on the elephant, he began his answer: 'How different is the elephant from the mouse, which. . . .' I have this excuse for expatiating on the Algerian mouse, that there is no elephant. This case, then, is a standard whereby to judge Soviet influence.

The Front de Libération Nationale, which came to power in July 1962, is a revolutionary, non-communist, anti-bourgeois, left-wing party which insists on a monopoly of state power. In its period of war with France it was recognized as a government principally by China, and China also provided most of the material help it received. Yet there are today no People's Communes—quite the contrary, they are thought of with horror. The Yugoslavs did indeed recognize the FLN much before the USSR and its European allies— which did so only after the cease-fire in March 1962. Belgrade suffered in consequence a technical rebuff by French diplomacy. But its services were not on a Chinese scale, so it is clear that political gratitude, that rare commodity, played a very small part in subsequent events.

Workers' councils, or self-administration, have some traditional roots in the Algerian countryside, but not many. There is a parallel here to the Aztec and Spanish experiences of collective farming,

---

[61] I have used principally F. d'Arcy, A. Krieger, and A. Marill, *Essais sur l'Economie de l'Algérie Nouvelle* (Paris, 1965); Pierre Bourdieu, *Sociologie de l'Algérie* (Paris, 1961). The Yugoslav quotations were kindly supplied by my colleague Mr Ljubo Sirc.

which made possible and natural the *ejidos collectivos*. On the land Islamic law was theoretically paramount, and this is unequivocally— and most uneconomically—in favour of private peasant farms, coupled with indefinite parcellation in order to keep the share of each heir equal. In practice the sedentary Kabyles simply refused to apply the Islamic law of inheritance to female heirs, in order to prevent land going outside the tribe. For the rest, members of the tribe had a restricted right to alienate their land, which they culti- vated family by family. The Kabyle was thus on the whole an econo- mic man and individualist. Arabic-speaking peoples, nomadic at least in principle, evaded rather than denied Islam, with a primitive rural co-operation based on the small tribe. This permitted com- munal *pasturage* by separately-owned livestock; but where crops were concerned it went no further than the periodical redistribution of the privately cultivated farms (the *arch* system). That much col- lectivism is standard form among primitive peoples. More relevant is it that in all cases the unit of *management* was the nuclear family. The extended family, ruled by a patriarch, was strong, but did not settle the details of cultivation. Whether the tribe or the family *owns*, whether indeed ownership can be spoken of at all, is surely less important than this. In fact the land of the extended family was burdened, much as the equity of a capitalist company, by innumerable claimants to aliquot parts of the proceeds. This was one of the main results of French capitalist legalism, which tried for a hundred years to bring order of its own kind into the native tenure systems. The extreme and ludicrous individualism of these arrange- ments was perhaps a stimulus even in the eyes of the peasants to collectivism. But in fact much of the land was held capitalistically by the French, and it was *this* land, not the decaying Arab communal tenures, that was turned over to true collectivism.

At Tripoli in June 1962, that is, already before taking power, the movement[62] wanted state farms with workers' control. But the idea was only one among many, and it did not receive great emphasis. Immense impetus was given to it in the same month, however, by the flight of great numbers of French entrepreneurs and owners. The new government was instantly faced with a big problem of managerless enterprises. In these circumstances workers' control

[62] Strictly not the FLN, which was then much more moderate, but the National Council of the Algerian Revolution. The Tripoli resolution was Ben Bella's. Subsequently he took over the Politbureau of the FLN.

became a grass-roots movement, and a practical necessity. As in Russia in 1917, the workers simply took over the management of their previous places of employment with, however, the difference that they had no bosses to expel.

In such a situation Lenin would have at first hypocritically encouraged the movement, but with his profound distrust of all 'spontaneity' he would have simultaneously built up some fair-seeming alternative (in Russia in 1917, the trade unions). At a suitable later moment he would have overwhelmed the workers' councils and substituted his own centralizing instruments. In Poland in 1957 Gomulka did much the same. Ben Bella, on the contrary (who finally defeated his more moderate enemies in September 1962), favoured this system wholeheartedly, and encouraged it by supplementary government decrees.

Looking at this situation from the governmental, as opposed to the grass-roots, point of view, a foreign model for legislation was very useful. Ben Bella had not been 'got at' or 'nobbled' by the Titoists; he simply found their experience useful since he faced the same problems.

Certainly the number of parallels is remarkable. In both countries local government units, called Communes, play a very large part in financing and inspiring self-management in the enterprises on their territory. In both countries the manager represents the element of order, responsibility, and state hierarchy; and in both the Commune nominates him to the enterprise (though in Yugoslavia the workers' council may reject the nomination). Beneath the Algerian committee of management there stands a larger and less powerful representative body, the workers' council; in Yugoslavia it is the same, except that the committee of management is nominally a mere emanation of the workers' council, and there is no legal distinction of their powers and responsibilities.

All historical events are highly particular. Ben Bella's adoption of Titoism is no exception. First, he did make some changes; Algeria did not become a carbon copy. Thus the chairman of the workers' council is a much greater figure in Algeria than in Yugoslavia; it is possible for him to dominate the director. My guess is that this is because Algeria is not a communist country, and did not arrive at self-management via the rejection of Stalinism. The new system was not super-imposed on an existing statist hierarchical structure, but upon a vacuum. Also in part it grew from below: it was not wholly imposed from above, as in Yugoslavia.

Again, Algerian self-management is essentially agricultural, but agriculture is the one field that in Yugoslavia is not subject to self-management (except for a few state farms). The Yugoslav peasant has indeed the tradition of the extended family as a co-operative unit (*zadruga*), but by 1945 this had been highly attenuated. Essentially capitalism had taken over, and it was individualistic peasants whom the new communist regime had to persuade that collective—not state—farms were better. Persuasion did not work, and the act of collectivization in 1949 was scarcely less violent than in the USSR in 1929. By 1953, however, the Soviet model had been completely rejected, and Yugoslav agriculture was de-collectivized, just after the introduction of self-management in industry.

What do Algerians and Yugoslavs say officially about this imitation? Diplomacy and common sense require that both sides should play it down, and I have not been able to dig up a straight claim that any particular element was a copy. The usual line is concisely expressed by Hadj Ben Ala, member of the Politbureau and President of the National Assembly:

> The 'self-government' movement, which made its appearance immediately after the realization of independence on lands abandoned by the colonists, was expressive of the desire of the working people for self-assertion in the political and economic field.
>
> Self-government in the economy of the country made it imperative to expand the scale of nationalization of agriculture and industry, as well as to reorganize internal and external trade and the banking system. To prevent hostile agencies from usurping the national heritage, the government *sanctioned the trend* mentioned above by its Decree of March 1963.
>
> However, one can have effective self-government—which in the case in point means improved economic management and increasing productivity in the self-managing industrial establishments and on farms—only by educating the workers to it.[63]

Ben Bella himself was always more cagey. He saw to it that 'self-management' occurs only in the preamble of the Constitution.[64] Just before Tito visited Algeria, Ben Bella, interviewed for a Yugoslav journal, said: 'Our rapid pace along the road towards socialism is not being dictated by any *a priori* idea, ready-made formula or blind imitation of foreign experiences, even the most valuable.'[65] After the visit the Tito-Ben Bella communiqué ranged over the whole

[63] *Review of International Affairs* (Belgrade), 5 January 1965 (my italics).
[64] *Neue Zürcher Zeitung*, 18 December 1963.
[65] *Review of International Affairs*, 5 April 1965.

world, but did not mention self-management. It had only this to say on internal affairs:

> The two delegations, confident that socialism was developing into a universal system, considered that the ways of building up this system differed according to the specific conditions prevailing in each different country and nation. There was no single road leading to socialism, but only the road suited to each nation and its needs.
> The two sides expressed the view that the experiences of Algeria and Yugoslavia should be judged in conformity with the actual conditions prevailing in each of these countries. By the practice of exchange of information and views, the peoples of Yugoslavia and Algeria were helping to enrich their own indisputably original experiences.[66]

If we look away from Algeria's actual administrative structure, the country in the most similar situation was Cuba. There too there had been foreign-owned latifundia, there too the economy was grinding to a halt owing to the withdrawal of foreign capital and technicians. Castro too had created state farms with a modicum of self-management on the confiscated property. Ben Bella's diplomatic warmth towards him was due to his fellow-feeling, and he may have taken some of his general ideas from Cuba.

Nevertheless he did not copy the single improvement that Cuba has made in the socialization of agriculture. Castro's regime had paid some attention to the effect of agricultural nationalization on the distribution of income among farmers; a matter the USSR had completely neglected. State farms were set up only where the main activity was livestock raising. On sugar plantations, however, cooperatives were established, and these were more like Soviet kolkhozy. The distinction was made in order to encourage and reward labour in the latter case; for sugar is an extremely labour-intensive crop, and there is so little capital that small social injustice is done if the income from it is divided among the workers. But livestock is itself an expensive item of capital, and it would be unjust if the worker on the farm benefited from taking over all this investment. So he is paid a straightforward wage. This Cuban distinction is a very crude one. It would have been much better to levy a tax on the precise amount of capital, no matter what the farm did, and above all to exact a rent on the land.[67] But even so Cuba had made

[66] *Ibid.*, 5 May 1965.
[67] Cf. René Dumont, *Cuba, Socialisme ou Développement* (Paris, 1964), pp. 38–40.

an advance on Soviet, Chinese, or other brands of collectivization. Algeria did not imitate this, however—which perhaps shows more clearly than anything the Yugoslav inspiration. For Titoist workers' control resembles Soviet collectivization at least in this, that differences of site, fertility and capital employed cause differences in income. Such differences are great also in Algeria.

But wherever we seek for parallels it must not be in the USSR. The Tripoli resolution of June 1962 has much to say, for instance, about the capture of the commanding heights in industry, banking, and foreign trade. But there is little about planning, and no attempt has been made to introduce a command economy. Indeed, as this goes to press there still remain some private banks. Algeria has, very wisely in view of its limited administrative resources, left the market more or less alone. This, of course, is also Titoism. In a general way, too, it would appear that Titoism has struck fairly deep roots. Col. Boumediène, who replaced Ben Bella in a coup for purely personal reasons, has strongly reinforced the system of self-management.

XIV. *Why the USSR has lacked influence*

Why has our enquiry produced such negative results? Why is socialism elsewhere so extremely un-Soviet in practice? Partly, Soviet influence has been small for the same reason that all imperialist influences, unless backed by actual sovereignty, are small: other people are cussed, and the nation-state is independent. But that is not enough. Such capitalist institutions as two-tier banking systems, resting on a single central bank linked to the rest by a money market; as stock exchanges and public companies with limited liability; as patents and patent law; as the income-tax—all these have spread clear across the world. Without the least political pressure these social devices have been imitated very precisely.

It seems that two features distinguish these capitalist social devices from Soviet devices, and render the latter *magis admiranda quam imitanda*. The first is their obvious and exact suitability for the job in hand. They are not some dictator's brain-child, they are not *voulu*. They may well not be right; indeed many practitioners and theoreticians of capitalism have passionately opposed them; but they are *natural*. But suppose the aspiring foreign socialist asks a Soviet communist, why not have state farms instead of collective farms? Why give an enterprise this kind of indicator rather than that? How do you contain inflation? He will get—or would until recently have got—an answer distinguished by neither candour nor logic. Perplexed, he does not abandon socialism, but he chooses his own way.

So the first reason why the USSR has had so little detailed influence is the arbitrary and unconvincing nature of its own arrangements. The second reason is cognate; indeed it is almost the sole cause of the first. Soviet social science is at an extremely low level of intellectual achievement and common honesty. Until very recently everything was decided at the top, by the political leaders. The task of the social scientist was to support the new top decisions, even if they reversed previous top decisions, and to criticize everybody at lower levels for not carrying them out. Since nearly all interesting questions were controversial, and controversy was dangerous, virtually no interesting research was carried out. Moreover social science was under especially heavy censorship, and censors have to understand what they are reading. So they did not allow techniques to develop that they could not understand, and technique stagnated completely. Not even the most obvious faults could be admitted— unless indeed it was the party line to admit them, and then a sudden spate of self-criticism would flow. But here too the stilted and uniform phrasing showed that the source of self-criticism was not candour but expediency.

Nor was this all. Social science is nowhere so highly developed as to monopolize social initiative. Quite the contrary; academic preoccupations and attitudes tend to freeze thought in the freest countries, and most innovation is made by inspired amateurs or by people pursuing their own group interests in the actual social process. But here too the USSR was at a singular disadvantage. There was no mass initiative; hardly any practical suggestions and no serious reforms at all originated from free public discussion or open pressure groups. Even if they had, no foreign socialist would have been allowed contact with such 'dangerous elements'.

Serious contact with, and understanding of, the Soviet system was thus possible for only two categories: academic Sovietologists and foreign communists. The former were for various obvious reasons beyond the pale—your average communist writes them all off as CIA agents. And indeed an excessive prejudice against things communist is the very natural *déformation professionelle* of the Sovietologist. As to the foreign communist, it is of interest that since about 1925 he has in fact been denied close insight into the system to which he devotes his whole life. He is in all Soviet domestic concerns on the wrong side of the iron curtain. Only when his party comes to power is he admitted to the *arcana imperii*, for then he has to run the system himself.

Imagine, for instance, a socialist politician from the Central Afro-Asian Republic who wishes to collectivize his country's agriculture. He goes to Moscow and says, how did you do it? May I see the files? Here, by the way, are my research assistants and may I borrow a photostat machine? Clearly the man will have to be deported at once, he is nothing but an imperialist spy. Whereas when Latin Americans in the inter-war period went to Washington to study the Federal Reserve Board they were welcomed with open arms. The West keeps only technological secrets, the USSR keeps social secrets too. If you are yourself ashamed of or incapable of rationally explaining what you do, you can force another country into imitation, but you cannot persuade it.

There is a third and still more powerful reason for the lack of Soviet influence: the high and unreasonable prerequisites for Soviet approval. It is the essence of Leninism—but not of Marxism—that it must be swallowed whole. For Lenin[68] as much as for Stalin there was only one correct or even possible path of moral rectitude and social development: the exact imitation of the USSR. Until the middle fifties a foreign government had to:

> have come to power through revolution,
> be waging active class war, and
> be wholly dominated by a single totalitarian party,

before it was recognized as worthy of advice and help. This has been invariably found too high a price to pay. In particular, nearly all non-communist governments have refused to wage class war; though Ben Bella and Nkrumah came very close to it.

To choose this or that part of Soviet economic policy while rejecting these essential prerequisites was in Soviet eyes an ontological absurdity, and indeed all sorts of ontological distinctions were invented to justify this all-or-nothing attitude. Thus nationalization and planning by a pre-revolutionary bourgeois government were

---

[68] Compare his Twenty-One Conditions, all of which had to be fulfilled by a communist party in order to join the Communist International (cf. E. H. Carr, *The Bolshevik Revolution* (London, 1953), ch. 25).

'state capitalism'; things not bad in themselves, indeed a historically necessary stage on the way to the proletarian revolution, but all the same class measures carried out in the interests of the bourgeoisie, and by no means beneficial to society as a whole. Similarly, the capitalist welfare State has never been dignified by that name; it is merely deception and bribery of a small favoured section of workers, designed to split the proletariat and blunt its revolutionary zeal.

This being the general attitude, no pre-revolutionary government or politician was encouraged to imitate the details of the Soviet economic system. This would still have been so even if the details had not been arbitrary and embarrassing to explain. For bourgeois society was governed by different laws. If the laws seemed to be the same then again ontological distinctions were drawn. Thus it might be held by the superficial that there is one problem of 'scarcity' or optimal resource allocation, common to the human condition as a whole. But no, the law of value applied only to capitalism; under 'socialism' it became 'the transformed law of value'.[69] Or again one might have cause to admire the Soviet fiscal system, with its heavy emphasis on indirect taxes and its very light income tax; surely this gave a greater incentive to work? But here again the discriminating admirer found his way barred by irrelevant distinctions of terminology, designed to imply differences where there really are none: the income tax was a 'tax on the population', but the very much heavier taxes on sales turnover and socialist-sector profits were 'not really taxes, only differences between cost and price'.

XV. *The Influence of other communist countries*

These theses are confirmed when we contemplate the influence of other communist countries. The second great communist power, China, has made the same mistakes. That is, having the same domestic rigidities it has the same iron curtain, and so has been unable seriously to influence the detailed policy of non-communist countries. Recently indeed, while the USSR has become a more open society and thus tended to gain influence, China has further frozen over and suffered heavy diplomatic setbacks.

Yugoslavia, however, has had influence out of all proportion to its mere eighteen million people. Now in large part this is because its institutional model is much more attractive. Most socialists con-

[69] And was not applied, we might add!

18

sider the capitalism of small peasants inevitable; that the socialist sector should run on market principles, not those of central command, is more practicable and more rational; and workers' councils are a superficially still more attractive feature.

But salesmanship has its role too, and the Titoists are the best ideological salesmen in the world. They have in particular understood that the salesman's best ploy is the trip round the works; the serious client will not buy something he has not seen being made. Yugoslavia, then, is an open country, at least as concerns its economy. Its statistical service is more honest, its enterprises are more open to inspection, even the sacred cow of workers' control is fairly openly discussed and criticized. A prospective imitator can genuinely inform himself and as a result quite specific influence can be traced in Algeria (as we have seen) and in Egypt.

I would not be misunderstood as having said that Yugoslavia is a politically free country, or one entirely without hypocrisy, or even an economically successful one. On the contrary, there is, even after the most recent reforms, very little freedom and much hypocrisy, especially on the subject of workers' control. But the basic, long-run sincerity of the most dyed-in-the-wool Titoist is scarcely in doubt. Here, the visitor feels, is a group of ex-Stalinists who are seriously bothered by the moral and intellectual shiftiness to which their position compels them. Here is no principled mendacity, no automatic secretiveness—merely the necessarily high minimum that the regime's survival requires. Whatever can with safety be done decently and freely is so done.[70]

The Soviet model itself has been best propagated by another nation less prone to secretiveness, hypocrisy, and self-deception: Poland. What distinguishes Poland from the USSR is not so much its uncollectivized agriculture—though that is indeed vital—as the high education and personal accomplishment of its social scientists. The Polish bourgeoisie was not entirely liquidated by Stalin and by the war, but survived in large numbers to take over again, under Gomulka, the nation's intellectual life. Since 1956 Polish university standards have been nearly those of the western world: infinitely higher than Soviet and considerably higher than Yugoslav standards. There is a long Polish tradition, less well known than

---

[70] For two discussions, from very different viewpoints, of this curious atmosphere, cf. Wolfgang Leonhard, *Child of the Revolution* (London, 1957); Wiles, 'A Voyage to Laputa', in *Encounter*, December 1957.

the insurrectionary one but quite as respectable, of collaborating
with a dominant Russia in order to ensure the nation's survival.
Entirely within this tradition, a galaxy of highly gifted but excessively
supple and accommodating intellects has revised and refined Marxism
and the Soviet institutional model so as to make it plausible to people
not under party discipline. Where Yugoslavia has its outgoing,
freedom-loving hero-politicians, who have turned Marxism-
Leninism upside down, Poland has its civilized professors, who have
packaged the orthodox product for export.

There is no lack of hypocrisy also in this venture. A Polish
professor is certainly not free to say anything he likes; but he does
like to keep insincerity down to the indispensable minimum. Curiously enough, too, the commodity he sells is not Poland, as Yugoslavs sell Yugoslavia; it is Marxism-Leninism. For he is to a remarkable extent an export commodity only. The Polish communist
politician is, with notable exceptions, a run-of-the-mill *apparatchik*
with few new ideas or attractive characteristics. He tolerates most—
not all—professors but pays them very little heed: let them edit
their learned journals within reason—he will run the country, and
conservatively at that. So domestic frustration and a human desire
for hard currency drive the professor abroad on missions. The
great case was precisely Oskar Lange himself in India, as we saw
above.

The doctrine thus exported is by no means uniform—professors
are never that—and by no means acceptable to Russians. It excludes
agricultural collectivization and class war, and sometimes also the
command economy; it subjects all dogma to discussion; it is lenient
and reasonable. But it is probably the best that can be made of
Marxism-Leninism if people are to be *persuaded* to adopt it.

XVI. Western influence on the USSR

It is at least as instructive to ask what has been the influence of
the capitalist world on Soviet economics. Until Stalin's death this
influence was even more indirect and general than its counterpart.
Not only was Stalin a paranoid isolationist; all communists assumed
as an article of faith the superiority of their social science and their
social organization. Imitation, too, was physically dangerous to the
imitator.

Since 1953, and even more since Khrushchev fell in 1964, changes
have been very great. They prove that western influence on the

USSR is much greater now than its converse. They also testify to a seriousness, flexibility, and willingness to act that stand in striking contrast to the unadventurous rigidity of most western countries. The belief in an imminent capitalist breakdown has been tacitly abandoned. The social sciences have been immensely developed and allowed a quiet and partial independence of Marxism. Mathematics and computers, long kept at bay, have been encouraged and even over-encouraged. The individualized consumer durable, and its concomitant hire purchase, have been declared ideologically clean. Decentralization *in principle* has come at last, called at last by that name, and reaching meaningfully down to the price, technique, and output decisions of the enterprise; mere Khrushchevian tinkering with the administrative hierarchy is no longer accepted as a substitute, nor is there any pretence that this is a temporary retreat as in the NEP. Equality of income is taken seriously again, and practical approaches towards it have been made. In innumerable complicated measures the kolkhoz peasant is receiving a new deal. Millions of prisoners have been released from forced labour.

Many of these developments are a more sincere flattery of the capitalist West than the latter has ever shown in reverse. To abandon the breakdown theory is to admit that Keynes was right and Marx wrong. It even brings us close to admitting that the capitalist State is above classes and can act, even in peacetime, in the interests of the whole nation; and that real wages are rising under capitalism. But the denial of these points is the very cornerstone of Marxism as a political movement. It is not too much to say that a public, official admission of their validity would bring communism, in the sense of a hostile, trouble-making force, to an end. Neither is it too much to say that they will one day be admitted, since they are true.

Not less important is the new freedom of the social sciences, and the application to them of mathematics. This hits two ways. First, it is ideologically disruptive. On this it suffices to say that if Marxism is Holy Writ, this is the Higher Criticism; the labour theory of value has proved especially vulnerable, and prices are more and more being fixed on capitalist principles. Second, it is politically disruptive: the party stalwart, long extruded from technological decisions, now finds that the social decisions have also become too difficult to grasp. He is left only with the power of appointment. Moreover, with the single exception of Kantorovich's invention of linear programming, all this development comes from the West, or results from competition with it.

The same is true of the consumer durable. With sewing machines the Russian communists were familiar at their mothers' pre-revolutionary knees; and this no doubt is why they have been so grossly overproduced. But the private motor-car is a post-revolutionary development unknown in old Russia. It will wreak big changes in landscape and human habits, all entailing the imitation of capitalism. It is, above all, poison to collectivism.

For one of these developments, we might argue, Yugoslavia may take primary credit. For all the mathematics and computers and sophistication of Novosibirsk or MIT, the way to economic rationality is still through decentralization and a market. Surely the USSR followed the friendly Marxist pioneer here, not the capitalist enemy? Plausible as this is, it is doubtful. Unlike east Europeans, Russians seem to know and care little about Yugoslavia. Even Khrushchev, an exception here, did not at all like the Yugoslav type of decentralization. Soviet eyes are for ever on Germany and the United States, where they feel that their country, as another developed industrial giant, has most to learn. Like Germans and Americans, they are power-and-size snobs. The 'Big Russian Brother', as he traditionally calls himself, cannot decently go to school in Belgrade. Accordingly the USSR has not accepted a free socialist market as desirable, and has found its own way to such less radical decentralization as suits it. Moreover in this new set-up the manager is the boss; there is only the palest imitation of the workers' council. In general Yugoslavia has been an irritant, not an example, to the USSR; but in eastern Europe it has been both.

For yet other developments it looks as if internal necessity was almost the sole cause. This is especially true where the strong Russian sense of fraternity and justice, or the strong socialist tradition of equality, was offended. We need not look abroad to ask why the peasants are getting a better deal, or the individual contract of employment is more fair to the worker, or why the prisoners have been released, or why minimum wages and old age pensions have been raised. No doubt there is an element of competition with the West here, just as internal necessity was clearly not absent from the reforms previously listed. But native moral revulsion was still paramount. It is true that in the case of the kolkhoz the regime is still the captive of its own shibboleths, and has shrunk from the required radical change—which is of course to break up the kolkhoz, as far as technology permits, into individual farms. If foreign example or advice, Yugoslav or capitalist, had been heeded, we should have seen far greater changes.

XVII. Foreign aid and its influence

Let us finally look at that interesting mixture of imitation and competition, foreign aid. The USSR rendered minuscule amounts of military aid to the Kuomintang in the twenties, and of economic aid to Turkey in the thirties. But this was no example to the West: by that time 'colonial development', the earliest name for public economic aid, was already old in the West, and of course public military aid and the export of private capital date very far back indeed. That the new communist countries should aid or be aided by the USSR after the war was only common sense, and again we need seek no western example. Nor need we here go into the extent of the initial Soviet exploitation of the new satellites, the failure to aid China, and the subsequently much fairer distribution of the intra-communist aid burden.

Our concern is with the post-Stalin decision to aid non-communist underdeveloped countries. First, of course, there had to be a change of ideology. Once released from colonial bondage, such countries were not after all simply capitalist or inevitably headed for a pro-letarian revolution after a long period of capitalist accumulation. They could on the contrary choose their path, so it was the plain duty of Soviet foreign policy to help them. Nor was this unorthodox doctrine if the Marxian tradition be taken as a whole. Though the author of *Das Kapital* would have been shocked, the Marx who corresponded so politely with the Russian Populist Vera Zasulich said much the same thing, and so of course did Lenin. It was Stalin who had condemned Nehru as an out-and-out bourgeois and British agent, and his successors were disagreeing with him, not revising the doctrine.[71]

Nevertheless it can scarcely be doubted that cold-war competition took easy precedence over ideological rectitude. Stalin's policy was

---

[71] Some of the most recent (1963) formulations are, however, revisionist vis-à-vis Lenin's doctrine of the party. These stipulate that in one-party non-communist States communists should not try to form their own party, but should in-filtrate other parties individually. Cf. Richard Lowenthal in *Survey* (London), January 1966.

missing opportunities and losing influence: the contrast with western public aid was glaring. But if these were the reasons for giving aid, the actual methods have rather differed from those of capitalist countries, and these differences must be understood before the aid's effectiveness is estimated.

Nearly all aid-givers show political bias in terms of the *countries* that they aid: we do not aid our enemies. But even granted a friendly foreign policy, there is also the question of how the giver may influence the recipient's domestic social and political structure. In this respect at least two principal western aid-givers have a distinct right-wing bias. United States public aid, even though mostly to foreign governments, is designed to lay the groundwork for capitalist development; and the International Monetary Fund is of course interested in monetary stability and convertibility. In addition much western private aid is the direct investment of large international oil companies. West European public aid, on the other hand, is 'blind'. It balks at communism and at other forms of open diplomatic hostility, just as Soviet foreign aid does not go to Formosa; and it is concentrated on ex-colonies where the aider is an ex-imperialist Power. But that is all: the borrower chooses what institutions please him. There is also a great flow of western private capital to public borrowers in underdeveloped countries, in the sense that the bonds of such borrowers are bought for private portfolios.

Soviet foreign aid, however, is fully as biased as that of the IMF. It never goes to private enterprise or to currency stabilization. It is almost all directed to setting up public enterprises, thus expanding the socialist sector. In this way one great unwisdom of capitalism is avoided: the actual capital transfers are all at fixed interest, and what is acquired is not ownership but debt. The Soviet aid team comes in specifically to set up the enterprise and get out again. This cuts most of the ground from under accusations of imperialism. No doubt in part this lesson was learned not from the failures of capitalist imperialism but from the unpopularity of Stalin's mixed companies in the satellites.

So why have not the walls of Jericho fallen down? Why has the steelworks at Bhilai not turned India communist? Not, surely, because in this case also Soviet purposes are evidently dishonest. They are certainly no more dishonest than American, British, or French purposes. All four countries alike seek not only to do good but to aggrandize themselves.

Seemingly the big explanations are the commercial inefficiency of the aid—for every story of American waste and delay there are several of Soviet waste and delay—and the extremely small size of the total effort. Indeed, as a percentage of national income Soviet aid is quite derisory by western standards. True, it is none the less an impressive phenomenon, since many countries at the Soviet level of productivity and income are still in the queue for aid. If in the past it might have truly been objected that the USSR was drawing capital in one way or another from its satellites, then their performance in turn becomes remarkable. But today the Soviet balance of payments receives little or no such adventitious aid, and in addition the USSR sits at the centre of a formidable empire, of which it bears the main defence burden. But these are considerations for the scholar or the moralist, not the harassed Indian planner. What he wants is large quantities of usable goods, and these he does not get.

A subordinate reason for lack of effect we have already met in other connections: the iron curtain. The Soviet technician carries, though decreasingly, his own iron curtain around with him. He keeps himself apart after hours, haunts his own embassy, and generally fails to enter into the spirit of things. His descriptions of life back home are constrained and peculiar. Compared with the drunken, bottom-pinching, tax-dodging, and perhaps racist American technician, his behaviour is faultless, and that is just what is wrong. It does not even help that he is specially selected by his government as an outstanding citizen, while his American counterpart tends to be self-selected as a failure at home. Where there is no candour there can be no trust. A closed society can exercise power abroad, but only an open one can influence.

XVIII. *An optimistic conclusion*

One very pleasant conclusion emerges: human beings respond to candour and reason. You can examine the Bank of England or the New York Stock Exchange or the Office du Plan. You can argue with a Polish economist and you can cross-question the chairman of a Yugoslav workers' council. In none of these five cases will you get the whole truth. There is *always* something discreditable to hide. But by and large the serious enquirer is told what he wants to know, and can then make up his own mind. In the absence of this elementary human prerequisite he takes his enquiries elsewhere. He even prefers to borrow capital elsewhere.

Here then is the root cause of the Soviet failure. A powerful nation, armed to the teeth, exporting both education and capital, and fully engaged in propaganda and diplomacy, has a messianic sense of mission and a highly distinctive social system to sell. It has subdued many neighbours and imposed its system on them. Its foreign agents have taken power even without military assistance, and again—for a while—imposed the system. But it lacks common honesty; so of independent imitation, the only genuine compliment, it has received almost none.

Now, however, Soviet communism has stepped into the world market of ideas, as we saw in sec. XVI. It gives and takes advice as well as aid, and so has to make a detailed case for everything it *actually* does, especially for its recent drastic changes. This necessity has not been the least important cause of the ideological thaw. The mere increase in higher education, and the eventual recognition of the system's unsuitability to domestic needs, have been of course paramount. But missionary activity is also bad for faith. 'Do you believe all that?' said the Zulu neophyte to Bishop Colenso, in reference to another faith. The bishop described this exclamation as a turning-point; he was later deprived.

The Model of the Totalitarian State

RICHARD LOWENTHAL

I. The Origin of the Model

Fifty years ago, the Bolshevik Party seized power in Russia in the name of the Soviets of Workers' and Soldiers' Deputies. For months before, 'All Power to the Soviets' had been their central political slogan. For many years afterwards, they propagated the 'Soviet system' as the specific political institution of the new regime—the only adequate political form for the rule of the working class, the 'dictatorship of the proletariat' envisaged by Karl Marx. The new Russia was proclaimed a 'Soviet Republic' and soon extended into a 'Union of Soviet Socialist Republics'. When the Communist International was founded in 1919, it was to the Soviet banner that it rallied the most militant revolutionaries of Europe, and it was for the creation of Soviet rule on the Russian model that communists were subsequently to fight and die in Germany and Hungary, in the Balkans and the Baltic States, and even in distant China. But the Soviet system did not, in fact, spread to other countries—not even to those which came, after the Second World War, to form part of the 'Soviet bloc'; and even the Chinese communists, who had copied the institution in the shifting rural areas controlled by them after 1928, did not in the days of their final triumph restore the name which they had abandoned under their 1937 anti-Japanese alliance with Chiang Kai-shek.

This failure of the efforts to spread the 'Soviet system', and the ultimate abandonment of those efforts by the Russian Bolsheviks themselves, did not, however, prevent the political forms of their new State from having a worldwide impact; only it was a very different set of political institutions that proved of major historical importance as an international model. It is as the first totalitarian single-party State, rather than as the first Soviet State, that the new type of government developed by the Bolsheviks has attracted imitators—not only among those who share their ideological goals, but also among their most bitter enemies and among people who are quite indifferent to those goals. Thus while the Bolsheviks, in stressing the Soviets as their most important political contribution, selected the institution that expressed most clearly the *legitimation* of their power by its alleged social content, the course of history has selected the institution that embodied the *reality* of their power— independent of any social content.

In the completed form which it reached in Russia from about 1921, and in which it has made its way around the world, the totalitarian single-party State may be defined by four main institutional characteristics. The first is the monopolistic control of the State by the ruling party, excluding the toleration of other, independent parties in opposition or even as genuine partners in coalition, and leading logically also to a ban on the formation of organized tendencies or 'factions' *within* the ruling party; this amounts in effect to a monopoly of political initiative and decision for the inner leadership of that party, and ultimately to a monopoly of decision for a single leader. The second is the party's monopolistic control of all forms of social organization, depriving these organizations of their role as independent interest groups as exercised in non-totalitarian, 'pluralistic' societies and converting them into as many tools for the mobilization, education, and control of their members by the ruling party; this enables the totalitarian regime to supplement the levers of the state bureaucracy for controlling the actions of its subjects 'from above' with a network of organizations enveloping them from cradle to grave, while preventing the formation of any independent groups. The third is the monopolistic control of all channels of public communication, from the press and other mass media to all forms of education, of literature and art, with the aim not merely of preventing the *expression* of hostile or undesirable opinions by a kind of censorship, but of controlling the *formation* of opinion at the source by planned selection of all the elements of information. The fourth is what Lenin himself used as the definition of dictatorship—'the removal of all legal limitations on state power', in other words, the possibility to use state power in arbitrary and terroristic ways whenever this is deemed expedient for the purposes of the regime. It is essentially the combination of these four characteristics which has enabled the totalitarian regimes of our time to extend the effectiveness of state power beyond anything that was deemed possible before 1917.

This institutional scheme had not been conceived by the Bolsheviks in advance. We may apply to it the words of J. L. Talmon about another regime with which their rule has often been compared: 'Jacobin dictatorship was an improvisation. It came into existence by stages, and not in accordance with a blueprint. At the same time, it corresponded to, and was the consequence of, a fixed attitude of mind of its authors, intensified and rendered extreme by events.'[1]

In the Bolshevik case, however, this attitude of mind had long created its appropriate body in the centralistic organizational structure of the party that seized power on 7 November 1917. Lenin had consciously created his 'party of a new type' as an instrument for the revolutionary conquest of power; and even though, in writing *What is to be Done*, he had been far from envisaging the concrete forms that party's domination was to take fifteen or twenty years later, the possibility of a totalitarian party dictatorship was implied in the shape of that instrument. Without the pre-existing 'party of a new type', the first State of the new type could not have been built up; with that party once victorious, the tendency for its leaders to establish dictatorial, monopolistic rule was given—to be brought out 'by events'.

To understand how the truly epoch-making new system of government became possible, it is therefore necessary to recall how unusual were the basic features of Lenin's concept of the revolutionary party. Up to 1902–3, a party had been generally understood to be the organized expression of a part, a section of society—of a particular economic or social interest or current of ideas. Even the socialist parties of western and central Europe that based themselves on the revolutionary teachings of Karl Marx were supposed merely to express the actual ideas and aspirations of the industrial working class of their respective countries; in Marx's own view, his theories could be gradually assimilated by these parties only in the course of their experience, and it was for each of them to draw its own conclusions on the best road to power in accordance with national conditions. Yet Lenin, in writing *What is to be Done* as a platform for the reconstruction of the Russian Social-Democratic Party organization in 1902, and in forming his own 'Bolshevik' faction over the question of centralized control during its 1903 congress, started from the assumption that no mere 'interest group' of the industrial working class would be able to overthrow Russian Tsarism; that the coalition of all discontented classes and

[1] J. L. Talmon, *The Origin of Totalitarian Democracy* (London, 1952), p. 122.

groups necessary for this crucial task could be forged only by a conspiratorial organization of professional revolutionaries specifically devoted and adapted to the conquest of power; and that this organization needed links in all oppositional classes and groups as well as in the state machine, even though the industrial workers must furnish its main base. Such a party, being not an expression of a social current, but the instrument of a will to power and of a strategy for achieving it, could not grow democratically from its roots, but must be planned and built 'centralistically' by its founders. Its local committees must be appointed by the central leadership, its members admitted only after scrutiny by the local committees, selection from above rather than election from below must be its principle all along the line: only thus could the historically conscious, 'scientifically' Marxist leadership use the party to carry out its strategy and bring about a result which the historical process might fail to yield 'spontaneously', that is, without such planned intervention.

As Lenin's Marxist critics—Plekhanov, Axelrod, and Martov, Trotsky and Rosa Luxemburg—protested at once, this concept of the party had its roots not in Marxism, but in the tradition of the Russian revolutionary conspiracies of the nineteenth century, and particularly in the theories of those of their members who professed so-called 'Jacobin' principles, that is, the primacy of the conquest of power and the need to adapt the revolutionary organization to this overriding purpose. In reply, Lenin proudly accepted the model of such revolutionary organizations as the *Narodnaya Volya* and its predecessor, the (second) *Zemlya i Volya*, pointing out only that they did not confine themselves to conspiratorial activities, but combined those activities (such as the infiltration of the state machine and the preparation for armed insurrection) with open revolutionary propaganda; and he also defiantly accepted the Jacobin label, going as far as to define the revolutionary social-democrat of his dreams as 'a Jacobin inseparably linked to the working-class movement'.[2] The view that both the Leninist party and the

[2] For Lenin's proud, if critical acceptance of the tradition of the revolutionary organizations of the 1870s, see *What is to be Done*, in Lenin, *Selected Works* (London, n. d.) vol. II, pp. 148–50, 182; the latter passage includes an explicit tribute to the importance of Tkachev's ideas for that tradition. For the Jacobin definition of the revolutionary social-democrat, see *One Step Forward, Two Steps Back*, ibid, p. 433.

Bolshevik dictatorship were largely re-enactments of the earlier model set by the Jacobin Club and the rule of the Comité du Salut Public—a view equally widespread among the apologists and the critics of Bolshevism, and also encountered among historians and political scientists—goes back to those early debates; but this interpretation overlooks the fact that all the parties to the dispute confused the historical reality of Jacobinism with the later legend created by F. M. Buonarroti, and as a result gravely underestimates the true originality of the Bolshevik achievement.

In fact, and contrary to that legend, the dictatorial climax of the French Revolution was not, and could not be, a party dictatorship of the Jacobins, because the Jacobin Club never was the kind of disciplined, centralized, and ideologically homogeneous party that could have played that role.[3] It started as a broad forum for politicians ranging from liberal monarchists to intransigent republicans; it became more radical by the secession or expulsion of the more moderate elements just as the National Assemblies changed their political colour; the secretary in charge of correspondence with the provincial clubs changed frequently and had no power to enforce conformity with the views of the centre; and when centralized dictatorship did in fact develop, it spread from the centralization of government—through the *commissaires en mission*—to the clubs and not vice versa. The idea that the clubs should control state appointments was voiced by the Hébertists but rejected by Robespierre, and a temporary majority in the Jacobin Club did not protect the Hébertists from being wiped out by the holders of the real power, the Committee of Public Safety. Conversely, the rule of that committee was eventually overthrown in the Assembly by deputies who belonged to the Jacobin Club—although Robespierre had not previously lost his majority there.

But while the French Revolution never produced the reality of a party dictatorship, it did produce the idea. That idea arose among the defeated extremists in the prisons of the Thermidor: the concept of the 'revolutionary vanguard' was born as a dream of the defeated rearguard of revolutionary extremism. The first attempt to put the dream into practice—to create a party and a regime which would avoid the 'weaknesses' of the Jacobins and of Robespierre—was made in the conspiracy of Gracchus Babœuf; and it

[3] For a documented analysis of the political and organizational history of the Jacobins, see Crane Brinton, *The Jacobins* (New York, 1930).

was a survivor of that conspiracy, Filippo Buonarroti, who later launched the legend that Robespierre and the Jacobins had themselves set the example for that attempt.[4] From Buonarroti, the concept of the conspiratorial revolutionary party aiming at an 'educational' dictatorship passed to Louis-Auguste Blanqui and to the Russian 'Jacobins' of the nineteenth century, notably to Blanqui's friend Peter Nikitich Tkachev. It was in that sense that the founder of Bolshevism was accused of being a Jacobin, and that he accepted the label.

Even so, Lenin at first sincerely rejected the implication that he was aiming at a party dictatorship in Russia. We do not know just when he came to regard such a regime as the necessary political form for the 'dictatorship of the proletariat,' but we do know that up to the First World War he considered that a dictatorship of the proletariat was not yet on the agenda of Russian history. During the revolution of 1905, he aimed at the overthrow of Tsarism by an alliance of workers and peasants, and at the formation of a coalition government of Social-Democrats and Social-Revolutionaries as its political expression. It was only the shock of the war of 1914 that convinced Lenin that a socialist revolution had become an immediate task internationally, and that it was therefore the duty of socialists even in backward Russia to go beyond the overthrow of Tsarism and the establishment of a 'bourgeois-democratic' regime and to set up the power of the proletariat in order to contribute to the fulfilment of the international task.

When Lenin, after his return to Russia in April 1917, began to propagate this new concept, first within and then beyond his party, he did so under the slogan 'All Power to the Soviets'. Yet while he emphasized the Soviets as the direct organs of proletarian rule, the opposition of all other socialist parties to this programme convinced him that the establishment of that rule depended on the Bolsheviks acquiring control of the Soviets first. In the course of 1917, the Bolsheviks ceased in Lenin's mind to be merely the most enlightened and energetic representatives of the interests of the Russian working class and became, to him, the *only* party of the Russian

---

[4] The main source both of the real Babouvist tradition and of the Jacobin legend based on it is F. Buonarroti, *La Conspiration pour l'Egalité dite de Baboeuf*, last reprinted in 1937. Cf. also J. L. Talmon, *op. cit.*, who properly distinguishes between 'the Jacobin improvisation' and 'the Babouvist crystallisation'.

proletariat; and this implied that the 'dictatorship of the proletariat' must in fact take the form of a Bolshevik party dictatorship.

This crucial identification of party and class appears as a matter of course in all Lenin's writings during the months immediately preceding the seizure of power. It becomes most explicit on the very eve of victory in his pamphlet *Can the Bolsheviks Retain State Power?*, in which the Soviets—the directly elected representatives of the workers, soldiers, and peasants—are openly and unceremoniously treated as the new 'state apparatus' by means of which the victorious Bolsheviks will exercise and maintain *their* power and carry out *their* policy. It was a consequence of this outlook, not yet understood at the time even by many leading Bolsheviks, that Lenin after 7 November consistently rejected all proposals for a coalition with the Mensheviks and accepted as temporary partners in the new regime only those Left Social-Revolutionaries whom he regarded as representing the peasants in the process of agrarian revolution. It was another consequence that he dispersed the Constituent Assembly, elected *after* the Bolshevik assumption of power, when its large non-Bolshevik majority refused to vote a blanket endorsement of all the revolutionary measures already enacted by the new regime.

By the time of the October Revolution, then, Lenin was determined to establish a revolutionary dictatorship of his party. But this did not mean that he had, even then, a plan or blue-print for a totalitarian single-party State. What was clear in his mind was the last of our four characteristics of such a State—the rejection of any legal limitations on the revolutionary power. This was sufficient to enable him to suppress resistance to his policy as the need arose. But as resistance developed into civil war, determination to break it was no longer enough: to maintain and defend the revolutionary government, a new state machine had to be created.

It had been an essential part of Lenin's revolutionary programme, explained most fully in his pamphlet on *State and Revolution* and based on Karl Marx's analysis of the Paris Commune, that the victorious proletariat could not use the bureaucracy, army, and police which had served its exploiters as a machine of oppression, but must smash them. Before 7 November, he had also followed Marx in arguing that the new proletarian regime had no need to put another *professional* state apparatus in their place: part-time workers' delegates in the Soviets, part-time voluntary organs of workers' control in economic life, a part-time workers' militia would be enough.

Yet after victory, and especially with the spread of civil war, the creation of a new, revolutionary army, police, and bureaucracy became imperative if the Soviet regime was not to follow the Paris Commune also on the road to defeat. The new, professional state machine had to be staffed with reliable cadres at least in the key positions; and in the conditions of party dictatorship, reliable cadres could only mean Bolsheviks. From being the leading force in the Soviets and the government, the party thus developed into the backbone of a new state machine: its monopolistic control of the new State became entrenched in practice before it was proclaimed in theory. In fact, as Leonard Schapiro has shown,[5] the party was so little prepared for this task that its provincial organizations were temporarily almost paralysed by the absorption of the most active cadres in the work of the new Soviet bureaucracy. When the need for central control of the assignment of party members to state jobs was recognized by the spring of 1919, the central party apparatus was still quite inadequate for this new role: it had to be expanded from a mere 15 persons to 600 within two years.

Even so, during the entire period of the Civil War, the Bolsheviks never argued in principle that they should be the only legal party; nor was there any hint of that doctrine in the constitution of the RSFSR adopted by the fifth All-Russian Soviet congress in July 1918. But they did argue that they would not tolerate any bourgeois parties opposed to Soviet rule in principle, nor parties working for the armed overthrow of the new regime, even if they professed a socialist programme; and they claimed that the central and local organs of Soviet rule, including the Cheka, must not be hampered by any legal safeguards in deciding whether any party, newspaper, or individual was guilty of such counter-revolutionary activity. In practice, this led not only to the suppression of parties and groups that were actually supporting armed insurrection against the Soviet power—such as the Right Social-Revolutionaries when they set up a counter-government in Samara in June 1918 in the name of the dissolved Constituent Assembly and under the protection of the Czech legionaries, or those leaders of the Left Social-Revolutionaries involved in the assassination of the German Ambassador and the abortive Moscow revolt of July of that year; it also produced a cat-and-mouse game of arbitrary harassment of parties and groups

[5] L. Schapiro, *The Communist Party of the Soviet Union* (London, 1960), pp. 241–6.

that explicitly and consistently placed themselves on the ground of the new Soviet Constitution and the defence of the Soviet regime, but claimed the democratic rights of competing for influence and criticizing the authorities on that basis, such as the Mensheviks led by Martov and some breakaway groups from the Social-Revolutionaries. In the absence of legal standards, the only maxim underlying that practice was clearly that no party, however loyal to the 'Soviet system', must be allowed to become strong enough to endanger the effective power of the Bolsheviks: whenever and wherever that seemed to threaten, newspapers were shut down, opposition candidates arrested on the eve of elections, newly elected Soviets with opposition majorities dispersed, elected trade union boards replaced by appointed communists—and it was a mere matter of expediency whether the arrested leaders would quickly be released again, deported by administrative order, or—in rare cases—brought to trial on trumped-up charges.[6]

Yet while the Bolshevik regime of the Civil War years was clearly a terrorist dictatorship—'Red Terror' was officially proclaimed as a policy after the attempt on Lenin's life in August 1918—and while the dictatorial party increasingly merged with the new state machine in process of construction, it did not yet create a totalitarian single-party State as we have come to know it since. As late as 1920, there were many hundreds of Mensheviks in the provincial Soviets, and Martov himself was able in the Moscow Soviet to voice their protest against the arbitrary suppression of 'working-class democracy' and to advocate their programme for economic recovery that anticipated the later New Economic Policy of the Bolsheviks. Important trade unions were still under Menshevik control, and the Bolshevik leaders were under no illusion that the influence of their critics among the workers was increasing as the Civil War drew to a close. Discontent and indiscipline had moreover affected so many of the Bolsheviks' own militants that spontaneous co-operation between Mensheviks and those undisciplined Bolsheviks produced surprise majorities against the 'party line' in Soviets or trade unions more than once. It was only after the end of the Civil War, in early 1921, at a time of growing unrest among both workers and peasants culminating in the Kronstadt rising, and simultaneously with the decision to introduce the New Economic Policy, that Lenin decided

[6] L. Schapiro, *The Origin of the Communist Autocracy* (London, 1955), pp. 192–204.

to put his regime on a more secure institutional basis. To understand the decision that produced the first modern totalitarian regime, we must try to envisage the problems that faced him.

The classical tasks of a Jacobin revolutionary dictatorship had been fulfilled. The counter-revolution had been defeated, the power of the former ruling classes broken for good. But the expectation that the Bolshevik victory in Russia would be the immediate prelude to socialist revolutions in the advanced countries of Europe had not come true: the 'dictatorship of the proletariat'—in fact of a minority party claiming to represent the proletariat—had remained isolated in a backward country in which the proletariat formed a minority, and in which, as Lenin knew and recognized, the economic and cultural preconditions for a socialist system were lacking. To overcome the discontent born out of economic paralysis, to begin the work of recovery after the devastations of war and civil war, major economic concessions to all the remaining non-proletarian strata—to the peasant majority above all, but also to the traders and technicians—were inevitable; the 'war communist' fantasies of a straight leap into Utopia had to give way to a policy of patiently creating, in cooperation with all classes, the productive resources which elsewhere had been created by capitalism, and which alone could eventually form the basis for a socialist economy. It seemed the typical situation for a 'Thermidor'—for liquidating the revolutionary dictatorship that had done its work; and that was indeed what the Mensheviks suggested with growing confidence in their own judgment.

Yet Lenin drew a different conclusion. He agreed on the need for a break with utopian dreams, for material concessions to all productive classes, for shifting the emphasis in Russia from political revolution to economic evolution; but he insisted that the 'proletarian' dictatorship must be maintained during the new phase as well, in order to ensure that evolution was accomplished by what he termed state capitalism—under the control of a State which would maintain Russia's independence from the capitalist world and prevent the restoration of a class of capitalist owners, even while accomplishing the task which capitalism had fulfilled in the advanced countries, and would thus preserve the foundations for the later transition to socialism as well as a stronghold for the international revolutionary movement. The Bolsheviks must hold on to their dictatorial power—no longer primarily as a revolutionary dictatorship, but as a special type of a dictatorship of development. It is from this decision that the truly unique course of the Russian Revolution begins; it is from this decision, too, that the need to create a system of totalitarian institutions has resulted.

The new need, as Lenin saw it, was no longer the comparatively simple one of fighting the class enemy arms in hand: it was to harness the economic energies of non-proletarian classes for a constructive task, to grant them a place in society for a whole period—yet to prevent them from influencing the direction of economic and social development. As Lenin had once conceived the 'party of a new type' as an instrument to make the social forces of discontent converge in a revolutionary direction which they might not otherwise take, so now he conceived the State of a new type as an instrument to guide the millions of independent peasants, the private traders, the industrial technicians of bourgeois origin, in a socialist direction which ran counter to their natural tendency to evolve a capitalist social structure. To foil that tendency, it was not enough that the State kept firm control of the 'commanding heights' of the economy; the alien classes must be permanently excluded from any possible access to the levers of political power. The unique purpose of forcing an entire society to develop not in the direction corresponding to its inherent trend, but in the direction dictated by the ideology of its ruling party, required a unique institutional form, closing all channels of political expression to the existing social forces: no plurality of political parties, however vestigial; no organized interest groups or publishing media free from party control; and finally, as a logical extension of this principle, no plurality of organized tendencies *within* the ruling party, as in the absence of opposition parties such factions would tend to become the channels for the pressure of non-proletarian class interests.

Oddly enough, no formal ban on all remnants of non-communist parties was passed even then. But mass arrests of their central and local leaders destroyed their organizations for good in the early months of 1921, so that in the summer of 1922 even the Menshevik leadership, by then in exile, explicitly renounced any further attempt to put up candidates for Soviet elections. Moreover, a formal ban on factions within the ruling party *was* passed at its tenth congress in March 1921—the same congress that introduced the NEP—on Lenin's proposal, and explicitly based on the grounds stated above—

thus showing that the final destruction of the other parties at this moment was a deliberate decision. By November, on the fourth anniversary of the Bolshevik seizure of power, Zinoviev could state publicly that the Bolsheviks had been 'the only legal party' in Russia for some time past. The remaining Menshevik-controlled trade unions were 'reorganized' under appointed communist leaders during the same year, thus proving that the regime could in fact not afford to tolerate the independent advocacy of the interests of the industrial workers any more than of any other class; and by the time of the twelfth party conference of the Bolsheviks, in August 1922, the need to extend the principle of *Gleichschaltung* to all 'so-called social organizations', as well as to the universities and publishing firms, was proclaimed on the ground that otherwise those legal channels could be used by the now illegal 'anti-Soviet parties' for their dangerous propaganda.[7]

The first totalitarian State thus did not arise either as an automatic result of revolution and civil war, or as a mere instrument for the accelerated economic development of a backward country: it was the product of the decision to use the dictatorship resulting from the revolution in order to twist the development of society in the preconceived direction indicated by the ideology of the ruling party. As Lenin saw it, however, that politically directed development would henceforth proceed by evolutionary methods, without further violent upheavals. The emphasis in the writings of his final years was on the need to raise the economic and cultural level of the Russian people—including in particular the cultural level of the new bureaucracy—by steady, patient efforts within the given political framework; Lenin's last pamphlet on the agricultural co-operatives in particular, which Bukharin was later to describe as his political testament, pointed to the growth of co-operation rather than capitalist differentiation in the countryside as decisive for the evolution of Russia in a socialist direction, but envisaged that growth as taking place voluntarily on the basis of the peasants' material self-interest, parallel with the progress of the agricultural machine industry on one side and of the peasants' educational level on the other.

This evolutionary vision of the state-guided development of Russian society was also generally accepted by Lenin's heirs, at

[7] Ibid., pp. 204–9.

least as long as the problem of post-war recovery dominated economic life. As for Stalin in particular, he continued to oppose the idea of reviving the internal class struggle against the peasants for several years after first Trotsky and then Zinoviev and Kamenev had called for it. When, in 1925, he undertook to define the task of the totalitarian regime in terms of a distinction between the 'bourgeois' and the 'proletarian' revolution, he explained that the former had only had to remove the pre-capitalist 'political superstructure' after the new capitalist economic and social 'basis' was already fully developed, whereas in the case of the latter the political seizure of power—the creation of the new 'socialist' superstructure—was a *precondition* for the development of the new basis, the socialist economy and society.[8] But while this formula brought out with striking clarity the originality of the task bequeathed by Lenin and the extent of his departure from the Marxist tradition, it contained no hint that the creation of the new basis would require further crises of a revolutionary character.

Yet as the period of recovery drew to a close and the problem of financing Russia's industrialization—of the primitive socialist accumulation of capital—pressed to the fore, the hidden, inner contradiction of Lenin's vision of the guided socialist evolution of a society containing a majority of small, independent producers became obvious and confronted his heirs with a dilemma. The financing of socialist industrialization by peaceful, evolutionary methods—by encouraging the peasants to earn surpluses and to lend their savings to the State—as advocated by Bukharin, was *economically* possible and indeed rational; but, as experience showed by 1928, it was bound to increase the *social* weight of the individualist peasantry and to lead to a growing dependence of the formally all-powerful party-state on the informal but effective organizations of the village, typically led by the most efficient, near-capitalist peasants. The more successful the evolutionary road in terms of production and savings, the less likely was it to lead in the desired direction of preventing a capitalist development of the village and its growing impact on Russian society as a whole—the more it would therefore undermine the purpose and ultimately the power of the totalitarian regime. Conversely, the alternative road of financing socialist industrialization at the expense of the peasants, by syphoning off their surpluses more or less forcibly, as originally advocated

[8] J. V. Stalin, *Problems of Leninism* (Moscow, 1947), pp. 129–30.

by the 'Left Opposition', might effectively stifle the tendency towards capitalist development in the village and maintain the course required by the regime's ideology; but it was bound to provoke peasant resistance to an extent that could be broken only by the massive use of state power—in other words by the abandonment of peaceful evolution.

In launching the 'liquidation of the kulaks as a class' and the forced collectivization of agriculture, which he himself later described as a revolution 'equivalent' to that of October 1917, but distinguished from it by being 'accomplished from above, on the initiative of the State',[9] Stalin decided in favour of the primacy of the totalitarian regime and its ideological goal: he recognized what Lenin had not foreseen—that a totalitarian regime can fulfil its task of diverting the development of society from its 'spontaneous' course in an ideologically preconceived direction only by repeated recourse to revolutionary violence. The dynamics of the permanent, or at any rate recurrent, revolution from above as developed by Stalin are the necessary complement to the ideological goals set and to the totalitarian institutions created by Lenin: they, too, were not part of a blueprint, but they grew out of a fixed attitude of mind—and out of the institutions in which it had been embodied—under the pressure of events.

There is no need for us at this point to discuss the later development of Soviet totalitarianism under Stalin and its post-Stalinist fate; for it is the form given to the single-party State in the final years of Lenin's rule and the early period of Stalin's that has become effective as an international model and that is still regarded as 'classic' in the Soviet Union today. What concerns us here is the degree of success obtained by the Bolsheviks by means of those institutions in achieving their objectives, the impression made by that success in different regions of the world, and the reasons both for the domestic success and for the spread of the model.

To begin with a negative statement: the Bolsheviks clearly did *not* succeed in achieving the goals that had originally inspired their revolutionary dictatorship—in establishing the social power of the proletariat or in approaching an egalitarian society. Both ideological goals were, of course, strictly incompatible with the immediate task

[9] *Short History of the CPSU* (Moscow, 1939), p. 279.

of state-directed primitive accumulation, which required massive material sacrifices on the part of all productive classes, including the industrial working class; and the ruling party, being potentially independent of its original proletarian basis by its centralistic structure, used its dictatorial power to impose these sacrifices on workers and peasants alike, and to identify itself in outlook and composition increasingly with the 'new class' of bureaucrats and technicians who were both indispensable for the process of state-directed industrialization and few in numbers, and therefore had to be privileged.

But the Bolsheviks *did* succeed in achieving the goals that had inspired their transformation of the original revolutionary dictatorship into a totalitarian single-party State: in maintaining their own dictatorial power, far beyond the revolutionary crisis that had enabled them to seize it, by turning it into an engine for the state-directed modernization of their country, and in changing the direction of Russian social development to a considerable extent from the course it would otherwise have taken. Their experience showed that even the most powerful State could not force society to conform to aims that were inherently utopian; but it also proved that a new type of State specifically geared to the purpose of directing social development could alter the 'natural' course of that development far more effectively than had previously been believed possible.

Ever since, in the eighteenth century, the first western thinkers began to conceive of the economy as a self-regulating mechanism, and of the development of society as following immanent historical laws, modern thought about the relation between State and society had been dominated by the concept of the limits of political force. However much Liberals and Marxists might later disagree about the *content* of the laws that controlled social life, they did agree that these laws were objectively given and could not be altered by political fiat; nor did either school show much awareness that their supposedly universal laws were in fact generalizations based on the experience of modern western societies alone. Conservative thinkers, too, while more wary of this type of generalization, tended to minimize the 'manageable' element in society by their emphasis on the limits of legislation and on the necessary ineffectiveness of any attempt to interfere with the organic growth of a historical entity. To all of them, the Bolshevik experiment seemed foredoomed to failure— because it violated the canons of economic rationality, because it tried to leap ahead of the stage reached in Russian social development, or because it was contrary to the character and traditions of the Russian people.

Yet the Bolshevik regime, by following political investment priorities and by brutally forcing the mass of the people to bear the cost of its often grossly irrational economic methods, succeeded in building up the industrial apparatus of a modern great Power with remarkable speed—at the price of depressing the standard of living of the Russian people for decades. By deporting millions of 'kulak' families to break peasant resistance, it succeeded in suppressing the inherent tendency of the individualist peasantry to competition and capitalist differentiation, and in shepherding the bulk of the rural population into state-controlled collectives—at the price of causing a catastrophic loss of livestock and condemning Russia's agriculture to abysmal stagnation for a quarter of a century. By exposing an entire generation to a combination of harsh bureaucratic pressures, based on the threat of dire penalties for trifling offences against labour discipline or for failure to fulfil the delivery quotas, with intense educational remoulding through an all-embracing network of party-controlled organizations and publications, it succeeded in changing the 'Russian character', the typical attitudes to work and leisure, to rationality and superstition, to family and State, far more quickly than the combination of Reformation, Counter-Reformation, and Enlightenment with the brutalities of early capitalism had brought about comparable changes in the West—at the price of creating a 'reserve army' of state slaves in its labour camps and of drastically narrowing the mental horizon of the entire nation.

Moreover, the unprecedented concentration of political, economic, and ideological power by the totalitarian institutions (which caused Trotsky to write at the end of his life that Stalin could truly make the claim '*La Société c'est moi*'), did not only enable the ruling party to create a social structure of a completely new type, consisting of the four classes of the ruling and managing bureaucracy, the state workers, the collective peasants, and the labour slaves in the camps. It also enabled it to combine the prevention of any organized resistance to state-imposed sacrifices and party-directed mental remoulding with the active mobilization of the people to share in the society's transformation and their own. The party-controlled Soviets, trade unions, and other mass organizations, long deprived of any independent role as organs of self-government or of the advocacy of group interests, proved effective organs for broadening mass participation in the administrative execution of decisions handed down from the top; the institutions of the Union Republics and the smaller national units, barred from attempting independent national policies or even from developing a true cultural autonomy at the risk of counter-measures ranging from wholesale purges of political and intellectual leaders to the verge of genocide, proved nevertheless effective in giving large numbers of members of these nationalities, including not a few who had been illiterate only yesterday, the chance to learn to help administer their own affairs in their own language— always in accordance with central directives. In the end, totalitarian oppression proved compatible with, if not conducive to the growth of a truly felt 'Soviet patriotism', a genuine allegiance of the citizen to the State in whose greatness his blood, sweat, and tears had been invested by the rulers.

Last and not least, the party regime has succeeded in maintaining for half a century, in the face of several crises of leadership succession, dramatic policy turns, murderous purges, and the supreme test of a world war, both its power over its subjects and its internal cohesion. No ancient or modern dictatorship of revolutionary origin can boast of a similar record. The Russian achievement has been all the more remarkable because, while the nature of the totalitarian single-party State requires a single leader with uncontested authority (so as to stop the inevitable disagreements within the inner circle from leading to the growth of organized factions), the nature of communist ideology has prevented the Bolsheviks from admitting this need and seeking an institutional solution for the problem of succession. Yet on the other hand it is that same ideology, the common faith inspiring the cadres of the ruling party, that must be regarded as to an important degree responsible for the longevity of the regime—not only because it has helped again and again to maintain its *political* cohesion in the face of crises, power struggles, and tyrannical crimes that would have been intolerable to non-believers, but also because it has helped to maintain its *moral* cohesion in the face of the innumerable temptations of dictatorial rule. Soviet bureaucracy, including the party bureaucracy, has of course had its full share of the corruption inseparable from the exercise of arbitrary power, but a comparison with some other modern dictatorships will at once show the vital difference of degree: in fifty years of Bolshevik rule, corruption has never reached the point of endangering the cohesion of the system. For an ideology that has had to be adapted to such far-reaching changes of situation, policy, and generation as the communist one, that, too, is a remarkable achievement.

The experience of the first totalitarian regime has thus shown that the impact of the political will, of modern state power wielded in the service of an ideological faith, on the development of society, can be far more profound than either liberal, Marxist, or conservative thinkers had believed possible before the 1920s. The 'limits of political force' could be stretched far beyond the imagination of the nineteenth century by a revolutionary party in power—on three conditions. It must be inspired by an absolute, unquestioning belief in its idea and determined to act on it with the utmost ruthlessness. It must know how to utilize the new totalitarian engine, to combine the employment of a state machine freed from legal restrictions with a monopoly of political, organizational, and educational activity, in order to prevent the formation of independent social groups and to mobilize the people in its service. And it must know how to make hard choices when the necessities of maintaining power come into conflict with some aspects of its ideological beliefs, and yet preserve its ideological cohesion.

For the stretching of the limits of political force did *not* mean, as it might have appeared at first sight, that *anything* was now possible to a skilled and ruthless political manipulator. Limits still did exist, and they had repeatedly forced the Bolshevik leaders to change their policies and revise their ideology accordingly. As we have seen, it had proved inherently impossible to create in any real sense the dictatorship of the proletariat which they had set out to establish. It had proved impossible to combine the forced industrialization of Russia with an approach to egalitarianism, or the imposition of sacrifices on all classes with freedom of discussion and organization. The Bolsheviks survived in power because, under Lenin as under Stalin, whenever they were confronted with the dilemma of choice between the needs of forced modernization and the vision of Utopia, they gave preference to the former: they succeeded in extending the range of the possible because they did not persist in attempting what was really impossible.

It may be seen as a reflection of this feature of the Bolshevik achievement that the impact of the totalitarian institutional model on the working-class movement of the advanced industrial countries

has on the whole been less durable and far-reaching in its consequences than has been the impact on the nationalist elites of non-
western countries with major unsolved problems of development,
and even the impact on the anti-democratic and anti-labour extremists of some western countries in the throes of major social crises.
Communist ideology might well hold out the example of the
October Revolution to western proletarians in a temporary mood of
acute despair and utopian expectation, but the very strength of such
expectations tended to act as an obstacle to successful imitation of
Leninist practice in periods of potentially revolutionary crisis;
and as with the lapse of time the essence of Leninist-Stalinist totalitarianism as an engine of forced modernization of a special type
became increasingly obvious to communists and non-communists
alike, it also began to appear increasingly irrelevant to the needs of
the working classes of advanced industrial societies. In the course
of half a century, no communist party beholden to the Bolshevik
model has succeeded by its own strength in winning power in a
western industrial country; and the only remaining western communist parties of importance, those of Italy and France, are by now
so convinced of the hopelessness of the attempt that in recent years
they have issued programmatic statements to the effect that they no
longer regard the model as applicable in advanced western countries
with democratic traditions.

By contrast, some non-western nationalist leaders have been
far ahead of the western communists in recognizing the importance
of Russian totalitarian institutions as an engine of state-directed
social development, and in viewing this instrumental function as
completely separable from the egalitarian and internationalist goals
of the communist ideology with which these institutions had been
historically bound up in their Russian origin. It was nationalist
leaders of this type who were to make the first attempts at a selective
imitation of the Russian model of the single-party State.

II. *The Nationalist Modernizers*

(a) *Kemalist Turkey*

Kemal Ataturk is generally considered the first national leader
to have successfully practised such selective imitation of the Russian
model—to have built up a single-party dictatorship without accepting
the communist ideology. As he proclaimed his intention to found

the 'People's Party' at the end of 1922, shortly after his decisive victory in a 'war of national liberation' in which the Soviets had given him substantial support against the 'imperialists', the assumption that he was consciously learning from the system of government of his erstwhile allies is indeed plausible, and there is ample evidence that the ideas and institutions of revolutionary Russia had been much discussed in revolutionary Turkey during the war years.[10] Yet in contrast to what was to happen shortly afterwards in the case of the Chinese Kuomintang (and also to a legend occasionally found in print),[11] there was no direct Russian advice to Kemal on the building of his State.

In fact, Kemal could build in part on the indigenous foundation of the Young Turk conspiracy, the Committee for Union and Progress, of which he had been a member, and of its later party rule, of which he had been an increasingly bitter critic. They had been the first to unite the modernizing elements of the officer and civil servant class with the most active part of the urban intelligentsia in a political organization around a programme of national salvation by constitutional modernization on the western model; and, finding that growing opposition in the country threatened their parliamentary rule, they had suppressed their critics step by step until, by 1914, they ended up with a single-party parliament. But the outcome had not then been a revolutionary party regime, but rather a wartime military dictatorship, and it collapsed as a result of military defeat in the First World War.

When Kemal Pasha decided in 1919 to engage his military prestige in starting a national resistance movement not for the

[10] These discussions were reflected chiefly in the syncretistic ideas of the abortive Ankara Communist Party (also known as the 'Green Apple') which tried around 1920 to provide political leadership to the pro-Kemalist, but undisciplined peasant partisan movement known as the Green Army. Its ideologues, Hakki Behic and Hikmet, sought to combine Kemalist and Soviet ideas in a 'National Bolshevik' type of programme, but were repudiated as imposters by the Comintern. Cf. E. H. Carr, *The Bolshevik Revolution 1917–23*, vol. III (London, 1953), pp. 299–300; Walter Z. Laqueur, *Communism and Nationalism in the Middle East* (London, 1956), pp. 208–10.

[11] The legend originated in China in the middle twenties, when both Dr Sun Yat-sen and later Marshal Chiang Kai-shek repeatedly hinted to their followers that Borodin and other Soviet advisers to the Kuomintang had previously performed similar duties with Kemal. This could be true for some *military* advisers; it is almost certainly untrue for Borodin, as there is no known evidence for the presence of Soviet *political* advisers with Kemal at any period.

recovery of the decayed Ottoman empire, but for the sovereignty of the Turks on their national territory proper, the Association for the Defence of Anatolia and Rumelia formed under his leadership was largely based on the same type of notables, and not infrequently on the same individuals, who had formed the backbone of Union and Progress in the provincial towns. But he made them forswear any attempt to revive that defunct party, explaining that they must have no programme narrower than the defence of the national territory; and it was only on the ground that the Sultan was in enemy hands and no longer a free agent that he brought the Association, and the Grand National Assembly based on it, to commit themselves in the spring of 1920 to the principle of popular sovereignty. To the end of the war, the Association saw itself not as a political party with a common ideology and discipline, but rather as the organ of a non-party provisional administration set up to deal with a national emergency—as the civilian arm of the army of resistance, whose members might hold widely different ideas on the future form of State and society.

Throughout this period, revolutionary Russia was important to Kemal chiefly as an example of successful struggle against the victorious western 'imperialists' and as a powerful potential ally against them. It was their common interest in eliminating the independent Caucasian States as a focus of western influence in the area that formed the basis of their early establishment of diplomatic relations in 1920 and of their treaty of friendship of March 1921; and it was arms supplies and international support rather than advice on his system of government that Kemal requested, and received, from the Bolsheviks during the remainder of his struggle for national survival.[12] Indeed, when the Russians did send a group of Turkish communists along with their first diplomatic mission, the Kemalist authorities had them drowned in January 1921; and though a Turkish Communist Party was authorized in March 1922, during the period of closest Russo-Turkish military co-operation, it was suppressed again in October, immediately after the war had been won.[13] Conversely, Kemal's decision to move towards a single-party State of his own, though evidently inspired by the Russian model, was taken during the critical months of the Lausanne peace negotiations, at a

[12] Carr, *op. cit.*, pp. 247–50, 294–8, 473–5; Louis Fischer, *The Soviets in World Affairs* (Princeton, 1951), ch. 12.

[13] Carr, *op. cit.*, pp. 298–9, 301, 475–6; Laqueur, *op. cit.*, pp. 210–11.

time when relations with Russia had cooled considerably, and without any assistance from Soviet experts.

It had been victory in the war of liberation that, by ending the national emergency, had put the future of Turkey's system of government on the agenda. To many of Kemal's wartime associates, a return to traditional legitimacy by a compromise with the Sultan-Caliph seemed the obvious solution. But to Kemal, the national revolutionary and unbelieving rationalist, the wartime conduct of the Defender of the Faith had been the final proof that the Turkish nation could be renewed and modernized only by a radical break with the monarchy and indeed with Islamic traditionalism. Under the fresh impression of his military triumph, he forced the National Assembly to take the first step by voting the abolition of the Sultanate; and the initial resistance he encountered among the deputies convinced him of the need to transform the Defence Association into a disciplined political party, pledged to a programme of national modernization and unity under his leadership against all 'traitors', and apt to become the instrument of the secularist revolution he intended. Now Kemal understood clearly that the only alternative to a traditionalist regime deriving its title from the will of God was a revolutionary regime deriving it from the will of the people; yet while wishing to mobilize the people for the struggle for modernization and for the democratic legitimation of the regime, he also feared that a pluralism of political parties and organized interests would be dangerous to national unity, or rather to the speedy achievement of his revolutionary goals. To a leader thus seeking to combine democratic legitimation with a refusal to permit freedom of organization, the Russian single-party State offered, by the turn of 1922–3, a ready-made prescription.

Thus Kemal toured the country in the early months of 1923, calling on the local committees of the Defence Association to transform themselves into units of the new party and to broaden their membership; in February he summoned an Economic Congress of traders, farmers, artisans, and workers, and used it to appeal for the concentration of all efforts on the economic development of the country and to give warning against a class war which Turkey could not afford; he combined this campaign of mobilization with a series of repressive measures, tightening control of the press, banning public meetings, and even seeking to lift the Assembly members' immunity from arrest. When the Assembly, defending its rights and rebelling against Kemal's obvious attempt to prolong his dictatorial powers beyond the term of the wartime emergency, sent a deputation asking him to give up leadership of the new party because 'the head of State must be above party', he replied openly that the People's Party he had founded must be the *only* party because of the continuing need for national unity, and that it was a point of honour for him to combine leadership of party and State.[14]

The new system, however, proved more difficult to create than Kemal had expected. Elections to the new National Assembly took place in June, before the party was properly organized; the first party congress was held only in August, on the eve of the Assembly's first meeting; and though it adopted the principle of voting discipline on penalty of expulsion from the party, it could not assure uniformity in the new Assembly. When, at the end of October 1923, Kemal asked the Assembly formally to proclaim the republic and to adopt a presidential system of government making him independent of its confidence, the proposal was voted only by 158 out of 286 deputies—40 per cent of the elected representatives abstained.[15]

It was on this precarious basis that Kemal and his party, now named the Republican People's Party, began the new phase of the revolution, the struggle for the secularization of the country, with the abolition of the Caliphate and of the religious courts and schools in March–April 1924. Within a few months, the convergence of economic and religious sources of discontent proved so strong that Kemal found himself unable to prevent the formation of an opposition party, the Progressive Republican Party, led by the opponents of his personal power within the Assembly.[16] Attempts to intimidate the opposition by terrorist acts, including the murder of a deputy by the chief of Kemal's bodyguard, backfired so badly that Kemal had to break up that formation and to appoint a government of conciliation before the end of the year; a motion drastically to reduce the presidential powers was only narrowly defeated in the

[14] H. C. Armstrong, *Grey Wolf* (London, 1937).
[15] Bernard Lewis, *The Emergence of Modern Turkey* (London, 1961), pp. 255–6.
[16] Some recent writings tend to describe this early opposition party as if it had been deliberately encouraged by Kemal, like the Liberal Republican Party of 1930. In fact, the Republican Progressives of 1924 were not an experiment conducted from above, but a true political rebellion from below. Cf. Lewis, *op. cit.*, p. 260, and Arif T. Payaslioglu's chapter on the Turkish party system in Robert E. Ward and Dankwart A. Rustow, *Political Modernisation in Japan and Turkey* (Princeton, 1964), p. 419.

Assembly. Only the outbreak of a major rising of the Kurdish minority, led by religious fanatics, in February 1925, enabled Kemal to rally the bulk of the nation against all 'traitors', to get dictatorial emergency powers voted by the Assembly, and to use them for dissolving the opposition party, setting up emergency tribunals, and closing down the religious orders. Even so, resistance among the leaders of his own party still prevented him from impeaching the leading opposition deputies, some of whom had been among his closest comrades-in-arms during the national war. It took the discovery of a murder plot against him in June 1926 to give him a chance for show trials in which these former military leaders were discredited and driven from public life, while a number of other opposition leaders were hanged.

By 1927, the single-party dictatorship was at last complete. The new National Assembly elected in that year consisted exclusively of members of the Republican People's Party bound by strict discipline, and it extended the dictatorial powers for another two years. A party congress to which Kemal gave a triumphant account of his road to power in the famous 'six-day-speech'[17] elected him leader for life; it also resolved that all public appointments in the political, economic, social, and cultural fields, down to the village headmen, should henceforth be subject to the approval of party inspectors.

In step with this decisive political breakthrough, the secularist revolution made further major strides. The famous campaign to abolish the fez was forced through under extreme pressure. The western calendar and clocktime were introduced. Most important, the introduction of the Swiss civil code in 1926 finally replaced the religious laws on matters of marriage and divorce, and by legally ending polygamy and repudiation laid the foundation for the emancipation of women. By 1928, the constitution had been amended to remove the last references to Turkey as an Islamic State. Parallel with these measures, an educational movement to develop the Turkish national consciousness, going back in part to pre-war efforts, had since 1924 been encouraged to found 'People's Houses' in the provincial centres and had held a first national congress in 1927. In 1928, a further major step both to cut the links with Islamic tradition and to increase literacy was taken with Kemal's introduction

---

[17] *A Speech delivered by Ghazi Mustapha Kemal, President of the Turkish Republic, October 1927* (Leipzig, 1929).

of the Latin alphabet for the Turkish language, based in part on the alphabet that had been introduced a few years before for the Turkic-speaking peoples of the Soviet Union.

By the beginning of 1929, the legislative programme for the secularization of Turkey had been more or less completed; and it now became apparent that the ideology of nationalism and modern-ization, as so far developed by Kemal and the Republican People's Party, comprised no further revolutionary task. In the circum-stances, continuation of the party dictatorship no longer appeared justified to Kemal himself: by March, the emergency powers were allowed to run out, and after some preparation an old friend of Kemal's was encouraged in 1930 to start a Republican Liberal Party as a loyal opposition. Yet the popular response showed quickly that a few years of forced enlightenment might transform the politi-cal, legal, and educational system, but could not break the hold of religious traditions on a large part of the people; and in a situation when the world economic crisis led to a drastic fall in Turkish export yields and forced a corresponding tightening of imports, economic misery easily combined with religious opposition to form a powerful counter-revolutionary potential. Toleration of criticism thus quickly led to riots and risings, and within a few months the emergency powers had to be restored and the loyal opposition dis-solved itself.

The experience convinced Kemal that, compared to the legislative and bureaucratic aspects of modernization, both the economic and the educational had been neglected, and that in both respects he could still learn from the model of Russia, just then in the throes of its first five-year plan. By 1931, the slogan of 'etatism', defined as the responsibility of the State for speedy economic development as a vital interest of the nation, was listed among the basic principles of the Kemalist movement;[18] and the practice of the following years made it clear that while Kemal continued to reject the communist programme of wholesale nationalization and particularly of agricul-tural collectivization, he had resolved to go beyond the piecemeal mercantilist measures of the early period and to try to supplement the insufficient private initiative of the Turkish middle class by planned state investment in the creation of new industries. A first Turkish

[18] Article one of Kemal's Manifesto of 20 April 1931, describes the Republican People's Party as 'republican, nationalist, populist, etatist, secularist and re-volutionary'. Lewis, *op. cit.*, p. 280.

five-year plan came into force in 1934, and a Russian loan contributed to it.

During the same period, the party was reorganized to broaden its social composition and adapt it more effectively to tasks of mass education as distinct from pure administration. The People's Houses were taken over by the party in 1931; recruitment among the lower classes was pushed, leading to the election of some ninety workers, artisans, and shopkeepers to the new National Assembly in the same year; and special women's and youth organizations of the party were developed.

In this way, the Kemalist regime continued as a dictatorship of economic development by *étatist* methods and of nationalist and secularist education to the death of its founder in 1938, and under his successor Ismet Inönü to the end of the Second World War. The party's monopoly of political activity and its monopolistic control of social organizations were maintained for more than twenty years, and they accomplished profound changes in the country's economic and social structure, its legal system and its educational level. But, to the end, Kemalism remained different from the totalitarian model of Bolshevik Russia not only in its concrete political goals, but also in its institutional means.

First of all, being exclusively concerned with a task limited in time and space—the establishment of a modern society on the national territory—it did not have to work out an all-embracing ideological system and did not need a monopoly of information to enforce conformity: the political censorship it imposed remained compatible with some freedom of discussion in the intellectual sphere. Second, the party sought to combine administrative with educational tasks, but never struck strong roots in the villages and succeeded only to a limited extent in activating the lower social strata; the official classes and intellectuals continued to form its backbone throughout, and their relation to the masses always remained somewhat paternalistic—a factor which limited the depth of the party's impact on the countryside. Finally, in contrast to all true totalitarians, the Kemalists never idealized their single-party rule as the only true democracy, but insisted on its provisional and educational character; and this enabled (and to some extent compelled) them eventually to repeat the attempt to end the monopoly and admit opposition parties in 1946, and this time to go through with it to the free elections of 1950 which ended their rule.

The degree to which they have achieved their goal of modernizing Turkey may be disputed in the light of subsequent developments, but appears nevertheless impressive in comparison with other Middle Eastern Islamic nations that started on a similar level. But their most remarkable contribution to the history of systems of government consists in the proof that a single-party dictatorship may voluntarily surrender its monopoly of power—provided that it has founded its legitimation not on worldwide, utopian goals, but on a task that is by definition limited in space and time.

(b) Kuomintang China

While Kemal Ataturk founded his monopolistic party in order to transform the military power he held as a wartime national leader into a peacetime revolutionary dictatorship, Dr Sun Yat-sen had to go the opposite way: he had to transform the organizational structure of his long-established, revolutionary party, the Kuomintang, in order to enable it to gain at last a military power base under its secure control. Having repeatedly failed, despite his immense prestige as a patriotic leader, to build up a stable governmental structure by his own devices, Dr Sun thus needed not only Soviet diplomatic and military support against the 'imperialists' and the Chinese warlords linked with them, but Soviet advice on the problem of revolutionary political and military organization. Yet in seeking to learn from the Russian model of the single-party State, he wished to reject the communist goals and the doctrine of the international class struggle, and to replace them with his own programme of national sovereignty and modernization; and it was in part the example of Kemal that convinced him that such selective imitation was possible.[19] The Soviets in turn, who had accepted a Kemal *in* power as a valuable ally even if he suppressed the communists, were able to use their support of the Kuomintang's struggle *for*

---

[19] There exist some important ex-parte accounts of the Kuomintang regime and some studies of specific aspects of it, but no comprehensive scholarly treatment of the Kuomintang's history has so far been published in any western language. What follows is based mainly on an unpublished manuscript by my Berlin colleague, Dr Jürgen Domes, which attempts such a treatment on the basis of Chinese as well as western sources and which will shortly be published under the title *Vertagte Revolution*. I wish to express my gratitude to Dr Domes, without whose massive work I should not have been able to come to the conclusions presented here; yet my conclusions inevitably at times diverge from his, and he should not be held responsible for them.

power to press for a legal role for the communists in its regime—
with the result that this regime carried from birth the contradiction
between a single-party concept and a two-party reality.

Dr Sun Yat-sen had first become known as the leader of the
nationwide conspiratorial movement against the Manchu dynasty,
whose programme of national sovereignty, republican constitution,
and agrarian reform he had propagated from his Tokyo exile, and
had become the first president of the Chinese republic after the
monarchy was overthrown. But the legal National People's Party
(Kuomintang) which he founded after resigning his office to Marshal
Yuan Shih-kai had quickly eluded his control as many of its office-
seeking representatives made their individual compromises with
the military power, and Sun withdrew into exile and renewed
revolutionary plotting in 1913. Returning to Canton in 1916 after
Yuan's death, he became by September 1917 head of a counter-
government opposed to Peking's entry into the war; but when
his military 'subordinates' settled their differences with Peking in
May 1918 they abandoned him and a third term of exile began.
It was on 10 October 1919, the eighth anniversary of the overthrow
of the monarchy, that he refounded the Kuomintang in Shanghai,
in the midst of the ferment of national protest against China's
impotence and her humiliation by the imperialists that had been
aroused by the decision of the Versailles Powers to hand the former
German protectorates in China to Japan. In the following years,
both before and after his acceptance of the invitation of the general
in control in Canton to assume the presidency of the regional government there, he began to develop his political ideas into a system,
to look for the lessons of his political disappointments, and in
particular to take a growing interest in the Russian Bolshevik
revolution, the apparent kinship between its anti-imperialist spirit
and his own, and the reasons for its success.

Dr Sun's famous 'three people's principles'—national sovereignty,
popular power, and people's welfare—had been sketched out by him
before, but were now elaborated in the light of recent Chinese and
international experience. He came to see the struggle for China's
national unity and for the abolition of the unequal treaties as part
of a common anti-imperialist struggle of the exploited nations. The
programme of a democratic constitution with an elaborate division
of powers was now interpreted as a final stage, the realization of
which must be preceded first by the military unification of China

and then by a limited 'tutelary' period of educational dictatorship by the revolutionary party. The plan for raising the people's welfare by a policy of modernization and social justice, on the other hand, was given greater precision in conscious contrast to the Marxist idea of class struggle and to communist policies of wholesale nationalization: state ownership of natural resources, banks, and transport, and state investments for development were to be combined with a moderate agrarian reform by taxation, rent control, and promotion of co-operatives, and with a general redistributive social policy designed to promote class harmony in a framework of predominantly private property.

Dr Sun's contacts with the Soviets clearly influenced the elaboration of his doctrine both positively and negatively. A first letter from Chicherin, the Soviet Commissar for Foreign Affairs, suggesting friendship, trade relations, and anti-imperialist co-operation, reached Dr Sun in June 1921 when he was president of the Canton government; and his reply, dated August, contained an urgent request for detailed information on the organization of the Soviets, the Red Army, and particularly on Soviet methods of political education: 'Like Moscow, I should like to anchor the foundations of the Chinese revolution in the young generation, the workers of tomorrow'. He was to receive some of the information he desired in two conversations with a Comintern official, the Dutchman Sneevliet (Maring), later that year; and Maring was the first to urge Dr Sun to transform the Kuomintang into a disciplined mass party and to set up a military academy for the technical and political education of a new type of officer in order to create a politically reliable armed force. Before Dr Sun could act on this advice, its soundness was borne out: the revolutionary ideologue was once more toppled from nominal power by one of the formally subordinate generals on whose support he had hitherto always depended. The Canton commander who had made him 'president', embarrassed by Dr Sun's plans for a military expedition to unify China, overthrew him in June 1922.

It was when he arrived in Shanghai in mid-August, once more a powerless fugitive but still the nationally famous leader of a party of some 150,000 members, that another Comintern official offered him a united-front pact with the tiny Chinese Communist Party, which had just agreed at its second congress to co-operate with the 'bourgeois nationalists' of the Kuomintang on a basis of mutual independence, as suggested in Lenin's theses of 1920. This Dr Sun rejected: if the communists wanted to support the national revolution, they were welcome to enter his party. Now Maring once again took a hand and persuaded the Chinese communist leaders to try the policy which came to be known as the 'bloc within'—joining the Kuomintang as individuals without concealing their continued membership in a separate Communist Party. By the end of the month, one of the communist founders, Li Ta-chao, made a test application and was accepted. Other leaders followed, and the new policy was officially confirmed by the fourth congress of the Communist International in November 1922, and by the third congress of the CPC in June 1923.

Meanwhile Dr Sun made a first attempt to reform the Kuomintang in the sense suggested by Maring—that of the Bolshevik model of a disciplined, centralistic party with links to a net-work of 'mass organizations'. A committee in whose work the Communist Party secretary Chen Tu-hsiu took part published a new statute for the Kuomintang on 1 January 1923; yet in the absence of an effective party machine operating from a secure power base it hardly reached the membership. But the conditions for a real transformation improved decisively when later in January a visit to Dr Sun by a representative of the Soviet government, A. A. Yoffe, led to a formal pledge of Soviet political support for the Kuomintang and to an informal promise to send advisers, and when just at that time the general who had expelled Dr Sun from Canton was overthrown by other generals who recalled the exile and asked him to form a 'national government' in their city. By July, a Kuomintang delegation headed by Chiang Kai-shek, Dr Sun's personal chief of staff, left Canton for Moscow, where it was to study Soviet military and political institutions; and in early October, a group of forty Soviet advisers arrived in Canton to help Dr Sun to reorganize his party and to establish a military academy. It was headed by Mikhail Borodin, who had previously worked for the Comintern but was now accredited by deputy foreign commissar Lev Karakhan as representing the Soviet government, and it included the Soviet general Blucher (Galen).

The first effect of Borodin's advice was Dr Sun's decision to call the first party congress ever held by the KMT, and to charge a provisional executive committee of nine, including one Chinese communist, with drafting a new party programme and statute for submission to it. Borodin took a prominent part in its deliberations; and after the outlines of the reorganization plan had been published in mid-December, he was officially appointed 'adviser to the KMT'. The congress, composed of 113 appointed and 83 elected delegates, met on 20 January 1924 in an atmosphere of friendship and admiration for Soviet Russia. It adopted a manifesto which criticized the party's past failures as due to insufficient 'links with the masses' and called on the Chinese workers and peasants to join its ranks; it combined a programme of national unification and democratic and social reform with a clear warning that a democratic constitution could come into force only after the complete victory of the revolution, and that while it was in progress its opponents would not enjoy democratic rights. The new party statute closely followed the model of Bolshevik 'democratic centralism'. New entrants were to be sponsored by two party members and to pledge themselves to disciplined execution of party policy; local, district, and provincial units were each to elect an executive committee and a control commission, while the national congress, to meet annually, was to decide policy, to elect a Central Executive Committee (CEC) and a Central Control Commission; the CEC in turn had power to give binding instructions to all regional and local units and to fix the method of delegation to the congress; it was also to set up central departments for dealing with various types of activity, including organization, propaganda, mass organizations, and military affairs. There was one major deviation from the model, however: Dr Sun was made lifetime leader of the party by statute, with the right to preside over both the congress and the CEC, to veto any decisions of the latter, and to demand obedience from all members—a role familiar from Bolshevik practice but never admitted by communist theory.

The Chinese communists played an important part in making the 'new model Kuomintang' work. With only 300 members at the time, compared to the KMT's 170,000, they not only gained substantial representation in the Central Executive Committee; despite the misgivings uttered by some old KMT leaders before, during, and after the congress, the communists succeeded with Dr Sun's help in occupying positions of great importance for the transformation of the party organization and its link-up with a network of 'mass organizations'—notably in the central departments dealing with personnel appointments, with the peasant movement, and to a lesser extent with the trade unions. As the national revolutionary movement expanded in the following years, the control of those key positions greatly helped the Chinese communists to turn the 'mass organizations' into their strongholds.

Meanwhile the creation of another vital element of KMT power, the 'party army', began with the new military academy which opened in June 1924 under Chiang Kai-shek's direction, combining military and political training for enthusiastic volunteers from all over China. Here Russian military experts introduced the Russian model of organization, including the dualism of commandants and political commissars; Russian funds had to finance an institution which the local generals regarded with understandable suspicion; and Russian arms arrived at a crucial moment to permit the newly trained cadres to form the first units under their command. But the Chinese commanders, political commissars, and teachers at the academy were in the main non-communist, and the CPC never succeeded in gaining a major share in the new army's control. It was in October, in a clash with a 'Volunteer Corps' armed by Canton merchants, that Chiang Kai-shek's cadets first used their training and their Russian arms to put a reliable force at the disposal of Dr Sun, securing for him undivided control of the city; and in February 1925 they defeated for the first time the mercenaries of a provincial general and brought much of Kwantung province under the rule of the KMT. After Dr Sun's death in March, during a visit to Peking, some other generals rebelled in June and the performance had to be repeated—no longer in the name of the leader, but of the primacy of his movement. Chiang's renewed victory proved beyond doubt that the 'new model army' had at last established a solid basis for the power of the 'new model party'.

Dr Sun had undertaken his last journey in a vain attempt to persuade a new ruling group in Peking to join him in summoning a broadly representative 'national convention' for the peaceful unification of the country; when it failed he reaffirmed his revolutionary concept in a 'political testament' and in a message to the Soviet authorities which he signed on his deathbed. The CEC of his party reacted to his death by two major changes. It decided not to invest any of the survivors with the powers of lifetime leader, but merely to elect a technical chairman of the collective leadership in the person of Wang Ching-wei; and it proceeded to replace Dr Sun's personal rule by the creation of a formal government designed to administer the territory under the party's control and to claim authority over the whole national territory in its name. The ministries of defence, foreign affairs, and finance, which formed the nucleus of the new state apparatus, were staffed with KMT members and remained responsible to the party as the only organ of popular representation.

In May and June 1925, a series of clashes between striking Chinese workers and Japanese and British police in Shanghai and Canton led to a nationwide mass movement of strikes, demonstrations, and boycotts directed against the unequal treaties, in which the KMT successfully took the lead. This breakthrough to the masses, and the part played in it by anti-imperialist slogans and communist organization techniques among the workers, helped to strengthen the influence of the left-wing revolutionary nationalists in the Canton leadership and to increase the misgivings of the more con-servative leaders, many of whom left Canton for Shanghai or Peking during the winter of 1925–6 and even attempted to set up their own rival 'KMT' in the North. Chiang Kai-shek, riding with the left wave, used it to achieve the unification of all the Canton govern-ment's armed forces into a 'National Revolutionary Army' under his command; by the time of the second KMT congress in January 1926, this army controlled the whole of Kwantung province.

The congress was marked by enthusiasm for the Soviet alliance and anti-imperialist world revolution, as well as by the emphasis put on winning the active support of the workers and peasants, and it led to a further strengthening of communist positions in the central party machine. By this time, moreover, some of the Soviet military advisers had assumed positions of direct command, while the Chinese communists controlled the armed workers' militia created to enforce the anti-British boycott and had begun to gain positions as political commissars at least in some army units. This led to the first crisis of the alliance when Chiang, soon after the con-gress, began to prepare for a military expedition to conquer Central China which the Soviet advisers regarded as premature. Taking advantage of Borodin's temporary absence, Chiang suddenly moved on 20 March 1926 to arrest the communist political commissars and disarm the workers' militia, keeping the Soviet officers under house arrest during the coup; he subsequently assured Borodin on his return of his continued loyalty to the Soviet alliance, but asked and obtained the recall of the 'interfering' Soviet officers. The simultaneous departure of his civilian colleague Wang Ching-wei for a health cure in Europe left Chiang in sole control of army, party, and government, and he used it to remove communists from key positions and to demand from them pledges to refrain from any criticism of Dr Sun's ideas and to submit all their party instructions to a mixed committee.

The Northern expedition, begun in July, soon yielded major victories, and by October Wuhan on the middle Yangtse had been taken. Yet while success increased Chiang's military power and prestige, it also led to the incorporation of entire non-political army units under unregenerate local warlords into the Revolutionary Army, when their commanders came over for opportunist reasons; at the same time, communist-controlled peasant leagues and trade unions that had helped to disorganize the enemy rear acquired growing influence. Soon Wuhan, where the government had been transferred on Chiang's own prompting, became the centre of a coalition of communist and ex-warlord forces led by famous names of the KMT Left and directed against Chiang's dominant position in the name of the primacy of civilian party power. In March 1927, when Chiang was on the point of taking Shanghai and Nanking, a CEC plenum held in his absence in Wuhan asked for and obtained his resignation from the leadership of the central party organs and for the first time entrusted two communists with ministries, those of agriculture and labour.

By this time, however, Chiang Kai-shek had made up his mind to shake off all dependence on the Soviets, to break with the communists, and to use the leverage which control of Shanghai, China's economic centre, would give him for achieving recognition by the other Great Powers. Hardly had a communist workers' rising delivered the city into his hands when Chiang proclaimed a local state of siege, imposed a ban on unauthorized arms-carrying, and encouraged the formation of an anti-communist 'movement for the protection of the party and the salvation of the nation' throughout the region controlled by forces loyal to him; and on 12 April 1927, he began to disarm, dissolve, and massacre the organizations of the Communist Party and the communist-controlled trade unions from Shanghai right down to Canton. He followed this up by forming a counter-government to Wuhan at Nanking, in the name of a purified KMT which would embody the only true alternative to either warlordism or foreign-inspired red terrorism, and by stating that co-operation with the Soviets was justified only so long as it could be conducted on the basis of equality and non-interference in Chinese internal affairs.

The Wuhan government, now led by the returned Wang and backed by a majority of the CEC including the communists, had first reacted to Chiang's moves by 'expelling' the members of the Nanking counter-government from the party. But the conflict with the communists, which both they and Wang wanted to avoid, was forced on Wuhan as forcible land seizures by the peasant leagues and equally violent counter-actions by local military commanders and secret societies spread on its territory. When at last the communists reluctantly moved, in agreement with the even more reluctant Stalin, to press fo the adoption of a revolutionary land policy and the punishment of the commanders in question, Wang and his associates realized that they would have to break with the CPC unless they wanted to lose that part of the army on which they had so far relied. By the end of June, army units disarmed the workers' militia in Wuhan and the communists withdrew from the government; by mid-July, they were expelled from the Kuomintang— and Borodin was sent home.

The communists expected that Chiang's and Wang's 'betrayal' would end the Kuomintang's role as bearer of the national revolution. The KMT leaders expected that the crushing of the communists would open the road to a true nationalist single-party State. In fact, the élan of the movement for national unification was not broken, and the KMT gradually did succeed in unifying China in the following years; but the break with the communists changed the structure and composition of the party once again as drastically as Soviet advice and communist co-operation had changed it before.

Henceforth, the mass organizations became suspect objects of restrictive control, permitted to engage in little more than professional training, with the result that in many areas they dwindled into insignificance; local party branches were largely reduced to groups of notables from the landowning and official classes, while the party machine suffered from a persistent shortage of civilian full-time cadres which the creation of a central party school could mitigate but never overcome. As national unification came to appear rather the result of military campaigns and military bargaining than of an ideological and social revolution, the role of the military within the leadership of party and government was bound to increase correspondingly—carrying with it the seeds of a new military regionalism *within* the Kuomintang regime. The bitter regional conflicts of the following years were different from the earlier warlordism in that all the rival commanders now had to base their claims on the common principle of party legitimacy; but this was possible because the political leaders themselves were so divided into rival factions and clans that party legitimacy could again and again be interpreted in a variety of ways. Centralist discipline remained the party's constitutional rule in theory, but in practice the unity of will, the authority of the single leader, and even the monopoly of legitimate force were achieved only gradually, with repeated setbacks, and incompletely. Under the cloak of single-party rule, regional and factional pluralism retained so much vitality that the one-party State of the KMT was never completely one-party, and perhaps never completely a State.

The immediate consequence of the break with the communists was a compromise between Nanking and Wuhan, negotiated by the more conservative second-rank military and political figures on both sides with little regard either for their leaders or for party legitimacy. Chiang resigned all his offices to demonstrate that he would not stand in the way of unity, and Wang withdrew in protest with his left-wing followers when leadership was transferred to a 'special committee' of all factions including right-wingers he had once helped to expel from the party. But this group proved unable either to cope with the unrest from below, fomented not only by ill-prepared local communist risings but also by Wang's demand for a new plenary session of the 'legitimate' CEC elected by the 1926 party congress, or to provide effective leadership against the warlords who still dominated China north of the Yangtse. As the demand for Chiang's return as Commander-in-Chief grew, he made the resignation of the 'special committee' and the recall of the CEC a condition of his acceptance and achieved both at the turn of 1927–8; but by then, the abortive communist rising in Canton, Wang's stronghold, had so much weakened the Left that the CEC session now confirmed not only all anti-communist measures, but also the dissolution of the KMT's department for mass organizations, the cancellation of all earlier pro-communist resolutions, and the readmission of those on the right who had earlier been expelled for their premature anti-communism.

It was thus an army commanded and a party and government dominated by Chiang that resumed the Northern expedition at the beginning of March 1928 to achieve national unity under Kuomintang rule; but it was also an army, party, and government that had been able to preserve their own unity only by granting considerable autonomy to the most important regional military leaders through the creation of 'regional bureaus' of the Central Political Council. Full and final victory over the Northern warlords was achieved within three months; in early June, Chang Tso-lin withdrew to his Manchurian domain only to be assassinated there, and Kuomintang troops entered Peking. The military campaign for the unification of China was over, and by December the decision of Chang Hsue-liang, the son and heir of Chang Tso-lin, to join the Kuomintang and accept its rule in Manchuria, put the seal on its success.

Now the creation of effective political institutions—the 'educational dictatorship' conceived by Dr Sun—and the recovery of external sovereignty by the revision of the unequal treaties became the principal tasks. Chiang did not envisage their solution as a continuation of the revolutionary process depending on the active participation of the people, but as a work of constructive reform legislation from above within China, and of patient diplomatic negotiations without; so he rejected all proposals from the Left for reviving the mass organizations and accepted the ideas of Hu Han-min, the most conservative among Dr Sun's principal lieutenants, for the provisional organization of the State. Dr Sun's plan for the creation of five parallel organs of the central government—the executive, legislative, judiciary, examining, and inspecting bodies—was to be carried out immediately; but when the new 'Organization Statute of the Republic of China' was completed in October, it showed that the composition of all these organs was to be decided by a single Council of State, whose chairman would act both as chief of State and as commander-in-chief: thus the technical division of labour between the five organs would not in fact amount to a political division of power. Moreover, the 'Principles of Educational Dictatorship' adopted at the same time made it clear that the theoretical sovereignty of the people was to be exercised for that entire period by the ruling party, represented between congresses by its

CEC and entitled to give policy directives to the government: in fact it was the CEC that appointed the first Council of State, with Chiang as chairman.

The substitution of party dictatorship for popular sovereignty, characteristic for all single-party regimes but disguised in most of them, was thus openly admitted by Kuomintang China from the start—admitted, that is, as a temporary necessity pending the education of the people for democratic self-government. Yet the regime as now constituted showed little aptitude or inclination for promoting such education in practice. At the third congress of the KMT held in March 1929, 285 out of 399 'delegates' had been appointed, not elected; small wonder that the majority rejected the left-wing view that the needed social reforms could not be carried out by bureaucratic methods alone, without organized popular activity, and approved the principle of confining all 'mass organizations', in the interests of social harmony and internal peace, to tasks of professional training. The new CEC consisted of a solid majority of followers of Chiang and Hu, with regional generals and politicians making up the minority.

In fact, while the party dictatorship was overt, party centralism was still largely fictitious. Outside the territory occupied by Chiang's own 'central army', agreements on the proportional demobilization of all regional armies after the end of the civil war were being ignored; so were central directives aimed at preventing arbitrary tax extortion by local authorities or at stopping landlords from passing on the tax burden to their peasants. It was at the same third congress that Chiang gave the first sign of his determination to come to grips with this new intra-party warlordism. On his demand, three generals from Kwangsi were expelled as 'rebels' for having deposed a provincial governor who had dared to pass on taxes to the central government. When he had driven them from most of their territory within three months after the congress, Chiang openly proclaimed his intention to centralize the government: he now dissolved the regional bureaus of the Central Political Council which he had conceded on the eve of the decisive battle against the old warlords. It was the beginning of a new series of armed conflicts, but this time between Chiang and other generals belonging to the KMT and claiming to fight for its true principles.

Between May 1929 and January 1930, Chiang defeated five successive regional rebellions, all claiming to act in support of Wang

Ching-wei's 'left' faction and its demand for a new, genuinely elected party congress, but all in fact representing little more than the struggle of various regional commanders to maintain their independence. But as all the rebels used the slogans of the Left, Chiang came to treat all propaganda of the real Left, and indeed all public criticism, as if it were armed rebellion, and his increasingly harsh repression provoked increasingly bitter opposition among the intelligentsia. In the atmosphere thus created, Chiang's military rivals and civilian critics from both left and right finally coalesced in the spring of 1930 into a common front against what they regarded as his personal despotism. They formed a joint High Command in April, set up a rival party leadership under Wang in Peking in July, and finally a counter-government on 1 September. But Chiang had already defeated the Southern branch of the rebellion by mid-June; in October he triumphed over his most formidable opponent in the North, Feng Yu-hsiang, and in November the coalition dissolved.

By the end of 1930 Chiang was thus completely victorious and in effective control of almost all China; but he was also shrewd enough to realize that repression had passed the point of diminishing returns. The most articulate part of the nation, the intelligentsia, had for the first time begun to turn from a party that seemed increasingly identified with the rule of the army and the bureaucracy; during the summer of 1930, Wang had responded to that mood by calling for an end not only to Chiang's despotism, but to the 'educational dictatorship' of the party, proposing instead the early election of a national convention with open competition between several parties. The consolidation of the communist 'Soviet Areas' and partisan armies in spite of the repeated 'annihilation campaigns' by Kuomintang troops, amounting to the revival of a danger that had seemed totally crushed in 1927, was another indication of the weakening popular basis of the regime. So Chiang decided to launch his own programme for carefully controlled liberalization—a limited political amnesty and the summoning of a national convention with broad non-party participation which was to draft a new provisional constitution. The next plenary session of the CEC, which crowned the victory of centralism and laid the foundation of financial reform by at last abolishing all internal customs, also approved the calling of the national convention; the electoral law, announced on 1 January 1931, was based on a kind of corporative franchise, with candidates to be chosen not only by the party, but by all legal professional bodies, including registered trade unions and peasant leagues as well as educational associations and universities. The amnesty, however, was crippled by the resistance of Hu Han-min, who successfully insisted on excluding from it not only communists, but all 'ringleaders of rebellion' so as to prevent a possible reconciliation between Chiang and Wang. By the time Chiang broke with Hu and forced his resignation by putting him under house arrest, the chance of a genuine relaxation had passed; the basis of the regime had, in fact, further narrowed.

Even so, some 40–50 million voters are said to have participated in the elections of March–April 1931; moreover, these elections, though obviously managed to a high degree, did not take place on a single-list system, and the deputies elected included known critics of Chiang. In its one and only session, held on twelve days in May, the convention passed a new 'Basic Law for the Period of the Educational Dictatorship' which set out the stages for the gradual building of local and regional self-government from below, with the introduction of full constitutional democracy as the final stage. In the meantime, the party dictatorship was to continue in the form of a presidential regime.

By the time this law was passed in Nanking, a new coalition of Chiang's political opponents, backed by a group of Southern generals, was once more forming in Canton; at the end of May, they proclaimed a counter-government headed by Wang. But this time, the country's disgust with civil wars had become so strong that each side hesitated to march against the other; instead, they began to compete with promises for a new party congress and protestations of their desire for a true national reconciliation. After the Japanese occupation of Manchuria which started with the 'Mukden incident' in September 1931, the pressure for compromise became overwhelming. In October, negotiators from both sides agreed to hold separate congresses in their respective territories, to form a new party executive in agreed proportions, and to reorganize the government on a more collective basis. The Nanking congress promptly ratified these terms; in Canton, some of Chiang's military enemies at first resisted, and agreed only on condition of his resignation, which took place in December. But once the new executive was formed at the turn of the year, Wang and his followers began to side with Chiang's men against their former regionalist allies. A personal reconciliation between the two leaders followed quickly under pressure of the double threat from Japan and from the popular clamour for a war for which both knew China to be unprepared; by March 1932, a true division of power was established between them, with Wang as Prime Minister and Chiang as chief of staff and chairman of the Military Committee. In this form, the party regime was to last without major crisis until the eve of open war with Japan.

It would be wrong to conclude from the foregoing that during its early years, the Kuomintang regime had produced nothing but victory over regional rebellions and some constitutional fictions of doubtful practical importance. On the contrary, in the midst of all its political troubles, the government found the time and energy to frame a number of modern legal codes and made them effective at least in the major urban centres of the south and east; to reform the tax system and abolish the internal customs; to unify and improve the standards for higher education; and to recover control over the external customs and reduce greatly the extra-territorial and extra-jurisdictional privileges enjoyed by the imperialist Powers (with the exception of Japan). But general economic progress was hamstrung both by the lack of internal peace and by the shortage of funds; and major changes in the social structure were excluded by a regime which lacked an administrative machinery distinct from the economically privileged groups, and was afraid to mobilize the masses. This applied above all to the crucial issue of land reform: a moderate but useful reform law was passed early, but its execution was delayed pending an 'implementing law' that was held up until 1935; moreover, the land of all holders of public office and all serving officers was in principle exempt.

With all this, the party members, bureaucrats, and officers—and the latter two groups now made up a vital part of the party membership—could still feel that they were truly serving the rebuilding of the nation. The Japanese occupation of Manchuria marked a turning point by cruelly showing up the national impotence of the regime; it thus came into conflict not only with the social aspirations of the masses, but with the nationalist emotions of the very elites on which it most wished to rely.

The establishment of the Chiang-Wang duumvirate had been welcomed as promising a change in the character of the regime which would leave greater scope for public discussion and criticism. In fact, while communist activity continued to be mercilessly suppressed as far as the power of the government reached, non-revolutionary opposition groups and even 'parties' were henceforth permitted, in an effort to restore the dialogue between the regime and the intelligentsia. Beginning in 1932, a number of them quickly developed among the professors and students of Peking, Tientsin, and Shanghai—the same groups that had started the nationalist movement of the 4th May 1919, and with largely similar anti-Japanese, liberal, and modernizing slogans. But now their nationalism led them to attack the Kuomintang government for failing to offer effective resistance to Japan.

Prima facie, the charge was justified. Chiang Kai-shek and Wang Ching-wei had been driven together not only by the common threat of Japanese invasion, but by their common conviction that China lacked as yet the strength for a war against the only Great Power in East Asia. As their appeals to the League of Nations proved the unwillingness of the western Powers to restrain Japan, while the Soviets were prepared to encourage Chinese resistance by the resumption of diplomatic relations but not to offer substantial support, the Kuomintang adopted a policy of yielding to Japan under protest and looking for some accommodation with the moderate elements in the Japanese government: it refused to recognize the Japanese puppet State of Manchukuo, it even authorized armed resistance when the Japanese attacked in Shanghai, but it preferred to react to each local defeat by concluding a military armistice rather than by a war that might spell the collapse of all it had achieved so far. In the opinion of Chiang and Wang, the paramount need was to delay all-out conflict while building up Chinese strength and consolidating national unity—and this included the destruction of the 'Soviet Areas': it was necessary to defeat the communists before a serious confrontation with Japan.

But this was not the kind of argument to convince Chinese nationalist intellectuals or even many of the younger officers. When the government called a 'National Emergency Conference' in April 1932 to discuss its response to Japanese aggression with its intellectual critics, a number of the latter refused to attend, some representatives of the Shanghai bourgeoisie among them. New nationalist opposition groups mushroomed, and though their membership remained small, their influence among the students and through them on public opinion kept growing. Moreover, their anti-Japanese demands were given constant public backing by the Canton regional government under Hu Han-min.

It was an even more serious warning sign when in the autumn of 1933 the 19th Army, nationally famous for its resistance to the Japanese in Shanghai and now stationed in Fukien province, rose against the Kuomintang and called on the left-wing nationalist leaders of the socalled 'Third Party' to form a counter-government around a programme of resistance to Japan, political democracy, and radical social reform, offering military co-operation to the communist partisan armies. Despite a preliminary agreement, the communists never implemented that co-operation, and the revolt was crushed within two months; but it had demonstrated how dangerous a weapon anti-Japanese nationalism, once abandoned by the regime, could become in the hands of its opponents.

Nevertheless, Chiang and Wang were not be be shaken in their determination to crush the 'internal enemy' first. In the cities, the three parallel political police organizations of the regime—one of them, the dreaded 'blueshirts', directly dependent on the headquarters of the KMT—were remarkably successful in hunting down communists. In the countryside, where several campaigns against the 'Soviet Areas' had failed, the government revived in 1932 the system of universal registration, under which groups of families were held responsible for mutually checking on each other's loyalty—a system first used by General Tseng Kuo-fan in fighting the Taiping rebellion in the nineteenth century.

But Chiang and his immediate circle were well aware that the regime could not in the long run maintain its cohesion and destroy the communist partisan forces by repression alone—without an ideology which would give a moral backbone to its officials, a sense of mission to its officers, and hope for progress to the peasants in the contested areas. It was this search for an ideology that brought a number of the younger generals trained by Chiang to form the 'Rebirth Group', and it was one of them who started in 1933 the first 'special force' of volunteer officers for fighting the communist partisans by political as well as military means: they were to ensure the pacification of reconquered areas by combining refugee relief, educational and health work, and control of the army's conduct towards the population, with their police and intelligence duties. The special forces thus felt themselves to be a true political and moral elite of the army, and they scored considerable initial successes.

The young generals of the Rebirth Group, being nationalists engaged in fighting communism, were inclined to take inspiration from the Japanese militarists and from the victory of national-socialism in Germany. But Chiang, while impressed with what appeared to him as the spirit of community and national sacrifice displayed by the fascist States, finally decided against adopting a variant of their ideology. One reason for this was that the Rebirth Group recommended the fascist model chiefly on account of its 'leadership principle', appealing to him to abolish the committee system in party and government in favour of open one-man-rule for life, as once established by Dr Sun Yat-sen. But during the years in question—1934–6—Chiang was more convinced than ever of the need to maintain unity with the important regional leaders by negotiation and compromise, and he regarded committee leadership in party and government as a tried and proven method for achieving this purpose in Chinese conditions—all the more so as his prestige assured his ascendancy in any committee.

Another, more fundamental objection was probably that an ideology of the fascist type required the open exaltation of militant nationalism, and that was incompatible with the tactical flexibility Chiang's diplomacy required at the time: an anti-Japanese nationalism would have prevented a continuation of his efforts to secure a modus vivendi with the aggressor and precipitated war, while an unconditional commitment to pro-Japanese nationalism would not only have been extremely unpopular, but would have disarmed the Kuomintang on the eve of its most serious attempt to reach a settlement with Tokyo. In fact, during the second half of 1934, parallel with Chiang's final offensive against the Kiangsi Soviet area, the KMT leaders hinted to Japan that they were willing to support her in any future conflict with the West or with Russia, if only Japan would respect China's territorial integrity and treat her on a basis of equality. The negotiations resulting from this offer dragged on far into 1935, leading as a by-product to government measures against the anti-Japanese movement, until the determination of the Japanese military leaders to create a series of protectorates on Chinese soil finally ended this prospect.

Whatever the reasons, the fascist type of ideology was finally rejected by Chiang in favour of a neo-Confucian revival that was more comparable to the ideas of the Moslem Brotherhood, or even to an Asian version of Moral Rearmament: an effort to ensure the devotion of officials and officers to a programme of national discipline and orderly reform from above not by a commitment to any sort of revolutionary nationalism, either Kemalist or fascist, but by a moral regeneration based on a new interpretation of the values of the Chinese tradition. This was the essence of the 'New Life' movement launched by Chiang in the spring of 1934. Its origin was linked closely with the largest, and ultimately successful, military campaign against the principal Soviet area in Kiangsi: it was the 'special forces' that were charged with training students from all over the country to become 'leaders towards rebirth'. As their basic text they were given a pamphlet written by Chiang himself, which outlined the qualities needed by the elite that was to regenerate China—honesty and social justice, respect for authority, discipline and self-discipline, cleanliness and dedicated activism—and derived them from the classical Confucian virtues. By July 1934, the movement had become organized on a nationwide basis with Chiang as leader, and the official cult of Kung-tse was reintroduced during the same year. Campaigns to clean the houses and the cities and to fight the sale and consumption of opium followed, the latter supported by anti-drug legislation specially directed towards curing officials and officers of the habit.

The adoption of this ideology set the seal on the Kuomintang's alienation from the modernizing intelligentsia. Despite its reformist elements, the movement was essentially conservative and quite incompatible with nationalism of the Kemalist type; it was thus less suited to a new-style party dictatorship aiming at the re-education of the people and their active participation in the reshaping of society than to an old-style authoritarian regime based on the bureaucracy and the army. Yet this was what the rule of the Kuomintang, under the impact first of the conflict with the communists and then of its inability to fight the Japanese invasion, had in fact largely become by the middle thirties. Of the 1.2 million members to which the ruling party had swollen by the time of its fifth congress in 1935, some 700,000 were in the army; of the remainder, it is safe to assume that about half were party and government officials, including state-employed teachers, and most of the other half urban and rural notables from the same families from which the bulk of the officers and civil servants were drawn. Far from controlling the army and the bureaucracy, the party no longer had a separate existence from them: it was now simply the meeting ground where the various military and bureaucratic cliques made their deals.

It was characteristic of this transformation of the regime that during the same years, Chiang increasingly relied on concessions to regional leaders to avoid conflict and promote national unity. At the CEC meeting in December 1934, which celebrated the liquidation of the Kiangsi Soviet area, agreement was reached to increase the power of the provincial governments in the execution of national laws, the maintenance of local forces, and the selection of officials. The policy was successful in reducing friction, and a final revolt of Kwantung and Kwangsi generals after Hu's death in 1936 was quickly reduced without serious fighting; but it meant that when the 'implementing law' to the land reform was finally passed in 1935, it left the fixing of maximum holdings to the provincial authorities— with the result that nothing serious was attempted except in parts of Chekiang and the reconquered areas of Kiangsi.

The fifth congress of the Kuomintang met in November 1935 under the impression of new Japanese attempts to create 'autonomous' areas in Inner Mongolia and North China, and of a rapid expansion in the scope of the anti-Japanese movement. Before the congress, Wang Ching-wei had offered his resignation in an effort to commit Chiang to a continuation of the policy of appeasement, but as he was seriously hurt in a nationalist attempt on his life, he could not attend; and Chiang, while calling for priority for internal construction and patient efforts for an understanding with Japan, gave a first hint that there were limits beyond which he would not yield to pressure. In the following weeks, anti-Japanese mass demonstrations, centred in the universities, culminated in the formation of a 'National Salvation Union' which called for an end to the civil war with the communists, a government of national unity, armed resistance to all further Japanese encroachments, and a speed-up of armaments; and Chiang thought it wise to meet the delegates of this organization and plead with them. Yet efforts to negotiate with Japan were continued, in increasingly hopeless conditions, to the middle of 1936, and some of the student associations that had organized the demonstrations were dissolved as late as April.

The turn towards resistance seems to have begun with the Japanese proclamation of a 'Military Government of Inner Mongolia' at the end of June 1936. By August, Chiang had fixed for himself the point beyond which he would not yield, even at the risk of national catastrophe, and by mid-November that point had been reached with the occupation of parts of Suiyuan province by Japanese auxiliaries: the province was reconquered on Chiang's orders by units of the central Army while Japan was warned of the acute danger of war. Yet even then, the KMT leaders strove to complete their monopoly of internal power first: Chiang ordered a new offensive against the communists in Shensi, where they had organized their new base after the 'Long March', even though they had by then made a number of offers for a united anti-Japanese front—including offers to 'dissolve' the Soviet government and subordinate themselves to a national government following national elections. Seven leaders of the National Salvation Union were arrested in Shanghai late in November—a move that contributed much to the later rapprochement between the communists and the intellectual opposition.

The famous 'Sian Incident' of December 1936, in which Chiang was arrested by the regional commanders he had ordered to attack the communists—headed by the Manchurian exile Marshal Chang Hsue-liang—showed the risks of this policy in the new conditions. But the rallying of opinion against the coup, and the recognition by the Soviets, and in their wake by the Chinese communists, that Chiang's authority was indispensable for mobilizing united national resistance to Japan, forced Chang to release his captive and submit to his discipline, so that Chiang emerged once more with a free hand for his future policy. He subsequently dissolved the units that had revolted, and at the next CEC meeting in February still repeated his readiness to negotiate with Japan on a basis of Chinese equality and territorial integrity, and his demand for the liquidation of the Chinese Soviet government and Red Army and for the cessation of all 'class struggle'. But as the communists were by then offering to turn their territory into a regional government, and to subordinate their army to any national government that would resist Japan, without any longer insisting that a 'democratic' reconstruction of the government must precede that move, Chiang's demands seem in fact to have been the prelude to secret negotiations with them—though even then the negotiations were accompanied by the transfer of loyal elite troops to the neighbourhood of the communist base. It was only the Japanese attack on Peking in July that finally persuaded the KMT to conclude new agreements both with the Soviet Union and with the Chinese communists—after a break of ten years.

When the war with Japan, which the leaders of the Kuomintang had striven so long and so hard to avoid, was forced on them at last, it did not bring the total collapse of Chinese statehood which they had feared; but it did finally foil their hopes of ever completing their programme of internal reconstruction.

On the most formal level, this was shown in the indefinite postponement of their plans for ending the 'educational dictatorship' and passing to the 'third stage' envisaged by Dr Sun Yat-sen— full constitutional democracy. In fact, the bureaucratic, authoritarian regime had in the intervening years made no real progress in creating the conditions for such a transition laid down in the provisional constitution of 1931—the fostering of local and provincial self-government. Nevertheless, various government bodies had been working on the draft of a democratic constitution since the spring of 1934 and had adopted a final version in May 1936; it provided for a national assembly to be elected once in six years and to elect in turn a president for the same period who would appoint and head his government, while the assembly would select the legislative and inspecting bodies and meet at rare intervals as a revising chamber. The debates on this draft and the plan to hold elections to the first national assembly in November 1936, then in November 1937, sounded curiously remote from reality in view of the lack of progress on the local and regional levels and the real pressing problems of those years; when war broke out, the 'educational dictatorship' was prolonged for the duration.

On the level of actual organization, the war brought a further narrowing of the leadership by the defection of Wang Ching-wei, and a vital weakening of the administrative structure by the transfer to the front of the young officers who had been the only promising cadres for reform from above. With the economic strain of war added to the other unsolved problems, the lack of a civilian elite now led to a rapid growth of bureaucratic corruption and a corresponding loss of political attraction and cohesion for the regime.

Finally, on the level of real power, the understanding with the communists meant the *de facto* renunciation of the Kuomintang's monopoly of power at the very moment when it was *de jure* extending the period of its 'educational dictatorship'; for though the communists had nominally accepted the subordination of their territory and their armed forces to the National Government and High Command, it was obvious that Mao Tse-tung was unwilling to carry out this pledge and Chiang unable to enforce it. Henceforth, a Kuomintang and a communist government were in fact developing side by side, first in limited cooperation and then in increasingly hostile mutual toleration, on different parts of China's territory—in addition to Wang Ching-wei's pro-Japanese government which both were fighting.

While the Kuomintang started the competition with a vast advantage in the extent and wealth of the territory controlled, the size and equipment of its armed forces, and the recognized legitimacy and national prestige of its leader, the communists were enabled gradually to neutralize this advantage in part by their greater capacity for survival in fighting the superior Japanese enemy by prolonged partisan warfare in primitive conditions, and in part by the greater ideological cohesion of their cadres. When, after the victory over Japan, talks about a national coalition were started between the two rival one-party regimes on the initiative of the Great Powers, neither had the slightest belief in the possibility of such a solution; and the inevitable outcome was the renewal of their civil war, in which an effective communist one-party regime finally defeated a degenerated non-communist one.

As this account would seem to suggest, that outcome was neither due to an inherent inferiority of national revolutionary regimes, nor a purely external effect of the damage inflicted on the fabric of Chinese life by Japanese aggression: it was primarily caused by the successive deformations produced in the Kuomintang first by the initial participation of the communists and the scars of the break with them, and then by the period when it had to avoid an open stand against Japan. The first crisis crucially weakened the modernizing and socially progressive aspects of the ideology of Sun Yat-sen's party, the second its nationalist aspects, until it had lost the substance of the mass appeal on which a modern one-party State can alone be built.

(c) *The new African States*

After a long interval, the model of the single-party State as an instrument of development returned to the agenda of history with the emergence of a number of ex-colonial States in Africa in the second half of the fifties. Most of the creators of the parties in question probably did not plan from the outset to establish a party dictatorship, but they were consciously influenced by the communist type of party organization and at least by some aspects of communist ideology—notably the Leninist doctrine of imperialism and of the need to organize democratic revolutions against colonial rule. On the other hand, none of these 'Afro-Marxist' parties was communist in the sense of accepting the doctrine of class struggle and the leading role of the proletariat for their own countries, of identifying themselves as proletarian class parties, or of wishing to submit to the leadership of an international communist centre.

In the framework of the present essay, it is not possible to give a comprehensive survey of these parties and the regimes created by them, many of which have proved highly unstable and are still in a state of flux. But a few of the outstanding examples will be briefly discussed.

The first parties of the new type were created from 1946 onwards in French West Africa; they had their common origin in the *Rassemblement Démocratique Africain* founded in that year at Bamako by Félix Houphouet-Boigny and his associates with the active assistance and advice of the French Communist Party. It was from the communists that the RDA and its regional sections, notably the *Parti Démocratique de Guinée*, the *Union Soudainaise* and the *Union Démocratique de Cameroun*, learned the need to base their struggle for self-government and eventual liberation on a mass organization with professional organizers and propagandists and with branches formed, if possible, down to the last village.

The alliance between the new parties and the French communists had been concluded at a time when the latter formed part of the metropolitan government and were able directly to aid their progress. But when in the course of the Cold War the French communists turned to violent and embittered opposition, the tie with them was transformed from an advantage into a handicap, and by 1950 the RDA preferred to ensure its future legality by a clean break with the PCF. Its type of organization, however, was not affected by this development, and it continued to gain in electoral strength whenever the colonial authorities gave an opportunity for voting.

Of the one-party regimes that eventually arose from this development, the most important has been that of the PDG in Guinea. Its peculiarity is based on the fact that Guinea, alone among the States emerging in the former territory of French West Africa, has a semi-revolutionary origin: Sekou Touré and his party were alone successful in rejecting membership of the new French *Communauté* during the 1958 plebiscite, and paid the penalty in the form of a sudden and complete withdrawal of French administrative cadres, assets, and aid. As a result, the new sovereign State of Guinea had to be built up from scratch by the victorious party; the new administration was simply the party organization under another name, and there was never any question of permitting other parties. According to the official doctrine, the State has no existence separate from that of the people, and it is the party that organizes and leads the people.

In fact, there is no selection procedure for party membership, and a very large part of the adult population are nominally party members, though the organizational skeleton appears to consist mainly of intellectuals and semi-intellectuals. The party is organized on the communist principle of democratic centralism with strong emphasis on 'collective leadership'. While Sekou Touré's unique position as party leader is undisputed, he has not permitted the type of 'personality cult' in which Kwame Nkrumah used to indulge, but the collective principle seems most important in the intermediate and lower committees as a safeguard for ensuring disciplined execution of central directives.

All 'mass organizations' are controlled by the party in conformity with the communist model. It was an attempt at communist infiltration of two of these organizations, the youth league and the teachers' union, that led to a crisis in Guinea's relations with the Soviet Union in December 1961. Since then, the Soviets have made it clear that they will not support any competing communist parties in 'progressive' African one-party States of this type. On the basis of this assurance on one side, the general renunciation of the principle of single-centred international discipline by Moscow on the other, loose, semi-fraternal relations have since developed again between the PDG, the CPSU, and some other communist parties, as shown by mutual representation at party congresses.

Similar relations also exist between the CPSU and the Union Soudainaise, the ruling party of Mali whose regime appears to come closest to that of the PDG in its type of organization and ideology. They share not only the early Marxist training of their leading cadres, but also the origin of their States in conditions of conflict. In Mali, the break of the original federation with Senegal has left, though to a lesser degree, similar traumatic effects as Guinea's break with the *Communauté*. As a result, these two States have shown, despite their grave and recurrent economic difficulties, rather more political stability than most of the other new single-party regimes in Africa.

The communist model of organization has also played an important role in the development of the party that created the first of the new African States—the Convention People's Party of Ghana. In this case the model first made its impact not through any direct inter-party relations at an early stage, but through the formative personal influence which an ex-communist, George Padmore, exerted on Kwame Nkrumah during his years in Britain. In converting from communism to Pan-Africanism, Padmore had rejected Moscow's authority and the communist class analysis for Africa, but had retained anti-imperialism and a belief in the communist technique of organization. On his return to the Gold Coast in 1947, Nkrumah carried this plan with him, and it was his attempt to transform the then most representative party of that colony, the United Gold Coast Convention, from a party of notables into a militant mass organization, that led to a split and to the formation of the CPP.

Independent Ghana, however, was not born as a single-party State. The transition to sovereignty was peaceful, and as the administration remained intact and was only gradually africanized, the party never completely merged with it. Rival parties were at first tolerated, generally on a tribal basis. Nor was the CPP itself originally monolithic; its congresses and press showed open factional differences, and these were reflected in waverings of government policy.

But as the young State experienced its inevitable economic and political difficulties, Nkrumah reacted to every crisis by a tendency to crush the opposition, and his authority and the power of his party were strong enough to accomplish this. Between 1959 and 1961, the opposition party was gradually harassed out of existence, its leaders driven into exile or arrested. Parallel with this, control over the mass organizations was tightened to the point where they lost all separate identity; in 1960 they were given formal representation in the party's central committee; in 1961 the membership cards of the trade unions, peasant organizations, women's and youth organizations, etc. were abolished and exchanged for cards directly issued by the party. While the party thus reached a nominal strength of two million, it became more amorphous rather than more effective; this was shown in 1961, when a combination of economic difficulties and government infringement of trade union rights led to a spontaneous general strike called against the will of the official union leaders. The suppression of all parliamentary and trade unionist opposition was followed by acts of terrorism and by an all-pervading fear of plots, for which various right-wing and left-wing factions within the CPP and the government were held responsible.

By the time the party monopoly had at last been embodied in the Constitution, the party itself had also become formally monolithic by the elimination of all potential opponents of Nkrumah's personal rule, while the glorification of the leader as a semi-divine saviour of his people assumed an increasingly central part in official propaganda. As this transformation of the regime was not accompanied either by success in the solution of the country's problems or by an effective adjustment of the party's organizational structure to the growth of its nominal membership, what developed in fact below the façade of monolithic despotism was a widening gulf between the regime and the people. When in 1965 Nkrumah was overthrown, during his absence in Peking, by a military coup, the almost total lack of resistance showed that the party regime had long ceased to be a reality and that he had created a void around himself. It also showed that the Afro-Marxist ideology which Nkrumah had propagated in his own peculiar version had penetrated rather less deeply in Ghana than in Guinea.

By the time the bulk of the new African States obtained independence in 1960, the model of single-party government appeared to be well established by the three West African precedents discussed above, and so was no longer considered as necessarily linked with its origin in the communist world. Some of the new leaders tended to regard single-party rule simply as a convenient means of national integration and mobilization during the period of development, without linking it with Marxist or Leninist ideological tenets; in some cases single-party rule even developed by the weaker party voluntarily joining the stronger in order to ease the transition to independence.

On the other hand, the absence of an initial struggle for power, with all its ideological concomitants, often meant that the need for an effective organization with reliable cadres was not grasped, and this led to a weak and unstable power structure. It is safe to say that some of the nominal one-party regimes, for instance in former French Central Africa and also in former British East Africa, bear as little relation to the real thing as some of the nominally parliamentary governments established in Latin America in the nineteenth century, and in some Asian States in the twentieth, bear to western democracy.

But even a party that has won power in a long and bitter struggle and has consciously built the new State on the foundations laid by its fighting organization may show an internal balance of forces very different from that of the 'classical' totalitarian model. This is shown most strikingly by the case of the Algerian FLN.

The men who founded this movement in 1954 were thinking purely in terms of a fighting organization to win independence from France by armed struggle. As the movement grew, they had to develop their various specialized organizations among the workers, the peasants, the students, etc.; they also had to set up a government in exile and to train a professional military force under its control. As they were fighting against a western Power and receiving aid from the communist bloc, their revolutionary nationalism naturally assumed an anti-imperialist and anti-capitalist tinge. At the same time they reacted to communist offers of a united front within Algeria with the argument of Dr Sun Yat-sen: the communists were welcome as members, but not as partners of the FLN.

On the eve of taking power in the country, the FLN at its Tripoli congress made it clear that it intended to establish itself as a party and the only party of the new Algeria, and that the government would be formed by that party as its organ. This was done; the communists were not allowed to exist officially, and the mass organizations were treated as affiliated to the FLN. But subsequent developments showed that the actual relations of power in the new regime were different from the formal ones.

The divisions and political instability in the leadership, and the lack of a common ideological training in an organization whose previous activity had been predominantly military, meant in fact that the mass organizations and the regular army were not strictly controlled from above but began to play the role of so many interest groups seeking to influence official policy: the FLN was for some time less centralistic and more democratic than it claimed to be. The communists in particular, while unable to compete with the FLN as a separate party, were able to gain key positions in some of the mass organizations and to exert considerable influence on FLN policy by this indirect means. Towards the end of 1963 the Algerian Communist Party and the Soviets recognized that this form of influence promised more success than any legal party competition could have offered, and accepted 'licensed infiltration' as their best strategy in the circumstances; in the spring of 1964, the CPSU established fraternal relations with 'Comrade Ben Bella'.

However, the balance of interests and influences within the FLN continued to be unstable, and with the overthrow of Ben Bella in June 1965, by Colonel Boumediène, the communists suffered a considerable setback. As in China in the twenties, the regular army had remained comparatively immune to their infiltration. At the same time, it proved not to be under the effective control of the party leadership, and Boumediène assumed control of the government before he bothered to legalize this step by a decision of the party organs. Resistance, partly inspired by the communists, continued for a time in some of the mass organizations, but it proved ineffective.

In the Algerian regime of today, then, control from the top would appear to be stronger than before since it has been taken over by the head of the army. But this means that it remains an open question how far we are dealing here with a genuine single-party regime or with a mixed form in which the army uses the party as an auxiliary for the exercise of its power.

(d) *Arab parallels*

The political development of the Algerian revolution has in many ways been more closely related to events in other Arab States than to those in Sub-Saharan Africa. Among the former, the case of Gamal Abdel Nasser's regime in Egypt is of particular interest as providing another type of mixture between a military dictatorship and single-party rule. In contrast to Algeria, however, Nasser's regime in Egypt was created by a purely military coup, and the attempt to underpin it by a monopolistic political organization followed only as an afterthought.

As early as January 1953, Nasser's Council of the Revolution created a so-called 'Liberation Front' for the express purpose of bringing the existing professional organizations, notably the trade unions and student associations, under the control of the regime. But this Front remained a mere co-ordinating board and never even attempted to recruit a membership of its own.

The next step was taken in the Constitution of 1956 when the—as yet non-existent—'National Union' was charged with the task of nominating the candidates for a national assembly. But this was still no more than a formal device for creating a sham parliament intended for acclamation rather than consultation. By the time the elections were arranged in 1957, only the executive committee of the National Union existed—and this was apparently considered sufficient for the purpose.

A more serious attempt to create an organization with roots in the country was undertaken after the establishment of the United Arab Republic in 1958. Nasser was unwilling to compromise with the existing political parties in Syria, but realized that he could not simply suppress them as he had suppressed the traditional Egyptian parties—the need for organized links between the regime and the population began to make itself felt. Though the new Constitution provided for the direct appointment of national assembly members by the president, the monopoly of organization of the National Union was proclaimed at the same time, and an effort to build up regional and local committees began in 1959. A national congress of the Union was held in July 1960, and Nasser selected from its ranks those members of the national assembly of the United Arab Republic who had not sat in the previous Egyptian and Syrian assemblies. Similarly, a law concerning local self-government provided for its organs to be composed of a minority of appointed government officials and a majority of representatives to be elected by the local units of the National Union.

Nevertheless, the creation of a genuine political organization by the fiat of the military dictatorship proved extremely difficult; it appears that most of the local committees provided for in the statute never came to life, and that the Union never acquired an active membership. A new start was made when, after the Syrian break-away and the dissolution of the United Arab Republic in 1961, Nasser took a decisive turn towards a policy of wholesale nationali-zation of industry. Under a decision promulgated in November of that year, a 'national congress of the popular forces' was to be formed by delegates of all professional organizations, to adopt a 'National Pact for Revolutionary Action', and then to arrange for the election of new local committees on this basis.

The National Union emerged from this attempt to put new life into it with a new name, the 'Arab Socialist Union'; but it has remained not only an auxiliary of the military regime, which was intended, but a remarkably inactive auxiliary. In addition to the basic difficulty of creating a state party for a regime that was already in power and had developed its bureaucracy without such a party,

22

Nasser seemed to be short of useful ideologists who would be able to justify the pragmatic twists and turns of his international and domestic policies by coherent and convincing systems.

This persistent weakness of the state party despite all its re-organizations, which Nasser increasingly recognized as an obstacle to the national mobilization and re-education needed for successful development, formed part of the background for the new rapproche-ment with the Soviet Union and the release and subsequent employ-ment of many pro-Soviet communists after 1963. The Soviets had by then come to accept Nasser's government as a progressive, non-capitalist regime which the communists should support rather than oppose, and to regard communist entry into the state party on the Algerian model as the most promising course for their weak Egyptian following. Nasser in turn responded after Khrushchev's visit of 1964 by using some of the released communists in his propaganda apparatus and permitting them to publish a Marxist review in order to stimulate discussion in his stagnating 'movement'.

In December 1964 a conference of representatives of 'the com-munists of the Arab countries' endorsed the project of 'transforming the Arab Socialist Union into an organization that would represent the interests of the toiling masses as completely as possible'. But the parallel to the Algerian development remained strictly limited, given the obvious concentration of the real power in Nasser's hands.

Finally, an Arab revolutionary party with a nationalist and socia-list ideology has conquered power repeatedly in Syria and once also in Iraq. The Baath, conceived by its Syrian founders as transcending the frontiers of the existing Arab States, was intended to achieve Arab unity and the social transformation of the Arab world by revolutionary means, and clearly aimed at a single-party regime whenever it had a chance. Composed chiefly of intellectuals and officers, the Baath has from the outset suffered from two weaknesses. First, it sought power as a party but could see no way of achieving it except by a military coup. Second, the lack of a generally recognized leader of Nasser's stature made every Baath government, once established in a particular State, the plaything of rival military and ideological factions. There has been no specific, consistent policy characteristic of the Baath: in Iraq, it was responsible for the fierce anti-communist suppression following the overthrow of Kassem, while in Syria in recent years it has adopted a marked pro-communist policy and even admitted communist representatives into the government.

(e) *Some conclusions*

The experience of nationalist one-party regimes in developing countries, widely dispersed as they have been in both time and space, permits some general conclusions. First, nationalist one-party regimes, even when started with active Soviet support and consciously leaning on the Soviet model, have generally been able either to reject communist goals altogether, or at least to set strict limits to communist influence and infiltration. Second, the success of these regimes in their positive task of development has been extremely uneven, depending on a variety of factors, ranging from the ideological aptitude to preserve internal cohesion and achieve mass mobilization, to the understanding of the organizational principles of single-party rule and to the presence or absence of a leader of outstanding authority and ability.

On one side, 'pure' nationalism without a concept of the revolutionary transformation of society is clearly not sufficient for a party dictatorship of development. On the other, a revolutionary ideology based on a syncretism of Marxist and nationalist ideas will not ensure success if the leaders of the movement do not know how to impose discipline on the mass organizations without paralysing them, if the lack of an outstanding personality tempts them into self-destructive rivalries, or if the leader neglects the concrete task of development and escapes from its problems into international demagogy and megalomaniac self-worship.

III. The Fascist Dictatorships

In the underdeveloped countries, as we have seen, the Bolshevik model of the 'party of a new type' and of the single-party State has been used for a purpose which, for all the differences of doctrine, is historically similar to their function in their country of origin: for mobilizing the masses in the process of modernization and conferring 'democratic' legitimacy on a dictatorial regime, while ensuring at the same time a concentration of national energies on its goals by a total suppression of all independent interest groups. The concept of 'totalitarian democracy', coined to highlight the links between Bolshevik totalitarian practice and Rousseau's definition of democracy as the rule of an indivisible *volonté générale*, thus applies to all the nationalist modernizers who learned from the Bolshevik model.

The situation is clearly different in the case of parties and party dictatorships of the fascist type, which bear a striking resemblance to the same model in their organizational structure and political institutions, yet are radically opposed in their doctrine to the egalitarian, rationalist, and humanistic values of the democratic tradition. Fascists and national-socialists believed that it was their historic task to root out the disruptive ideas that had come into the western world since the Enlightenment and the French Revolution, and to destroy all 'Marxist' movements, and Bolshevism in particular, as the most pernicious fruits of those ideas.

Yet a closer analysis of fascist ideology will show that the fascists agree with the Bolsheviks not only negatively in their utter contempt for the liberal aspect of the democratic tradition—freedom of discussion and dissent, protection of minorities and partial interests, security of individual rights under the rule of law—but also in basing the legitimacy of their regimes on the will of the people. The fascists are not traditionalists content to play an auxiliary role in the defence or restoration of God-given dynastic regimes; they are revolutionaries claiming to carry out the national will in destroying the rule of a conspiracy of alien or separatist interests. That national will is as authentic a derivative of the *volonté générale* as is the 'proletarian class-consciousness' of the communists: as with the latter, it is not to be identified empirically by a counting of votes, but is established *a priori* by the superior understanding of the party and ultimately the leader.

The fascist party and the fascist dictatorship, in pursuing their anti-egalitarian and nationalist goals, have thus to solve the same political dilemma as the communists in pursuing their egalitarian and internationalist goals: how to combine 'democratic' legitimation by a mass movement with suppression of freedom of discussion and of the representation of partial interests. It is this similarity of the problem that accounts for the similarity of the forms of party organization and state institutions. But because of the opposition of ideological goals and values, the fascist leaders were not originally conscious of the parallel, and were only gradually driven to adopt the organizational and institutional devices of their enemies.

(a) *Italian fascism*

The history of Italian fascism is usually dated either from Musso-lini's break with the Italian Socialist Party in 1915, or from the foundation of the *Fasci Italiani di Combattimento* in 1919; but no influence of the Bolshevik model on Italian fascism can be traced before the autumn of 1921, when the movement was transformed into the *Partito Nazionale Fascista* at its Rome congress. The change was more than nominal: it marked the emergence of a new concept out of a crisis both in the practice of the movement and in the ideas of its leader. Benito Mussolini had occasionally boasted that he was the true father of Italian communism because of the prominent part he had played as a leader of the radical wing of the Italian Socialist Party on the eve of the First World War. But the mixture of revolu-tionary Marxist and syndicalist ideas which he then held, while foreshadowing some aspects of his future in their stress on direct action and their contempt for parliamentary discussion and com-promise and for legal procedure, contained no original contribution to the problem of party organization.

In breaking away from the socialists in order to become an active propagandist of participation in the war, and in reorganizing his followers after the war as a 'fascist' movement to resist the militant internationalism and Soviet sympathies of the bulk of Italian orga-nized labour, Mussolini was not at first aiming at creating another party—not even a party of a new type. He rather hoped that his militant movement would give him a basis for concluding alliances with other organizations, notably ex-servicemen's associations, but possibly also with a trade union movement that might emancipate itself from the Marxist internationalist doctrine of the Socialist Party, and that a great new Labour Party would eventually emerge from this alliance.

The actual development of the fascist movement, however, turned in a quite different direction. On one side, the attempts to woo the trade union movement were completely unsuccessful, as Italian labour reacted to the post-war difficulties with an aimless radicalism expressed in theory by admiration for the Soviet system and in practice by an unprecedented wave of strikes, culminating in the famous occupation of the factories by the locked-out engineering workers in August–September 1920. On the other hand, the influx of nationalist and anti-labour former officers, ex-servicemen, and students, gave the fascist 'action squads' an increasingly right-wing complexion, and the landowners of the Po valley, hard pressed by agricultural labour unions working closely with the socialist municipalities of the region, began by the turn of 1920–1 to call on these action squads to destroy the 'subversive' unions, co-operatives, and municipalities by armed terrorism. A movement that Mussolini had conceived with an ideology combining nationalism and anti-Bolshevism with radical demands for social reform and production control of a syndicalist type, and which up to then had been a marginal factor in Italian politics, thus experienced at the same time both a rapid increase in membership and a transformation of its composition and outlook: between October 1920 and February 1921, the number of local *fasci* rose from 190 to 1,000 and reached 2,500 by the end of that year, but the rapid increase was linked to the role of the new organizations as armed executioners of the labour movement financed by the agrarians.

In the spring and summer of 1921 Mussolini still tried both to exploit the growth of his movement and to change its direction. The elections of May 1921 had enabled the fascists to enter parliament with a group of thirty-five deputies—a parliament in which the problem of finding a stable parliamentary majority was continually acute, because the traditionally governing liberal groups had lost their majority with the introduction of universal suffrage and proportional representation after the war, while of the two new mass parties, the Socialists and the Catholic Popular Party, the former refused all government participation on doctrinaire grounds.

Mussolini now argued that the 'Bolshevik danger' in Italy had been overcome by the successful intimidation of Italian labour, and that the tactics of violence must be ended by a 'peace pact' with the tamed labour organizations in order to make fascism respectable and open the road for its eventual participation in the government—preferably in a coalition with both the Catholics and the reformist wing of the socialists. But when he actually concluded such a pact at the beginning of August 1921, a right-wing opposition based on the strong fascist organizations of the Po valley, and headed by Grandi, Balbo, and Farinacci, denounced him at a regional rally as a 'traitor', and opposed the programme of a 'national revolution' and a corporative State to his parliamentary projects. Within a week, Mussolini had to resign his leadership of the movement.

At this critical juncture, Mussolini was still the fascist movement's only nationally-known leader and the owner and editor of its news-paper. He had proved himself an immensely effective propagandist, with great strength of will and ruthless ambition, but he had lost control of his organization; and though he considered breaking with it, he found that he would lose most of his value for possible political partners without its backing, while the organization could not get far without his ability. He emerged from the crisis with the convic-tion that he would have to adapt himself to the anti-labour instincts and interests of his movement, but at the same time to transform his unruly and generally non-political para-military organization into a disciplined party based on the primacy of the political over the military arm.

It was this that was accomplished at the Rome congress in Novem-ber 1921. Mussolini dropped the 'peace pact' as 'past history', and authorized the resumption of large-scale anti-labour terrorism, thus implicitly abandoning all plans for coalition with the democratic forces. Nationalism and anti-liberalism were made the cornerstones of the platform of the new party. It started with a membership of 320,000, with its cadres recruited largely from the upper and middle classes, among them a large contingent of students, while the lower ranks included the members of many agricultural and some industrial labour unions that had been forced to take refuge with the fascists after their own leadership had been destroyed.

At the same time, the party's new statute provided for subordina-tion of the action squads to the political leadership at all levels. Local *fasci* were to be founded only with central permission, and were to be grouped into regional federations, whose elected repre-sentatives were to form a central committee and a small central directorate of eleven, including one General Secretary, which in turn would supervise the regional organizations. Even the action squads were still supposed to elect their commanders at this time, though these would be subordinate to the 'general inspectorate' which formed a department of the party secretariat. Each local *fascio* was to include technical units of specialists in the public services for purposes of strike-breaking; in addition, special organizations for women, students, and young people were to form part of the party.

If this form of organization may be described as 'democratic centralism', the democratic element in it was still remarkably strong. The statute of 1921 provided no special position for the party leader, nor did it provide for the appointment of regional and local leaders from above; in fact, despite Mussolini's reconciliation with his opponents at the congress, they still insisted on transferring the headquarters from his seat, Milan, to Rome, and he reacted by refusing membership in the directorate. But they soon found that they could not conduct national policy without him, and the following months saw both rapid progress in the centralization of the local squads into a national fascist militia under a single command, and the beginning of the cult of the Duce. By early October 1922 all commanders were being appointed from above and the principle of strict obedience to superiors was in force. Mussolini had achieved this by arguing the need for centralized action for the conquest of power, though he did not in fact consider armed insurrection: he knew that all the successes in his undeclared civil war had been gained only with the tolerance of the army and police, and he remained determined to get into power by legally joining a coalition government—though now it could only be a coalition of the Right. What he really wanted and achieved was a party and a party army organized not for revolution from below, but for merging with the state machine from above—and this task required even stricter centralization.

The fascists thus became transformed into a true totalitarian party only during the last year before their 'March on Rome' in October 1922, brought off once again thanks to the non-resistance of the King and the armed forces, made Mussolini head of a coalition government. Some of the formal adjustments of the party statute to the leader principle were made even later: the Duce's right to confirm the election of regional party leaders was written in only in October 1923, the principle of their appointment from above transferred from the military to the political organization only in October 1926. The rule that membership in the party was incompatible with membership in a Masonic Lodge also dates from early 1923, the same period when the Nationalist Party, in many ways an ideological forerunner of the fascists, was finally annexed by them under the euphemistic name of fusion.

The fact that to the fascists, Bolshevism was a mortal ideological enemy who could not possibly be acknowledged as a model, naturally makes it difficult to judge how far this transformation had really been influenced by a study of the Bolshevik experience. We know, however, that precisely during the crucial period in 1921–2 Mussolini repeatedly referred to Lenin's change-over to the New Economic

Policy as proof that the trend of political developments was everywhere to the right, and that the superiority of the hierarchical over the egalitarian principle had been confirmed even in Soviet Russia. Mussolini detested Bolshevism but admired Lenin as a technician of power; and if he followed Russian developments as he did, he must have been impressed with the effectiveness of the centralized party and its monopolistic rule, which was only finally and formally established during this same period.

At the same time, the origin of the party in a political defeat of the leader by the conservative forces indicates a peculiar historical weakness of Italian fascism that was to remain characteristic of it right to the end. Italian fascism was not the creation of Mussolini to the same extent as Bolshevism was the creation of Lenin or national-socialism the creation of Hitler. Mussolini rose to power after abandoning his own original republican and anti-clerical aspirations, not only because this was a tactical precondition for being entrusted with the government, but also because these aspirations were not shared by decisive elements within his own party. Hence, while the compromise with the parliamentary regime, which meant nothing to the party hierarchs, could easily be abandoned in the next major crisis, the compromises with the monarchy and the church remained, to offer a basis of action to Mussolini's enemies in the testing hour of 1943: Italian fascism became the first totalitarian regime to be overthrown from within—because it had never been *fully* totalitarian.

The regime which Mussolini installed after the 'March on Rome' was still a mixture of a parliamentary coalition and an extra-legal party dictatorship. Other parties remained both within and without the government, and even the new electoral law passed in 1923, while providing for a two-thirds majority of seats for any party winning a quarter of the votes, did not eliminate them in principle. On the other hand, the fascist militia was made a state organ without even being sworn to the King, and the terrorism it used against active opponents of the regime, and particularly against the remnants of the labour organizations, became an essential factor in the elections. The contradiction led to an open crisis when the socialist leader Giacomo Matteotti was murdered in 1924, after a speech in parliament attacking the validity of the elections because of widespread intimidation; amidst a wave of nation-wide indignation, the opposition deputies left parliament as a sign of protest.

Mussolini's reaction to the crisis—he offered concessions and hesitated for several months—seems to indicate that he had not made up his mind in advance to regard his coalition as a mere transitional stage to a single-party regime; but he was clearly determined not to abandon power, and by the beginning of 1925 he realized that, as the extremists of his party had urged all along, he had no other alternative. Farinacci was now made General Secretary of the party, and within the next two years the remaining opposition parties were suppressed, their leaders killed, arrested, or driven into exile, the independent papers handed over to fascist editors, and the fascist 'trade unions' given a monopoly of organization. New legislation eliminated the parliamentary mandates of the opposition and obliged all civil servants to join the party, while the heads of municipalities were made appointed government officials. The head of government was given both exclusive control of the executive and the right to govern by decree, amounting to the union of executive and legislative power. The list of political offences was extended to 'thought crimes', and the penalties were increased by introducing the death sentence and creating concentration camps. Labour relations were based on the principle of the 'corporative State', under which the employers' organizations were given the dignity of state organs without a substantial change in their leadership, while the fascist unions, with their appointed leadership, were given a monopoly of labour organization, and co-operation between the two, including a ban on strikes, was imposed.

By the end of 1926, Italy was thus a totalitarian State except for the autonomy of the church and the continued existence of the monarchy, and even the prerogatives of the latter were curtailed by a law of 1928 giving the Fascist Grand Council a voice in the question of succession. At the same time, Italy was unique in combining a totalitarian political organization with an economy run on liberal capitalist principles. It was only the impact, first of the world economic crisis (during which the fascist State took over a considerable number of bankrupt enterprises), then of the League of Nations' sanctions during the Ethiopian war (leading to a number of austerity measures and stimulating the production of substitutes), and finally of the alliance with Hitler's Germany and the Second World War, which forced the gradual extension of state control over Italian economic life.

It is true that some of the early economic policies of fascism, such

as the building of motor roads and the efforts to increase the cultivated area by amelioration of marshland, showed aspects of a dictatorship of development; and it may be argued that even the suppression of a militant labour movement which, quite apart from its
'revolutionary' ideology, had been too strong for the state of the
Italian economy, may have promoted Italy's emergence from the
post-war crisis and its economic growth. But Italy in the middle
twenties was not as underdeveloped as Turkey, China, or even Russia
in 1917; moreover, the social composition of the fascist party made
it unwilling to tackle the truly structural obstacles to further development, such as the distribution of land-ownership, particularly in the
south. In common with all dictatorships of development, Italian
fascism described its programme as that of a nationalist revolution;
in contrast to successful dictatorships of development, it directed its
dynamism against organized labour rather than against the traditionalist obstacles to development, and towards expansion abroad
rather than to the transformation of the economic and social
structure at home.

It was this preoccupation with the expansion of Italy's territorial
and military power which, by driving the reluctant Duce into an
alliance with the much stronger Führer, ultimately led fascism to
its doom. In contrast to Hitler, Mussolini had not been willing *a
priori* to base his foreign policy on the ideological affinity with
nazism; and when the restrictions he had to impose on Italy's
economic life in the course of the world crisis made it more urgent
for him to obtain spectacular successes in foreign policy, he first
thought to gain them by obtaining the toleration of the western
democracies for his Ethiopian adventure in return for a measure of
co-operation with them in containing Hitler. Yet when the upsurge
of anti-fascist and anti-imperialist opinion, notably in Britain,
destroyed the basis of this 'Stresa diplomacy', Mussolini had no
option left but to walk into Hitler's wide-open arms; and in the
early stages of the Second World War, his military failure in Greece
turned the unequal partnership, which the Axis had been from the
start, into *de facto* subordination to nazi Germany.

By the time of the allied landings in Italy in 1943, the Fascist
Party, which had taken power in the name of national greatness,
had in fact led its country into a destructive war under foreign control.
The manner in which Mussolini's rule was ended by the Fascist
Grand Council, and the latter was abolished by a royal coup, proved

that both the leader and his party had completely isolated themselves from the people they governed; and the final revival of the 'Fascist Republic' under German occupation had no more political significance than any other Quisling regime.

(b) *German National-Socialism*

Supporter of a movement is he who declares his agreement with its aims. Member is only he who fights for it.

The supporter is won for the movement by its propaganda. The member is directed by the organization to co-operate personally in recruiting new supporters from whose ranks new members may arise in turn.

As support requires only passive acceptance of an idea while memberships demands its active advocacy and defence, there will always be only one or two members for any ten supporters.

These sentences could have been written as arguments for Lenin's draft of Paragraph 1 of the statute of the Russian Social-Democratic Workers' Party—the draft around which the Bolshevik faction was formed at the party congress of 1903. In fact, they stand in Hitler's *Mein Kampf*, in the chapter entitled 'Propaganda and Organization', the central importance of which for Hitler's concept of his party has been rightly stressed by Hannah Arendt. It is true that the second part of the chapter develops a doctrine which is in strict contrast to the Bolshevik theory of organization—the rejection of committee rule in favour of the principle of one-man responsibility at all levels. Yet by the time *Mein Kampf* was written in 1924, that principle had in practice been introduced into the administration of the Soviet State and its economy.

Nothing indeed is more striking about the beginnings of the National-Socialist Party, the NSDAP, than the clarity with which Hitler from the start recognized the basic principles of a centralistic party—even before he developed the clear concept that his party was to become the ruling force of a resurrected Germany, rather than a mere auxiliary of the army. Hitler had been delegated into Anton Drexler's German Workers' Party as a propagandist of the local Reichswehr command in 1919, and it was with Reichswehr funds that Dietrich Eckart bought the *Völkischer Beobachter* for the NSDAP in late 1920. It is highly doubtful whether Hitler consciously aimed at an independent seizure of power by his party before Mussolini's March on Rome set the example in October 1922. Yet it was in July 1921, before the Fascist Party was even founded, and at a time when Mussolini was forced to give in to his regional sub-leaders, that Hitler surmounted his first major inner-party crisis and forced his recognition as party president with unlimited powers by threatening resignation; and at the first party congress, in January 1922, he already proclaimed the principle that his Munich branch was to remain the model and centre for the entire party.

For all the radical opposition between Hitler's ideas of a 'natural' hierarchy of race and the egalitarian and internationalist goals of the Bolsheviks, and for all the bitter hatred of the 'Jewish Bolshevik World Conspiracy' shown by Hitler from the start, the parallel between Hitler's and Lenin's concepts of the party as the instrument of a single will to power, and between their practice in forging that instrument against every kind of resistance, is indeed extraordinary —once allowance is made for the difference of conditions in the development of an underground party in Tsarist Russia and of a legal party in the Weimar Republic. Like Lenin, Hitler had in fact to refound his party repeatedly—notably after his return from the Landsberg fortress in 1925—and to reassert his leadership by threatening or carrying out a split: he broke with the Deutsch-Völkische wing of the party at that time, and subdued the North German faction of the NSDAP with its anti-capitalist and pro-Soviet tendencies in the following year.

Like Lenin, too, Hitler defended the principle of the primacy of the political over the military arm—in a milieu where this was far more unusual and difficult: though some of his best cadres came from the Free Corps and the para-military leagues, he dissolved the SA in 1925 rather than allow it to become a non-political instrument of secret rearmament, organized the SS in the following year as a politically reliable elite unit, and refounded the SA only when its control by the party was assured.[20] Among the anti-democratic nationalists of Germany in the twenties, the idea that the nationalist cause could triumph only by subordinating the para-military organizations to a political party was as novel and startling as the idea that social-democracy could triumph only as a centralist conspiratorial organization was among the revolutionary circles of Russia around the turn of the century.

Yet while the parallel is striking, no direct influence of the Bolshevik model on Hitler can be traced. It is not only that he would

---

[20] The SA (Sturm-Abteilungen), Stormtroopers or brownshirts. The SS (Schutz-Staffeln), blackshirted, were started as Hitler's personal guard.

naturally have been reluctant to acknowledge any such influence; there is also no indication whatever that Hitler studied the Bolshevik experience, even to the extent to which Mussolini may have done in 1921–2. Hitler's socalled experts on Bolshevism, German expatriates from Russia like Rosenberg and Scheubner-Richter, saw in the Bolshevik regime nothing but the rule of a Jewish gang, based on the extermination of the native elite and the support of Mongol elements, and were quite incapable of even asking what might be the roots of Bolshevik strength; and those sub-leaders who began to recognize that strength and to show an interest in the problem by the middle twenties, like Goebbels and the Strasser brothers, found their ideas scornfully rejected by the Führer.

On the other hand, Hitler's early grasp of the principles of organizational centralism cannot be explained by his military background alone. No doubt it was army experience that had impressed him with the superiority of hierarchical discipline and individual responsibility over democratic election and discussion; but it was not there that he could have learned the importance of the primacy of political over military leadership. Even if the fact is taken into account that Hitler himself held no officer's rank and rose to influence by his gifts as a demagogue, the question remains of what model may have encouraged him to claim a role of leadership over his military betters.

The most plausible answer is to be found in a document the profound influence of which on Hitler's political imagination is beyond doubt: the so-called *Protocols of the Elders of Zion*. Here we have the model of a conspiracy aiming at world domination in the service of a political idea by the use of all means, but starting without direct control over military forces and making ample use of political intrigue and of the propagandist 'rape of the masses'. It is no accident that Hitler's description of the methods of the Jewish all-enemy reads so often like a recipe for his own actions: they constitute at the same time a projection of his ambitions and a model for their execution.

But we know that the *Protocols* were forged and used in the circles of the Tsarist secret police and of the ultra-reactionary Black Hundred organization, and that their original purpose was to discredit the Russian revolutionaries as tools of an anti-Russian conspiracy. Much that is said in the *Protocols* about the alleged methods of the Elders of Zion is thus a distorted image of the actual methods of earlier Russian revolutionary organizations, notably of the *Narodnaya Volya*: the Black Hundred were founded in 1881, after the assassination of Alexander II by that revolutionary organization. It was, on the other hand, the real experience of the *Narodnaya Volya* that Lenin took as a model for his theory of organization.

The *Protocols* thus take their place in a series of steps by which the revolutionaries and counter-revolutionaries of Europe may be shown to have learned from each other since the late eighteenth century. The secret order of the Bavarian Illuminati attempted to use for the aims of the Enlightenment the methods which it ascribed to the Jesuits. The Jesuit critics of the French Revolution sought to explain that entire historical event as due to a conspiracy of the Illuminati and the freemasons, with the Jews thrown in for good measure. The Russian revolutionary societies of the 1870s incorporated in their statutes the formula that 'the end justifies the means' which was regarded as a Jesuit motto, and the *Protocols* in turn pretended to reveal the secret international background of those revolutionary societies. Hitler's ideas about the relation of the struggle for power with specific organizational techniques are not derived from Lenin's, but the parallelism between them is not accidental: both were derived from different branches of this interacting tradition.

The common core of this tradition is precisely the combination of 'propaganda and organization'—in other words, recognition of the 'democratic' need for winning the support of the people, combined with organizational devices for making the party, and later its government, as independent as possible from particular interests and pressures from below.

The experience of Mussolini's March on Rome coincided with a marked acceleration of the German currency inflation and was soon followed by the profound crisis of German society caused by the French occupation of the Ruhr and the German government's decision to finance the policy of passive resistance. The crisis year of 1923 saw a Hitler who had clearly abandoned all thought of acting as a mere propagandist auxiliary—a 'drummer'—for the Reichswehr, and was determined to accomplish a national revolution under his own leadership and with his own party. The crucial months after the fall of the Cuno government in August in particular, during which passive resistance was liquidated while the chief of the Reichswehr, General von Seeckt, was invested with emergency powers, are characterized by Hitler's growing impatience with the various nationalist leaders and military commanders in Munich and Berlin, each of whom was openly hostile to the republic but waiting for somebody else to make the decisive move for its overthrow. Hitler's utterances of this period show his conviction that he alone had the political courage and vision to make this move and establish his dictatorship by a 'March on Berlin', but also his recognition that he needed the active support of at least the Bavarian military to ensure that there would be no resistance by the legal forces of order; as one of his advisers, Scheubner-Richter, wrote in a memorandum at the time, the real National Revolution could only start once the police had been brought under the control of the revolutionaries. In short, Hitler had learned from Mussolini both that it was necessary to take full power and that it was possible to do this only with the toleration of the army and the police, but he was not yet committed to the doctrine that this could be achieved only in the forms of 'legality'.

The events of 8 and 9 November showed that Hitler had under-estimated the strength of the republican institutions and over-estimated his own influence on the Bavarian right-wing leaders. As the crisis of State and society was overcome with the progress of economic stabilization, while Hitler disappeared for a time in the fortress of Landsberg, the NSDAP lost at the same time its leader and the respectable allies who had hitherto protected it. It became the prey of factional fights in which Hitler's authority seemed almost completely dissipated, and when he returned he had to start anew by building a secure base in Bavaria at the price of temporary political concessions to the Catholic regional government; it was this opportunism that led to his break with the strongly 'anti-Roman' Deutsch-Völkische who had in the meantime merged with his party. The real reassertion of his leadership came in a showdown with those North German regional leaders who had taken the 'socialist' element in national-socialism seriously enough to wish to support the left-wing parties in their referendum for the expropriation of the former German princes; in forcing them to accept his alternative that the 'foreign stock-exchange princes' should be expropriated first, he may have temporarily lost votes, but he ensured his party's chances of 'respectable' support in future crises. The successful reassertion of Hitler's leadership was sealed by the new party statute adopted by a full membership meeting held in Munich in May 1926:

it not only declared the party programme unalterable; it established the principle that the whole party was an extension of the Munich branch with the Munich leadership acting as national leadership and entitled to appoint all Gauleiters. Under German Association Law, the leader himself could not be made formally irremovable but the statute made his removal dependent on conditions that could hardly ever be fulfilled in practice; at the same time he was given power to appoint the heads of the various departments as well as the manager of the party headquarters, who would form a majority of the party executive. It was only after this formal establishment of the Führer principle that he started rebuilding the party's para-military force, the SA, but in the changed circumstances he took much greater care than in the early years to keep it within the limits of the law.

By the time the world economic crisis gave the NSDAP its second chance, Hitler's concept of the road to power had clearly matured. He was determined to achieve a type of single-party State in which the party cadres would occupy the nerve centres of the state machine, as was by then the case in fascist Italy as well as in bolshevik Russia; beginning as early as 1926 and accelerating with the approach of the crisis, the party had created, quite apart from its political organization in the country, a number of specialized central departments preparing plans and cadres for future government policy in such diverse fields as agriculture, education, defence, and 'racial health'. He was equally determined to take power legally, and particularly with the help of the Reichswehr; but he now realized clearly that the Reichswehr leaders did not want a revolution and would first have to be won over by the argument that the victory of the national-socialists was the only alternative to that of the communists. It was the turn of part of the industrial and land-owning classes to renewed opposition to the republic and to active nationalist propaganda which gave the National-Socialist Party its chance to overcome its isolation, from 1929 onwards, by an alliance with Hugenberg's German Nationalist Party, and thus to regain the subsidies and publicity needed for the propagandist exploitation of the crisis along with a new aura of 'national' respectability. The first great electoral victory in September 1930 confirmed Hitler on this road and opened a period in which every government crisis was accompanied by his increasingly frantic attempts to find a legal door to the key positions of power. Yet in repeated negotiations he consistently rejected any form of coalition which would have involved him in government responsibility without giving him an effective lever for casting aside his allies and achieving full power. It was for this reason that he allowed the negotiations with the Catholic Centre Party to fail and that he wrecked the tentative accord reached between General von Schleicher and his own lieutenant, Gregor Strasser. It was for the same reason that, in finally accepting a coalition with von Papen and Hugenberg in January 1933, he insisted on immediate new elections which would enable him quickly to change the terms of the coalition agreement.

With far greater clarity than Mussolini, Hitler had understood in advance that the legal road to a 'National Revolution' could be opened only by way of an alliance with the conservative forces— army and bureaucracy, landowners and industrialists—against organized labour: while Mussolini had had to be forced on to this course by his sub-leaders at the price of a loss of authority, Hitler forced the same course on reluctant sub-leaders, thereby strengthening his authority. But with far greater clarity than Mussolini, too, Hitler in 1933 formed a legal coalition with those conservative allies with the deliberate intention to transform it into an extra-legal dictatorship of his party.

As Hitler was able to profit from the experience both of bolshevism in 1917–21 and of fascism in 1922–6, he did in fact establish his single-party regime in a much shorter time. Immediately after the formation of the government and the calling of elections, his brownshirts were given the status of an auxiliary police force, so as to prepare the proper climate for the polls. The Reichstag fire of 27 February, though probably accidental and not expected by the nazis, was at once exploited for destroying the Communist Party and considerably weakening the social-democrats by a wave of terror, and for 'legalizing' the practice of terror by the 'Decree for the Protection of People and State'. Though the elections of 5 March still left the nazis dependent for a majority on their nationalist allies, the cancellation of the communist mandates promptly eliminated that dependence. The enabling law passed by the new Reichstag against the votes of the social-democrats removed further legal inhibitions, and within a few months the social-democrats too had been outlawed and the bourgeois parties bullied into self-dissolution. With Hugenberg's nationalists sharing their fate, the coalition was ended and single-party government achieved; the decree of 1 December

1933 formally established the 'unity of party and State', thus drawing the conclusions from the new state of affairs and providing the legal basis for the mass entry of party cadres into the bureaucracy.

This penetration of the state machine by the party, though much more thorough than in fascist Italy, never reached the completeness of bolshevik Russia, where the state machine had to be rebuilt completely after a genuine revolution from below; in different departments of the German government it was accomplished to a very uneven degree, as a result not only of the inertial resistance of the old bureaucracy, but also of the insufficient qualifications of many of the party members aspiring to bureaucratic positions. Success was most nearly complete in the vital area of police control, and here it was entirely due to the SS, which within a short time had developed into a kind of 'inner party' with much stricter standards of selection and discipline than the shapelessly swollen civilian party organization. It was the SS that within a few months took over the political police, the guarding of the concentration camps, and the creation of heavily armed mobile police formations; by 1936 Himmler and the regional SS leaders were at the same time placed in charge of the entire regular police force.

The most critical area for the fusion of party and State, on the other hand, was the army. Its wish to avoid a clash with the nazi movement had been decisive for Hitler's victory, yet at first it still owed loyalty to the non-nazi head of State, Field Marshal Hindenburg. The ambition of the SA leaders to have their para-military organization integrated in the regular army, and to be established there with ranks corresponding to their SA status, was liable to provoke the solid resistance of the professional soldiers rather than achieve the desired fusion. Hitler brutally solved the problem by the blood purge of 30 June 1934, which decapitated the SA and broke its ambitions, yet by the assassination of General von Schleicher and of a number of conservative critics demonstrated his determination not to tolerate any political independence on the part of military leaders. By taking the oath of allegiance to Hitler as Führer and Reichskanzler, the Reichswehr a few months later paid for the preservation of its professional monopoly; it was not until February 1938 that Hitler felt strong enough to attack its professional independence and to remove Generals von Fritsch and Beck. Indeed, his control of the army remained less perfect than of other branches of the state machine down to the conspiracy of July 1944.

The purge of June 1934 could not have been carried out without the existence of an armed force tied to no legal rules and owing loyalty to nobody but Hitler: the SS. As proof of the dictator's ability to wield the instrument of terror against a variety of actual or potential opponents at one and the same time, it is said to have profoundly impressed Stalin; according to Krivitsky, it was now the Bolshevik leader who began to learn from the nazi model for his own impending purges. It is arguable that a similar impact in reverse was also exerted on communist strategy by the example of the legal seizure of power: the undoctrinaire policy of the anti-fascist 'popular front' in the following years, and the experiments with the 'peaceful road' to communist power encouraged by Stalin after 1945, and used as a basis for a general theory by Khrushchev after 1956, owe more than a little to the successful demonstration of how thoroughly fascists and nazis were able to transform States of which they had taken control by methods which in form had been legal and parliamentary.

Conversely, it is certain that Hitler was profoundly impressed by Stalin's purges, and that by the late thirties he was no longer convinced of the weakness and instability of the 'Jewish Bolshevik' regime. He had come to admire its techniques of power and in particular its political control over the army, and during the war he expressed this admiration first by the order to kill all political commissars who were captured on the Russian front, and finally by creating a parallel institution in the shape of the 'NS-Führungsoffiziere' in 1944.

As with the Bolsheviks and in contrast to Mussolini, the clarity with which Hitler conceived of single-party rule as a system of total power was linked to the purpose of a total transformation of society in accordance with an ideological vision. But in the conditions of highly industrialized Germany, that purpose could not be connected with the process of modernization, as in Russia and in less developed countries. Here as there, political power was to be concentrated in a single hand in order to overcome a form of social stagnation—but it was not the stagnation of a semi-traditional society, but of an economic crisis resulting in paralysing social conflicts; and the transformation envisaged was the total mobilization for war and territorial expansion and the creation of an empire based on the principle of racial hierarchy.

As early as the summer of 1936 Hitler, in a secret memorandum on the tasks of the four-year plan, set the goal of making the army and the economy ready for war within four years. Without substantial interference with the legal forms of private ownership, the powers of the government were used to direct investment into the channels of a war economy—armaments, substitute raw materials, strategic roads. The control of the employers' organizations, the replacement of the trade unions by the Labour Front and of the peasant organizations by the Reich Food Estate, all of them co-ordinated under party discipline, served the same purpose. We know that in November 1937 Hitler explained to his inner council that war should not be postponed beyond 1943–5 at the latest. The change in the army command followed within a few months of this announcement and was followed in turn almost immediately by the annexation of Austria—the first step on the road to territorial expansion.

But in the framework of the nazi ideological vision war and territorial expansion were not conceived merely as means for increasing national power: it was the rule of the Nordic racial elite that was ultimately to be established, with the German nation fighting in the service of this vision because it had had the good luck to come first under the rule of this elite. Being an instrument rather than the ultimate goal of this scheme, the German nation had itself to be transformed in the process—not only in its economic and social structure, but in its biological substance. Hence policy measures that were 'rational' by the standards of classical power politics—rearmament, economic mobilization, conquest—were accompanied by equally systematic measures that by the same standards were 'irrational' in their wanton brutality, and meaningful only in relation to the racialist ideology: the racial health measures at home, the systematic destruction of national elites among the Slav peoples, and the extermination of the Jews.

The first law for the prevention of biologically inferior offspring was passed as early as July 1933, the decree about the killing of the insane on the opening day of the Second World War, and long-term measures for further 'improvement' of the biological substance of the nation were being prepared by the appropriate SS departments in the midst of war. The orders to destroy the leading strata of the Polish people were issued as soon as the campaign was over. The anti-Jewish measures were first put on the basis of the principle of racial purity by the Nürnberg laws of 1935, and pursued to the 'final solution' with unswerving energy, without regard to any political effects at home or abroad, or even to the strain on the war economy, from 1942 to the end of the regime.

German national-socialism may thus be said to have developed the possibilities of using the system of single-party dictatorship in the service of anti-egalitarian goals to their ultimate conclusion. Its unprecedented destructiveness, ending in what amounted to the self-destruction of the regime and indeed of the German national State, appears as the logical result of a utopia of racial domination that could in its nature not be approached, let alone achieved, without worldwide war and without measures of racial extermination.

IV. Concluding Remarks

The experience of the deeds and collapse of the Third Reich makes it appear improbable that the model of the single-party regime will again be used for similar purposes in an advanced industrialized country. It is indeed remarkable that the model has not so far been applied to any such country in its original communist form either, except for the case of its imposition on Czechoslovakia in 1948, when the situation of that country within the Soviet sphere of control was decisive for the outcome. The only countries in which communist parties have established one-party States after coming to power by their own strength in independent revolutions have been underdeveloped countries—Yugoslavia and Albania, China and North Vietnam.

Taking a broad historical view, it thus appears that the chances of successful application of the one-party system are best in countries which share with the Russian model the basic unsolved problems of development, yet are not underdeveloped to such an extreme degree that the necessary cadres for such a regime cannot be found, as seems to be the case in some African States. Given the 'proper' level of underdevelopment, the question whether a communist or a nationalist single-party regime emerges victorious, or whether the task of development is left to a regime of an altogether different type, seems to depend primarily on historical factors within each particular country.

What seems remarkable, however, is the possibility of the transformation of a nationalist into a communist one-party regime, that has reappeared in recent years. In a sense such a possibility was visible on the horizon in China before 1927, but it then faded from public discussion for more than three decades. It was the decision of Fidel Castro to throw in his lot with the communists, and to merge the remnant of his victorious but disorganized movement with their party, that reopened the question and, together with the radicalization of the Algerian and West African one-party regimes, caused the Soviets in 1963–4 to develop a political concept for achieving such transformations by means of a strategy of 'licensed infiltration' of nationalist one-party regimes by communists.

Yet while the pluralistic decay of the former organizational and ideological unity of the world communist movement has made it easier for a revolutionary nationalist leader to welcome the co-operation of trained communist cadres in his party, it may also have diminished the potential importance of such infiltration. If the communists in question continue to be tied to Soviet leadership, to internationalist doctrine, or even to a precise programme for the road to the classless society, their influence on the nationalist party is likely to remain in most cases severely limited; to some extent this is even confirmed by the special case of Cuba, where it is still an open question how far Castro's regime has really become a communist party regime in the classical sense, and how far it has remained a personal dictatorship using communist slogans and cadres as exchangeable instruments. If, on the other hand, the communists adjust their outlook to the national needs and the nationalist emotions of the countries concerned, their influence may improve the systematic quality but will hardly change the direction of the nationalist regimes.

The future role of the Bolshevik model of the single-party State in developing countries is thus likely to be most effective where the leaders using the model are most successful in emancipating themselves from the specific ideological beliefs that were linked to the model in its country of origin.

Index